Computers

Their Impact and Use

Basic Language

Computers

Their Impact and Use

Basic Language

Robert E. Lynch.
John R. Rice
Purdue University

Holt, Rinehart and Winston, Inc.
New York   Chicago   San Francisco   Atlanta
Dallas   Montreal   Toronto   London   Sydney

Copyright © 1975 by Holt, Rinehart and Winston, Inc.
All rights reserved

Library of Congress Cataloging in Publication Data

Lynch, Robert Emmett, 1932-
  Computers: their impact and use.

  1. Computers. 2. Computers and civilization.
3. Basic (Computer program language) I. Rice, John
Rischard, joint author. II. Title.
QA76.L89   001.6'4   74-9773
ISBN 0-03-088526-4

Printed in the United States of America

5 67 090 9 8 7 6 5 4 3 2 1

Preface

Objectives and Philosophy

A reader who studies this book will receive a *general appreciation* of what computers have done, can do, and might do in the future. The core of the book contains a selection of topics which provides a framework of knowledge upon which the reader can build in the future. These topics include descriptive material about the history, the scope, and the impact of computers on society. The remainder is concerned with some basic facts and skills of computer programming and specific features of current computer systems. It is our firm belief that one cannot appreciate the potential of computers without knowing a little about computer programming and having some experience in solving problems with a computer. Consequently, we feel that each reader should write computer programs to solve a few problems and have a computer execute the programs. A wide range of exercises are included, from very simple ones which test basic comprehension to ones that involve fairly complicated ideas. The reader should choose problems which are challenging and interesting to him.

Audience and Background Assumed

No previous knowledge about computers is necessary for a reader to understand the material in this book. Elementary mathematical concepts known by a typical high school graduate are needed at a number of places. It is helpful, but not essential, to have some knowledge about some of the examples which are discussed in detail, such as chess, English grammar, the stock market, urban problems, and so on.

Plan of Study

The material in this book does not have to be studied in the order in which it is presented. The dependency of the material in a specific chapter on the material in other chapters is indicated by the diagram inside the front cover; this diagram shows what should be studied before a specific chapter is attempted. Chapter 0 gives introductory material about computers and, unless one knows some fundamentals about computers, this should be studied first. The core material is contained in Chapters 1, 2, 5 and 6; this material is the minimum that one should study and as much of the remaining material as possible should be studied in the available time. The chapters following Chapter 0 are divided into two principal parts: Chapter 1 through 4 contain material on the *impact of computers on society*; Chapters 5 through 9 contain material on the *use of computers*.

Use as a Textbook

As indicated above, a number of different courses can be based on this book and the instructor has considerable choice on what to cover in the allotted time. Chapter 0 and the core material should be covered but this material alone does not make up a normal one semester course. If time is not sufficient for all the chapters, then an instructor might wish to emphasize *impact* or *use* and to assign some of the material which he does not cover as reading assignments. The material on computing programming in the *use* part of the book is sufficient for a standard introductory programming course. At the end of each chapter in the *impact* part is a list of suggested readings to supplement the material in this book. The use of these is adequate for an in-depth course in the *impact* of computers on society. Below we give several example course organizations to illustrate some of the possibilities.

Acknowledgements

A small part of the material in this book has been adapted from previous books by one of the authors and we acknowledge the many colleagues and students who have contributed to improving this material. We particularly thank: Robert Blissmer, Seymour Pollack and especially, Zamir Bavel who read various drafts of the manuscript and made numerous helpful suggestions; John Kirk Rice who helped in many ways with the text, figures, programs and production; Allan MacDonald who spent many hours to obtain a useable photo of the "bath tub" vortex; the many commercial firms and individuals who allowed us to use their photographs and who are specifically credited in the captions of the figures; the Purdue University Computing Center for use of its facilities on which all of the programs in this book were run; Wanda Michalenko, Martha H. Lynch and Nancy A. Rice for their expert typing of the many drafts of the manuscript. Finally, we express our sincere appreciation and thanks to our wives for their patience and understanding during the years of trials and tribulations.

Lafayette, Indiana   *R.E.L.*
July 1974   *J.R.R.*

vi

EXAMPLE COURSE ORGANIZATIONS

1. *Short course covering only fundamentals*

Chapter 0	Computers and Information
First part of Chapter 5	First Elements of Basic
Chapter 1	History and Scope
Remainder of Chapter 5	First Elements of Basic
Chapter 2	Impact on Society
Chapter 6	Program Construction and Debugging

2. *A course emphasizing the impact of computers on society*

Chapter 0	Computers and Information
Chapter 1	History and Scope
First part of Chapter 5	First Elements of Basic
Chapter 2	Impact on Society
Remainder of Chapter 5	First Elements of Basic
Chapter 3	Plausible Future
Chapter 6	Program Construction and Debugging
Chapter 4	Selected Applications
Selected readings and individual assignments	

3. *A course emphasizing the use of computers*

Chapter 0	Computers and Information
Chapter 5	First Elements of Basic
Chapter 1	History and Scope
Chapter 6	Program Construction and Debugging
Chapter 7	Problem Solving
Chapter 2	Impact on Society
Chapter 8	Intermediate Elements of Basic
Chapter 9	Languages and Systems

4. *Balanced combination*

Chapter 0	Computers and Information
First part of Chapter 5	First Elements of Basic
Chapter 1	History and Scope
Remainder of Chapter 5	First Elements of Basic
Chapter 6	Program Construction and Debugging
Chapter 2	Impact on Society
Chapter 7	Problem Solving
Chapters 3 and 4 (selected sections)	Applications and Future Development
Chapters 8 and 9 (selected sections)	Programming, Languages and Systems

5. *Full course beginning with impact*

   Chapter 0
   Chapters 2 through 4 with selected readings
   Chapters 5 through 9

6. *Full course beginning with use*

   Chapter 0
   Chapters 5 through 9
   Chapters 1 through 4 with selected readings

Contents

Computers

Their Impact and Use

Basic Language

O Computers and Information

0-1 INTRODUCTION

This book is about computers—what they do and how they do it. Hopefully, it will provide the reader with an appreciation of two things: *the impact of computers on society* (Part I) and *how one uses a computer* (Part II). (You may start with either Part I or Part II.) In order to study either of these parts, however, some minimal information about what a computer *does* and *can do* and about the *relationship between information and computing* is necessary. This introductory chapter is intended to provide such a background. It does not include all that one should know about these topics, rather only enough to proceed with the rest of the book.

Two distinct views of computers are presented in this chapter: first a rather mechanical, concrete view; and second an abstract functional view. This is followed by a discussion of the different ways information can be expressed or represented, and how it can be processed by a machine. The final section of this chapter illustrates the immense complexity of the information processing task by considering what happens when a political scientist uses a computer system and a data bank to study trends and patterns in voting. The flow of information through the system is illustrated in detail as the scientist starts his study.

0-2 COMPUTERS - A MECHANICAL VIEWPOINT

Computers are not unlike many more familiar machines such as typewriters, adding machines, and desk calculators (Figure 0-2.1).

FIGURE 0-2.1 **A simple adding machine (left) and a more complicated desk calculator (right). The desk calculator can add, subtract, multiply, and divide numbers entered into the keyboard.**

Consider a simple problem, the solution of which requires only arithmetic (done on a desk calculator). The step-by-step solution to this problem illustrates some of the simpler features of real computers.

Problem: You want to deposit $1000.00 in the savings bank so as to give you the most interest. You have a choice between two banks with the following interest rates:

Bank A offers an annual interest rate of 5.1% and credits your account.with the interest earned one time a year.

Bank B offers an annual interest rate of 5.0% and credits your account with the interest earned four times a year.

Which bank should you choose in order to have the most money at the end of one year?

This problem is solved by performing the following arithmetic calculations:

Bank A:

Original deposit			$1000.00
Interest paid at end of year	$1000.00 \times .051$	=	51.00
Amount at end of year	$1000.00 + 51.00$	=	1051.00

Bank B:

Original deposit			$1000.00
Interest paid at end of first quarter	$1000.00 \times .05/4$	=	12.50
Amount at end of first quarter	$1000.00 + 12.50$	=	1012.50
Interest paid at end of second quarter	$1012.50 \times .05/4$	=	12.65
Amount at end of second quarter	$1012.50 + 12.65$	=	1025.15
Interest pair at end of third quarter	$1025.15 \times .05/4$	=	12.81
Amount at end of third quarter	$1025.15 + 12.81$	=	1037.96
Interest paid at end of fourth quarter	$1037.96 \times .05/4$	=	12.97
Amount at end of year	$1037.96 + 12.94$	=	1050.93

Solution: You will earn more interest by choosing Bank A.

Now consider how you would tell a friend to perform these calculations. The friend may be thought of as a *computer* and the instructions you tell him may be thought of as a *computer program.* We make several suppositions about the friend:

1. He can do arithmetic accurately (using a desk calculator).
2. He will do exactly what he is told to do.
3. He will not do anything he is not specifically told to do.

The instructions for calculating Bank A's interest per year might be given as follows:

Multiply the numbers 1000.00 and .051 and add their product to 1000.00. Write the result on a sheet of paper putting 2 digits on the right of the decimal point and at most 6 digits on the left of the decimal point. Then give the paper to me.

The instructions for the Bank B calculation could be given the same way although many more words would be required. We see that these instructions would be repetitious because the calculations (but not the numbers) for each quarter are the same. How could you tell the friend what to do without repeating everything four times? To get the next quarter's result from the current amount you might say:

Divide the rate .05 by 4 and multiply this by the current amount and discard any fractions of cents that occur. Add the result to the current amount to get the new current amount.

This has the gist of the idea, but is still incomplete. For instance, your friend must be told how to obtain the first set of numbers to start the calculation, how many times to follow these instructions, and what to do after he has finished.

Suppose your friend has frequently done calculations for you and you have organized a method to give him instructions in a clearer, simpler, and less wordy manner. He knows to discard any fractions of cents that occur. He uses a sheet of lined paper to record the instructions and the results of his computation. Each line of the paper has a number (considered its "address") and the lines are numbered sequentially: 1,2,3, ... To conserve paper and also to get a realistic model of a computer, you give the following instructions to the friend for the computation for Bank B's interest per year:

Instruction

#1	Name line 14 "A" (for "amount")
#2	Name line 15 "R" (for "rate")
#3	Name line 16 "T" (for number of "times" interest is paid per year)
#4	Name line 17 "F" (for "factor")
#5	Write 1000.00 on the line named A
#6	Write .05 on the line named R
#7	Write 4 on the line named T
#8	Divide the number on line R by the number on line T and write the result on line F.
#9	Multiply the number on line A by the number on line F and add the product to the number on line A. Write this result on line A after erasing the number there.
#10	Subtract 1 from the number on line T and write this result on line T after erasing the number there.
#11	If the number on line T is not equal to zero, do the instructions starting at #9. Otherwise, go on to instruction #12.
#12	Write the number on line A on a sheet of paper with 2 digits on the right of the decimal point and at most 6 digits on the left of the decimal point. Give me the paper.
#13	Stop and wait for further instructions.
#14	
#15	

.
.
.

The sheet of paper with the instructions is given to the friend and he is told to follow the instructions starting with #1. (Note that the first eight instructions serve to "start" the calculation.)

Although these thirteen instructions are still very wordy, they are a model of a computer program. Note that when one instruction is carried out, your friend automatically goes on to the next one unless instructed otherwise.

The sheet of paper corresponds to the *memory* of the computer. The computer memory is the place where numbers (such as 1000.00 and .05) are placed and where instructions (such as "Write 4 on line T") are written. Each line is called a *word* in a real computer (its lines are not very long!) and each word has an *address* (the line numbers in this example). Once storage space in memory has been allocated for the numbers and the instructions and this space has been filled, the computer is told to start carrying out the instructions beginning at a certain place (address #1 in this example). It continues sequentially (unless told otherwise) until told to stop. Instructions (like #11) which break the normal sequence of following the instructions are called *transfers* or *jumps*.

The desk calculator that your friend uses corresponds to the *central processor* of a computer, the piece of equipment that does arithmetic and testing (such as checking whether the number on line T is equal to zero as required in instruction #11). Your friend himself corresponds to the *control unit* of a computer, the piece of equipment that interprets the instructions. Normally the control unit is physically a part of the central processor. Even though there is a useful logical distinction between *interpreting instructions* and *doing arithmetic*, both of these functions are performed by the central processor.

In summary, we have now identified three important elements necessary to calculate the solution to this problem (see Figure 0-3.1):

1. The *program*: A set of instructions to be followed.
2. The *memory*: A place to record the instructions and the numbers involved in the calculation.
3. The *processor*: A device that both interprets and performs the instructions.

The instructions that you gave the friend are still very wordy and actual computer instructions are much more compact and abbreviated. Figure 0-2.2 shows how the instructions for this calculation would appear in a particular programming language. This programming language is presented in some detail in Part II.

The instructions are given to the computer in a readable form for the machine, typically on IBM punched cards or by teletyping. (See the appendices for more details on this process.) The resulting program is called the *source program* and is written in a *programming language*. The language is very simple compared to English and its grammar is simple. Nevertheless, everything must be translated into *machine language* before the computer will begin to act. Each model of computer has its own special machine language. This translation is done automatically by the computer (with another computer program) producing the *object program*. This object program is a list of numbers which the central processor decodes or interprets. The computer then carries out the indicated operations. Machine language is more difficult to learn and more awkward to use than programming languages.

A computer program does the translation from a programming language to machine language. This program examines each of the instructions in the source program and "translates" it into an equivalent set of machine language instructions. This language

Basic Language Instructions	Explanation
50 LET A = 1000.00	Simultaneously names a word "A" and puts (writes) 1000.00 there. Corresponds to #1 and #5 above.
60 LET R = .05	Simultaneously names a word "R" and puts .05 there. Corresponds to #2 and #6 above.
70 LET T = 4	Simultaneously names a word "T" and puts 4 there. Corresponds to #3 and #7 above.
80 LET F = R/T	Names a word "F", performs a division and puts the result in F. Corresponds to #4 and #8 above.
90 LET A = A*F+A	Multiplies the contents of A and F, then adds the contents of A to this result and places the sum back into A. Corresponds to #9 above.
100 LET T = T−1	Subtract 1 from the contents of T and place the result back into T. Corresponds to #10 above.
110 IF T <> 0 THEN 90	If T is not equal to 0 then go to instruction 90. Corresponds to #11 above. The symbol <> is an abbreviation for "not equal."
120 PRINT A	Write the contents of A. Corresponds to #12 above. Elementary Basic language does not provide control over the number of digits printed.
130 STOP	Corresponds to #13.

FIGURE 0.2.2. The instructions given the friend are rewritten (left) in the Basic programming language. An explanation is given on the right.

translation program also allocates storage space in the memory for the instructions and numbers involved. A language translator is often called an *interpreter* or a *compiler.*

There is much more to the operation of large computers, but the foregoing description should do for now.

Computers vary tremendously in range of cost, power, and capabilities. Some examples of computers are listed in Table 0-2.1 along with five items of information. The data for each of the items (except word size) is only an approximate "average" value because these computers come in many variations. For instance, the speed of doing arithmetic may depend on the "sub model" considered or the particular situation that exists inside the computer at the time of the calculation. Note that one cannot accurately compare the power of these computers on the basis of the data presented here. There are many pertinent items missing and it is difficult to make comparisons even for the items listed.

Consider, for example, the capacity of main memory. This is measured in terms of words and the length of a word is measured in terms of bits. The term *bit* is a contraction of *binary digit.* A bit is a piece of information that can be represented by a "0" or "1" digit (and nothing else). Thus a 32 bit word might contain the number 11110000111100001110000 but this number could not be put into a 16 bit word. Note that many manufacturers use other measures in their advertising and descriptions. Thus, IBM uses *bytes* (which are 8 bits) and others use *characters* (which vary from 6 to 8 bits). In many applications the 600,000 words of a CDC 6600 provide more memory capacity than 1,000,000 words of an IBM 360/85 because the CDC 6600 words are longer.

TABLE 0-2.1
Some characteristics of a number of common computers. Most of the values given are only approximate averages or ranges and are not precise. Arithmetic speeds are not strictly comparable because some smaller computers have shorter numbers and are limited to integers.

Computer	Monthly Rent	Word Size Binary Digits	Main Memory Computer-words	Arithmetic Operations per second Addition	Multiplication
PDP-8	$300— 3,000	12	4,000— 32,000	400,000	20,000
IBM 1130	$700— 1,800	16	4,000— 8,000	2,200	1,200
IBM System 3	$1,200— 2,500	8	1,000— 32,000	4,000	500
IBM 360/20	$1,500— 4,000	32	2,000— 8,000	2,000	400
Honeywell 200/200	$3,000— 15,000	48	4,000— 16,000	16,000	2,000
IBM 370/125	$5,000— 15,000	32	48,000— 64,000	20,000	5,000
IBM 360/40	$8,000— 25,000	32	4,000— 65,000	25,000	9,000
DECsystem 10	$10,000— 25,000	36	64,000—4,000,000	250,000	100,000
IBM 370/145	$10,000— 25,000	32	40,000— 125,000	160,000	60,000
Xerox Sigma	$10,000— 30,000	32	8,000— 132,000	300,000	150,000
Burroughs 5700	$10,000— 33,000	48	16,000— 64,000	200,000	100,000
IBM 360/65	$35,000— 60,000	32	32,000— 250,000	400,000	220,000
Honeywell 8200	$40,000— 60,000	48	32,000— 125,000	150,000	125,000
Burroughs 6700	$40,000— 60,000	48	132,000—1,000,000	1,000,000	300,000
Univac 1108	$45,000—100,000	36	65,000— 250,000	700,000	400,000
CDC 6600	$60,000—150,000	60	32,000— 150,000	1,000,000	800,000
IBM 360/85	$85,000—200,000	32	125,000—1,000,000	4,000,000	700,000
CDC 7600	$125,000—300,000	60	500,000—1,000,000	1 to 10 Million	.7 to 7 Million

There is a rough correspondence between IBM's newer 370 line of computers and the older 360's. The model numbers for the 370's are all in the hundreds (125, 145, 168, 195.) An IBM 370/145 should be comparable to the IBM 360/40 in the sense that it is somewhat more powerful and slightly more costly.

0-3   COMPUTERS - A FUNCTIONAL VIEWPOINT

Most people view the computer as some sort of machine, which, of course, it is. However, it is more than just a collection of physical parts. One of the three essential elements of a computer (see Figure 0-3.1) is rather abstract, the program does not have a physical existence in the same way that a gear or motor or vacuum tube does.

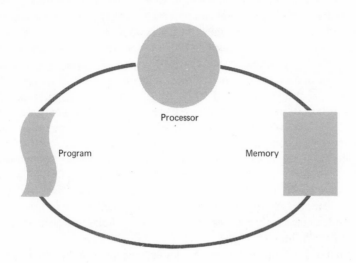

Program

Processor

Memory

FIGURE 0-3.1   The three essential elements of a computer.

The *memory* of a computer is a device where information is stored, for example, the elements of a payroll: workers identification numbers, rate of pay, hours worked, deductions, and so forth. There are two key properties of a memory: its *size* and its *speed*. The size of a memory is easy to visualize and the larger the memory, the more information (or, data) one can place there. The speed of a memory is a measure of the time it takes to locate a piece of data that is in the memory (or to discover that it is not there). The nature of computer memories is such that if one substantially increases the size (or capacity), then one decreases the speed (or *access time*). Fairly small computer memories can be extremely fast and yet contain the same amount of information as a short text book. In many circumstances a "fact" can be located in less than a millionth of a second. In other situations, it may take much, much longer to locate a piece of data. Compare this with a person looking for a fact in the public library. If he knows that a particular page in a particular book contains the fact, and if he knows the exact location of the book in the library, then he can obtain the fact quickly. If, on the other hand, he does not know whether the fact is in a book on economics or a book on statistics or one on the history of science or in a newspaper published many years ago, then it might take weeks or even months to locate the fact.

Another relevant property of computer memories is that they are one of the most expensive parts of a computer, especially if they are both large and fast.

The *processor* is the part of the computer that carries out operations. Obviously, one of the things it does is to process information in the memory; but it is not restricted to this. It can control other machines of various kinds, it can sense and store in memory new information of different kinds. The information might be the time of day, the temperature, the speed of a plane, the weight of an iron bar, or the fingerprint of a man.

The speed at which a computer can process information is so great that it is hard to comprehend and appreciate. A computer might examine and act upon *millions* of pieces of information in a minute. The speed at which it does other things depends on the type of things involved. For example, it can control the keys on a typewriter at a rate of only 200–300 words a minute because of the mechanical limitations of a typewriter. On the other hand, special printers designed to be controlled by a computer can "type" the equivalent of 100,000–200,000 words a minute. Within a few years we expect to see devices that operate at 10 times this rate. This entire book then could be printed in much less than a minute by a computer.

The third and unique element of a computer is the *program*. A program is simply a set of instructions for the processor. It is a particular kind of information much like a recipe for fixing pizza or fried chicken, and hence does not have a fixed physical existence like a motor or typewriter. Of course a program must have some sort of physical existence, perhaps as words on paper or as holes punched in a card or as magnetized spots invisible to the eye.

A computer program embodies the knowledge of how to do something. It is difficult to overestimate the impact of this facet of computing, and we are only beginning to see its utilization. We interpret this ability as follows: suppose an expert (an engineer, a doctor, an economist, a banker, and so forth) discovers how to solve a certain problem or to accomplish a certain task. He can then write down a set of instructions (a program for a computer) which, when followed, accomplishes the task. The program can then be made available very rapidly throughout that part of society concerned with the same problem or task. This means that the expert's knowledge and technique can be made available *throughout* society, rapidly and reliably. An illustration of this is shown in Figure 0-3.2. This allows one to hope that someday the average person can obtain cheaply and rapidly the benefits of a diagnosis by a leading brain surgeon, advice from an expert investment banker, legal aid from a lawyer and so forth by using programs written by such experts. These things will not happen immediately and the realizations will no doubt not work quite as effortlessly as predicted, but the *potential* is clearly present. As potentially significant as this development is, it is still *only one* of the several developments involving computers which will have a significant impact on society.

It is important to keep in mind that programs control the actions of a computer and programs are created by people. People can write bad programs much more easily than good ones and a common result of a bad program is some absolutely stupid action or result, that is, a "computer goof." Some of these "computer goofs" are highly publicized and many people and organizations tend to blame all kinds of mistakes on the *computer*—even when they are due to *human* errors and some of them never involved a computer at all. This process is illustrated in Figure 0-3.3, note the similarity of this process with that illustrated in Figure 0-3.2.

FIGURE 0-3.2   A schematic diagram that illustrates the potential of the computer to transmit information, knowledge, and know how. Large teams of experts prepare programs that answer questions in their areas of special knowledge. These programs also incorporate methods to solve many of the common problems in the experts area. These problems might range from calculating one's income tax, to trouble-shooting for a misbehaving TV set, to trigonometry and higher mathematics.

FIGURE 0-3.3   The computer carries out the instructions of the program. If someone (the programmer) has left "bugs" in the program then strange things may happen. In the case illustrated above, the computer insists that Mr. Smith owes an income tax of $27,411.89 even though Mr. Smith only earned $12,450.00.

One last but crucial point to be made is the following. *There is a distinct difference between being able to do something and knowing exactly how it is done.* For example, Bach, Beethoven, or Brahms could compose great music, but they could not give exact instructions about how this is done. Likewise, Albert Einstein could explore the fundamental laws of physics, but he could not write a program to do it. Finally, most readers of this book can work crossword puzzles but they are completely unable to write a computer program that can work even easy crossword puzzles (nor will they be able to after studying this book). However, some people know exactly how to calculate the weekly payroll of a company or the path a rocket should take to land on the moon. These people have been able to write computer programs to do these calculations.

0-4 INFORMATION AND ITS REPRESENTATION

How a computer is told to do something and *how* it can process information is most important. The key idea is the *representation of information* and the *representation* may change rapidly and radically as the processing and computation goes on.

One of the important concepts in the study of information is *the difference between information and a representation of this information.* This difference is seen in everyday life in cooking, for example. The recipe for cooking young wild pigeons with olives can be written in English, or in French, or in Amharic, or in Chinese. Even though we might have four different pieces of paper with writing, we have only one set of information. These four writings are thus only different ways to express or represent this information. Given one representation, another can be obtained by a *translation*. The change of representations back and forth is called the *encoding* and *decoding* of the information.

We do not try to say precisely what information "is." We simply feel that it is something abstract that does not have any physical existence. Thus, the fact that it snowed three days ago on Prince of Wales Island is a fact of information that does not depend on whether or not it is recorded anyplace. And, if it is written down, it does not depend on how it is recorded.

An elementary piece of information is called a *bit*. A bit is a piece of information that can be represented by one of the two words "yes" or "no," or by one of the two digits "1" or "0." Note that we do not attempt to say what a bit is directly but that we consider only how we can express it, represent it, or test for it.

The fact that it snowed on Prince of Wales Island is a bit of information. We can represent this fact by the single word "yes" or by the single digit "1." The reason that we can do this with a single digit is that we are in a very specific *context*, that is, someone has posed, either directly or indirectly, the question: "Did it snow on Prince of Wales Island?" Without this context, the information cannot be represented by 0 or 1. Thus we see that a representation consists not only of bits, but also of a context of interpretation. In other words, there must be a scheme for *encoding* and *decoding* the information into and out of the bits.

The symbols 0 and 1 can be used to represent bits and hence all information. However, we feel more comfortable if we use a larger set of symbols, namely,

$$0\ 1\ 2\ 3\ 4\ 5\ 6\ 7\ 8\ 9$$

We can combine these symbols (or characters) into the decimal digits of numbers and represent many bits of information by a relatively short number like 47907 (this ZIP code specifies Purdue University, West Lafayette, Indiana). This number might represent five bits of information or hundreds of bits. It depends on the encoding scheme used.

Computers are often thought of as machines that only process numbers and hence as only giant calculators for arithmetic. They can be used to process all sorts of information because one can represent this information in a numerical form. In fact, there are many different ways to represent numbers as shown below:

decimal	octal	binary		decimal	octal	binary
1	1	1		9	11	1001
2	2	10		10	12	1010
3	3	11		11	13	1011
4	4	100		12	14	1100
5	5	101		13	15	1101
6	6	110		14	16	1110
7	7	111		15	17	1111
8	10	1000		16	20	10000

We see that the number fourteen (which we just represented using 9 letters of the alphabet) is represented in three ways as follows (* denotes multiplication)

$$14\ =\ 1*10 + 4 \qquad\qquad\qquad\qquad \text{decimal (base 10)}$$
$$16\ =\ 1*8 + 6 \qquad\qquad\qquad\qquad\quad \text{octal\quad (base 8)}$$
$$1110\ =\ 1*2^3 + 1*2^2 + 1*2 + 0 = 1*8 + 1*4 + 1*2 + 0 \quad \text{binary\quad (base 2)}$$

No matter which representation is used there is only one piece of information involved the number "fourteen."

These different representations are only samples of the many possibilities. Eight more examples of representation are given for the three numbers 120, 1.5, and 1/20.

		120	3/2	1/20
1.	Rational	120	3/2	1/20
2.	Decimal (base 10)	120.0	1.5	0.05
3.	Octal (base 8)	170.0	1.4	0.03146 . . .
4.	Binary (base 2)	1111000.0	1.1	0.000011001100 . . .
5.	Floating binary	.1111000*2^7	.11*2^1	0.110011 . . .*2^{-4}
6.	Floating decimal	.120*10^3	.15*10^1	.5*10^{-1}
7.	Chinese characters	一二〇	三／二	一／二〇
8.	Arabic characters	١٢٠	٣\٢	١\٢٠

The *floating point* representations are common in computing. One writes the digits of the number after a decimal or binary point and then multiplies by an appropriate power of the base. Thus multiplication by 10^3 or 10^{-1} moves the decimal point three places right or one place left, respectively. Similarly, multiplication by 2^7 or 2^{-4} moves the binary point seven places right or four places left.

These eight ways of representing a number are samples of the unlimited number of possibilities. No matter which representation is used, there is only one number, that is, one piece of information, involved.

We now consider how one can represent letters and other symbols in a numeric form. The idea is to assign pairs of digits to each letter, symbol, or *character*. One such scheme is as follows

Letters	Punctuation	Digits
A ∿ 00	, ∿ 26	0 ∿ 30
B ∿ 01	. ∿ 27	1 ∿ 31
C ∿ 02	; ∿ 28	2 ∿ 32
.	blank ∿ 29	.
.		.
.		.
X ∿ 23		7 ∿ 37
Y ∿ 24		8 ∿ 38
Z ∿ 25		9 ∿ 39

This allows us to encode any combination of these 40 characters as a number. Examples of words and phrases encoded this way are:

ACE   ∿ 000204   X,Y,Z ∿ 2326242625
BECKER   ∿ 010402100417   71.9 ∿ 37312739
HE IS OLD ∿ 070429081829141103

This scheme results in a representation that is hard for humans to understand, but it is suitable for computers. The character sets of most higher-level languages have from 48 to 64 items. Many computer systems have facilities for 128 characters *even though several of these have no written or visual representation.* They are referred to by words like "end-of-record mark" or "0-2-9 mark."

An extremely important consequence of this approach is that *all written information can be represented by combinations of bits* (or as binary numbers). This means that computers are able to do much more than act as gigantic, whirlwind adding machines. They can process almost any kind of information imaginable: words, numbers, pictures, maps, and so forth.

It is convenient to imagine that computers process numbers, but numbers are abstract mathematical objects without a physical existence. This means that they cannot be processed directly but rather their physical representations are processed. People use visual representations (marks on paper, blackboards, or TV screens) and mental processing. One of the most common physical representations is by means of *holes* punched in cards. The familiar IBM card is shown in Figure 0-4.1 and each of the letters, digits, and special characters is encoded in the card by a combination of holes.

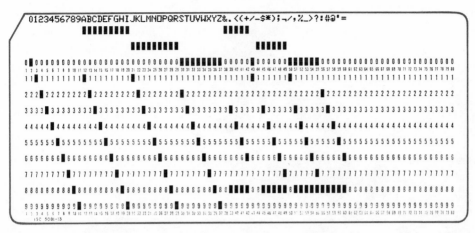

FIGURE 0-4.1 An IBM card which shows how digits, letters and special characters may be represented as punched holes. The "blank" is represented by no holes at all. There is a total of 63 different characters in this encoding scheme.

Computers are electromagnetic machines and thus information inside a computer is represented by patterns of magnetized spots, voltages, and so forth. It is a worthwhile exercise to follow a short piece of information as it passes from a computer user through a computer system. We mention the particular devices involved, but it is not important here what the devices are. A few of the devices involved are shown in Figure 0-4.2. We follow the path of a single character, say "A."

Form of Representation	Remarks
"A" written on paper	An instruction in the users program.
mental image	The user reads his program as he sits at a keypunch machine.
"A" key depressed	The user hits the A key.
electrical current in a keypunch	The depressed key activates a current which, in turn, activates a punch and print mechanism.
holes in a card	A pattern of holes has been punched.
electrical current in card reader	Brushes are passed over the card and they make contact through the holes.
voltages in a small computer	The current is sent to a small computer.

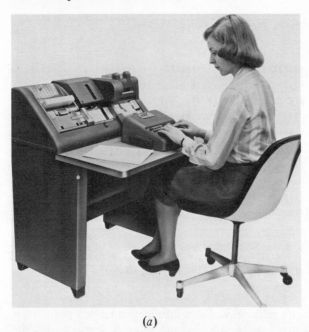

(a)

(b)

FIGURE 0-4.2   Five of the physical devices involved in getting the letter A from the programmer to the memory of a large computer. (a) An IBM 026 keypunch machine, (b) a card reader, (c) a magnetic tape unit, (d) a small IBM 360/20 computer, (e) a magnetic disk unit. (Courtesy IBM Corp. and Control Data Corp.)

(*c*)

(*e*)

(*d*)

electrical current in a tape unit	This computer sends, at an appropriate time, the information on to a unit that reads and writes on magnetic tape.
magnetized spot pattern on a tape	The tape unit magnetizes the tape.
electrical current in a tape unit	Another tape unit controlled by a large computer is reading the tape.
voltages in a processor	The information is now inside a computer, but not for long.
magnetized spot pattern on a disk	A current is sent to a disk controller which records the information on a magnetic disk. The information waits there.
patterns of magnetization in arrays of magnetic cores	The computer has asked the disk for the information, currents are sent, and, after manipulation, used to magnetize tiny metal doughnuts (cores) that make up the computer's memory.

At this point the character "A" has been represented 13 times in 9 essentially different physical situations. As the computer processes "A," it is shifted back and forth between currents, voltages, and magnetized patterns. If "A" is finally to return to the user, it starts back along a path that might well involve another half dozen changes in representation. We conclude that information goes through an almost bewildering sequence of transformations in the course of being processed by a computer. One of the primary objectives of the computer system is to allow the user to ignore all (or at least most) of these transformations. In fact, most users of computers never have to consider information except in visual (handwritten or printed) form.

So far we have concentrated our attention on small items of information that is, numbers, letters, and words. It is equally important to realize that large, coordinated bodies of information must be represented and processed. One of the primary examples of this is the information about how to do something. In particular, a computer program is a representation of the information about how to do something with a computer. Programs in a programming language are one representation and this representation is changed when a language translator takes the source program and produces an object program in machine language. Later in this book we discuss applications of computers that involve placing large bodies of coordinated, organized information into a machine and then having a program to manipulate this information in various ways.

0-5 ILLUSTRATION: A POLITICAL SCIENCE APPLICATION

The purpose of this section is to illustrate some of the complexity and action of computers. The situation described here is not one of everyday (or even common) occurrence at the present time (1973). All of the devices now exist and the programs could be written to create this situation. However, other factors (primarily cost) force us to wait a few years before this illustration becomes reality.

We consider a political scientist who wants to study certain aspects of voting behavior. His source of information is a large set of statistics about voting that has been gathered and placed in a computer memory device. This set of statistics in the computer is called a *data bank*. The political scientist uses a console (described below) to communicate with the computer. This console is located away from the computer (perhaps a hundred yards, perhaps a hundred miles) and a connection is made by a telephone line.

A real computer system has many separate devices but we show only four of them here. (Figure 0-5.1) One is a *communications controller* that connects with the incoming telephone lines (there may be hundreds of them). The main computer is shown along with two auxiliary memory devices. One of these is a *program library* where a large number (perhaps 500) generally useful programs are kept. Since most programs have

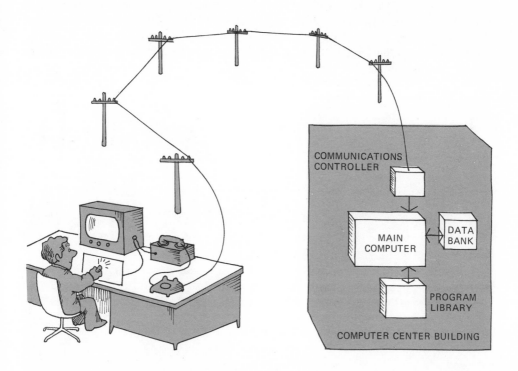

FIGURE 0-5.1   The general situation when a political scientist is analyzing voting trends from a computerized data bank. He communicates through a TV console and tablet with the computer which gives him access to the data bank.

several hundred lines (or statements) and many have 20,000 to 50,000 lines, this memory device must have a very large capacity. The most common devices used here have capacities that range from 500 thousand to 500 million *words* of memory. The data bank is essentially the same as the program library except that data is kept there rather than programs.

The console has two parts, one is a display screen almost identical with an ordinary television set. This is how the computer transmits information to the scientist. The other part is a special kind of tablet, called a *Rand tablet* because it was developed by the Rand Corporation. The function of this tablet is simple: one writes on the tablet and the result appears on the console screen. This is how the scientist transmits information and requests to the computer.

The tablet has a simple function, but it is an extraordinarily complex piece of equipment. Consider what happens to the letter "A" between the time it is written on the tablet and it appears on the console screen. There are three distinct steps:

1. Sensing the handwritten letter and transmission of the information to the computer.
2. Computer analysis of the pattern received to identify the letter.
3. Transmission of the letter's identity to the console and display on the screen.

We do not describe the analysis in the second step because it is beyond the scope of this book. It is an extremely complex and delicate analysis and the user must make well-formed letters in his writing in order for them to be recognized. Some of the subtleties of the problem are indicated in Figure 0-5.2 where we see how variations of the letter A can become B or R or H.

FIGURE 0-5.2 **Various ways in which the letter A can be written so as to look like another letter such as B, R, or H.**

The processing for the first step in shown in Figure 0-5.3. The handwritten letter is magnetically sensed as the "pencil" goes over a grid inside the tablet. A real tablet has a much finer grid than shown here. The tablet can sense whether or not the pencil passed over a particular square and this information can be represented by an array of 0's and 1's. The "1" is used for "yes, the pencil passed here." This large array or *bit pattern* can

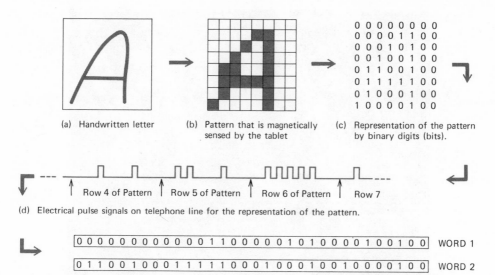

(a) Handwritten letter   (b) Pattern that is magnetically   (c) Representation of the pattern
                                        sensed by the tablet   by binary digits (bits).

(d) Electrical pulse signals on telephone line for the representation of the pattern.

│ 0 0 0 0 0 0 0 0 0 0 0 0 1 1 0 0 0 0 0 1 0 1 0 0 0 0 1 0 0 1 0 0 │ WORD 1

│ 0 1 1 0 0 1 0 0 0 1 1 1 1 1 0 0 0 1 0 0 0 1 0 0 1 0 0 0 0 1 0 0 │ WORD 2

(e) The bit pattern inside the main computer in the form of two 32-digit binary numbers.

FIGURE 0-5.3   **The process of transmitting representations of the letter A from the political scientist to the main computer. A real system would use a finer grid to sense the letter and hence lead to more computer words in the representation. Note that the two numbers are 3012144 and 14437042204 in base 8 (or octal) or 791652 and 1685865604 in ordinary base 10.**

then be sent over a telephone line as a series of "blips" or pulses for "1" and no pulse for "0." The scheme illustrated here starts with the top row of the array and ends with the bottom row.

As the pulses are received by the communications controller, they are represented again by 0's and 1's and sent on to the main computer. There the bits (0's and 1's) are placed into computer words. These words are 32 bits long so that one computer word holds four rows of the bit pattern. The 32 bits in the computer word can now be considered as a binary number and we can, in turn, represent these numbers as an octal or decimal number as follows:

binary	*octal*	*decimal*
00000000000011000001010001100100	3012144	791652
01100100011111000100010010000100	14437042204	1685865604

We see that the decimal representations of these numbers is much shorter and more familiar. More significantly, we have been able to represent what is written on the tablet by two decimal numbers. One can regard the decimal numbers as being analyzed at Step 2 in order to identify the letter written, no matter what the computer does internally.

Note that the computer does not have numbers "written" in the words as ordinary visual marks. Rather another magnetic scheme is used which involves a large number of *cores* or little metallic doughnuts strung on a system of wires (See Figure 0-5.4). These cores can be magnetized either in a "left-hand" direction or a "right-hand" direction and the direction is used to encode a "1" or a "0." The wires are used to sense in which

FIGURE 0-5.4   View of a section of core memory in a computer. The wires through the cores are finer than a hair. The horizontal and vertical wires carry pulses to change the magnetized directions of the cores, while the diagonal wires are used to sense the directions. (Courtesy of Honeywell, Inc.)

direction a core is magnetized and to change the directions. Sensing the directions corresponds to reading the word and changing the directions corresponds to writing a word. Current computers have from 12 to 60 bits in one word (32 is the most common) and from 4,000 to 250,000 words in their main memroy. Thus a large computer has up to 10 million of these little cores. These memories are very expensive because they must be extremely reliable and fast. The speed of a memory is measured by the time it takes to read or write a word in the memory. This time may be 1/10 of a millionth of a second (.1 microseconds) or even less.

Assume now that the main computer has analyzed the information received and identified the letter as an "A." It now tells the console what to display on the screen. Assume that four blanks as well as an "A" are to be displayed. We adopt the code of the previous section and place the codes for five characters in one computer word as seen in Figure 0-5.5. The process that sent information to the computer is reversed and the number 2929292900 is sent back over the telephone lines and placed in a word in the console. The console also has a memory and in many instances it is a kind of small special purpose computer.

Once the information is in a console word, it must be displayed on the screen (see Figure 0-5.6). The word is broken into five parts (the codes for five characters) and these parts are passed on to a *character generator* which creates the display with a single letter as shown. The character generator has a special electronic circuit to display each character. A typical console may have from 60 to 125 of these character generation circuits. The actual circuits are quite small, perhaps the size shown in Figure 0-5.7. The circuits shown are comparable with those of a good radio in complexity and capability.

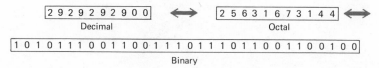

(a) The pattern of 4 blanks, then A (blank = 29, A = 00) in numerical
     representations as numbers inside the main computer.

(b) The pulse pattern sent back to the console over the telephone line.

```
2 9 2 9 2 9 2 9 0 0
```

(c) The pattern of 4 blanks, then A as represented inside the console.

FIGURE *0-5.5*   **The computer recognizes the bit pattern received as an "A"
and sends the console a string of 4 blanks and an A to be
displayed on the screen. The change from numerical representation to pulse pattern and back is illustrated. The computer
and console use binary numbers exclusively, but people find
octal and especially decimal much easier to understand.**

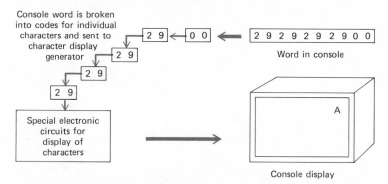

FIGURE *0-5.6*   **Diagram of the process that converts a word (number) in the
console into a visual display on the screen. The code for blank
is 29 and for A is 00. The displays are enlarged in this
chapter. A typical console has 40 to 75 lines with 50 to 80
characters per line.**

We have seen that the processing of a single letter from the tablet to the computer
and back to the display is a very complex operation. It is only practical because of the
fantastic speeds with which computers and other electronic devices operate.

Let us follow the interaction between the political scientist and the computer
system through five distinct steps.

1. User sign-on and identification.
2. Choice of computing that the user wishes to do.
3. Request for data from the data bank.
4. A simple computation with part of this data.
5. Request for a graph of the computed results.

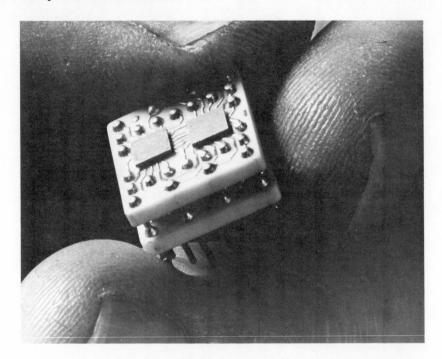

FIGURE 0-5.7 Two examples of highly miniaturized, complex electronic circuits as used in computers. (Courtesy of the IBM Corp.)

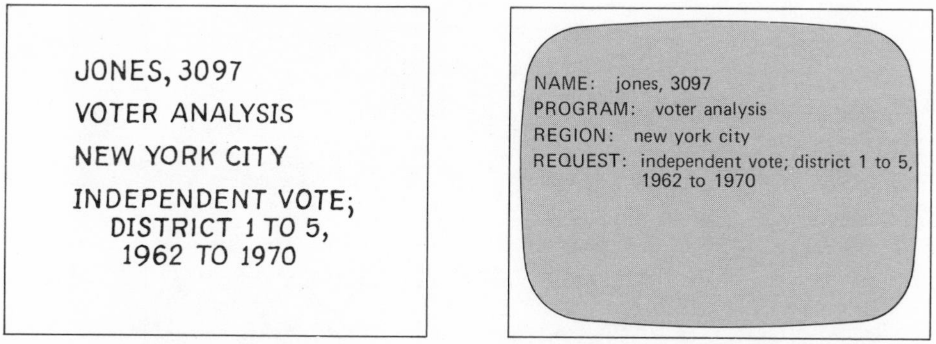

JONES, 3097

VOTER ANALYSIS

NEW YORK CITY

INDEPENDENT VOTE;
DISTRICT 1 TO 5,
1962 TO 1970

Things written on the tablet by
the political scientist

NAME: jones, 3097
PROGRAM: voter analysis
REGION: new york city
REQUEST: independent vote; district 1 to 5,
1962 to 1970

Things displayed by the computer on the console.
Capital letters are from the computer program,
small letters are things taken from the tablet.

FIGURE 0-5.8   A typical dialog where the user identifies himself and his account number. He then
states he wants to use the voter analysis program and this program processes his
request to see the data on independent votes in districts 1 to 5 for the years 1962
through 1970.

During these steps we examine various displays on the console. The tablet with
handwriting is shown on the left and the display is shown on the right. What is written by
the computer on the display is shown in capital letters while the user's writing is
displayed in lower-case letters. The first three steps are shown in Figure 0-5.8.

After the console is turned on, the computer displays the message "NAME:" The
user responds with "JONES, 3097" written on the tablet. The computer processes the
handwriting and displays it on the same line as its message. The number 3097 is a charge
account number and the computer makes a check that Jones is an authorized user of this
account. Presumably only the authorized people know the account number.

Once Jones is signed on and identified, the computer asks him which program he
would like to use. He replies "voter analysis" and this program is obtained from the
program library. *At this moment an important change takes place.* When Jones started, he
was interacting with the "general purpose" system of the computer, the one that
everyone uses to start with. Now the control of his console is turned over to the voter
analysis program and he then works in interaction with this special program.

The voter analysis program asks for the region that is to be studied and once this is
specified it asks for the user's request. The political scientist wants to start by examining
the independent voting trends in certain areas of New York City and this request is made
of the voter analysis program. It responds with a display of the percentage of independent
voters for the years and districts specified (Figure 0-5.9). The numbers shown are
ficticious.

Before proceeding any further, let us consider how the program library and data
displayed are obtained. We already know how the computer receives the message to get
the voter analysis program. Once the "general purpose" system recognizes that the voter
analysis program is needed, it searches for it in the program library. This library is
actually a set of disks (similar to phonograph records) as sketched in Figure 0-5.10. The
information in this library (and also in the data bank) is arranged on *tracks* around the
surface of the disk. One track is shown enlarged and we see that the information is

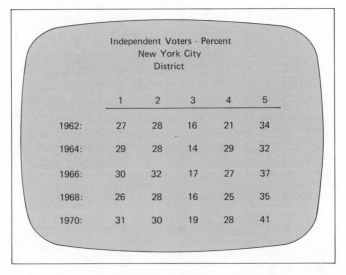

Independent Voters - Percent
New York City
District

	1	2	3	4	5
1962:	27	28	16	21	34
1964:	29	28	14	29	32
1966:	30	32	17	27	37
1968:	26	28	16	25	35
1970:	31	30	19	28	41

FIGURE 0-5.9 The display of information as a result of the requests made. The data for this display is taken from the data bank by the voter analysis program. The numbers actually shown here are fictitious.

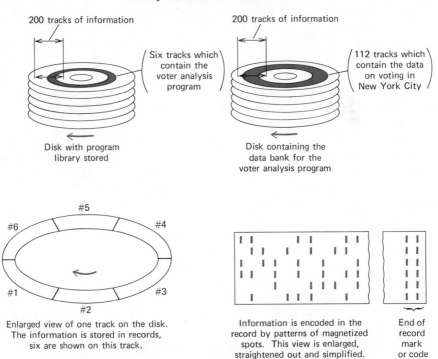

200 tracks of information

Six tracks which contain the voter analysis program

Disk with program library stored

200 tracks of information

112 tracks which contain the data on voting in New York City

Disk containing the data bank for the voter analysis program

#5 #6 #4 #1 #3 #2

Enlarged view of one track on the disk. The information is stored in records, six are shown on this track.

Information is encoded in the record by patterns of magnetized spots. This view is enlarged, straightened out and simplified.

End of record mark or code

FIGURE 0-5.10 A configuration of two disk units which might store the program library and data bank for the computer system. Enlarged views of a track and a record are also shown. Typical sizes for such disk units are from 750,000 to 50 million words of storage capacity.

further broken down into *records*. Records are the basic unit in most computerized information systems and the name comes from (pre-computer) business information systems where it has the same meaning.

A small portion of a record is shown and we see that the information is finally represented as a bit pattern along the record. The "1" bits are indicated by magnetized spots and the "0" bits by unmagnetized spots. The magnetic principles are similar to those used for tape recorders. A photograph of a disk is shown in Figure 0-5.11. A disk has a fixed reading head which can only read information directly next to it. Thus there can be a delay in obtaining information because one has to wait for the disk to turn. Even though these disks spin at 15,000 revolutions per minute (rpm), these delays can cause significant problems because they are very long compared to the electronic speeds of the rest of the computer system. A car would have to be traveling 1200 miles an hour for its wheels to spin at 15,000 rpm.

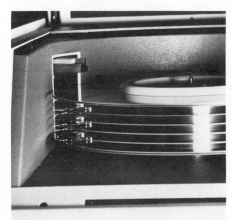

FIGURE 0-5.11 (Above) Close up of a disk of the type used for program libraries and data banks of computer systems. (Left) A collection of disk units.

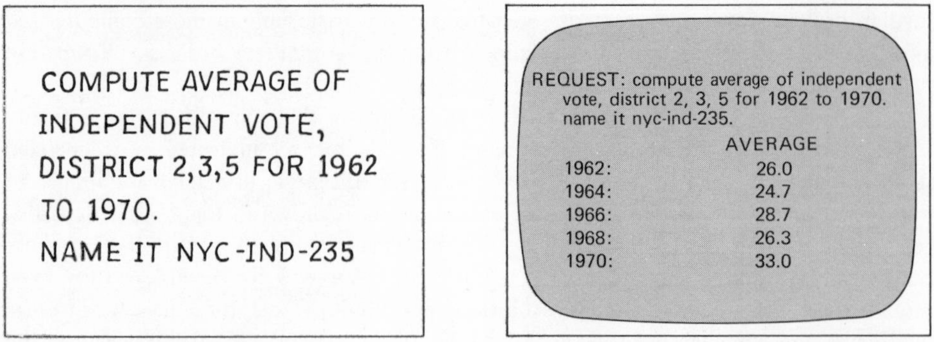

```
COMPUTE AVERAGE OF
INDEPENDENT VOTE,
DISTRICT 2,3,5 FOR 1962
TO 1970.
NAME IT NYC-IND-235
```

Things written on the tablet
by the political scientist

REQUEST: compute average of independent
vote, district 2, 3, 5 for 1962 to 1970.
name it nyc-ind-235.

	AVERAGE
1962:	26.0
1964:	24.7
1966:	28.7
1968:	26.3
1970:	33.0

Things displayed by the computer on the console.
Capital letters are from the computer program,
small letters are things taken from the tablet.

FIGURE 0-5.12 **An example of a typical request that requires some processing of the information in the data bank.**

When the voter analysis program has control of the console it also has control of the disk with the data bank of information on voting. Jones' request results in a search of this data bank and the information is transmitted to the main computer and then on to the console for display. During this process the representation of the information is changed many times.

Let us suppose now that Jones decides to examine some average values of the numbers displayed for him. The computer writes the word REQUEST and he responds as shown in Figure 0-5.12. We assume that the voter analysis program is designed to handle a request like this and the result is also shown in Figure 0-5.12.

If the voter analysis program did not recognize the request for computing the average, it would print a message to that effect. It might, perhaps, display

"COMMAND ERROR: AVERAGE NOT RECOGNIZED"

Such messages also occur when words are misspelled or when the writing is too poor for the words to be recognized. Programs of this nature normally require rather simple and stylized requests and demand that the punctuation be correct.

Recall the discussion earlier about the instructions that one must give a computer in order to have some calculations made. One of the chief functions of the voter analysis program is to take a request like that in Figure 0-5.12 and to generate the computer instructions to carry out the request. The first few such instructions for this request are indicated in Figure 0-5.13. The actual process required to obtain this list of instructions is quite complicated, but it is important to realize that *every request must be translated into this simple-minded language.* The voter analysis program must keep track of where everything is located. For example, the 25 numbers of the first data display are located on lines 31 through 55 and the number for 1962, district 2 is on line 36. The results being computed are placed on lines 61 to 65.

All this computation takes place inside the main computer. Once the averages are found, they are transmitted to the console along with *all* the details about the display to be made for the user.

1. Count the number of items for the average and write the number on line 22.
2. Get line 36 (data for 1962, district 2) and write it on line 23.
3. Get line 41 (data for 1962, district 3) and add it to the number on line 23.
4. Get line 51 (data for 1962, district 5) and add it to the number on line 23.
5. Divide the number on line 23 by the number on line 22 and write the result on line 61.
6. Get line 37 (data for 1964, district 2) and write it on line 23, after erasing the number previously written on this line.
7. ————

FIGURE 0-5.13. **The initial segment of the computer instructions that the voter analysis program must use in order to process the request for some average values. In this example, the number 3 is written on line 22, the number 78 = 28 + 16 + 34 is written on line 23 and finally 26 = 78/3 is written on line 61.**

Once Jones has seen these numbers, he can decide to have a graph (or plot) made. Actually, he gave these averages a name (he chose NYC-IND-235) just so he could later request that something be done with them. The request to plot these averages and the resulting graph are shown in Figure 0-5.14. This console has the ability to draw straight lines as well as to display characters and a nice graph is possible.

The information about the graph must be encoded into a representation for the console to process. We assume that any point on the screen is located relative to the lower

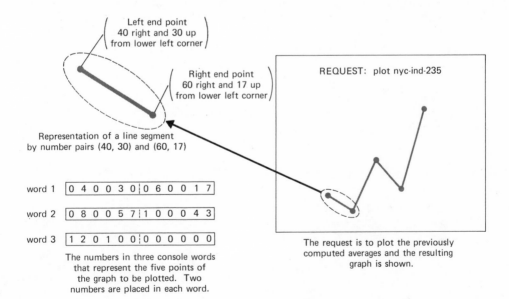

FIGURE 0-5.14 **The political scientist requests a graph of the averages just computed. The graph is represented by numbers in the console words (two per word). The numbers are fed to special electronic circuits that draw the specified lines on the screen.**

left-hand corner of the screen. Thus 40-30 is 40 units to the right and 30 units up from the bottom, likewise 127-196 is 127 units right and 196 units up. These pairs of numbers can be combined into one number of six digits, that is, 040030 and 127196. These six digit numbers represent points on the screen and a list of them represents a broken line graph. The numbers are placed into console words two at a time and thus the entire graph is represented by the three words as shown in Figure 0-5.14. The numbers are processed by special circuits which display the required lines on the console screen. These circuits are similar although more complicated than those that display a character.

We leave Mr. Jones as he continues to search for clues to the behavior of the voting public. He becomes familiar with the computer as a helpful tool as he uses and converses with these programs during his study. He soon forgets, if he ever knew, the intricate operations and massive information transfers of the computer system. The voter analysis program communicates with him at a level that is natural and easy. This is, of course, the ultimate aim of a computer system; to harness its fantastic speed and capacity and make it into a useful, productive tool. Great strides have been made in harnessing the computer, but there is still a great deal to be done.

1 The History of Computer Development

1-1   ANCIENT HISTORY (2500 B.C. TO 1880 A.D.)

The history of computing properly starts with man's first efforts to develop the concept of numbers and counting. After many centuries the concepts were firmly established and the ancient Greeks and Egyptians realized the need to perform more complex operations—to take square roots, to find the value of π (the ratio of the circumference of a circle to its diameter), and to solve simple trigonometry problems. Nevertheless, even the simple operations of addition and multiplication could be carried out only by leading scholars. Multiplication tables were much in use. One of the main reasons for the difficulty was the cumbersome number systems used. Consider what a Roman was faced with when he wished to add 147 and 244, or multiply 1539 by 38:

$$\begin{array}{r} \text{CXLVII} \\ +\ \text{CCXLIV} \\ \hline ? \end{array} \qquad \begin{array}{r} \text{MDXXXIX} \\ \times\ \text{XXXVIII} \\ \hline ? \end{array}$$

It is no wonder that few Romans did anything with numbers besides counting and inscribing them on buildings. The addition is not as hard as it might appear but multiplication with Roman numerals is extremely complicated.

The Arabic number system, the one we use today, provided the key to efficient arithmetic calculation. In the seventh through twelfth centuries, Arab and Hindu mathematicians perfected algorithms for addition, multiplication, and division. The word *algorithm* is derived from the name of one of those ninth century Arab mathematicians. An algorithm is a sequence of logical steps which, when carried out, yields the solution of a problem. The actual symbols 1, 2, 3, 4, . . ., 9, 0 were introduced in Europe before 1000 A.D. and came from Hindu, not Arabic, symbols for the digits.

The first mechanical aid to computation was probably the abacus. (Figure 1-1.1). Although its origin is unknown, it was used over 2500 years ago by the Chinese. The abacus is remarkably effective and a skilled user can compete quite successfully in speed and accuracy with a mechanical desk calculator. In spite of its effectiveness, the abacus was not widely adopted outside the Orient and computations elsewhere were made with

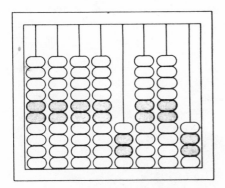 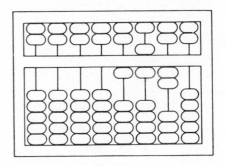

FIGURE 1-1.1   **A typical modern abacus.**

the help of pebbles or the familiar paper and pencil. Or, for instance, the multiplication and addition tables we memorized as children were intended to create a "built-in" calculator in our minds.

There were several unsuccessful attempts to mechanize arithmetic from the eleventh to the sixteenth century. However, a significant aid to paper and pencil calculations was introduced by the Scottish mathematician John Napier in 1614 when he published his tables of logarithms. Logarithms enable one to replace multiplication or division by a single addition or subtraction. His tables, and later variations of them, were widely used in scientific circles to aid computation. Logarithms are the mathematical basis for the slide rule (Figure 1-1.2), the calculating aid that is (or at least once was) the trademark of the engineer.

FIGURE 1-1.2 **A slide rule is a device which allows one to perform calculations involving multiplication, division, exponents, trigonometric quantities, and so on, with great rapidity. The accuracy is limited by one's ability to read the scales.**

In 1623 Wilhelm Schickard, a professor of biblical languages and astronomy, designed and built a machine which was able to add, subtract, multiply, and divide. Like its predecessors, however, it was considered impractical. The model was ruined in a fire and never replaced.

The world's first mechanical adding machine was constructed in 1642 by a 19-year-old French genius, Blaise Pascal. The machine used a scheme similar to the system of wheels and gears on an automobile speedometer. It was made for Pascal's father, an accountant who did extensive calculations in order to compute taxes. Pascal recognized the potential use of calculating machines and went to considerable effort to build and sell them commercially. (See Figure 1-1.3) He obtained a "droit de la roi," or king's rights, on

FIGURE 1-1.3 **One of the original calculating machines built by Blaise Pascal in the middle 1600s. (Courtesy of The IBM Corp.)**

the machines and built more than 50 of them. However, because they were rather expensive and delicate, the commercial venture failed. Pascal went on to do pioneering work in many areas of mathematics and statistics as well as in philosophy and literature.

Another young genius, Gottfried von Leibniz, took the next step and constructed a mechanical device that could add, multiply, divide, and extract square roots. The machine was built in the 1670s when Leibniz was about 25 years old. He was aware of the delicate and sometimes unreliable nature of Pascal's machines and a machine built by Samuel Morland in 1666. After studying their designs, Leibniz produced a machine that was reliable and accurate. He also went on to do pioneering mathematical work, including (along with Isaac Newton) the original development of calculus. These machines established the principles involved in the mechanization of calculation, but they did not have an impact on the computation problems of business or science.

A machine called the arithometer was designed in 1820 by the Frenchman Charles X. Thomas. It too was somewhat delicate but nevertheless was widely adopted by commerce throughout France. Improvements in the mechanical design continued to be made and in 1885 William S. Burroughs invented the printing calculator, a machine which printed the results of its calculation on paper. The next year Dorr E. Felt invented a calculator called the comptometer, a machine without rival for many years. By the end of the 1800s calculating machines were a standard fixture of business and commerce.

Mechanical problems also plagued the first attempt at a more ambitious calculating machine. In 1822 Charles Babbage received funds from the British government to develop his "difference engine." (See Figure 1-1.4.) It's purpose was to calculate the various powers (x^2, x^3, x^4, . . .) of a given number x. He constructed one such machine and while in the process of perfecting it, he conceived the idea of an "analytical engine," a general purpose calculator which could be "programmed" to evaluate a wide range of arithmetic and algebraic formulas. Lady Lovelace, the daughter of the poet Lord Byron, and a close friend of Babbage, had a scientific bent which led her to become deeply interested in his machines. She prepared many programs for the analytical engine earning the title of the

FIGURE 1-1.4 **A model of one of Charles Babbage's "calculating engines' built in the middle 1800s. Although correctly conceived, the engines never worked reliably. (Courtesy of The IBM Corp.)**

world's first programmer. Babbage spent many years on these machines, but the level of machine technology at that time simply could not provide reliable operation. The papers and drawings that he left show that his design was logically and mechanically correct.

The analytical engine's design included provisions to "store" up to 1000 fifty-digit numbers. The "mill" or "central processor" would perform additions or subtractions of such numbers at the rate of one per second and would multiply two such numbers in one minute. Other components included a typewriter-like device to print results and a mechanism to read or punch holes in cardboard cards. Babbage probably used punched cards because of their use in automatic looms, or weaving machines (Figure 1-1.5). The system of controlling looms by using punched holes in a metal drum was introduced in 1741 and in 1790 Joseph Jacquard modified the system to use punched cards.

Although Babbage's difference engine was not perfected, George Schentz used the design as the basis of one he constructed in Stockholm. Schentz' machine was used in the 1850s to calculate a number of tables. A better difference engine was built in the 1870s by the American George B. Grant. It weighed 2000 pounds and had more than 15,000 parts. Grant also made important contributions to the development of advanced calculating machines.

FIGURE 1-1.5 **A modern Jacquard loom controlled by metal "punched cards" seen at the top of the loom. These cards contain the information about the pattern to be woven.**

1-2 MIDDLE HISTORY (1880 TO 1945)

The impetus for the next step in computing, or more exactly, in data processing, was the U.S. Census. It took almost nine years to process the information obtained in the 1880 census and it was clear that it would take over ten years for the next one if data processing techniques were not improved. Herman Hollerith, a statistician and inventor, joined the Census Bureau in the mid-1880s and developed a new system to record and process the census data using punched cards. The original data was punched into cards (with a hand punch) and these cards were processed by tabulating machines. For example, a card sorter was developed which could sort cards into one of twelve groups at the rate of 300 cards per minute. After much experimentation the system was perfected. The data of the 1890 census was processed in less than three years.

The original card that Hollerith designed had 45 columns, round holes, and was the size of a dollar bill. The same size cards are used today; the dollar bill has changed size since the 1880's, not the card. Punched cards had been used in weaving machines for over a century and Babbage used them in his analytical engine; Hollerith claimed, however, that the idea crystalized in his mind after watching a conductor punch his train ticket. The current card format of 80 columns and rectangular holes was introduced by IBM in 1928.

Two of the modern computer companies originated from these Census Bureau efforts at data processing. Hollerith formed the Tabulating Machine Company around 1900 and in 1912 it merged with some other companies to form the Computing-Tabulating-Recording Co. The name was changed in 1924 to International Business Machines. James Powers was Hollerith's successor at the Census Bureau. He, in turn, left the Census Bureau in 1911 to form the Powers Accounting Machine Co. which became part of the Remington Rand Corporation.

Punched card equipment or *unit record equipment* was widely adopted for business data processing in the 1930s. This equipment included machines to punch cards, to print on them (interpreters), to print their information on paper, to sort them, and to perform short, simple arithmetic calculations. As this technology was being assimilated by business and industry, the seeds of the next technology were germinating.

A. M. Turing developed theoretical models of computation and machines that could perform them; his work prepared the ground for automata theory. He was mainly interested in exploring the theoretical limits of calculation and computers. His results form one of the cornerstones of automata theory.

At the same time, there were practical efforts to build general purpose calculating machines. The first successes were *differential analyzers* which are computing machines used to solve a certain class of scientific problems. The principal worker in this area was Vannevar Bush who by 1930 had working differential analyzers at the Massachusetts Institute of Technology. He wrote articles in the mid-1940s about the general nature and potential of computing which were extremely perceptive and are still relevant more than 25 years later. Bush became one of the leading scientific figures in the United States and a principal scientific advisor to President Roosevelt during World War II.

Other efforts were made to build computing machines much as Babbage had envisioned them. The basic component was changed from wheels and gears to electro-magnetic relays. Such relays were widely used in telephone switching and the Bell

Telephone Laboratories built at least two such computers between 1938 and 1943. The first of these was a special-purpose computer, designed to handle one specific task, but the second was general purpose, capable of solving a wide variety of problems, although it was built to perform ballistics computations. These two computers included many of the features (or direct ancestors of them) of modern computers.

The best known computer of this era was the Mark I at Harvard University. The idea of building a general purpose computer had been suggested by several people and in 1937 Howard Aiken of Harvard University became interested in the possibility. The construction of the Mark I was supported by IBM (out of their advertising budget) and much of it was done in their plants. It was finished in 1944 and many people consider the Mark I to be the first realization of Babbage's concept of an analytical engine. The Mark I was more than a prototype model; for many years it provided productive computations on mathematical and scientific problems.

1-3 MODERN HISTORY (1945 TO PRESENT)

The primary emphasis is on the United States because the bulk of the research and development of computers in this period was done here. By 1970, however, there were many important projects in progress throughout the world. We mention only a selection of the significant computers—those which seem to have set the more important trends.

There are two points that can reasonably mark the beginning of the modern era of computers. One is the introduction of the electronic devices and the other is the introduction of the internally stored program.

A calculator using electronic devices (vacuum tubes) was started about 1940, well before the Mark I was completed. It was constructed at the Moore School of Electrical Engineering of the University of Pennsylvania under the direction of John Mauchly and Presper Eckert. This calculator was called the ENIAC, an acronym for Electronic Numerical Integrator and Calculator. The ENIAC, finished in 1946, was a huge machine with over 18,000 vacuum tubes and 1500 relays. (See Figure 1-3.1.) It was able to perform an addition in 1/5000 of a second. Although this rate was dwarfed by later computers, it was already large enough to make one wonder about the need for so much speed in addition.

The ENIAC and earlier calculators were externally programmed. That is, the instructions about the operations to be performed were outside of the machine and fed, one at a time, to the machine via some device like a punched card reader or paper tape reader. It was a formidable task to write a program for early computers whether they were internally or externally programmed. It required complete familiarity with the details of the machine's operation, considerable ingenuity, and a great deal of patience. After reviewing a coding (programming) manual for such a computer, one contemporary wrote:

> As it is, coding appears to be an almost insurmountable barrier between the machine and the mere mathematician with a problem to solve.

Even as the ENIAC was being finished, the advantages of the internally programmed calculator were realized. Indeed, it is the internally stored program that distinguishes a computer from a calculator. Thus the instructions for a computer are

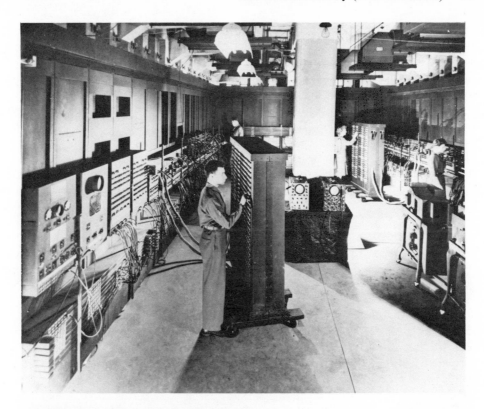

FIGURE 1-3.1 The early vacuum tube computers were huge machines that filled a good sized room. Shown are (top) the ENIAC (circa 1947) and (below) the EDSAC (circa 1951). Modern computers the size of a small desk are much faster and more powerful than the ENIAC.

stored, electronically or magnetically, inside the machine and they can be interpreted, executed, and modified if need be at electronic speeds. The chief proponent and developer of the stored program concept was John von Neumann. Perhaps the most eminent mathematician in the United States, he was convinced that computers could solve many important unsolved problems in applied mathematics.

Von Neumann joined the ENIAC group along with H. H. Goldstine. Together they directed the construction of the EDVAC (Electronic Discrete Variable Automatic Computer) for the U.S. Army Ordinance Department at the Aberdeen Proving Grounds. The EDVAC project was started in 1946, but delays postponed the completion of the computer until 1952. The first computer EDSAC (Electronic Delayed Storage Automatic Computer) went into operation in May 1949, at the Mathematical Laboratory at Cambridge University, England. The development of EDSAC was directed by M. V. Wilkes.

Eckert and Mauchly left the EDVAC project soon after it started (one reason for the delay in EDVAC) to form a company to produce another computer, the UNIVAC (Universal Automatic Computer). The UNIVAC was the first computer designed for business rather than scientific applications. The first one was sold to the Census Bureau in 1951.

Although IBM was heavily involved in the business machine field and had sponsored the Mark I, it did not enter the computer field until 1953. The first IBM 701 (Defense Calculator), delivered in 1953, was, for that time, a large scale scientific computer. It had a 2048-word high speed memory on a cathode ray tube (TV screen) backed up by both magnetic tapes and a magnetic drum. In the same year IBM announced the IBM 650 computer, a smaller machine useful for either scientific or business applications (Figure 1-3.2). The IBM 650 is discussed in more detail in Chapter 9 where it is used as a model for the first generation of computers, the simple computers. Earlier, in 1949, the CPC (Card Programmed Calculator) was introduced by IBM for business applications. It was not a computer, however, since it did not have an internally stored program.

The first "super computer," the NORC (Naval Ordinance Research Computer), was delivered to the U.S. Naval Weapons Laboratory in 1955. A computer is classified as super if it is significantly bigger, faster, and more powerful than its contemporaries. Super computers provide a great deal of excitement in the computing community even if sometimes their overall impact is slight. The NORC could perform an addition of two decimal numbers in 15 microseconds (15 millionths of a second); which is about thirteen times faster than the addition time of the ENIAC. The actual increase in power is much greater because the ENIAC could only add integers and, even though it could do one addition in 1/5000 of a second, it could not add 5000 integers in one second because it was externally programmed and could not receive instructions at a rate comparable to its calculating speed. On the other hand, the NORC could perform 67,000 additions in one second. At the time the NORC was built most computers required from three to ten times as much time for a multiplication as for an addition; the NORC's multiplication time was only twice its addition time. Furthermore, the NORC had a form of machine language which, on the average, results in faster operation that the form of machine language used on earlier (and on most current) computers. The simple machine language described in Chapter 9 is the most common form. Only one NORC was built.

FIGURE 1-3.2 The IBM 650 was the most widely used computer in the world during the middle 1950s. (Courtesy of The IBM Corp.)

The period from 1956 to 1958 saw three significant developments in computing: magnetic core memories, higher level languages, and the realization of a need for a "system" for operating a computer. The magnetic core memories were larger, had faster access (the time required to obtain a number from memory), and were more reliable than the earlier vacuum tube memories. They were also cheaper, though still very expensive.

The computing community has had several painfully costly lessons by adopting new approaches that are incompatible with preceding ones. Sometimes, of course, the incompatibility is unavoidable and occasionally it is even advantageous; but changes in machine languages particularly seem to create confusion and headaches.

Fortran, the first of the higher level languages, was issued in 1957 for the IBM 704 which was IBM's current large scientific computer. That first version of Fortran was rather crude compared to the current Fortran IV language now widely used.

The original Fortran language had a whole array of illogical and unreasonable features (not unlike the irregular verbs, strange spellings, irregular formation of plurals, and so forth, of the "natural" languages like English or French). These features make the languages difficult to learn and probably add little, if anything, to their usefulness. Many of these disagreeable features of the original Fortran have disappeared in later versions. Figure 1-3.3 illustrates the evolution of languages for communicating with computers (programming).

FIGURE 1-3.3 Languages for man-computer communications have evolved steadily since 1950. The direction has been consistent: to make computer languages closer to natural ones. A persistent difficulty, illustrated above, is that one must know *what* to say (or ask) as well as *how* to say it.

The computing community recognized the value of higher level languages and the problem of machine dependence. A program written in early Fortran was likely to run on an IBM 704 only. This, of course, meant that the program was useless when another, probably better, computer was installed. As a result, an international effort was organized to define a language for computing independent of a particular computer. The resulting language is Algol (algorithmic language), first defined in 1958. A modified version of Algol appeared in 1960 and has been widely adopted, especially outside the United States.

The third development of this period, and perhaps the most significant of the three even though higher level languages have had a profound influence on computing, was the widespread appreciation of the necessity for a "system" for operating a computer. Many systems were developed, most of which were of the "batch-processing" nature (discussed in some detail in Chapter 9). The systems areas of computer science has emerged as one of the central, most fruitful and most challenging areas of research and development.

The second generation of computers started with the introduction of transistorized computers. This technological advance permitted smaller, cheaper, faster, and more reliable electronic circuits. The first of these, the IBM 7090, was delivered late in 1959 and was followed shortly by the CDC 1604, the Philco 2000, and the second "super-computer," the Remington Rand UNIVAC LARC. The addition time for the IBM 7090 was about 4-1/2 microseconds (1/220,000 of a second) compared to 24 microseconds for its vacuum-tube twin, the IBM 709. The third "super-computer," the IBM Stretch, was delivered in 1961 to the Atomic Energy Commission. This super computer, however, did not meet its design specifications by a fair margin and only seven of them were built.

The third generation of computers was announced in 1964 by IBM with its 360 line of computers, although it is not clear what distinguishes a third generation computer from a second generation one. The technological advance of integrated circuits in the hardware is one possibility, or the provision of facilities for time-sharing, multi-programming, or other new concepts discussed in Chapter 9. In any case, almost all computers introduced after 1965 are declared by their manufacturers to be third generation computers, although some have been advertized as fourth generation. It is even less clear what distinguishes third and fourth generation computers from one another besides the advertising. This does not mean that technological advances or computer system advances are not continuing to be made. It is just that one cannot single one item that is important enough to mark a new generation.

The next "super-computer," the CDC 6600 (shown in Figure 1-3.4), was delivered by the Control Data Corporation to the Atomic Energy Commission in 1965. This computer executes about 3,000,000 instructions per second, an increase of almost 200 times the speed of the first super-computer, the NORC, introduced only ten years earlier. More super-computers being built in the early 1970's include the CDC 7600 and Star by the Control Data Corporation, the IBM 360 Model 195 by International Business Machines, and the ILIAC IV by the University of Illinois. The internal design of these computers is such that they can execute up to 5, 10, or even 100 million instructions per second by very high speed circuitry and extensive use of parallel, or simultaneous, computations. The ILIAC IV, for instance, is to have 64 synchronized and coordinated computing processors.

Two new and potentially very important trends, both of which are aimed at providing personalized computers, emerged in the early 1970's. The *mini-computers* are simply small (in cost and in size) computers able to provide effective and inexpensive computing services for a broad group of users. The costs of mini-computers have fallen dramatically in a few years and further large decreases are expected. At the same time, their power and flexibility have increased substantially.

The *computer network* or *computer utility* is the name applied to the system of connecting dozens or hundreds (or, someday, thousands) of individual consoles with a

FIGURE 1-3.4 A general view of a CDC 6600 computer system. This was the world's most powerful computer when it was first delivered in the middle 1960s. (Courtesy of Control Data Corp.)

(usually very large) computer. The goal is to provide the user with the equivalent of a small computer for his personal use. There are already nationwide networks, such as the ARPA (Advanced Research Projects Agency) network. Anyone on the network can, from his personal console, use any computer, any program, or any data bank on the network. Of course, he must learn how to use and be authorized to use the network resources. It seems certain that both of these trends will flourish in the future.

1-4 THE SIZE AND SCOPE OF COMPUTING

The historical development given above is centered around scientific and technological themes. In this section we consider some of the other aspects of the development of calculating power and computers.

The developments of Pascal, Leibniz, Babbage, and so forth, had negligible impact outside a very narrow line of scientific development. The middle history period (1880-1945) saw two separate types of development. The first of these was the perfection of the earlier ideas and their widespread dissemination throughout the scientific and business world. By the 1930's the ideas of Pascal and Leibniz had led to commonplace tools of society—a wait of about 300 years. The pace of technological development had quickened dramatically and some ideas conceived at the beginning of the middle history period (such as punched card data processing) were perfected and in widespread use—a wait of only 40 years. Even so, it was only at the end of this period that serious efforts were made to perfect the last ancient history idea, the analytical engine of Babbage. It is probably fair to say that the idea could not have been perfected and reduced to practice much earlier because this had to wait for technological developments in other areas. Thus, at the end of this period, most of the ancient history ideas had become integral parts of society, especially in scientific and business circles.

The other type of development in the middle period was to lay the ground work for the modern period. This activity parallels that of the ancient period. A number of important ideas on the mathematical nature and practice of computation were conceived. Equally important were technological developments in other areas (such as electronics) that would make it possible to build the first computers.

The modern period began with the completion of the ideas of the early innovators, the general purpose, flexible calculator. It also began with one of the key concepts of computing, the concept of the internally stored program. One can visualize two streams of development which started at this point. One of these was a huge amorphous activity, business data processing. It was based on the work in the ancient and middle periods, but had little awareness of its historical background. The other stream was a tiny rivulet, a few isolated groups of scientists interested in tools to solve very complicated scientific problems. The two streams were hardly aware of each other's presence and only a few people sensed that they would someday merge.

For instance, the original orientation of the Association for Computing Machinery formed in 1947 with 246 members was mathematical and scientific. The general public was unaware of computers except for a few Sunday supplement stories about "giant brains." The impact of computers even in the scientific community was still small and restricted to a few areas. The explosive growth was not far away though.

By 1951, however, the UNIVAC was on the market. The Census Bureau immediately acquired one for its huge data processing activity, the General Electric Company acquired one for its business data processing and the business application of computers was started. The computing community had grown and over 900 people attended the first joint computer conference in 1951. This conference was organized by several societies whose memberships were primarily electrical engineers or "pure" scientists. The activities at the conference were almost exclusively oriented toward science and engineering.

When IBM entered the computer business in 1953 its sales from office equipment and punched card processing equipment were $410,000,000. This represents a fabulous growth from its sales of $4,000,000 in 1914 and most of its growth was yet to come.

It was only a few years until the computer became an indispensible part of a number of scientific areas, for example, aerodynamics, space technology, atomic energy, hydrodynamics, vehicle dynamics, and so on. Computers were solving many difficult problems in these areas and opening many new areas for research and development. In the background was the steady introduction of computers into business applications. This event was not very exciting because little innovation was present. One merely did the same accounting and payroll operations using a computer to replace the punched card equipment in earlier use. The size and scope of the computing effort grew and attracted some attention in the general public although computers were still considered esoteric scientific research tools.

In the early 1960s the expansion of the use of computers exceeded even the most optimistic predictions of a few years earlier. Computer manufacturing established itself as one of the major industries in the United States. In 1961 some thirty large companies began to make their quarterly reports on Social Security taxes by magnetic tapes. For most of these companies over 1000 typewritten pages of reports were eliminated. The demand for trained and knowledgeable people was high and a few universities instituted graduate programs in Computer Science. Up to this time all of the professionals in computing (which by then numbered in the tens of thousands) had originally been trained in some other discipline.

In the midst of this explosive growth arose an awareness of the changing nature of computing. The esoteric scientific tool could do millions of calculations to solve a problem at the frontiers of science. The general public found it difficult to evaluate the significance of these problems, but they took it on faith that these problems were actually worthwhile (some of them were). Computing the payroll for General Motors and spewing out 500,000 checks every week or so was the stereotyped view of business applications of computers. A simple tabulation of the number (or value) of the computers in use showed that the business use of computers had grown far beyond the scientific use. Even more significant than the awareness of the shift of emphasis was the awareness that the stereotype business application was out of date. Computers were no longer solely being used to do the old things faster. They were being used to do things that had not been done before and it became clear that they were going to revolutionize many aspects of business operations. Many exciting and some successful innovative ventures were undertaken in business applications. Some of these are described in Chapter 2 and 4.

The change in the nature of computing was a significant shift away from science and engineering. On the other hand, it represents a significant shift of business management and operation toward science—or at least toward the use of the scientific method. Many of the novel applications of computers forced businessmen to formulate mathematical models of their operations and to analyze them in a rational, objective manner. Business was not the only area of application for computers; many others range from agriculture to literature to psychology to music to library science and so on. It almost seemed as if there were a contest to find the most implausible area in which to apply computers.

Computers were firmly established as an integral part of society in the United States by 1965. There were over 30,000 computers in the U.S. and the general public had become familiar with the punched card as an ingredient of everyday life. (See Figure

1-4.1 and 1-4.2.) There were over 5400 computers in the Federal government (either used directly or by defense contractors) compared to ten only twelve years earlier. Computer Science had a firm foothold in the Universities. In 1965 there were several universities which offered a complete program of Bachelor's, Master's, and Ph.D. degrees in Computer Science. Over 1100 computers were in use at universities by 1966. The value of the computers delivered in the United States in 1967 was almost six billion dollars. The sales of IBM had reached five billion dollars and although this includes office equipment and other noncomputer items, IBM dominated the market with 75 percent of the total sales.

FIGURE 1-4.1 A modern insurance company operation where clerks have direct access to the company's records and files using computer consoles. (Courtesy of Bunker Ramo Corp.)

FIGURE 1-4.2 The computerized reservation system of Pan American Airlines allows them to check for available seats, status of reservations, and so forth, for any of their flights. The system responds to a request for information in a few seconds. (Courtesy of Bunker Ramo Corp.)

By comparison, the value of automobiles delivered in that year was about 25 billion dollars, less than five times greater than computer sales. The Association for Computing Machinery had almost 20,000 members in 1967, and in just a few years its membership goal rose to 100,000.

By 1970 the expansion of the computing field had again exceeded predictions made only a few years earlier and its growth continued unabated. Over 200 universities offered degree programs in Computer Science and some universities predicted that it would be the largest single department on the campus in only five more years. There were perhaps 60,000 computers installed in 1970 of an almost limitless variety. They ranged in cost from only a few thousand dollars to the neighborhood of $15,000,000. The growth and economic impact is illustrated in Table 1-4.1 and Figure 1-4.3.

TABLE 1-4.1.
The growth of computers measured by the number installed and the cumulative value of the computing equipment.

Year	Number installed	Value (in $ Billions)
1945	1	–
1950	20	–
1955	1,000	.7
1960	6,000	1.5
1965	30,000	10
1970	60,000	22
1975 (est)	95,000	50
1980 (est)	145,000	80

Some experts estimate that the computer industry will surpass the automobile or oil industries in size by the early 1980s.

Figure 1-4.4 gives a "time-line" illustration of the history, development, and growth of the computer and its applications.

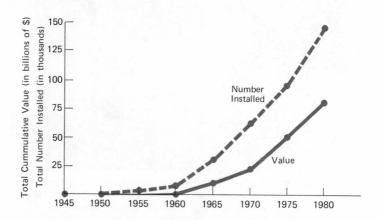

FIGURE 1-4.3 **The growth of computing in terms of total number installed and total cumulative value (in billions of dollars) of the computers installed.**

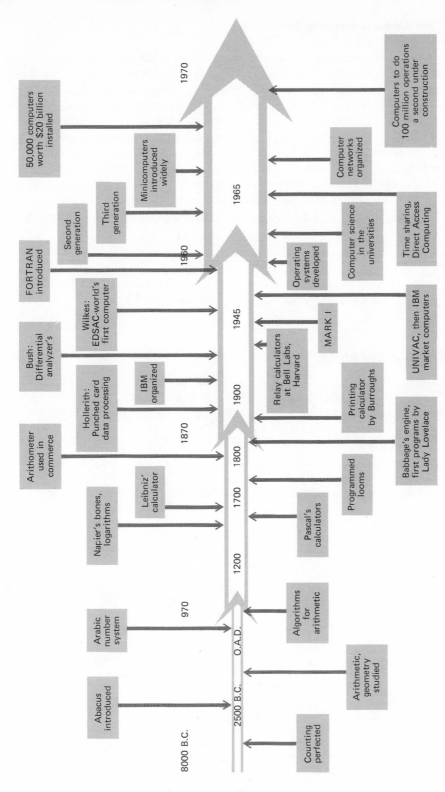

FIGURE 1-4.4 A portrayal of the development of computation and computers from antiquity up to 1970. Note the time scale is chosen so that the last decade is half the length of the last century which, in turn, is half the length of the last millenium.

By 1970 the computer impact was felt in almost every corner of society. Diverse applications included the war on poverty, chess playing, credit card buying, stock market speculation, national elections, arrangement of dating, the exploration of the moon, and many others. Computers were viewed with a combination of fear, awe, distrust, and reverence by the general public who did not understand them and attributed almost magical—or demonic—powers to them. Prophets had erred on the conservative side so often that now utterly fantastic forecasts were being made and only a few were able to judge which of these were nonsense and which were reasonable. It was clear that man had developed an enormously powerful tool to remold his world and his society. And, as with his other tools, he had to assume the responsibility to use it wisely and rationally.

The principal goal of this book is to provide a basis of understanding upon which to judge the uses made of computers.

SUGGESTED READINGS

An annotated list of readings is given at the end of Chapter 4. Several of these books are good sources of additional information on the topics in this chapter. Particularly pertinent from this list are the following:

Bemer, Robert, *Computers and Crisis.* Association of Computing Machinery, 1971.

Bernstein, Jeremy, *The Analytical Engine: Computers Past, Present and Future.* New York: Random House, Inc., 1966.

Communications of the Association of Computing Machinery, Vol. 15, No. 7, July 1972.

Pylyshyn, Zenon, *Perspectives on the Computer Revolution.* Englewood Cliffs, N.J.: Prentice-Hall, Inc., 1970.

2 *The Impact of Computers on Society*

2-1 INTRODUCTION

The proceding chapter shows that computing has had an explosive growth over the past twenty-five years. This chapter explores the nature of the impact of computers on society, specifically on science and technology and business and industry.

The area of science and technology was first and perhaps most affected by the computer. Calculating machines were first developed for business purposes and it is natural that business and industry have incorporated computers into their operations. Computers have already become an essential tool for modern business operations. Except for these two large segments, much of society is untouched by the computer. There are a number of areas where the impact of computers is just beginning to be felt and some of these are discussed in the fourth section of this chapter. The present discussion is of a general nature; more detailed examples are included in Chapter 4.

Section 5 considers the role of computers in policymaking. Even though policy is made by people, not computers, computer applications have resulted in some significant shifts in policymaking. The causes of these shifts, and some of the possible unfortunate consequences, are discussed. The final section explores a number of viewpoints that are widely held about computers and discusses some of the reasoning behind these viewpoints.

2-2 COMPUTERS IN SCIENCE AND TECHNOLOGY

Many of the scientific areas have incorporated computers and computing techniques into their very fabric; it is no longer feasible to work in these areas without some contact with computers. Modern educational programs in science and engineering include computer science as a basic required course, along with mathematics, physics, and chemistry. In spite of the already widespread adoption of computers in science, the impact of computers on science is really only beginning to be felt. (See Figure 2-2.1.)

The computer is a *tool* for the scientist and engineer to use. Unlike many tools, it does not have a specialized mode of use or restricted area of application. Its versatility allows it to assume completely different appearances as it is used in different ways. Let us look at three of these possibilities: the computer as a *calculating tool*, as a *design tool* or a *tool for theoretical exploration*, and as an *experimental tool.*

Calculating Tool

The first computers were intended to be used as calculating tools in science. Through the years, science and technology have used mathematical formulas and equations as an essential part of the language *to express the theories and results obtained.* Numerical answers in simple theories and applications can be computed with paper and pencil, slide rules, desk calculators, and/or special numerical tables. As science progressed theories became more complicated, as did the mathematics. Many theories were so complicated that no amount of mathematical analysis could produce specific numerical answers. Some of the required computations would take many centuries to perform by hand and, since one calculation depends on the results of a previous one, teams of people

FIGURE 2-2.1   The liftoff of the Apollo 16 mission to the moon (April 16, 1972) with astronauts Duke, Mattingly, and Young aboard. Such scientific explorations would not be possible without modern computing facilities. (Courtesy of NASA)

working simultaneously was no help. By the 1940s, progress in many areas of engineering and science (hydrodynamics, aerodynamics, antenna theory, nuclear power, elasticity and plasticity of materials, lubrication theory) was blocked by this problem. The builders of the first computers, well aware of these computational problems, enthusiastically hoped to remove some of the road blocks to progress in these areas. They were successful; the use of computers as purely computational tools continues to be a major application in science.

It is difficult for a nonspecialist to visualize how or why one would want to add, subtract, multiply, and divide millions of numbers, especially to obtain only a few numbers (perhaps only one) in the end. It is even more difficult to imagine that a problem might run for many hours on a very fast computer, but such situations exist and there are still some unsolved problems which are well beyond our current computing capacity.

To help visualize such situations, consider the problem of determining how long it takes to empty a full bathtub of water. A computer allows us to *calculate* this time rather than *measure* it. The theory of hydrodynamics provides us with formulas and equations for the flow of fluids and all the pertinent data and mathematics for modeling the emptying of a bathtub can be written on one or two pages. Recall what happens when the plug is pulled. At first the flow takes place near the bottom leaving the surface undisturbed. After a while a small vortex appears which is rather unstable. Have you ever wondered why the vortex always goes counter clockwise? The vortex expands as the water level drops and finally the flow separates and an "air hole" appears that goes down into the drain. (See Figure 2-2.2.) At the very end the vortex motion stops and the water simply flows to the edge of the drain and over the side as in a waterfall. Now consider the complexity of the path of a particular drop of water and the thousands of different paths there are. Each path must be found in order to know the flow of the water and, in turn, to compute the single number desired—the time required to empty the tub. Scientists

FIGURE 2-2.2 A view of the fluid flow pattern which develops when the plug is pulled from a drain. The counter-clockwise motion is seen from the dye being dropped on the surface of the vortex. (Courtesy of Alan McDonald, Purdue University.)

knew in principle how to compute this number many years before they could actually make the computations.

Of course, it is inefficient and unnecessary to use a computer to determine how long it takes a bathtub to empty. A much faster and easier way is just to fill the tub, pull the plug, and use a stop watch to measure the time. But what about studying the flow that results from a break in a major dam, or the time it takes to empty a fuel container on the moon, or the flow of molten iron in a yet-to-be-built steel mill? It is sometimes extremely difficult or even impossible to directly measure and observe the processes one is studying. In these instances a theoretical calculation using a computer may be the only way to obtain the desired information.

A selection of frames from a computer-generated movie is shown in Figure 2-2.3. The fluid flow depicted is the result of a suddenly narrowed throat in a pipe full of water. The frames show the turbulent flow that results at various times after the smooth flow has been disturbed by the throat.

Design Tool and Tool for Theoretical Exploration

The use of the computer as a design tool or as a tool for theoretical explorations grew rapidly in the 1960s and many people predict even greater growth in the future. The first section of Chapter 4 gives some specific illustrations, but this use of computers is described only in general terms here. Large numbers of calculations are involved with such a use of the computer. There is a significant element of interaction between the computer and the man using it. A typical application involves some objective, for instance the design of a bridge, the layout of the streets in a housing development, or the development of a theory of the geological structure of the moon. In any case the computer is first given a set of basic programs relevant to the objective. These programs, either written by the user or part of a standard set of programs for specialists in the area involved, provide two things: the set up of lines of communication between the user and the computer, and the means to carry out (normally automatically and without specific commands) all of the basic computations.

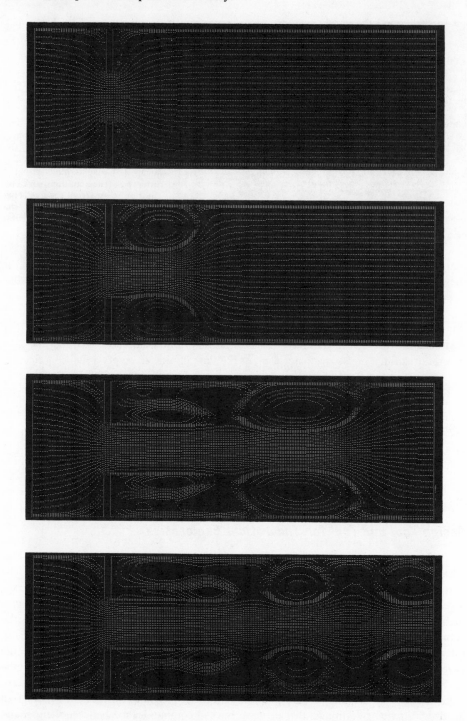

FIGURE 2-2.3   Selected frames from a movie produced as part of a study of the dynamic behavior of fluids. (Courtesy of Professor Manro Greppi)

An interchange between the computer and the user might then be as follows: The user describes some initial situation that he wishes to consider, perhaps a sketch of the arches and columns of a section of a bridge, a sketch of a street network and indication of the location of a park and two schools, or the specifications of three layers (of some particular thickness and composition) and a core for the moon. The computer carries out the necessary computations to examine the situation. If some essential element has not been provided, it requests more information from the user. Once the details of the problem area are complete, the computer returns a summary of the user's initial situations. The summary might consist of a picture of the bridge along with the maximum load it can carry, a plot of the housing development that includes individual lots for homes and a traffic flow analysis, or graphs of the vibration transmission behavior of the moon in standard situations. It is likely that the initial solution proposed has some serious defect, for example, the bridge might collapse from the weight of a single car, but the basic communication programs allow the user to modify the initial proposal and view the new results. Or the user might ask for details on a point that were not given him in the first summary. This interaction continues until the objective is achieved or (perish the thought) until the user gives up.

Experimental Tool

The final role for a computer considered here is its use as an experimental tool or instrument similar to a telescope or seismograph, for example, a microscope to study the atomic structure of complex molecules like the DNA molecules which carry *all* the genetic information about a person. A diagram of this microscope is shown in Figure 2-2.4. It is formidable, but still practical, to calculate the molecular structure from the x-ray diffraction patterns. Once the structure is "known" or represented internally in the computer, pictures of the molecule can be displayed on a television screen for a person to see. The molecule can be displayed from various angles, so that a person might examine cross sections, enlargements of various parts, or even see a slowly rotating picture of it.

One can argue that this is not really "seeing" and, to prove it, one could create the diffraction pattern, have the computer analyze it and then remove the molecule and the person would still see views of the molecule. A narrow and limited definition of seeing would also rule out photographs (especially infrared or ultraviolet ones) or "live" television, but such limitations really serve no useful purpose. It is easy to mentally extend this situation to the point of viewing the dynamics of a chemical reaction involving several molecules and where the movement seen on the television screen is essentially similar to the actions of the molecules.

The principle behind this microscope holds out the possibility that instruments might be built which allow humans to sense (see, hear, even smell!) things which cannot be sensed by direct approaches similar to microscopes or telescopes. Thus we can hope to see earth quake shocks traveling through the center of the earth, the nuclear reactions inside the sun, or "thoughts" traveling through the brain. The principle involved is simple even if its implementations might be fantastically complex and delicate. The information about specific events is contained in *some* physical form, for example, in x-rays, in magnetic field patterns, in nuclear radiation, or in pressure waves. The information might

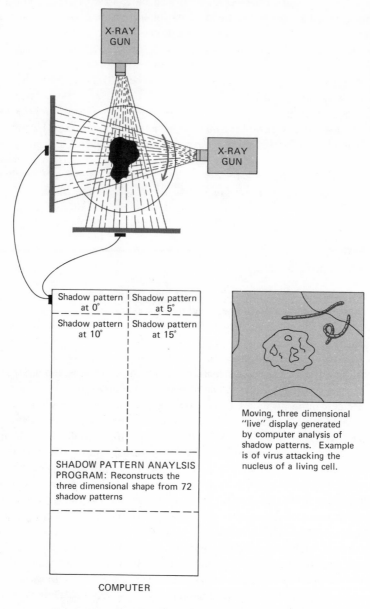

FIGURE 2-2.4 Schematic diagram of a microscope to study the atomic structure of molecules.

be (and often is) thoroughly scrambled in this physical form, but nevertheless, some device senses the physical output from the event, transmits this to a computer which unscrambles the information and then puts it in a form that a person can sense. The most acceptable form of sensing for people is seeing, but there is no reason that one could not feel the molecules or hear the earthquakes in the center of the earth or taste the thoughts in a brain, if these were the senses that one wanted to use.

2-3   COMPUTERS IN BUSINESS AND INDUSTRY

The early developers of calculating machines were motivated primarily by applications in the business world. The business machine industry was established by the middle of the 1800s and by 1950 there was an impressive array of machines available to aid in the calculations and bookkeeping of business and industry. The computer is a natural *calculating tool*, but it has also had considerable use as an *operations control tool* in which it takes on some of the activities of middle management, and is increasingly used as an *information and decision tool* for top management. These three uses of computers in business are not all inclusive, but they show that the impact of computers has already been felt throughout the business community, from junior clerks to corporation presidents.

Calculating Tool

The nature of the original calculating applications in business and industry differs from that in science. The business applications involved a large number of essentially identical, short and simple calculations. Each of these simple calculations processed a few items of information to produce a few new items of information. Thus, instead of millions of calculations to produce a few answers as is common in science, we have many thousands of calculations to provide thousands of answers based on thousands of items of data. The same computer program is often used over and over in these business applications while many scientific applications are "one-shot" computations. The nature of the business calculations led to the name *data processing* which suggests the fact that organizing and handling the data going into and coming out of the calculations is a very important part of this use of computers.

Examples of this use of computers occur in the billing of customers, recording of payments from customers, paying of dividends to stockholders, and so forth. One of the most familiar uses is paying employees—a problem used to introduce computer programming in Part II of this book. Several items of data are needed about each employee: name, identification number, rate of pay, time worked, and usually some other items about deductions for taxes, insurance, savings plans, and so on (see Figure 2-3.1). Given these items, the calculations are short and require perhaps a minute or two with a manual desk calculator. Even so, several numbers are produced which must be recorded or passed on to others: for example, take-home pay, taxes withheld, money to

356040 PURDUE UNIVERSITY

CHECK NUMBER 035 1285

DATE: MO. DAY YR. 12 14 73 33700943 307-64-9547

TO THE ORDER OF:

CATHERINE E HOUSTIS

DOLLARS CENTS $149.50

LAFAYETTE NATIONAL BANK
LAFAYETTE, INDIANA

DATE PAID MO. DAY YR. 12 14 73

PURDUE UNIVERSITY

CATHERINE E HOUSTIS

SOCIAL SECURITY NUMBER 307-64-9547

GROSS PAY 150 00

STATE TAX 50

NET PAY 149 50

IF YOUR COUNTY OF RESIDENCE OR WORK HAS CHANGED SINCE
1 JULY 1973 YOU NEED TO COMPLETE A NEW COUNTY OPTION TAX
CERTIFICATE, FORM WH-4, TO BE EFFECTIVE 1 JANUARY 1974.

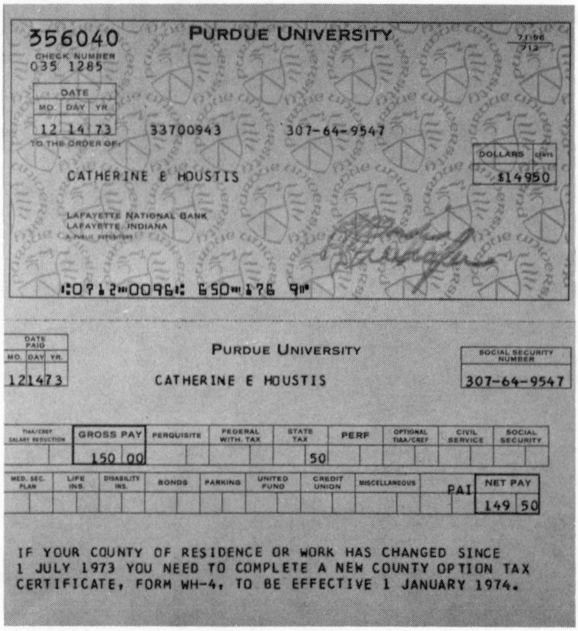

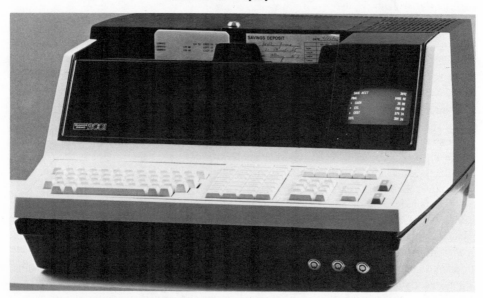

FIGURE 2-3.1 An example of a check that is printed by a computer on special forms. The numbers are computed internally and put directly on the checks without any person copying them. At the same time the numbers are entered into the permanent records of the company.

FIGURE 2-3.2 A computer terminal for a bank or savings and loan association. Such terminals give faster service to the customers and reduce the bookkeeping efforts of the bank (and reduce the number of bookkeeping errors). (Courtesy of Bunker Ramo Corp.)

be put in a savings account, and so forth. Figure 2-3.2 shows a modern computer terminal that automatically completes a savings account transaction, including recording all the information in the permanent records of the bank.

It is worthwhile to consider the facilities needed for efficient performance of this task. First a large memory is useful to store all the data going into and out of the calculations. A fast processor is, of course, required to carry out the calculations and to move the information around in the computer. Finally, and perhaps most important, fast and high volume lines of communication need to be established between the outside world and the computer. Note that each time the payroll calculation is made, *all* of the information about the employees must be put into the computer and *all* of the various results must be taken out at the end. In the first attempts to use computers in this way, the communication problem was the most troublesome. These early experiences led to the practice of permanently keeping the employees data in a form that can be directly read by the computer—or even keeping it in the computer memory itself. The computer now also controls printing devices so it can print the payroll checks directly. Some of the other information produced goes into the company records in a form that the computer can access directly.

At one time the following chain of events was not uncommon. A company's computer calculated and tallied the money withheld from employees for federal taxes. Every three months this information was printed out by the computer—over 1000 typewritten pages for some of the larger companies—and reported to the government. Government keypunch operators then prepared the information for the computers to process. This practice has been changed. Reports now are submitted in computer readable form (usually magnetic tapes) and one might say that a company's computer reports to the government's computer. It is only a matter of time until this is literally true and the report is made via a direct connection between the two computers perhaps by telephone lines as illustrated in Figure 2-3.3.

One of the obvious effects of this use of computers is the elimination of large numbers of clerical jobs. In many instances 80 or 90 percent of the clerks and other employees are no longer needed. This has led to widely publicized and real fears of computers causing widespread unemployment. Yet systematic studies of this problem show that such unemployment is relatively rare and isolated and that most companies have a steady or even increasing clerical force after computers are introduced. The two most important reasons for this are: first, that the clerical force becomes better trained and more skilled and thus able to take on more responsible and demanding activities, and second, that the amount of clerical work required increases due to the expansion and diversification of the activities of business and industry. An apt illustration of the various effects occurs in the occupation of telephone operators. At one time *all* telephone calls were handled by operators; by now, automatic switching exchanges (which are really specialized computers) have eliminated thousands of jobs. Yet still over half of the telephone companies' employees are clerical workers (primarily telephone operators). It has been said (and is probably true) that if the manual switchboard system was still used by telephone companies then *all* employed women in the United States would have to be operators in order to handle the current telephone traffic. However, because computers and automation have not yet caused widespread unemployment does not mean that it cannot happen in the future.

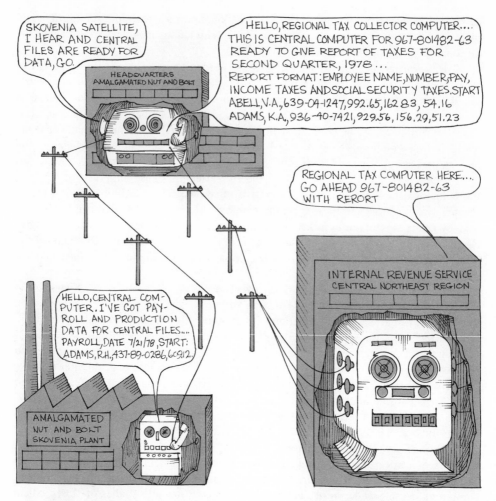

FIGURE 2-3.3   Schematic diagram of a computer network for financial and business use. The branch plant at Skoveenia has a computer that makes periodic reports to the computer at the headquarters of Amalgamated Nut and Bolt. This central computer makes the information available to management and also automatically makes reports (and transfers money for the taxes due). The Internal Revenue Service Computer is capable of receiving reports from many sources at the same time.

Operations Control Tool

Computers have also automated manufacturing processes. Figure 2-3.4 shows a modern computer-controlled weaving machine. Weaving has been automated for 200 years (see Section 1-1) so the impact on employment is not likely to be great in this area. However, some other manufacturing processes, especially assembly lines for mass production, have become highly automated in recent years with a resulting decrease in employment. A positive view of this development is that there is a resulting increase in the productivity of the workers.

FIGURE 2-3.4 A modern version of the 200 year old Jacquard loom. The metal "punched cards" are replaced by a magnetic tape (computer prepared) which, in turn, runs the weaving machine in the background. (Courtesy of North American Rockwell Electronics Group)

One of the primary functions of middle management in industry is to control the routine or standard operations of a company. For example, they:

1. Schedule work and assignment of personnel in a plant machine shop.
2. Maintain adequate inventories of basic items in a company warehouse. Figures 2-3.5 and 2-3.6 show a highly automated, computer-controlled warehouse designed to maintain adequate inventories at a minimum cost.
3. Choose the mixture of petroleum products to be produced at an oil refinery.

The role of middle management is to evaluate the current situation, to direct the activities, and to carry out the established policies. The computer aids (and occasionally replaces) middle management because it can rapidly evaluate the current situations in detail and calculate the effect of a whole range of possible actions. It then can indicate the action that optimizes the objectives established for this activity by top management.

There are three requirements for the profitable use of computers here. First, there must be a well-defined objective. For the above examples these might be:

1. Maximize the utilization of the machines (most jobs require several different machines).
2. Minimize the amount of money invested in inventories while keeping the risk of running out of some items at an acceptable level.
3. Maximize the total value of the products produced from a given variety of raw material. For example, the make-up of crude oil varies considerably and a refiner has the choice of making more of one product, say gasoline, by making less of another, say kerosene.

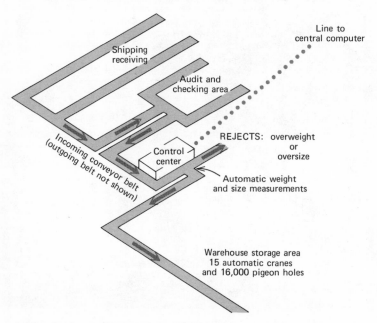

FIGURE 2-3.5 **Diagram of the operation of an automatic, computer controlled warehouse. People are only in the areas of shipping, receiving, and material checking.**

FIGURE 2-3.6 A computer controlled stacker crane in a narrow aisle of the "Automove" warehouse. The computer automatically answers requests for delivering or storing parts and simultaneously keeps records of the warehouse inventory. (Courtesy of Rohr Industries.)

Second, one must have accurate information about the various aspects of the possible actions and one must know the interrelationships between the subactivities involved.

Finally, the situation must be complicated so that the choices are not obvious (otherwise neither middle management nor computers would be needed). In such complicated situations, one often makes a number of calculations to try to determine which of a number of alternatives is best. A computer can do the computations much faster than a human, and without arithmetic errors. Consequently, in a given time interval, a computer can explore many more possibilities than a human, and determine the best choice—or at least a better choice than might be found by a human. Note that the cost of examining several thousand possibilities with a computer might be only a few cents.

Information and Decision Tool

The use of computers as an information and decision tool for top management has been under intensive development since the mid 1960s. One of the objectives is to provide speedy and accurate information about what is happening in a company. Figure 2-3.7 shows two corporate executives examining the steps required to develop a new

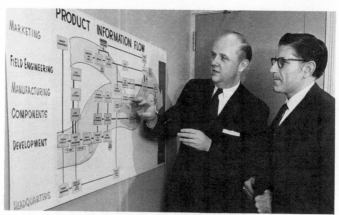

FIGURE 2-3.7   An example of the high level analysis of the operation
of a company. A computer program is written based
on this chart and it keeps top management informed
on the progress and costs of the development of a new
product. (Courtesy of S.D. Catalano and P.D. Walker,
IBM Corp.)

company product. This is no easy matter in an operation involving many factories, wholesale outlets, retail outlets, and so forth, and it is not uncommon for management to have several months of delay in discovering that sales of a product or production at a plant have sagged. Serious losses may occur before management is aware that a problem exists. The need for *accuracy* is illustrated by the fate of a rather large company (Standard Packaging, now absorbed in another company) which experienced rising profits and sales throughout 1969. Management and the stockholders were, of course, very pleased and various expansion programs were initiated. Then, one day, it was discovered that the computerized accounting programs were full of errors, the company was losing money at a rapid pace and the expansion programs were just expanding the losses.

In addition to providing timely information for decisions, computers are able to help management project and analyze the effects of various alternatives. In order to do this, a set of equations and data are derived which accurately describe the company's internal situation and its relationship with external economic forces. These are embodied in computer programs and then the computer can project future developments by following through, month by month or even day by day, all the detailed interactions within and outside the company. A president might experiment with raising and lowering the price of a product to see the effect on sales, on production capacity, on competitors sales, or on profits. (See Figure 2-3.8.) Or he might study the effect of borrowing $10 million to build a new plant to double the production of some items. Or he might examine the effect on his company of a 10 percent general slowdown in the economy. Programs that operate this way are called *simulations* and they essentially imitate the company and its situation in the economy. The imitations or simulations are, of course, not perfect and the user must take this into account in evaluating the results presented by the computer. Nevertheless, computer simulations can be much more detailed and reliable than projections prepared by a team of staff members working for a period of several weeks. Furthermore, the president can have the computer projections almost immediately and he can study many widely different possibilities in one afternoon.

UNITED RADIOLOGICAL SUPPLY CORP.

TANTALUM INVESTMENT SIMULATION - 20 YEAR

CASE 1:   MAINTAIN CURRENT PRODUCTION

CASE 2:   EXPAND NEW MEXICO PLANT - $50,000 CAPITAL COST

CASE 3:   BUILD NEW PLANT AT UTAH MINE - $400,000 CAPITAL COST

YEAR	CASE	PRODUCTION POUNDS/MO.	DIRECT COSTS PER MONTH	INTEREST COST PER MONTH	CASH FLOW PER MONTH	PROFIT PER MONTH
1976	1	280	29800	0	3600	2415
	2	350	35400	400	2400	2380
	3	500	57600	1240	-1400	1260
1977	1	280	30200	0	3800	2480
	2	370	34600	398	3950	2860
	3	570	54200	1232	2950	2630
1978	1	280	30600	0	3970	2530
	2	370	35000	396	4180	2960
	3	600	53600	1228	5840	5680
1979	1	280	31000	0	4120	2610
	2	370	35500	393	4390	3040
	3	600	54000	1208	6080	5870

FIGURE 2-3.8   A hypothetical computer analysis of an investment decision for the president of a company. The company president would have to compare these possibilities with other investments in new production facilities.

2-4   EMERGING AREAS OF THE COMPUTER IMPACT ON SOCIETY

The preceding sections discussed two segments of society greatly affected by computers. The current impact is still small in some other areas but it is likely to grow as new ideas and techniques are perfected. In other instances (banking and accounting for example) there are major, even revolutionary, effects.

The military organizations and large government units (the federal government and many of the largest and most modern state and city governments) have felt a substantial impact from the computer. The use of computers in these two areas is rather similar to the use in science and in business and industry so it is not discussed in more detail here. There is, however, a section in Chapter 4 on the potential use of computers to help solve the "urban crisis." The section surveys several areas where intensive efforts are under way to apply computers.

Education is one of the largest activities in this country and there are experiments under way to bring the power of the computer to the educational process. (See Figure 2-4.1.) However there is great controversy inside and outside of the educational establishment about the need for computers in education. The opinions vary from "It's just another gadget like slide projectors or colored chalk; these gadgets are useful but

FIGURE 2-4.1 A group of junior high school students make use of a computer-aided educational system. All the consoles are connected to a single computer. (Courtesy of Bunker Ramo Corp.)

really don't change things." to "Within 10 years the teachers, the classrooms, the whole operation will be replaced by computer directed educational programs." There is a rather detailed discussion of this problem Chapter 4; some of the possibilities and obstacles are analyzed.

Another area of considerable interest discussed in Chapter 4 is the use of computers to play games. These efforts are not likely to have a large direct impact on society but there is considerable philosophical interest, for example, in the real possibility that a computer might someday be the chess champion of the world. On the other hand, people do not seem particularly impressed by the fact that the computer has been the arithmetic champion of the world for many years.

Finally, there is a discussion of language translation in Chapter 4. Great hopes and efforts to use computers to rapidly and accurately translate languages (Russian to English, for example) have fallen far short of the original goals and recent progress has been slow. The nature of some of the obstacles encountered are explored.

Of the many emerging applications of computers we discuss three here. First, we consider applications where the principal requirement is the recovery of relevant information from a very large collection of information and a subsequent analysis of the various facts obtained pertaining to the specific problem. Medicine and law are two areas where a significant impact can be made by such a computer capability.

Information Retrieval

When one visits a doctor or a lawyer, there is an initial discussion during which the "expert" is provided with a basic set of facts. These facts might be a medical history, temperature, age, blood pressure, areas of pain, pulse rate, and so forth; or they might be a summary of the provisions of a contract such as money involved or actions required and a statement as to what part of the contract has been broken. At this point the doctor or lawyer uses his professional knowledge and training to organize this information into a whole and then match that against a background of literally thousands of possibilities (ailments, diseases, court decisions, laws passed, and so forth). Once some tentative guesses are made, he then probably asks for more information. If a firm conclusion cannot be reached then he probably seeks both more facts (additional medical tests or legal documents) and more background knowledge (reading his books and journals, consultation with colleagues, and so forth). (See Figure 2-4.2.)

There is considerable hope and evidence that this process can be made much more effective with the aid of a computer. A computer program can compare the facts of a particular situation with thousands of possibilities in a few seconds. The doctor or lawyer can also do this, but there are real advantages to the use of a computer. The computer never "forgets" to check any possibility in the program. Once programmed, the computer can contain information about hundreds of obscure diseases (or laws) and about extremely recent medical discoveries (or court decisions). The various parts of the

Well, uh, I think I had better consult another computer before I go ahead with an operation.

FIGURE 2-4.2

program can be written with the help of the very best specialists. These computer programs will not eliminate the need for doctors or lawyers, *they will rather greatly magnify their skill and ability.* It is realistic to look forward to a time when a doctor could quickly treat a disease *unknown* to him before the patient entered his office. The computer program might diagnose Mandolanian Monkey fever and recommend a treatment with hypoglyposuthiomilate and an exteriovarisolvency procedure described on page 1129 of volume 103 of the Journal of Incommunicable Diseases and state that this article is available from the computer as Medimemory item MMF-6042. Information like this is useful only to a highly skilled physician.

Modeling and Simulation Tool

The second emerging application of computers we discuss is that of computer modeling or simulation of political and sociological situations. The idea is much like that discussed above where a company president uses simulation to experiment with various lines of action. The most important differences, however, are that this application:

1. involves more complex situations,
2. involves a large number of emotional and psychological factors which are hard to quantify for a computer program,
3. has many important effects over which one has no control and some of these might change dramatically and at random at any time,
4. can normally only influence, not control the situation and thus at times one is unable to take highly desirable actions.

These aspects are all seen in the discussion in Chapter 4 of the applications of computers to the urban crisis. (See Figure 2-4.3.) In spite of the difficulties involved, this application is already in considerable use and has produced concrete results. Furthermore, it has motivated additional research efforts in the qualitative analysis of mass psychology, personal psychology, economic interactions, political behavior, and so forth. New results in these areas will allow more reliable and accurate computer simulations to be made. Equally valuable is the fact that these studies have shown that some important aspects of society are not controlled by anyone and cannot be controlled within the current political-sociological framework. Examples of this are "urban sprawl," the "inner-city decay" in many places, pollution of rivers and streams, unemployment in Appalachia, and technological development.

Another thought provoking and potentially very important discovery is the possibility that some, perhaps many, sociological processes are *counter-intuitive.* The discovery of instances of this are not entirely due to computer studies, but computer simulations using realistic models of society have shown such behavior and this greatly increases the belief that counter-intuitive processes do exist. The phrase "counter-intuitive process" implies that the results of an action are not what one expects, but something completely different, perhaps even the exact opposite. Science has provided so many counter-intuitive processes that people are no longer surprised by many of them. We routinely accept the fact that objects weighing hundreds of tons can fly, but in the

FIGURE 2-4.3 A utopian view of how computers might harness technology in order to solve the problems of the urban crisis. The fulfillment of this vision is not very likely to occur in the near future.

1880s one of the world's leading physicists stated that this was impossible and completely ruled out by the laws of physics.

Several examples of *possible* counter-intuitive processes are listed below (also see Figure 2-4.4).

1. The construction of expressways in large cities may increase the traffic congestion rather than decrease it. (See Figure 2-4.5.)
2. The tearing down of slums and building good housing in their place might not eradicate slums, but rather spread them and causes a net increase in them.
3. The social welfare aid given to families to help them "get back on their feet again" might, in fact, cause them to stay on welfare permanently.
4. The import quotas on foreign oil to preserve the United States oil industry in case of a future national emergency might, in fact, cause oil reserves to be used up much faster and thus increase the dependency on foreign oil sources in a future national emergency. (*Added in proof*: This counter-intuitive process became intuitive in late 1973)
5. The strongly stated warnings about the dangers of drug addiction might increase the number of people who experiment with them.

One can write books (and people have) about the arguments that support or contradict these statements. The significant fact here is that one's natural intuition about such matters might be completely wrong and that deep and thorough studies are needed to better understand them.

An interesting and increasingly significant application of this type is in the computer modeling of the electorate by politicians running for election as president, senator, or governor. The first step is to obtain a breakdown of the population according to age, sex, race, creed, color, and national origin—all those characteristics that should not

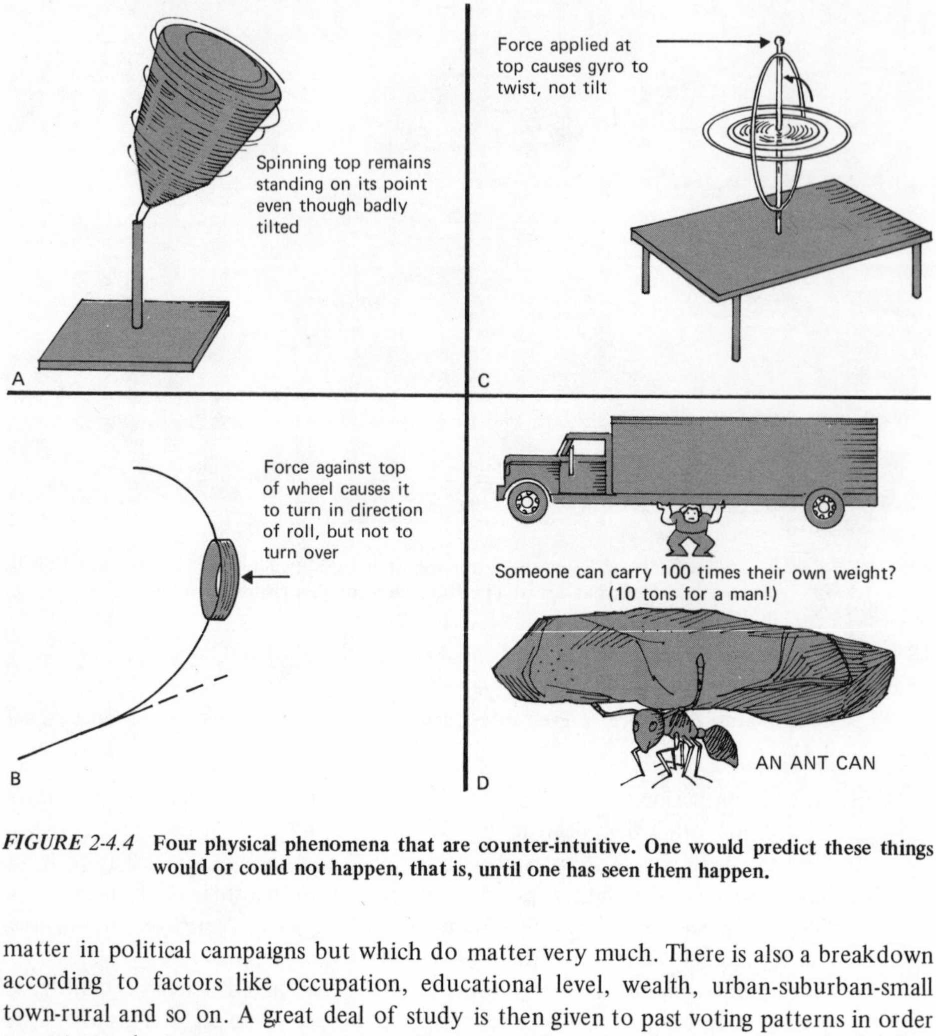

Spinning top remains standing on its point even though badly tilted

Force applied at top causes gyro to twist, not tilt

A

C

Force against top of wheel causes it to turn in direction of roll, but not to turn over

Someone can carry 100 times their own weight? (10 tons for a man!)

AN ANT CAN

B

D

FIGURE 2-4.4   Four physical phenomena that are counter-intuitive. One would predict these things would or could not happen, that is, until one has seen them happen.

matter in political campaigns but which do matter very much. There is also a breakdown according to factors like occupation, educational level, wealth, urban-suburban-small town-rural and so on. A great deal of study is then given to past voting patterns in order to estimate how various positions on the issues affect the voting of the various groups. The model rapidly becomes quite complex and a thorough analysis is possible only with the aid of a computer. The politician now has a framework within which to work and his task is to take a position which is compatible with his principles and which gives him over half of the votes. The situation is not nearly so simple and the computer simulation is only one guide in the determination of a campaign strategy. Unfortunately, the way a man combs his hair, delivers his speeches, wears his clothes might be more important in deciding the outcome of the election than his record or his position on the issues.

FIGURE 2-4.5   (opposite page) A schematic sequence that illustrates the possible counter-intuitive results of improving roads in large cities. As the roads improve, there are more cars, people make longer trips and there is little, if any, improvement in the traffic flow.

Tool in the Creative Arts

The last emerging application of computers considered is in the creative arts: music composition, painting, and sculpture. Drawings by a computer program are shown in Figure 2-4.6. Values in these areas are very subjective and the music composed by a computer may be beautiful for one person and horrid for another. The first attempts in these areas tended to be the simple random combination of elements (colors, tones, sizes, instruments) and the computer merely supplied the random selections. Even so, some people found the results striking. Much more sophisticated attempts have been made since the first efforts and a wide variety of "computer-creations" now exists. Some of these are totally new and different (if that is possible) while others are more traditional. Detailed studies of the music composed by Beethoven, Bach, et al. have discovered systematic patterns used by the composers. As more of these patterns are recognized, there is hope that a computer program can compose music in the style of Mozart. It is, of course, something else again to compose symphonies with the quality of Mozart.

The extent of the computer impact in the creative arts is yet to be determined, but there is no doubt that much experimentation will take place. Figure 2-4.7 shows the use of a computer as a musical instrument. The history of the creative arts shows many changes of fashion and style and it is plausible that computer music or computer sculpture will at some point become *the* fashion whether or not it has any enduring and

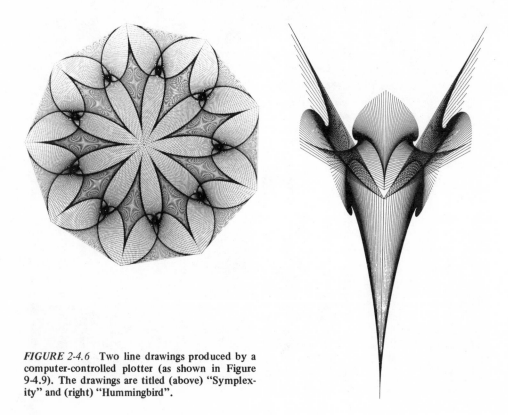

FIGURE 2-4.6 Two line drawings produced by a computer-controlled plotter (as shown in Figure 9-4.9). The drawings are titled (above) "Symplexity" and (right) "Hummingbird".

FIGURE 2-4.7 A computerized organ. This is a special-purpose computer in that all it can do is to detect the keys depressed and then operate the appropriate parts of the sound mechanism. It cannot, for example, add two numbers. (Courtesy of North American Rockwell Electronics Group.)

intrinsic value. The first great American mathematician, George David Birkhoff, spent many years (before computers) in the study of a mathematical theory of art and design. He tried, for example, to isolate those characteristics that made some Grecian urns beautiful and others not. His hope was to quantify the principles of beautiful and elegant design and he made some progress. One can expect further efforts (and, hopefully, progress) along these lines which might eventually lead to computer programs that are able to produce original and beautiful design for everything from goblets to dishwashers.

2-5 COMPUTERS AS TACIT POLICYMAKERS

Computers have changed the way many things are done in business, industry, and government resulting in the establishment of new policies and procedures. Many of these new policies are made only after careful considerations, but there are many others that are made quietly without study by (or even knowledge of) the usual policy-making groups in the organizations. Some specific instances of the latter are discussed in Chapter 6. We briefly consider two ways that computers lead to quiet, and often unintentional, policymaking and the consequences of this tacit policymaking.

Policy is made by people, not by computers, but the kinds of policymaking considered here are often "blamed" on computers. The decisions are usually made in one of two situations: either when procedures are instituted to make the use of computers easier or more efficient, or when the procedure, or issue, is considered unimportant. The former are made by a middle management person, a person who is knowledgeable about both the general policies and the detailed operation of the computing system. The decisions are, of course, necessary and usually harmless, sometimes even beneficial, but occasionally they cause unforeseen problems.

Decisions made in the second situation are usually encountered in the writing of the computer programs and the choice is made on the spot by the programmer. Needless to say, the consequences of the choice are not studied in detail and occasionally a poor choice is made for a point that is more important than it appears.

One of the most publicized and irritating examples of this situation occurs when computer systems are used to send bills to customers and warning or threatening letters to customers whose accounts are overdue. Disputes invariably arise over the bills and sometimes the error is due to an error made by the company sending the bill. The sequence of events might be: you receive a bill for $1,433.60, $27.35 of which is yours. You have been charged $1,416.25 for three rooms of furniture that you did not buy. So you send a check for the $27.35 that you owe with a note stating there is an error in your bill. The clerk who opens the payments places your note on the desk; it is soon lost. Next month your bill includes an interest charge and a nice reminder that it is overdue. You write a letter saying that you do not owe this amount. A clerk opens the letter, looks in your file (contained in the computer's memory) and it shows that you do owe the money (remember your lost note!) This letter is thrown away and the next month you get another bill with another interest charge and a reminder that your credit rating will drop to zero if you do not make an immediate payment. Now you are angry and you write a strong letter stating your views. A clerk opens the letter, looks in your file again (which still confirms the bill) and then, since you are so angry, looks through the sales slip file to check that you, K. Lehman on 500 Sammarkland Ave., did, in fact, buy this furniture. A sales slip exists that says you did, so no further action is taken. The next month your bill contains more interest charges and a statement that court action is to be started against you if you do not pay immediately. Finally, after two more letters are ignored, you demand to talk to someone in authority. A thorough check is started which reveals (after six weeks and two more very nasty letters) that the furniture was purchased not by you but by Karl Lehmann on 506 Summerland Ave., and the entire problem was caused by the sloppy handwriting of a sales clerk. The credit manager calls you to apologize profusely and to make remarks about how these computers are taking over everything and causing all kinds of trouble. He assures you that everything will be taken care of.

The fight is now half over. The next bill you receive shows your account credited with $1,416.25 but you still owe $108.36 for finance charges even though your balance has not been over $50 for the past year. Several letters, telephone calls, nasty notes, and months later the credit manager agrees that something must be done. However, they cannot redo *all* the accounts for the past year and they do not have a program to recalculate just one account. Furthermore, no one in the credit department is quite sure how to calculate interest charges and the people in the computer section are too busy to bother with such a trivial matter. And, even if they did know how much to credit your account, they are not sure which of the company's own accounts should be charged. Finally, with some desperation, the credit manager cancels all of your finance and interest charges and you are relieved that it is all over, at last. Three years later your banker says that before he approves your loan, he would like an explanation of why a company had to threaten court action in order to get you to pay for your furniture.

No company would deliberately adopt a policy of this type, yet decisions were made that resulted in this policy. The decision to ignore the initial letter in favor of the computer's records was made by middle management because ninety-eight times out of a hundred the computer's records are correct. Even after the company suspects an error the nasty computer generated letters continue because no one, management or programmer, thought to provide a switch to stop these letters in spite of a large overdue balance in the records. The problem in removing the finance charges is caused by a lack of anticipation that such action would be needed. No one asked for a program to recalculate just one account in order to adjust the finance charges and the programmer of the billing program found it convenient not to save the quantities needed for an easy adjustment by hand. Thus a number of small, individually unimportant decisions created an extremely frustrating and irritating experience for a customer and a bad name for a company.

One can give many other examples of such occurrences and their surrounding circumstances might be called the "We can't do that because the computer . . . " syndrome. Those who make such statements make them with complete honesty. They are not knowledgeable about the local computer operation and the experts find it much easier to tell an uninformed person that "you can't do that" rather than to explain to him why it is difficult or trouble or a nuisance to do it. Many requests that result in "We can't do that because the computer . . . " statements could, in fact, be explained by "Our computer programs don't do that and they don't because our programmers don't want to take the time and effort to write them that way." Sometimes, of course, the explanation is that it is bothersome to grant the request and the computer is used as an excuse.

The two main points made in this section can be summarized by two sentences. People write the programs and these people deserve the *credit* and the *blame* for the resulting actions. Computers are extremely flexible and versatile tools for business, government and industry; there is no need to establish rigid, inflexible procedures. Indeed, one of the great promises of computers for the future is that they can provide extremely diversified and individualized services for society.

2-6 HOW THE GENERAL PUBLIC VIEWS COMPUTERS

Almost all adults in the United States are aware of computers and have some opinion about their nature and capabilities. Their opinions are important first, because some uses of computers require that the general public cooperate in some way ("do not fold, spindle or mutilate") and widespread antagonism could rule out these uses; and secondly, the general public controls—usually indirectly—the decision makers for society and computers are becoming more involved in these decisions. The exercise of this control is occasionally direct but more often quite indirect and amorphous. Nevertheless, it is there.

Four distinct views discussed here are somewhat extreme in nature. The view held by most people is a combination of these, a combination that is only vaguely formulated. The names are suggestive of their nature: the *magic machine*, the *impersonal enemy*, the *servant of society*, and the *mechanic's tool*. There is considerable evidence that the least realistic of these, the magic machine view, is the most widely held by the general public.

The magic machine view of computers is primarily due to news media (newspapers and television) reporting. The reports are generally shallow and even when an in-depth analysis is presented it is usually ignored. The news media, of course, emphasize "news worthy" events which are somewhat different than "significant" events. Thus the fact that large companies use computers for their payrolls because it is faster, more accurate, and cheaper is considerably more significant but less newsworthy, than the fact that someone received a weekly paycheck of a million dollars because of a "computer error."

There are two principal (and inaccurate) components of the magic machine view. One is that the computer is an independent being which does some sort of thinking and has many human characteristics. It is a "giant brain" that might be grouchy in the morning and lazy in the afternoon. The second component of this view is the ignorance of the enormous human effort required in computer systems. Holders of this view are unaware of the nature of computer programs and the role that computer programmers and operators have. They feel that one presents a problem, almost any problem, to a computer and shortly it returns the answer without any outside aid or direction.

The impersonal enemy view is similar to the magic machine view in that it usually involves little knowledge of, or direct experience with, computers. This view is, of course, reinforced by personal experiences similar to the one described in the preceding section. Another contributing factor to this view is the general uneasiness that many people feel about the changes that technology is causing; the computer is a convenient target upon which to concentrate one's distrust and frustration. A provocative and early (pre-computer) presentation of this view is the 1872 novel *Erewhon* by Samuel Butler. A negative utopia is described where the population is split between the "machinists" who essentially control the world with advanced machines, and the anti-machinists. A civil war erupts during which all the machines are destroyed, the machinists are killed, and society returns to the simple agricultural level.

The servant-of-society viewpoint is frequently based on just as little knowledge or understanding as the magic machine and impersonal enemy views. Some who hold this view are simply optimists by nature and believe (or at least hope) that all the fantastic power that computers possess will be used to solve all the hard problems of the world.

The view of the computer as a panacea for all (or almost all) of the world's problems is also held by a number of highly knowledgeable although perhaps overly enthusiastic professionals in computer science. Whatever the reasons, there have been and continue to be exaggerated claims made by supposed authorities on computing. Exaggerated claims have raised the expectations for the computer in some areas to such a level that even significant advances are considered failures. It is difficult even for computing specialists to evaluate these claims because there is an element of real potential in most of them. The differences in opinion among the experts is more over the "when" and "how" than over the "whether" of these claims. The general public, of course, has almost no way to evaluate these potentials and if one accepts all the good news reported by the news media then it is easy to hold the servant of society viewpoint of computer.

The mechanic's tool view is usually held by those who have considerable direct experience with computers. The computer is considered as a machine which they can control in order to accomplish certain things. They are aware, of course, that this tool has great power and potential, but they do not attribute any magical, human, or demonic characteristics to computers.

The reader should keep in mind that the authors of this book hold this last view and thus they might be somewhat biased in the current presentation. We feel that the best view of computers is a combination primarily of the mechanic's tool view, a good deal of the servant of society, a dash of the impersonal enemy, and almost none of the magic machine. The inclusion of the servant of society and impersonal enemy components follows naturally from the view of the computer as a tool which can be used for both good and evil. One can conceive of the computer as the principal ingredient of a society more horrible than George Orwell's "1984" or a society bordering on utopia. The future depends on a complex array of factors and is likely to be neither utopia nor hell. Some of the plausible future developments closely related to computers are discussed in the next chapter and each person must assign his own values to these possibilities.

SUGGESTED READINGS

An annotated list of readings is given at the end of Chapter 4. Several of these books are good sources of additional information on the topics of this chapter. Particularly pertinent from this list are the following:

Baer, Robert, *The Digital Villain.* Reading, Mass. Addison-Wesley Publishing Company, Inc., 1972.

Bemer, Robert, *Computers and Crisis.* Association of Computing Machinery, 1971.

Bowen, Howard and Mangum, Garth, *Automation and Economic Progress.* Englewood Cliffs, N.J.: Prentice Hall, Inc., 1966.

Greenberger, Martin, *Computers and the World of the Future.* Cambridge, Mass.: MIT Press, 1962.

Martin, James, *Telecommunications and the Computer.* Englewood Cliffs, N.J.: Prentice-Hall, Inc., 1968.

Myers, Charles, *The Impact of Computers on Management.* Cambridge, Mass.: MIT Press, 1967.

Pylyshyn, Zenon, *Perspectives on the Computer Revolution.* Englewood Cliffs N.J.: Prentice-Hall, Inc., 1970.

Sackman, Harold and Nie, Norman, *The Information Utility and Social Choice.* Montvale, N.J.: AFIPS Press, 1970.

Taviss, Irene, *The Computer Impact.* Englewood Cliffs, N.J.: Prentice-Hall, Inc., 1970.

3 A Plausible Future of the Computer's Impact

The future is always uncertain and predictions are necessarily inaccurate. However, one should not be paralyzed by the fear of making errors. One must study seriously the future impact of the various technological and sociological changes that occur in society. There have already been some unpleasant surprises (automobile pollution, insecticides in fish, soapy rivers and so forth) and the continuing rate of change in society increases the chances of more unpleasant surprises. A number of thoughtful observers have become very alarmed about this situation and while we do not discuss their positions, the following metaphor summarizes them rather well:

> Society is rushing headlong down a track in a train of scientific, techno-
> logical, and sociological revolutions. This track has many branches leading to
> unknown destinations and for all we know there are demons at the switches.
> Yet most of society and its leaders are in the caboose, looking back at the
> scenery and only dimly aware that the train is even moving.

The purpose of this chapter is to explore some of the computer related developments that are likely to occur in *this century*.

There are two strategies in exploring the future. The conservative strategy is to look at those things which might occur very soon and which require little really new knowledge or technique. The other strategy is to think creatively, project far into the future, and contemplate the really fantastic potential for this century and the next. The conservative strategy is more accurate, more relevant, and less exciting. Some considera-tion of the far future (uncertain though it might be) is required to place the near future in a proper context, however. After all, why contemplate the possibility of a small, cheap, pollution-free internal combustion engine for the 2062 model automobiles if it is likely that there will be no gasoline left, probably no internal combustion engines in common use, a good chance that automobiles will be replaced by something else, and perhaps no people left.

The strategy in this chapter is conservative, some would even call it very conservative.

3-1   FUTURE HARDWARE CAPABILITIES AND IMPLICATIONS

Chapter Zero has presented a very limited definition and discussion of the purpose of the hardware (physical devices) of present computers. Further discussion of hardware is given in Chapter 9, but the fact is that most people (including computer users) neither know nor care much about hardware in spite of the fact that it is precisely what makes everything else possible. It is almost impossible for one person to learn the details and principles of all the devices in a complex technological society and we must rely on the specialists to invent, design, produce, and perfect the devices. In the meantime, we must learn the trick of considering and evaluating the capabilities of hardware (either current or future) without really knowing anything about it.

The important computer hardware capabilities are listed below, along with an indication of the nature of the capability or devices involved, and a projection of future developments.

Basic Operations

Such operations include putting a number or name into the memory, adding two numbers, testing the equality of two names, or sending a message out to a printer. The physical devices are primarily electronic circuits and the important properties of these operations are the *speed* at which the operation is performed and the *power* (or complexity) of the operation. Current devices allow 10 to 50 million operations per second and we expect the rate to increase to about 10 times that within a decade, and perhaps 100 times that by the end of this century. Such rates are, of course, available only in the most expensive computers; the smaller and cheaper ones operate at rates 50 to 1000 times lower. The power of a single operation is currently very small, perhaps not much greater than that of the computer operations in the 1950s. We can expect a dramatic increase in this property resulting in computational or processing power at least 1000 times greater than what is available now.

Currently, most computers perform their operations sequentially, that is one operation must be completed before the next one is started. We feel that there will be considerable increases in the ability to do simultaneous or parallel operations in the execution of a program. For some applications the total increase of computing power will be a factor of one million.

Memory

The memory is the part of the computer that contains the information, the instructions to the computer, the records of what it has done, is doing, and has yet to do, and so forth. The physical devices range from tiny magnetic donuts to magnetic disks and tapes to boxes of punched cards and on to film libraries. The key properties are *size* and *speed of access* and a major part of the price of the hardware of a large computer system is due to the cost of a memory that is both large and quick to access (*fast*). Current large computer systems have memory for many tens of millions of pieces of information, but the access time is *very* slow compared to the rate at which operations are performed. The memory of a computer system is made up of several components and types, for example, magnetic core (the magnetic "donuts"), magnetic disks, magnetic tapes, and so on. The sizes and speeds of these components vary. The fastest memory component has room for only 50 to a 100 thousand words. The performance of most sophisticated computing installations would benefit greatly by having 10 to 100 times as much of this fast memory. We certainly expect such increases in the size of fast memories of large computer systems, and multi-billion word memories with an access time of a fraction of a second will be available by the end of this century. A rough quantitative projection is shown in Figure 3-1.1.

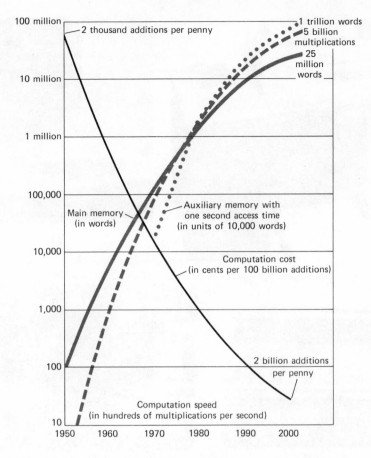

FIGURE 3-1.1 **Estimated growth in computation power and memory capacity of "large scale" computers. The units are chosen so that the rates of increase can be compared. Cost decreases are also shown.**

Consoles

Under the term consoles, we group all of the devices that allow people to communicate directly with computers. Most people, including the majority of regular users of computers, do not have any consoles now and do not interact directly with the computer. The present consoles are like typewriters (at the low price range—$800) or like a television set with a keyboard (at the medium price range—$3000) or are very elaborate devices costing up to $250,000. (See Figure 3-1.2.) The important properties of such consoles are convenience and flexibility. A telephone can and in fact has a limited use as a console at some places, but the messages to the computer are in the form of strings of digits dialed (or punched on a touch-tone phone). A reasonable level of speech recognition by computers is on the way which will greatly expand the telephone's

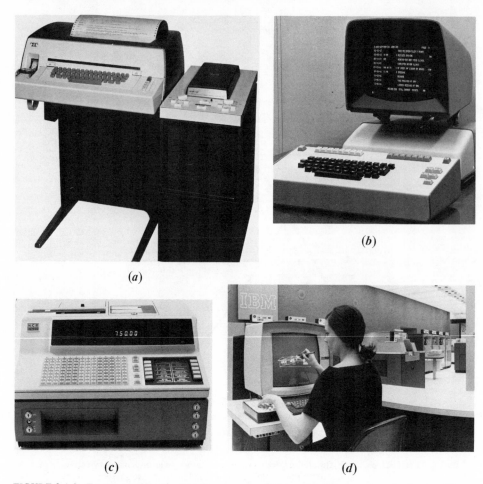

FIGURE 3-1.2 Four examples of computer consoles. The manufacturers and approximate costs are (a) Teletype ($1200 without the tape cartridge attachment), (b) Bunker Ramo ($4000), (c) National Cash Register ($10,000), (d) IBM Corp. ($250,000).

usefulness as a console. Some type of device will be available to add to a cable television system to allow one to use an ordinary television set as part of a console. Elaborate devices of all sizes, shapes, and forms will be available that give great convenience and flexibility in the communication between man and computer.

The main hurdle in developing consoles has been and will continue to be the cost. A reasonable console is not likely to be less complicated than a color television or an electric typewriter and thus a cost of several hundred dollars can be expected. When the services provided by a "computer utility" reach the point where the general public is ready to invest in a moderately expensive console then the mass consumption of computer power will begin—certainly before the end of this century.

Control Devices for Other Machines

Most computers now control a variety of machines that help transmit information to and from the computer. These machines include printers with tremendous capacity and readers for punched cards, magnetic ink checks, and standardized printing. Interface units (devices which allow communication between two computer components) are commonly used to sense and control the actions of a great variety of external machines (for example, oil refineries, space ships, trains, laboratory instruments, drill presses). It will be (and in many cases, already is) possible for a computer to control almost any mechanical device that has a fairly limited range of actions. By the end of this century we expect that one can build machines able to play ping-pong, run the vacuum cleaner, or put the dinner dishes in the dishwasher. Such machines will either contain a computer or use computing power from a computer utility through a computer network.

The capability to build such machines does not mean that they will, in fact, be built or be commonly available. The hurdle here, as with consoles, is cost, and the more versatile machines will be very expensive to purchase, maintain, and operate.

In summary, then, we feel that there will be dramatic progress in every important area of hardware for computers. Furthermore, the cost of any particular computation or operation will decrease steadily and significantly for the next several decades. The cost will be decreased at least by a factor of 100 and probably a factor of 1000. A smaller decrease will occur in the cost of consoles, perhaps only a factor of 10 or 20. Even so, this means that the cost of a very powerful computing system will be well within the price range of an average family. The software developments to come (discussed in the next section) will make this a useful and worthwhile (perhaps necessary) device for the average family. It may be that people do not buy computers but rather use a computer utility. In either case the computational power placed at our disposal will be many times greater, much easier to use, and much cheaper than at present.

3-2   *FUTURE SOFTWARE CAPABILITIES AND IMPLICATIONS*

It stands to reason that as improved hardware appears there also should be an increase in the capability to *use* the new machines. The widespread application of computers requires an array of computer programs to make the powerful hardware available to the user without years of study or months of effort to prepare a particular problem for computer solution. These programs, which permit humans to interact with a computer, form the *software* of a computer system, and its cost frequently exceeds the cost of hardware.

Four important software areas are described below along with a discussion of projected developments. Note that we are not discussing particular application areas yet; this software is general purpose and is involved in almost all applications.

Operating Systems for Resource Allocation

A sophisticated computer system has a wide variety of resources available for use and the *operating system* is a computer program to control the operation. The operating system is very large, very complex, and highly technical in nature. It's two primary objectives are to make an efficient allocation of the computer's resources and to be invisible to the ordinary user. It is an extremely challenging task to make an efficient allocation of all of the hardware and software resources which are, and will become, available. But our understanding and application of the theory of operating systems should increase at a fast enough rate to maintain the current level of efficiency (which is not exceptionally good) and perhaps to significantly improve it.

Language Processors

Each computer has its own *machine language* to control its basic operations and its various devices. These languages are very unnatural for humans, and one of the major software areas is devoted to bridging the gap between natural (human) language and machine language. Very important progress has already been made, but a large gap still remains. For example, the programming language presented in Chapter 5 is much easier to learn and use than machine language, but it is still clumsy, limited in scope, and unnatural. The basic task of a *language processor* is to translate a programming language into machine language. The difficulty of this translation process increases very rapidly as the programming language takes on the appearance of natural language. We can expect the appearance of what might be called *natural programming languages*, languages very similar to natural language with two restrictions. First, there are modest constraints on the sentence structure so that very involved, contorted, or obscure sentences are not allowed. Second, and more important, the language is limited to a specific subject area (for example, the weather, the design of expressway interchanges, advertising strategies for consumer products). Thus we can look forward to picking up the phone, calling a computer, and conversing naturally about various aspects of the weather (the forecast for tomorrow, yesterday's weather in New York City or Hong Kong, the likelihood of rain for a picnic next July and so forth). It is unlikely that this century will see a computer system that has a natural language processing capability resembling that of an average human. Of course, some people have developed the ability to carry on what seems to be an intelligent conversation about a subject where they have no knowledge or understanding. A computer program might be developed along these lines producing a computer which *seems* to have a natural language processing capability. Prototypes of such programs already exist.

Problem Solving Systems

The standard approach to solving problems with computers is discussed in Chapter 7, and it essentially consists of: (a) recognizing and studying the real problem, (b) constructing a model of the real problem, (c) finding a method to solve the model problem, and (d) writing a computer program to carry out this method. The aim of a problem solving system is the design and the writing of a computer program that already contains instructions to carry out steps (b), (c) and (d). Such a system accepts a statement of the problem and returns the solution. Problem solving systems already exist for many classes of rather standardized problems. We can expect such systems to be developed which are much more powerful and versatile and (when coupled with sophisticated language processors) which allow a person, not trained as a computer programmer, to solve a variety of significant problems. However, the user *must* know enough to describe the problem clearly and accurately; and the lack of a clear understanding of the problem is, and will continue to be, one of the principal sources of error in computer applications.

One can argue that problem solving systems will have a tremendous impact on society. The reasoning is as follows: A significant part of society's efforts is concerned with the transfer of knowledge from person to person and from generation to generation. A large part of this knowledge is related to problem solving. Book after book has been written for the purpose of giving others the ability to solve certain problems. The problem solving system is another means for one person to transmit this ability to another person, a means with characteristics different from a library of books and different from current educational systems. Such systems can materially raise the level of problem solving ability throughout the entire population and conceivably have an effect similar to several additional years of education or to an increase of 5 or 10 percent in the average intelligence. Such systems do not reduce the need for education because one must know and understand quite a bit in order to identify problems clearly.

Information Banks and Communication

The vastly larger memories of the future will allow most factual information of general interest to be placed in computer memories, that is, *information banks* will be created. This development has the potential of giving every man access to the accumulated factual knowledge (if not the wisdom) of mankind. This promise is much, much harder to fulfill than one might suppose. Intensive efforts have already been put into computer programs known as *information retrieval systems* which are designed to retrieve specific information from a general library in a computer's memory. Some people hope for near perfection and are disappointed by the rather mediocre performance of current information retrieval systems. This disappointment should be re-evaluated in light of the fact that current human-based information retrieval services are also mediocre and often much worse than current computer retrieval systems. There are reliable studies that indicate that between 80 percent and 90 percent of *all* research and development work is, in fact, the rediscovery of things already known. The information retrieval services used by people in this work is certainly not of high performance. In a large library one can spend many hours searching in vain for information sure to be there, if one only knew where to look. In summary, these information retrieval systems will not put all of mankind's knowledge at everyone's fingertips, but they will tremendously increase the amount of information to which we have quick access.

Software for communications will play a large, behind the scenes, role for information banks. Some information is in such constant demand that it will be available throughout the country. Most information, however, is required infrequently and thus will be placed in only a few (perhaps only one) computer information banks. Part of the information retrieval system will be dedicated to transmissions between information banks and computer users. An extensive communications network will exist to link together computers throughout the world.

Many persons are concerned (with justification) that highly personal information about them will be placed at everyone's fingertips. The question of *privacy* in computerized information banks will create considerable discussion and controversy in the future and we predict that the result will be as follows. Private and personal information about almost everyone will be in these banks and there will be rather elaborate safeguards against unauthorized use. A person sufficiently knowledgeable about the safeguards and with sufficient talent and resources will be able to circumvent them, and some invasion of privacy will result but it will probably be less than exists in our current society. The invasion will be of a different nature and the unanswered question is whether this difference will lead to unforseen and unpleasant consequences. Fortunately for most people, the private information about them is not worth the effort required to obtain it.

The impact of these projected software capabilities can be summarized by stating that the general public will be able to make real use of computers and that the amount of information and problem solving power made available will far surpass what was previously available. Computers will not, however, be infallible or idiot-proof and like the books, libraries, and educational systems which preceded them, there will be some who exploit them with great success and others who obtain little direct benefit.

3-3   *THE KIND OF THINGS TO EXPECT*

There are many specific developments that should not cause surprise in this century. All the items on the following list involve computers in an essential and usually dominant way. A projection about the future such as this must make some basic assumptions and we *assume* that no super-revolutionary or catastrophic events occur. Thus we expect revolutionary things to happen; but we rule out of consideration things like a war that devastates most of the earth, completely new forms of government, super-intelligence (either from outer space or developed by or in man), a world-wide anti-technology movement, immortality, and so forth. Paradoxically, a study of history shows that it is quite unusual to have a long period of time without a society-shaking event; that is, it would be very surprising not to be surprised!

Our assumptions, unfortunately, imply that large differences will remain between the developed and the underdeveloped nations. Our projections are for the most developed areas which will probably be Western Europe, North America, and Japan. The average level of education and wealth in these areas is assumed to be much higher than at present, perhaps by a factor of as much as three or four for wealth.

Our projections assume considerable advances in areas of technology outside of computers, yet these assumed advances are quite minimal compared to the projections for these areas. Since advances in electronics, materials, psychology, genetics, biology, and so forth, are also likely to be very significant, the interactions are almost sure to lead to situations where our projections are simply irrelevant. Thus, we might mention the future use of computers in the control of traffic and criminals, but developments in communication and transportation might eliminate traffic, and developments in psychology and genetics might eliminate most forms of crime.

Now that we have established that our projections are certain to be in error, we proceed to make them. The projections are divided into six groups roughly corresponding to the segments of society most affected. Space does not allow us to develop the arguments for (or against) these projections, and most of them are too technical in any case. However, it is worthwhile for the reader to select several of the projections and consider what impact they might have on society if they do indeed come to pass.

Projections Affecting the General Public

1. *Telephone Encyclopedia.* One will "dial the encyclopedia" and obtain quick access to a body of factual information at least as large as a good current encyclopedia. The requests are spoken and the response is either spoken or displayed on a visual communicaiton device (*video-phone*). Later, probably not in this century, a device the size of a hearing aid will give twenty-four-hour instantaneous access to even larger bodies of information.
2. *Household Robot.* One will be able to buy a device that can perform a variety of routine, standardized household chores. These include preparing some meals, cleaning up after meals, mowing the lawn, watching the baby, and washing clothes. The device will be expensive, but widely used in a wealthy society.
3. *Reliable Remote Identification.* A computer will be able to analyze a person's voice, handwriting, fingerprints, or perhaps even his picture, and make a positive identification. Presently, credit cards attempt to establish identification in several ways. See Figure 3-3.1. This ability will be coupled with extensive communications to make possible the *cashless society* (and checkless society) as discussed in the next chapter.
4. *Medical Advice and Diagnosis by Telephone.* One will "dial the doctor" and be connected to a computer program able to make a first level medical diagnosis. It will ask questions, prescribe pills, and give instructions on whether to go to the emergency room immediately or to the clinic tomorrow. More sophisticated versions will have access to a summary of a person's medical history.
5. *Automated Marketing.* One will be able to "dial the store" and obtain delivery on thousands of standard items from toilet paper to "Super-Soup" to screwdrivers to children's socks. Video-phones or similar devices will allow one to "shop by catalog" and obtain the bulk of one's needs without leaving home.

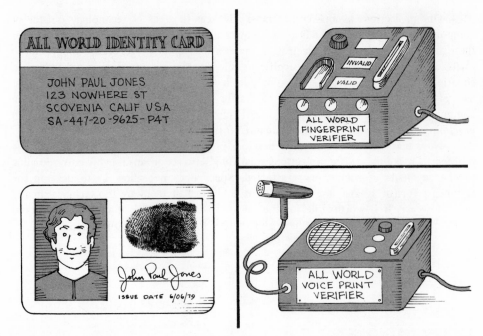

FIGURE 3-3.1   Illustration of card-based identification systems. Information about Mr. Jones is encoded magnetically on the card. When the card is inserted into the device, a check can be made to verify that the fingerprint or voice print agrees with that on the card. Much higher security results if a check is also simultaneously made with information from the central computer utility files.

Projections Affecting the Specialists

1. *The Professional Information System.* The professional information system is similar in concept to the telephone encyclopedia, but much more detailed and sophisticated. Separate systems will exist for each profession (or even specialty within a profession), and it will require considerable training and knowledge to make use of these systems. The lawyer, doctor, investment broker, and so forth, will have immediate access to information in greatly increased quantity, reliability, and timeliness.
2. *Sales Strategy Analysis* Complex computer models will be created for marketing and advertising strategy analysis. Madison Avenue experts will vary the blend of sex, elegance, snob appeal, youth, and exaggeration in their advertising, and then consider the resulting sales—at least as predicted by their model. Midnight oil will burn in crash efforts to counter the competition's latest product or advertising campaign.

Projections Affecting Business and Industry

1. *Simulated Prototype Production.* One will be able to have a prototype model of a new product "built" inside a computer using simulations. One can examine the model, see how much it weighs and costs, how well it performs, and so on, without ever actually building a model. Major and minor design changes can be made in the computer model and the results examined. This process will not be "quick and cheap," but it will be quicker and cheaper than building actual prototypes.
2. *Product Availability/Marketing Systems.* Product availability and marketing systems are similar in concept to the automated marketing systems for the consumer. A video-phone or similar device will allow a businessman to shop for wholesale quantities and to see specifications, pictures, and prices. A nationwide network of this type will become a primary component of the marketing system.
3. *One-of-a-kind Production.* Computer controlled design and production facilities will allow a growing variety of assembly line production of unique items. The permitted variations will not be unlimited, but a much greater degree of individuality will be possible in homes, clothes, furniture, insurance plans, vacations, and so on, than is possible with the mass production methods of the mid 1900s.
4. *Mobile Robot Workers.* Highly complex machines already exist that perform dozens of operations in a manufacturing process and these will develop into much more versatile mobile robots controlled by computers. The computers will analyze visual images in the control process and the robots will, in turn, operate less sophisticated machines.

Projections Affecting Science

1. *Exploration Robots.* Variations of the household and industrial robots will allow exploration in locations hostile to man. The temperature of the surface of Venus is about 800°, Jupiter has a poisonous atmosphere and crushing gravity, pressures on the bottom of the ocean can crush vessels with steel hulls several inches thick. Man is unable to explore these areas but robots impervious to heat, poisons, and pressure might.
2. *Weather Forecasting.* The weather is one of the most complex physical processes, but accurate analysis and prediction will be possible with the "super computers" to come. Once we understand the cause-and-effect relations of weather, then man can begin to explore means to modify it. Meanwhile, in this century we will have to take what nature gives us.
3. *Computers as Scientific Instruments.* Computers will be an integral part of instruments to allow man to see or hear phenomena that are outside the range of his senses even with sophisticated amplification devices. A device will sense the events in one of many ways, perhaps through magnetic fields, radio waves, heat, vibration, or pressure. These signals will be analyzed by a computer program and converted into visual images or sound patterns that a human can sense, examine and study.

4. *Problem Solving Systems.* Research and development in science involve a continuous stream of problems to be solved. Most of these are fairly well understood and yet it requires hours, days, even weeks to actually obtain their solutions. Computer systems will appear that will automatically solve all the routine, or nearly routine, problems encountered, and the scientist will be able to devote most of his time to the problems which require original analysis and techniques.

Projections Affecting Government

1. *Employment Information Systems.* Information banks and related facilities will gradually develop containing detailed information on available positions and persons seeking employment. By the end of this century these systems will cover positions at all levels and will be a major tool of the government in the analysis and control of the economy.
2. *Criminal Detection Systems.* The advent of reliable identification and automated payments of all kinds (the cashless society) will force criminals to be either unidentified or stay completely outside the main operations of society. The cashless society will, of course, eliminate some types of crime, but no doubt the human mind will be able to invent new ways to attempt to get something for nothing. Many other aspects of crime prevention and detection will employ computers, see Figure 3-3.2.
3. *Models of Election Strategies and Diplomacy.* Complex models of the voting patterns for various segments of society will be developed and used in all important election campaigns. The politician's problem will be to identify a position consistent with his principles that gives him a majority of the votes. Will the man without principles always win? Will the election go the party with the best models? the biggest computers? the most money? Voting is an emotional act and the emotions are fickle. National governments will develop similar models for international politics and diplomacy.

   We can visualize a nationwide communications network with every person connected (perhaps by telephone, perhaps by cable television). A politician could propose two alternative programs and then ask the people to respond with their preferences. His computers would tally the results and he would obtain "real" information about the people's desires. One can even visualize official voting taking place this way, but there are hard problems in the regulation of the vote.

Other Projections

1. *Robots that Play Ping-Pong.* It will be feasible to build a robot that plays an excellent game of ping-pong. A large amount of computing power is required for control and analysis and a specialized robot is envisaged. Such a robot probably will not be built (the cost is greater than the benefit), but similar abilities may appear in more productive robot applications.

FIGURE 3-3.2 A Maryland Highway Patrol officer uses a computer console to obtain instantaneous information on traffic violations, stolen cars, and so forth. (Courtesy of Bunker Ramo Corp.)

2. *Conversation Translators.* Computer systems will appear that combine voice analysis and language translation into a translator device for conversations in two different natural languages. The translations will be adequate for tourists, business transactions, scientific exchanges, and so forth.

The twenty projections made above are of an optimistic nature, and most people would call the things projected "good" on the whole. One can also visualize extremely unpleasant consequences of some of them. Society's efforts to control itself might make it possible for a tyrannical clique to obtain control. The elimination of work might lead to severe psychological problems for many, perhaps even most, people. Society is projected to become a much more interrelated and complex organization. It will be possible to immobilize this organization at any one of thousands of points. Unstable elements of society might appear and gain control of these points "shaking" society into a collapse back to a pre-industrial, farming (agrarian) society. No matter what values one assigns to agrarian society, it is extremely stable. It is possible that either heaven or hell on earth comes to pass, but not very likely. Thirty years or three hundred years from now man will still be challenged, frustrated, and struggling. The past will look primitive, but peaceful, and man's evaluation of the perfection of his current situation is not likely to change.

3-4   THINGS WE DON'T KNOW HOW TO DO (YET)

We have seen that computers can control all kinds of other machines, but our objective here is to examine limitations on the computer's own operations and not on the operation of machines controlled by computers. The essence of a computer's operation is information processing and as such can only be compared to the human mind. Thus consider the question: What can a human brain do that a computer cannot do? Note that computers can do some things (fast, accurate arithmetic, for example) that humans cannot do and there may well be other capabilities yet to be discovered.

Four facilities of the brain that have proved very difficult to duplicate with computers are *memory, pattern recognition, learning,* and *language*. We will not discuss the more philosophical questions of *creativity* for two reasons. First, there is no general agreement about the exact definition of creativity. Some definitions are so broad that almost every action (including those of computers) is creative and others are so narrow that only the greatest of men qualify as creative. Second, it is almost certain that creativity, whatever it is, involves the use of the above four facilities in significant ways and thus we must understand them before expecting to understand creativity.

It is important to realize that we have only a few inklings about how the brain operates. Thick volumes are required to record the mass of knowledge we have accumulated about the brain and yet most basic questions are still completely open. We do not know how specific pieces of information are retained; current theories center around either patterns of minute electric currents traveling along closed loops or complex molecules. Of course, if we do not know how the information is stored, we do not know the physical mechanism used to retrieve it. The information in the brain must be encoded in a special systematic way, yet we have only a few tentative conjectures on how the encoding scheme works. As we move to higher levels of operation the uncertainty grows and when we reach the analysis of the formation of emotions, creativity, and such psychological phenomena, there are many competing theories.

However the brain operates, it is certain that current computers operate in a totally different manner. This is perhaps best illustrated in the area of memory. Two crucial properties of a memory are its capacity and its speed (the time required to obtain a piece of information). The memory capacity of the brain is known to be enormous. Exceptional individuals have exhibited a memory capacity equivalent to the order of from 100,000,000 to 1,000,000,000 words of computer memory and there is considerable evidence that even these individuals utilize only a small portion of the brain. It is very probable that the brain uses an efficient encoding scheme which reduces the bulk of this information by a large factor. It would seem that the limitation on people's memory is not the storage capacity but rather the mechanisms that insert and/or retrieve information. Even so, the typical human brain has a working memory capacity that is much larger than that of a typical computer.

The speed of the brain is slow compared to a computer memory, at least from one point of view. It takes several hundredths of a second to obtain a piece of information from the brain while a computer can do this in a millionth of a second. *But there is a very important difference*. The computer requires that the location of the information be given while the brain has almost its entire contents available at the same speed. Thus a person can produce the name of the wife of his cousin who lives in Shawnee, Oklahoma in a split second and it would take hours for a current large computer to do the same if it had to search a file of information the size of an average brain's memory contents. We simply do not know how to organize information in a way to allow retrieval from memory as fast as the brain retrieves information. In fact, it seems very likely that a completely different process is required, one that has a *high* degree of parallelism or simultaneous operation. (See Figure 3-4.1 and 3-4.2) Current computers are essentially sequential in nature, that is they go through a file of information one item at a time. The first serious attempts at parallel operations in a computer are underway, but these are still far removed from the degree of parallelism that appears to be present in the brain's operation.

One of the key facilities, perhaps the most important one, of the brain is *pattern recognition.* In its simplest form, this is the facility the mind has for recognizing the letters A or B, the sounds of the words "dearly" or "daily," the tastes of bread or beans. In its most sophisticated form, the brain is able to recognize things that are given in a very incomplete form. For example, some handwriting can be read with ease even though 50 percent of the letters in the words are ill-formed or missing. A conversation can be followed where only a few words and sounds are clearly identifiable. In each of these

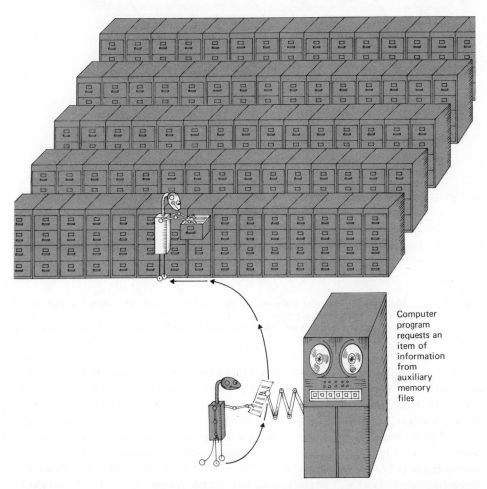

FIGURE 3-4.1 **Illustration of sequential searching of files of information. The search begins at the start of the files and proceeds until the requested information is located. Names, for example, might be alphabetized, but the request gives only an ID-number such as social security or driver's license.**

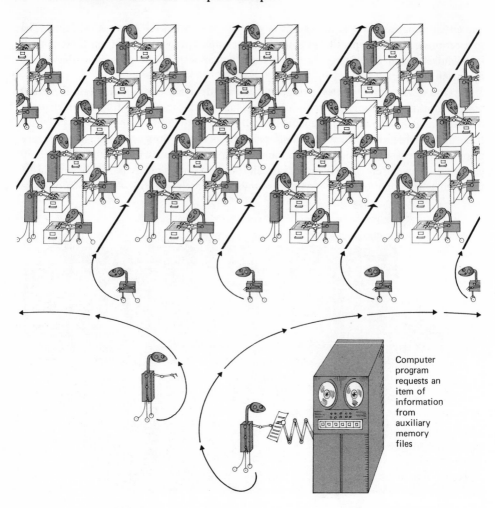

FIGURE 3-4.2 Illustration of parallel searching of files of information. The request is distributed throughout the memory by a system of "messengers." As soon as one searcher locates the requested information it is given to the computer program and the searchers wait for the next request.

examples, the information sensed by the brain forms a pattern and even though it is incomplete, the brain recognizes it and can then fill in the details from its own memory. This pattern recognition ability is highly developed in all normal humans and is used unconsciously in almost every action a person takes.

A great deal of effort has gone into the analysis of pattern recognition and it has been a major achievement to construct computer controlled equipment that can reliably recognize carefully written block capital letters. There is no doubt that improved pattern recognition capabilities will be developed, but it may require several breakthroughs in hardware, software, and theory before computers can be given a pattern recognition facility comparable to that of the human mind.

Pattern recognition is perhaps the most important tool the brain uses in *learning*. A great deal of the learning experience can be summarized as follows: The teacher presents the problem and explains how to solve it. At this point none of the students can solve the problem. The teacher then goes through the solution of several examples. At the end, many or most students can solve the problem. The next day another brief discussion is given and a few more examples are worked by the teacher and the students. By now almost all the students can solve the problem.

Where did the students learn how to solve the problem? It certainly is not at the original explanation even though *all* the pertinent information is given. The learning takes place in watching and doing the examples. *The brain recognizes the pattern of the solution process from these examples and thereby learns how to solve the problem.* Clearly this is not the only learning process the brain uses, but it is the most important in the area of learning "how to do things."

It is interesting to contrast this method of teaching with that which one uses to "instruct" a computer. A computer is instructed by a computer program which specifies, in detail, each step to be taken. This corresponds to the first (and least effective) step the teacher took in the above discussion. The later steps of doing examples have no effect whatsoever on the computer's performance. Research is underway to create computer programs that "learn" and some of the efforts have been publicized in the mass media. However, a careful examination of these efforts shows that the learning mechanisms are very rudimentary and we have a long way to go before the learning capabilities of computer programs is anything like that of the human mind.

The translation of natural language (English to Russian, for example) is considered in detail in the next chapter and this problem has been much more difficult than originally anticipated. A computer program has no trouble with vocabulary since it can use a dictionary with ease. The difficulty is to extract the correct *meaning* from a sentence even when the meanings of the words are known. Many common words have several meanings and thus a sentence may have different interpretations that are grammatically correct and which make sense. Some examples are discussed in the next chapter, but the classic example of such a sentence is the common metaphor: "Time flies like an arrow." This sentence has at least five different interpretations (see Section 4-4). Can you find them? An almost identical sentence is "Fruit flies like an apple" which has, in normal use, a completely different meaning. The brain extracts the correct meaning from a sentence by examining the *context*. Normally only one meaning fits the context and the brain immediately selects it. Its ability in this selection is nothing short of amazing. One can read a sentence on page 317 of a book whose correct meaning is determined by another sentence on page 88 and the correct meaning is selected without even slowing the pace of reading. The brain seems to have an image or pattern of the context and everything is matched against the context automatically. A straightforward approach to duplicate this facility in a computer program would lead to horrendously long processing times and in addition the results would probably be unreliable.

The conclusion to be reached from this discussion is that some very important kinds of information processing capabilities of computer programs are much inferior to those of the human brain. However, intensive research is in progress to create computer programs with improved capabilities. We have a long, long way to go but the pace of progress is rapid and we can expect the computer's capabilities to be improved many times over by the end of this century.

3-5 *MAN AND MACHINE*

We have just made a comparison of the information processing capabilities of computers and of humans. The computer's capability in this area is very small now, but might well rise some day to a level more comparable to that of the human brain. This possibility immediately raises the question: *What is the relationship between man and machine?*

Most people are not aware of the current relationship—or of the relationship in 1950 before computers were a significant factor. *The (so-called) advanced industrial societies can not exist without machines.* The societies of 1950 in North America and Europe would have immediately and completely collapsed if *all* the machines had been stopped. It is easy to see that we have become dependent on machines like automobiles, refrigerators, telephones, and drills. But even more basic items are machine products: paper, screws, electricity, guns, canned soup, salami. Man has already woven machines into the fabric of his society so that they cannot be removed without destroying that society.

Once we realize that our lives already depend (literally) on machines we can take a more relaxed view of the future of the relationship between man and his machines. The relationship is already one of *symbiosis* (a mutual dependence that is beneficial to both parties) and it will become even more so. Many people believe that man is unique because of his ability to use tools, an ability that he has exploited since before the dawn of history. The exploitation of tools (for example, computers) is viewed by some people as part of the natural evolution of the species. The computer has properties much different from other machines, but then so did the wheel, the cannon, the steam engine, the telegraph, and the atomic bomb. Its impact on society is already large and will become much larger but only time will show the real nature and significance of the impact. The impact will be greater than that of the Industrial Revolution during the last century.

A development that will have great impact on the relationship between man and machine is the "intelligent machine." Will such a machine be built? The answer is certainly yes, at least in some sense of intelligence. The reasoning behind this answer is as follows. A man of great talent will be able, with years of effort, to write a computer program that passes the ultimate intelligence test. That test is to place a machine in a room and a man in another room and then interrogate them. If the machine responds in a way that is indistinguishable from the man, then the machine passes the test and might be said to be intelligent. Note that a moron is human and thus the level of intelligence could be low. It is plausible that a team of men can some day write a program that is more intelligent than any one of them individually. The motivation and challenge to build an intelligent machine is great and one of low intelligence might appear in this century.

It is worthwhile to state precisely the nature of the development discussed above. We say that it is possible (and will happen) for man to *transfer some of his intelligence* to a computer via a computer program. We do not imply that a machine will be built which, when plugged in, is intelligent. Neither do we rule out this possibility, but it is certainly further removed than the transfer of intelligence to a machine.

It is also worth noting that we may be able to have intelligent machines (in the above sense) before we understand human mental processes. It is conceivable, even probable, that the information processing methods that make machines intelligent will be different, perhaps radically so, from those of the brain.

3-6   THE NEED: UNDERSTANDING

The theme of this section is contained in the following two statements:

There is a difference between being able to do something and knowing how it is done.

Once we understand, precisely and completely, how to do something then we can have a machine do it.

These two facts were stated in Chapter Zero but they are so significant that they deserve further attention.

In an earlier section we discussed a number of mental processes that everyone can do without really understanding. The first of the above two statements applies to this situation, but more significantly, it applies to a great variety of things that we have learned how to do, but still cannot say how they are done. Consider, for example, the following addition problem.

$$
\begin{array}{r}
347015 \\
27803 \\
57890 \\
31000 \\
\underline{192182} \\
655890
\end{array}
$$

One is taught how to do these problems as a child and most adults know how to add and can correctly obtain the sum for any test problem. Yet at least 99 percent of the people who can add and write cannot write down (in a reasonable time, say two hours) a set of instructions on how to do it. This is because they do not know *how* it is done. A common assignment in a beginning programming course is to write a program to add two integers just as people do. Most people are surprised at the struggle required to complete this assignment. The difficulty is not with the computer languages, for almost all of them are naturally suited for this assignment. The difficulty is that people are rarely able to organize and identify the steps of the process that they use in solving this problem. This phenomenon occurs over and over in computer programming even though many people never recognize the nature of the difficulties that they have.

There is an interesting experiment which illustrates the first statement. It is really a kind of a parlor game involving two players, *A* and *B*. Player *A* is to do exactly what player *B* tells him to do, nothing more and nothing less. The object of the game is for *B* to get *A* to accomplish some task by giving him *simple, direct* instructions about movement. The instructions allowed include: move your left hand up three inches, close your fist, close up your thumb and forefinger. Examples of instructions not allowed are: undo the button, grab the string, fold the top part over. *A* is the judge of the legality of an instruction and does nothing when an illegal instruction is given. Even very simple tasks provide a challenge as well as some fun. Some experiments are: undo a sleeve button, buckle a belt, pick up a pair of scissors and cut a piece of paper, untie a shoe and take it off, tie a shoe and so forth.

There is less subtlety in the second statement. Since computers can control other machines, the range of activities that can be computerized is enormous. However, this statement taken in conjunction with the first one implies that there are many things we do that cannot be computerized yet because we do not completely understand how they are done. And there is the crux of the exploitation of computers. We must obtain a better understanding of the real world and its activities. Some of the processes that we take for granted as natural are, in fact, extremely complex. The search for understanding in many computer application areas (education, election strategies, scientific instruments, robot control, for example) leads directly to some of the most fundamental and difficult questions about science, man, and his society.

3-7 BEYOND COMPUTERS, WHAT?

When one reviews *significant* increases in human understanding and technology, one sees a pattern. A group of people work together trying to solve a problem (for example: "How does one design a car that everyone wants^" or "What makes a daughter look like her mother^"). Each person focuses his full mental resources on the problem, but a significant advance occurs when *creativity* is introduced. All of a sudden, one of the investigators realizes that an essential ingredient is missing.

For example, it might be realized that a *new device* is needed. Whether or not the device can be made depends on the level of technology. (Recall that Babbage's analytical engine failed in 1840 because of mechanical difficulties, not because of weakness in his design). If the technology is right, then the device can be made and the problem solved (by the 1930s, it was practical to construct Babbage's analytical engine).

As a second example, it might be realized that a *new technique* or theory is needed. Newton's "Principia," written in 1687, presented a large body of knowledge, all organized around his famous Laws of Motion. One part of his book was subtitled "The system of the world (in mathematical terms)" and he literally meant to include everything from dewdrops falling from a leaf to explosions in the stars. This was the crowning achievement of a long study by many scientists. Newton stated his Laws in words because there was no mathematical way of expressing them. But, mathematics was necessary to use the Laws effectively, so Newton developed a new mathematics called calculus. His Laws could then be written as equations and analyzed with the techniques of calculus. This new mathematics and its new techniques were perhaps as important to the advance of science as his Laws of Motion.

In these two examples, a new device or technique was needed to achieve a breakthrough. Sometimes it is realized that the missing ingredient is in the problem itself. The problem needs a *new formulation* because some essential part is missing. Consider the automatic calculators of the 1930s and early 1940s; these could do arithmetic faster than instructions could be fed to them. At that time, the problem everyone was working on was: "How does one improve the mechanical and electrical mechanisms involved^" When the problem was reformulated to "How does one exploit a fast accurate arithmetic device^" it was recognized that the instructions for the calculator could be encoded as numbers and put into the calculator just like other numbers; this was a crucial creative idea. Once this idea occurred, then the next important step was to reformulate the problem again: "How does one represent information in a calculator?" The answers obtained from this formulation not only led from the old calculator to the modern computer, but also led to thousands of completely unforeseen applications of computers.

The authors have had many experiences watching people try to solve the "wrong" problem, that is, the problem was not formulated correctly. Unfortunately, it takes years for the average person to learn how to formulate problems correctly. A typical scene is as follows: A student comes to our office for help with a homework problem. A little probing shows that he has not formulated the problem correctly. A few leading questions usually lead the student to a correct formulation and he then leaves, knowing how to proceed towards its solution.

It is absolutely essential in problem solving, and particularly in computer programming, to be fully aware of what problem one is really trying to solve and exactly what are all the features which affect its solution.

We have indicated how breakthroughs have been made in the past and we discuss some problems in this and the next chapter where progress toward their computer solutions has not been very great. These problems tend to involve *patterns* (the pattern of chessmen on a chess board, the pattern of words and meanings in sentences, the pattern of clues in a detective story). A computer program and a human seem to play chess the same way: each examines the board and then chooses a move to try to improve his position. However, a good human player can make a choice in a few seconds which improves his position perhaps 10 or 20 moves later and a computer cannot. (See Section 4-3).

The key breakthrough here might well be another example where the formulation of the problem needs changing. Currently, the problem is stated: "How does one write a computer program which recognizes certain patterns?" It is true that various patterns can be encoded and placed in computer memories. The trouble seems to be that these encodings are not suitable for rapid processing. It is not too far from the truth to say that about all you can do with a computer representation of a complicated picture is to have the computer draw another copy of it. Perhaps the problem should be reformulated as: "How does one represent patterns so they can be processed quickly and manipulated easily?" The solution to this problem might require the invention of new devices and techniques; it certainly will require great creativity. The result of this solution (when and if it occurs) might lead to devices and techniques which are so significantly different from computing that they would have new names, and perhaps more important, they would open new horizons to us.

SUGGESTED READINGS

An annotated list of readings is given at the end of Chapter 4. Several of these books are good sources of additional information on the topics of this chapter. Particularly pertinent from this list are the following:

Bernstein, Jeremy, *The Analytical Engine: Computers Past, Present, and Future*. New York: Random House, Inc., 1966.

Carovillana, Robert and James Skehan, *Science and the Future of Man*. Cambridge, Mass.: M.I.T. Press, 1970.

Communications of the Association for Computing Machinery, Vol. 15, No. 7, July 1972.

Diebold, John, *Man and the Computer*. New York: Frederick A Praeger, Inc., 1969.

Ferkiss, Victor, *Technological Man, the Myth and the Reality*. New York: New American Library (Mentor), 1970.

Greenberger, Martin, *Computers and the World of the Future*. Cambridge, Mass.: M.I.T. Press, 1962.

———, *Computers, Communication, and the Public Interest*. Baltimore, Md.: Johns Hopkins University Press, 1971.

Martin, James and Adrian Norman, *The Computerized Society*. Englewood Cliffs, N.J.: Prentice-Hall, Inc., 1970.

4 *A Selection of Computer Applications*

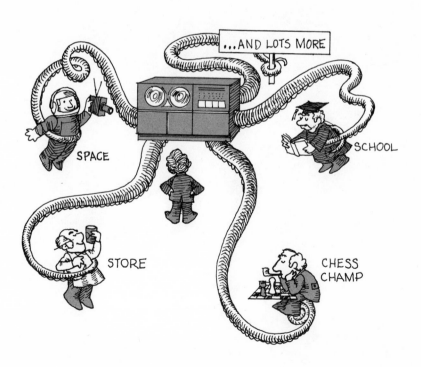

...AND LOTS MORE

SPACE

SCHOOL

STORE

CHESS
CHAMP

The computer applications presented in this chapter show the variety of ways that computers can influence our society. The applications considered are complex, real-world problems and computers are only one of several essential ingredients for success in some of these problem areas. The topics range from the almost frivolous (computers that play games) to the deadly serious (the urban crisis), from a smashing success (space travel) to a partial failure (natural language translations) from the everyday world (education and the cashless society) to the speculations of millionaires (playing the stock market). There is no special order in the presentations and the sections are essentially independent of one another.

4-1 SPACE TRAVEL

We consider three distinct applications of computers to space travel. The first is the design of the space vehicle and its components. The second and third are the planning of a mission and its operational control. We discuss the specific mission of a Mars landing for a motorized robot with instruments.

Component Design

Even though designing a space vehicle takes several years, it is a very dynamic process. Literally thousands of components are under simultaneous development, many of which have never been built before and whose final performance is uncertain. The project is broken into many subprojects, each of which is informed what the final performance will be of the components that affect this subproject. Each subproject uses this information as a basis of its own development work. There are two critical problems that arise and the solution of each requires a computer.

The first problem is the coordination of the subprojects and their progress. The projected performances of the components are only estimates and some may perform better (for example, a fuel tank might withstand higher pressures than anticipated so that 14 percent more gas will be available for maneuvers in space) and some may perform worse (the plexiglass in the viewing port may be weaker than anticipated and the size of the port is to be reduced from 18 inches to 15 inches in diameter). A way must be found to relay the current status of the vehicle design to *all* the subprojects. A steady flow of reports is one approach and is, of course, used. Another approach which supplements these reports is to have *all* the physical properties, sizes and shapes, incorporated into a *master computer model*. Once a design specification change is approved, that change is made on the master model and is immediately available to everyone concerned. A report is also issued describing the change, but most people receive more reports than they can read and it is easy to miss some essential item.

Aerospace research and development projects have the most sophisticated computer facilities. A subproject manager can request a drawing of the cross sections (at an angle of $37°$) starting at the #4 attitude controller and receive it in half an hour from a computer controlled drafting machine. This cross section will show every wire, nut and bolt including a recent change in the size of the viewing port. The master computer model contains data in addition to physical dimensions such as capacities (of tanks), strengths of key parts, electrical properties, and so forth. This additional data can be obtained on a computer printout or on a console (either typed or displayed on a television screen) even more readily than drawings.

The second critical problem is the testing of components whose operation depends on other unavailable components. Suppose, for example, a new design is proposed for the entry into a thin atmosphere such as the one on Mars. Theoretical analysis indicates that the entry vehicle will not burn up, but much more detailed information is needed for the design of landing gear, the specifications for the packaging of instruments, and so forth. It is obviously out of the question to build a prototype and then test land it on Mars. This leads to the creation of a second computer model of the space vehicle, one for operational or dynamic properties rather than physical dimensions. It simulates the operation of the vehicle in all important respects and consists of a large number of mathematical equations and relationships. These relationships describe the interactions of the forces and movements of the vehicle. The vehicle has a computer to help guide it, so the computer simulation makes all the calculations the actual computer would make. The simulations contain a segment that describes the properties of the atmosphere and these can be set to match those of Mars. The result is that the new entry vehicle design can be incorporated into the simulation model and then a simulated entry into a thin atmosphere is made. During this entry the desired data about acceleration, temperature, vibration, speed, and so on are gathered for use in further design and development refinements.

This simulated testing is not the same, of course, as real life testing, but in many areas of space exploration it is reliable enough to be used with considerable confidence. Needless to say, astronauts who risk their lives on the basis of these designs are very concerned that this simulation be checked, cross checked, and double checked. A single tiny error in a computer program has been known to cause a satellite launching to turn into a fireworks display. Few astronauts favor such an experience.

Mission Planning

Let us now turn to the second phase of computer application, the planning of a specific mission. For concreteness, let us consider the mission of making a soft landing on Mars with a motorized robot and instruments. At this point the space vehicle has already been designed and is a type that is assembled in an orbit 100 miles high around the earth. There are again two crucial questions to be answered: How can the vehicle be steered so that it reaches Mars, and how much cargo can it carry? The answer to the second question depends on the first because different routes or trajectories require different amounts of power for the same amount of cargo. (See Figure 4-1.1.)

The first problem then is to determine the trajectory to Mars that requires the minimum amount of power. Since the power of the vehicle is fixed, this trajectory allows the maximum amount of cargo or payload to be carried. Now it is not easy to determine any trajectory that results in a Mars landing, let alone the one with maximum payload.

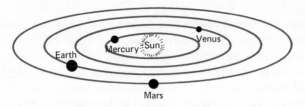

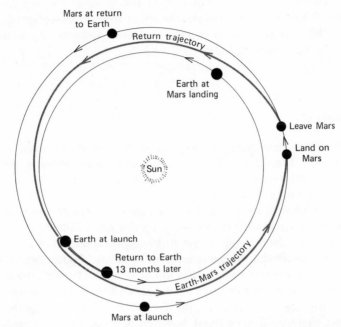

FIGURE 4-1.1 **A trajectory for a 13-month trip to Mars and back. Even though Mars comes to within 30 million miles of Earth, this trip is 800 million miles. Short, fast trips require rocket engines much more powerful than now available. Extensive computer calculations are required to time the launch so that one can get to Mars as fast as possible with a given rocket.**

The system of mathematical equations is very complex. These equations must take into account the positions, movements, and gravitational attractions of the earth, the moon, the sun, and Mars. Each of these is a complex function of time and affects the position of the space vehicle. Furthermore, the dynamics of the vehicle must be represented accurately and the performance of the rocket engines must be precisely included. And these are only some of the variables that must be included in the equations for a trajectory. The only hope of analyzing these equations is another computer simulation of the vehicle and its flight to Mars. This simulation is very similar to the operational one used in the design of the space vehicle. In fact, the same computer programs might be used in some instances.

The following procedure is used to determine the best or optimum trajectory for this mission. A first guess is made as to how to steer the vehicle. The people involved are very experienced and knowledgeable in this area and their first guess is likely to be a very good one. This guess is put into the computer simulation and a simulated flight is made to

Mars by the computer. The results of this first flight are analyzed and several variations are made on the first guess to obtain a better trajectory. These variations are then put into the computer simulation and more simulated flights are made to Mars. These results are then analyzed in order to determine further improvements in the trajectory. The making of systematic variations in order to obtain the best trajectory is a highly technical and mathematical process. The number of "flights" to Mars needed might be large and a great deal of computer power is consumed in this process. The end result is that a (hopefully) best trajectory is obtained and the rest of the mission is planned on this basis. For example, the amount of cargo is now determined and attention is turned to the selection of instruments to be included.

Mission Control

The third and final phase of computer application is the actual control of the mission's operation. The space vehicle and its payload are assembled in orbit and a very detailed plan for the mission is specified. At the precise instant planned the rocket engines are fired and the mission is started.

Things immediately begin to deviate from the plans. The deviations are quite small but even tiny errors are significant. An angle of a few hundredths of a degree is so small that the unaided eye cannot detect it, yet if the original direction of a 30,000,000 mile trip is off by such an amount the end result is off by about 25,000 miles. This would be a complete miss for a mission to land on Mars which is only 4200 miles across.

One's first thought is to get back on the planned trajectory, probably because on an automobile trip one keeps correcting the direction in order to stay on the road. This is not the correct strategy for space travel, however. A better analogy is made with a sled race down a huge, irregular mountainside. A sledder can start his sled anywhere along the top and his objective is to reach a certain point at the bottom as fast as possible. He surveys the mountain side very carefully and chooses a path that he believes to be the fastest. Suppose that partway down the mountain a hump turns out to be larger than he thought and he finds himself 10 yards off his planned path. If he makes a quick turn to get back on this path he will be slowed down by the additional friction and turning forces and there is no way he can regain this lost speed. The best thing for the sledder is to say "Somehow I've gotten here even though I didn't plan to, now what is the fastest path from here to the bottom." A real sledder may say this, but he does not have time to resurvey the situation and determine a new "best" route. This strategy might not be practical for a sledder, but it is for a space craft—provided enough computing power is available.

Let us review the facilities that are typically available for the control of a space mission. First, the space craft has an inertial guidance system that includes a miniaturized computer. This system senses the vehicle's motion and the computer compares it with the planned motion. When the deviations appear, the computer initiates changes in the steering that are intended to compensate for the deviations. The onboard computer is not powerful enough to compute a new "best" trajectory so there are larger computers on the ground to aid in the mission control. These computers receive

FIGURE 4-1.2   **Astronaut John Young collecting lunar samples on the Apollo 16 mission (April, 1972). It requires a tremendous amount of computer power for a space exploration mission to the moon and back. (Courtesy of NASA.)**

information from the inertial guidance system and from ground radar tracking and radio telescopes. These ground computers are large and fast and during a mission they do nothing but analyze the information and the progress of the mission. They periodically recompute a new "best" trajectory and these trajectories are sent to the space vehicles computer and incorporated into its steering control calculations.

After the initial main thrust is over, the computers determine the small "mid-course corrections" that may be needed to achieve a precise landing on Mars.

In summary, we see that space exploration projects are large consumers of computer power. While computers certainly do not deserve all the credit for the successes of space exploration, it is literally true that space exploration could not have gotten off the ground without computer power.

Impact on Society

The public probably does not appreciate the many benefits it has received from the successful (and expensive) space program. Many examples of new consumer products and devices can be given, but instead, we discuss a case where the benefit is computer technology know-how.

Consider the case of the reentry problem: a vehicle moves through a fluid, such as air or the atmosphere of Mars. One wants to know the details of its behavior, including its temperature, speed, vibrations, trajectory, and so forth. This extremely complicated problem is similar to the older and well understood ballistics problem: If one shoots that cannon, where does the cannon ball fall? However, the ballistics problem is much simpler since, for example, one does not care how hot the cannon ball gets. To solve the reentry problem requires, first of all, a complete understanding of all of the main items which affect its solution. This understanding is then expressed as a set of mathematical equations which are, in turn, put into a computer program to get a computer model of the reentry.

The intense study of the reentry problem resulted in new understanding, know-how, and computer programs. All of these can be applied to solve other problems involving fluids. These include the flight of airplanes, pollution in rivers, the spreading of smog, and even the flow of automobile traffic. One model of traffic flow regards the cars as smeared out along the highway and then traffic is like the flow of water in a pipe. Recall the "bangs" and "thumps" that occur in the plumbing systems of old houses. These come from shock waves caused by turning off faucets, just as airplanes cause shock waves (sonic booms) by violently disturbing the air. The tragic accidents on turnpikes which involve 10, 20, or 50 cars are exactly the same kind of shock waves. Less violent waves in traffic are seen in "slow down waves' or traffic jams that seem to occur for no reason at all. Thus, the better understanding of fluid flow gained from the space program can show up as benefits in a wide variety of situations, perhaps even in better highway designs. The example of fluids flows is only one of a number of examples where the space program has made significant contributions to practical problem solving techniques.

We do not want to leave the impression that the space scientists started from scratch on these problems, they did not. We *do* want to say that because of the space program many problems were restudied, the models (mathematical equations) were improved, new methods were found for solving the equations on computers, and all this knowledge can be (and is being) applied to many problems which affect the general public in everyday life.

4-2   *THE CASHLESS SOCIETY*

Before discussing how to eliminate cash from society, it is appropriate to discuss the nature of cash and money in general. Money originated from the commercial requirement to transfer wealth or value in some convenient and widely accepted form. The original forms of money were small items of value, primarily metal coins of gold and/or silver. The value of these coins was widely accepted and one could exchange them for other items. Since the coins were themselves valuable, they were widely used outside their country of origin. For example the Maria Theresa dollar, first minted in the late seventeenth century by the Austro-Hungarian empire, was widely used in Arabia and East Africa until 1940—long after the original issuing government had disappeared. Very few current coins (of any country) have significant value in themselves and those that do usually disappear quickly. For example, the price of silver rose in the 1960s until the United States silver coins were more valuable than the dollars they represented. They completely disappeared from circulation because both the government and individuals collected them.

Since modern (paper) money no longer has any intrinsic value, it is frequently considered as a certified receipt for money which does have intrinsic value. This view cannot be correct because there is not nearly enough gold and silver in the world to cover all of the money that exists. Note that money now exists in many forms, for example coins, bills, checking accounts, savings accounts, government bonds. Cash, in the form of coins and bills, is only one form of money, one which will gradually disappear as the monetary system evolves. Indeed, checks have already replaced cash in over 50 percent of the financial transactions in the United States. Not only cash, but checks, as well, will gradually be replaced. Perhaps the title of this section should be "the cashless and checkless society." We have a tendency to identify cash with money, just as the ancient Greeks and Romans identified gold and silver coins with money. Money itself will not disappear, it will only change form again. Figure 4-2.1 shows a few forms of money used in the past.

Another view of money is as a symbol (or receipt) for a contribution to the welfare of society. The government is charged with responsibility to certify and maintain the value of these receipts. This responsibility is not a simple one and some governments have totally failed in it. There were several examples of this in Europe in the 1920s. In one country it required 500,000 billion (that is half a quadrillion) pengös to mail a letter whereas it had required only ten pengös a few years earlier. The difficulty arose from the fact that the governments created new money simply by printing it and people lost their faith in its value. The value of money comes from society's acceptance of it as valuable. This may be rephrased by saying that money is a universally recognized equivalent of wealth and value, it is freely usable in exchange for other items of value and it is the standard measure of value. Money can be anything from bars of salt or pieces of paper to spots on a magnetic tape.

It is pertinent to point out that *everything* gains its value from the willingness of society to give it value. There is *nothing* that has an intrinsic value, that is a value that is inherent in its own existence or nature. This applies to everything from diamonds to peanut butter, from houses to education, and from shoes to sex.

What, then, is wrong with cash as a form of money? The primary problem is *security*, it belongs to whoever has physical possession of it. This means that one must continually guard against theft and accidental loss. A secondary problem is that it is a physical object which is sometimes inconvenient to transfer or to subdivide. Most money in the United States already exists in the form of checking accounts and this system gives a high degree of security and an easy means to send someone $117.38. It does not provide for the electronic transfer of money nor, more importantly, *checks do not have universal recognition as money.* That is to say, if you arrive in Des Moines, Iowa for the first time in your life and without any cash, you will have real difficulty buying a meal no matter how much money you have in a bank in California. A restaurant or bank in Des Moines is extremely unlikely to give you cash for a check no matter what you tell them or what you do.

FIGURE 4-2.1 Some of the forms of money that have been used in the past. Coins from ancient Greece (left) and Rome (center) are shown at the top. Money used in the 1800s included the huge stone wheels from Yap Island (center), the cross from Katanga, Africa (top right), the $1.00 bill from the United States (bottom left) and the money tree from Malay (bottom center) where one could make change by picking some leaves off. The whale's tooth is from the Fiji Islands (bottom right). (Courtesy of Chase Manhattan Bank Museum.)

There have been two significant means to solve the recognition problem for personal checks. One of these is the *traveler's check* (Figure 4-2.2) (or cashier's check) and the other is the *credit card* (Figure 4-2.3). Either one of these objects will allow a stranger to obtain cash someplace in Des Moines (or in Bangkok). Neither one is universally accepted, both require advance preparation, and both have limits on the amount of money that can be obtained. Even with traveler's checks one can underestimate the amount needed and be without money in Bangkok while having thousands of dollars in a bank at home.

Technical Requirements

There are three technical requirements for the evolution to a cashless society. These are positive *identification*, rapid *communication*, and rapid *accounting*. We discuss these requirements in reverse order.

Some banks already have sophisticated computerized accounting systems that give them rapid access to all their accounts. The elimination of cash will require all banks to have such systems and will require that these systems be extended to allow automatic transfers into and out of accounts. These extensions are not trivial but they can be completed within a few years. This technical requirement will not impede the evolution toward a cashless society.

A telephone network already exists which provides rapid communication between any two points in the United States. It is not clear that this network has the capacity for a cashless society. The number of money transactions made each day in the United States runs into the billions and if these were done by telephone, the number of telephone calls made in the United States could easily double. There has been a steady increase in the telephone system's capacity in the past but there has been an equally steady increase in

FIGURE 4-2.2 Traveler's checks are designed to overcome the problems of personal checks as they are guaranteed by a financial institution. They are almost (but not quite) as good as cash.

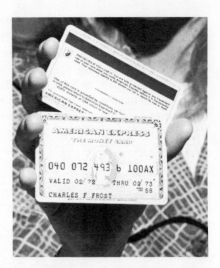

FIGURE 4-2.3 A credit card with a magnetic coded strip (black band on top of the back) for possible automatic processing. (Courtesy of American Express.)

the demand. It is likely that ordinary telephones will be only one part of the communications network for money transfers. There will undoubtedly also be a special interbank system and a collection of computers which have memories for items that are not urgent to direct the communications system. This will be one example of a computer network.

It is rather easy to visualize how the cashless society would operate. (See Figure 4-2.4). Mrs. Jones walks into Green Globe Shoes and buys a pair of sandals. The clerk has a connection to the banking system (probably a kind of telephone) and Mrs. Jones authorizes that $7.77 be transfered from her account to the Green Globe Shoes account. The banking system does this and, in the process, verifies that Mrs. Jones has $7.77 in her account. The final and most difficult technical problem arises here. How does the clerk (or the banking system) know that this is really Mrs. Jones? In other words, how do we achieve universal acceptance of this cashless system. The crux of the problem is to be able to positively identify people. The solution must be very reliable although it need not be perfect. After all, there are people who counterfeit cash and who forget signatures on checks. The losses suffered this way have been small enough so the present money system is workable. The cashless society money system need only do as well.

Let us consider some of the following possible means of positive identification (see also Figure 3-3.1):

> identification card
> visual comparison
> handwriting analysis
> finger prints
> voice analysis (voice prints)

The primary drawback to the ID card is that it depends too much on possession. Of course a photograph and signature can be added as well as an invisible magnetic code. Furthermore, the card could be semi-permanently attached as a bracelet or even placed under the skin and read magnetically. Thus we can visualize a card-based identification system which is very convenient and more reliable than any current document identification.

The other four means each involves comparing (by an elaborate computer program) some characteristic of a person against a standard reference kept on file by the computer. These are all personal characteristics which cannot be mislaid, which change slowly (if at all) and which are very difficult to duplicate. The "voice print" is particularly appealing as it could be recognized via a telephone connection. The transmission of visual images requires a better communications system and might well be no more reliable. These four systems of identification have some aesthetic appeal compared to the ID card but they each also involve a great increase in the computer processing power required to make the identification. None of these systems is foolproof and it is an interesting pastime to visualize ways to cheat them. Even so, there is little doubt that a satisfactory identification system will appear in the near future and the cashless society will be technically possible.

Even if it is technically possible, will it happen? Who is going to pay for those huge computers and the elaborate communications network? The answer is that it almost certainly will happen and the costs will be paid partly from eliminating the costs of the current system and partly by people (both consumers and businessmen) who desire the conveniences of the cashless society.

FIGURE 4-2.4 Example of purchase using a credit card. A device such as that shown could automatically credit the store's bank account from the buyer's account for the amount of the purchase. (Courtesy of North American Rockwell Electronics Group.)

Impact of a Cashless Society

The evolution to a cashless society will produce an impact, but it is unlikely to be spectacular. We examine this impact in four areas: the average person, business operations, crime, and government operations. The two principal advantages for the average person are:

1. He has nearly instant and continuous access to all his money.
2. There is no danger of losing money or of being robbed. However, one could be forced, say at gunpoint, to transfer all of one's money to someone else's account.

A total lack of cash causes one disadvantage: You cannot send your nine year old child to buy a loaf of bread. The child will not (or at least should not) have access to his parents bank account and thus cannot buy things. There are a number of solutions to this difficulty, for example, one could telephone an authorization to the bank for this one purchase. The most likely situation will be that cash does not disappear entirely but is still used for small transactions long after an essentially cashless society exists. One can easily foresee that banks will install automatic cash stations where one can obtain a few dollars at any time. Indeed, this event happened between the first and last drafts of writing this book. The operation of a cashless society might actually be cheaper than with cash, but if it is not, then the average person is one of those who will pay part of the extra cost.

The impact on business will be much greater, of course, but still evolutionary. The primary attraction is the elimination of bad credit, bad debts, and bad checks. The losses that business suffers in this area run into the billions and the costs of measures to guard against these losses run into more billions. Businesses that operate on a total cash basis also suffer huge losses from employees who take a few dollars from time to time. There is hope that these savings alone will more than pay for cost of the equipment and computer time for the cashless society. The elimination of mailing bills and receiving checks back will result in additional savings for business that will no longer need to give short term credit. It costs at least 25 cents to mail a bill (not counting the costs of accounting) and the customer must pay about 20 cents to mail a check back. This means that a cost of 45 cents per transaction in a cashless society, which seems very high, is no more cost than the standard operation of many businesses. There are a number of other advantages to businesses of a more technical nature that are associated with this operation. They arise when the sales transactions are also automatically and simultaneously entered into the accounting and record-keeping system of the business. This results in either a substantial saving in accounting costs or much better records; and this in turn can result in better inventory control, smaller working capital, better sales analysis, and a generally more efficient business operation. The mechanics of how these savings result is beyond the scope of this book, but they are a further motivation for business organizations to evolve toward the cashless society.

The possible impact of the cashless society on crime is very attractive indeed. A variety of crimes, many of them violent, are aimed at obtaining cash. These include robbing liquor stores and gas stations, purse snatching, mugging, pickpocketing, and taxi cab holdups. The elimination of cash will eliminate these crimes and result in a great saving to society in both financial and emotional terms. If the cashless society is based on the ID card, then one must protect that from being stolen. However, the ID card is much harder to use than cash and a person can freeze his bank account as soon as he is aware that the ID card is missing. Such petty crimes are primarily committed by the most unskilled criminals and the cashless society holds out the prospect of unemploying many of them.

While the unskilled criminals may be unemployed, computing opens up new horizons for the skilled criminal. A programmer has already been convicted of stealing fractions of cents from a bank. He wrote parts of a bank's program for savings accounts and operated as follows. In most calculations of interest there are fractions of cents involved. Thus the interest on $1,392.78 at 4-3/4 percent for six months is 33 dollars and 7.8525 cents. Most banks pay $33.07 and ignore the remaining 0.8525 cents. This man, however, wrote the computer programs so that $33.07 was credited to the proper account and the remaining 0.8525 cents was deposited to his personal savings account. Thus he never stole as much as one cent at any given time, yet he managed to steal several hundred dollars each month. There is growing concern that cleverer programmers might be able to steal much more, especially as all the financial institutions use more and more complex computer programs for their accounting.

There are at least two ways that the government can benefit from the cashless society and both of these involve the improved accounting system that is possible. First, better accounting means that the government has access to better records of income and expenditure for both individuals and businesses and thus it can collect more of the taxes that are due. There are several billion dollars in uncollected taxes each year because cash transactions are not recorded or reported. Second, the improved accounting system allows the government to obtain more detailed information (more rapidly) about the economic condition of the country. Since the government is responsible for keeping the economy running smoothly, it needs all the current information it can get. It seems likely that federal and state governments will not discourage (and will probably encourage) the evolution toward the cashless society.

Our discussion indicates that the cashless society is almost inevitable (which, in fact, the authors believe). There is not likely to be a particular day when one can say "the cashless society starts today," because the transition will be gradual. The transition has been in progress for many years now and there will simply be less and less occasion to use cash and more and more sophisticated methods to transfer money.

4-3 TIC-TAC-TOE, CHECKERS, AND CHESS

There has been considerable publicity and speculation about computers that play games, especially chess. The game of chess has long been considered a game that requires supreme intellectual ability and many people believe that if computers can beat people in chess, then computers must be as "smart" as people. The ability of computers to play chess well would not have a large direct impact on the world, but this ability has been taken as a guide for the general capabilities of computers in "intellectual" activities. The purpose of this section is to examine how computers play games or, more exactly, how people write computer programs that play games.

Tic-Tac-Toe

We consider the simple child's game of tic-tac-toe first, in some detail. It is well known that two reasonably capable players will always end the game in a tie or draw. Even so, it is fairly tedious to examine the game completely and prepare a computer program that will always win or draw.

The game of tic-tac-toe involves two players who take turns in putting marks in a pattern. One player uses circles (O) and the other crosses (X) and the object is to place three circles or crosses in a row (either horizontal, vertical, or diagonal). A complete game is illustrated in Figure 4-3.1.

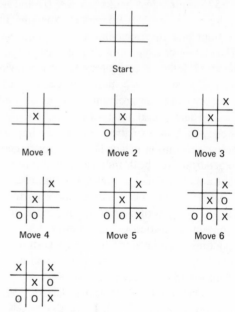

FIGURE 4-3.1 **Top, the pattern with nine positions for the game of tic-tac-toe. The moves of a game are shown, the player with the crosses wins on the seventh move.**

Move 7, the X-player wins

If we consider this game for a moment, we see that there are nine choices for the first move, eight for the second move, seven for the third and so on. Thus the total number of different games of tic-tac-toe is

$$9 \cdot 8 \cdot 7 \cdot 6 \cdot 5 \cdot 4 \cdot 3 \cdot 2 \cdot 1 = 362,880$$

This is a very large number, but common sense tells us that tic-tac-toe is not an intricate game so there must be a much smaller number of essentially different games. Consider, for example, the very first move. There are nine possibilities, but only three of them are essentially different as you see in Figure 4-3.2.

FIGURE 4-3.2 **The three first moves of tic-tac-toe.**

Center move   Corner move   Side move

The other six moves are equivalent to one of these. For example, if one starts in the upper right hand corner, the pattern (which is usually on paper) can be rotated until the cross is in the lower left hand corner and the game is unchanged. This simplification comes from the symmetry of the pattern and we will consistantly use symmetry below in order to simplify the analysis of the game.

We now wish to devise a winning strategy for this game. Then we could write a computer program to carry out this strategy and the computer would be unbeatable in tic-tac-toe. We assume that we play with the circles and our opponent plays with the crosses. We now have to specify a strategy to play the game. There are two obvious rules that determine about 75 percent of all our moves on defense.

Rule 1. If there are two circles and an empty space in a row, place a circle in the empty space. We win the game.

Rule 2. If rule one does not apply and there are two crosses and an empty space in a row, place a circle in the empty space.

To specify the remaining 25 percent of the moves, we have examined all the cases and selected a move for each of them. For example, on offense, we have selected as the first move to place a circle in the center. Our following selections on move 3, 5, and 7 are indicated in Figure 4-3.3. Note that two of the possible fifth moves as well as all of the winning moves are determined by the above rules.

In our analysis of the game we assume that our opponent also follows these two basic rules. He could make a mistake and give us an undeserved advantage. These two rules let us take advantage of our opponent's errors without explicitly considering them.

We consider two situations—offensive and defensive. In this game, offense (we play first) is much simpler than defense. We place the circle in the center to start the offense game. All of the possible games needed to present our strategy on offense are indicated in Figure 4-3.3. We have used symmetry to reduce the number of possibilities and we have not considered any blunders by either player. Note that we have a single fixed move in each situation. At move 2 and one of the fourth moves, the opponent has a choice. Of course, we must be prepared for each choice, so we have followed all the branches of the tree.

The defensive situation is much more complex because the opponent has the initiative and we must be prepared for any eventuality. We give no more than the tree structure of the possibilities because the space is limited. The reader might want to follow several of the branches in Figure 4-3.4 to see how the possible games develop. Note that the attack from the center position leads to the most complicated defense so we could say that this offense is the strongest. The other two opening moves lead to games which, after the third move, are governed almost completely by the two basic rules. Only one of these gives circles a chance to win (except if crosses makes a mistake) and that is the game that, after the third move, appears as follows

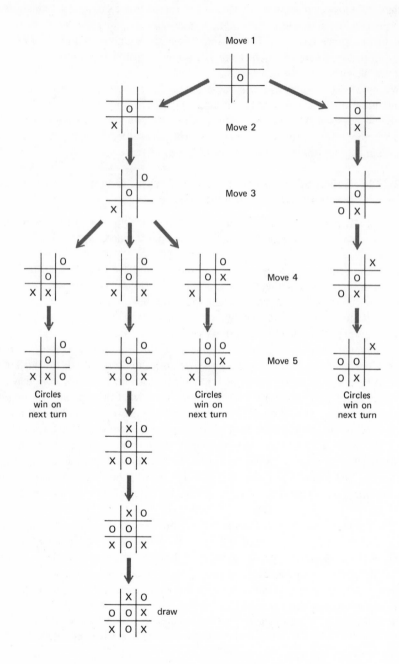

FIGURE 4-3.3 The tree of possible games for a winning strategy based on the first circle in the center position. There is only one successful defense for this offensive strategy.

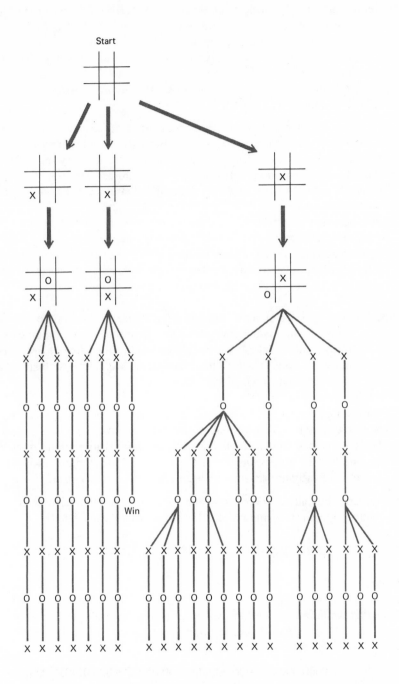

FIGURE 4-3.4 **The tree of possibilities for the defense strategy to be used for tic-tac-toe. There are 23 basically different games, 22 end in draws and circles wins one of them.**

If we assume that this analysis of tic-tac-toe is correct then we have obtained a completely automatic strategy (or algorithm) to play an unbeatable game. This strategy can be incorporated into a computer program and then one might say that the computer plays an unbeatable game of tic-tac-toe. It is more accurate to say that we (people) have written a computer program that plays an unbeatable game of tic-tac-toe.

There is still a considerable amount of work left to do in the writing of a computer program. The basic steps are:

1. Devise an internal computer representation of the information in the game. The computer program cannot process the visual pattern, so other means have to be provided for it to know where the circles, crosses, and empty spots are located.
2. Provide communication between this new internal representation and the external opponent. This might be done by a console, a Teletype, a printer, or some other device.
3. Put the complete information about the offensive and defensive strategies into the program. Recall that about 75 percent of the moves are determined by the two basic rules. The rest of the situations would be inserted one by one or other rules would be sought which further reduce the number of special patterns that must be examined by the program. Such a rule is:

Rule 3. With a choice on move 4 of the defense (rules 1 and 2 do not apply) move in the middle row or column if one of them contains two blanks and a circle. If the middle row and column are not free, then move to a diagonal that has a circle and two empty spots, placing the circle next to one of the crosses.

An examination of all the cases of this strategy shows that this rule (together with rules 1 and 2) determines all of the fourth moves.

4. Devise a method to detect when a particular game is a variation (by symmetry) of one of the games in the strategy. The strategy must then be varied appropriately (by using symmetry again) for this particular game.

To actually carry out all of these steps and to verify that they have been executed correctly requires a reasonable amount of patience and attention to detail.

Checkers

Now that we have seen how one can make a complete analysis for playing a simple game, let us turn to the game of checkers. (See Figure 4-3.5.) It has been estimated that the number of different checker games is

$$10^{40} = 10,000,000,000,000,000,000,000,000,000,000,000,000,000$$

This is a much larger number than the 362,880 games of tic-tac-toe. For tic-tac-toe we were able to reduce our examination to 28 games or one-thousandth of one percent of the possible number. Suppose for checkers that we could use symmetry and the

FIGURE 4-3.5 **A typical situation in the game of checkers.**

elimination of blunders to reduce the number of games considered to one-billionth of one-billionth of one percent. If you had that percentage of all the air on earth, you would have about as much air as the size of a large pea. That is out of an original blanket of air that is 14,000 miles long on each side and 50 miles thick. That still leaves 10^{20} = 100,000,000,000,000,000,000 games to consider.

A computer 100 times more powerful than current ones might be able to examine 100 complete games of checkers in a second. Suppose that you and every man, woman, and child in the United States had such a computer and used it to analyze the game of checkers. Suppose that everyone's computer works 24 hours a day, 7 days a week, 52 weeks a year for 50,000 years. At the end of this time all the games of interest might have been considered. Note that the games have merely been considered, one still has to select the unbeatable strategy. The conclusion to be reached from all this is that no imitation of the tic-tac-toe approach is ever going to be useful for the game of checkers.

What, then, does one do? A specific answer requires a detailed study of the game, but the general approach can be outlined. First devise a method to evaluate the strength of any situation that arises. Thus a position of – 35 might be very weak, a position of 0 nearly balanced, and a position of +40 extremely strong. Such an approach is widely used in the card game of bridge to evaluate the hands dealt. It requires a great deal of skill and effort to devise a useful evaluation method. It must be rather reliable and fairly easy to carry out.

Assume that we have a good evaluation method and we are in the middle of a game. There are usually about seven moves we could make and we could evaluate the situation after each of them and then choose the move that gives us the strongest position. This approach, however, is shortsighted and easily defeated.

So we decide to look further ahead in the game. We look at all seven of our moves, then all 49(=7·7) of the opponents and then all 343(=7·7·7) of our responses. We now want to choose the move that puts us in the strongest position, but we have no control over the opponent. We can use a tactic called *minimax* to attempt to achieve the best position. This tactic is best explained by an example. We simplify the situation by assuming that only three, rather than seven, choices of moves are available at any one time. We build a tree of the possible situations for three moves (two by us and one by the opponent). After each move we evaluate the strength of our position and record that number on the tree. A typical result is shown in Figure 4-3.6.

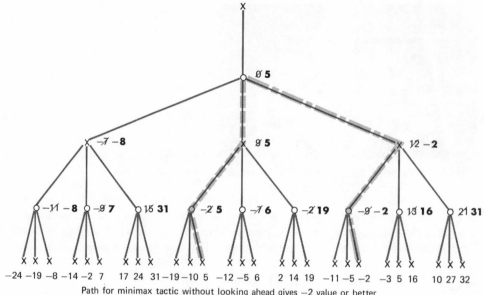

Path for minimax tactic without looking ahead gives −2 value or better
Optimum path gives +5 value or better

FIGURE 4-3.6 Illustration of the minimax tactic (with and without looking ahead) for selecting checker moves. Each position on the tree has a strength as indicated by the small numbers. The minimax look ahead is used and the "strengths" are replaced by values brought up from below. This leads to a better choice of more than simply picking the move with the most strength.

We now see along the bottom the results of all possible sequences of three moves. The shortsighted tactic of taking the strongest position next leads to choosing the right branch. That is possibly followed by a left-hand branch choice by the opponent and we again take the right branch to obtain a final strength evaluation of −2 which is weaker than the starting position.

The minimax strategy starts at the bottom with the following sequence of reasoning:

1. As our last move we choose the one that gives us the strongest position. Therefore the real strength of the opponent's last move is the *maximum* of the position values of our last moves which can follow this move.

The original evaluations have been crossed out and replaced by these maximum values in Figure 4-3.6 in the next-to-last line.

2. Our opponent might be as smart as we are, so he will choose his moves to give us the weakest position at the end. He does this by choosing his last move to minimize our strength on the next-to-last line. Therefore the end value of our next-to-last move is the *minimum* of the end values of the moves which follow from this one.

The original evaluations have been crossed out and replaced by these minimum values in Figure 4-3.6 on the second-from-bottom line.

This process of alternately minimizing and maximizing the evaluations at the next lower level goes from the bottom to the top of the tree. It gives the best end-result that we can obtain if our opponent plays the best game possible. We now choose as the next move the one that corresponds to this best end-result.

A real computer program to use this minimax strategy would normally consider several thousand positions, some of them perhaps 12 to 20 moves away from the current position. It would *not* consider all the branches of the trees. There are a variety of rules used to decide when a particular branch appears unfruitful and when to stop considering it. Note that with seven choices at each move we have about one million different possibilities after seven moves. We must somehow ignore most of them or the computer time required to choose a move would be too long.

The type of analysis that is actually made is illustrated in Figure 4-3.7. Some lines of play are followed for eight plays, but most of the possibilities are immediately eliminated at each move. Only 15 sets of eight moves are considered out of thousands of possibilities. The evaluation of the end values of each final position is shown in Figure 4-3.7 as bold face. These values are then transferred back up the tree by the minimax procedure. The best move is the one of the right branch which results in at least an end value of +6 compared to the current value of 0.

There are two essential elements necessary for a good strategy. First, and perhaps most obvious, is the computer power to quickly examine several thousand possibilities. Second, and clearly most important, is to devise rules and procedures which discard millions of "bad" lines of play and which retain the "good" lines of play for examinations. Thus, with a given amount of computing power, the deciding factor is the skill of the person who writes the computer programs to play the game.

By 1970 a computer program had been developed to the point of playing a very respectable game of checkers. It could almost always win against opponents who had not seriously studied the game. It challenged and occasionally defeated players with national rankings and its performance merited a national ranking. There are several levels of national rankings in checkers and this program performed at the lowest of these levels. It was unable to win against the best players in the United States. In summary, this program plays checkers at a level at which most people would be proud to play.

This program is the result of years and years of patient development and improvement. It represents a great accomplishment for the *persons* who wrote the program. These people have managed to incorporate a great deal of their ability and knowledge into the program so that the program together with available computational power is able to compete with people.

Chess

As a last example of game playing with computers let us consider chess. A typical situation in chess is shown in Figure 4-3.8. This game has long been considered the most difficult of intellectual games (the Japanese game of Go is as difficult but not widely known in the west). Each chess piece is allowed different moves so the game is much

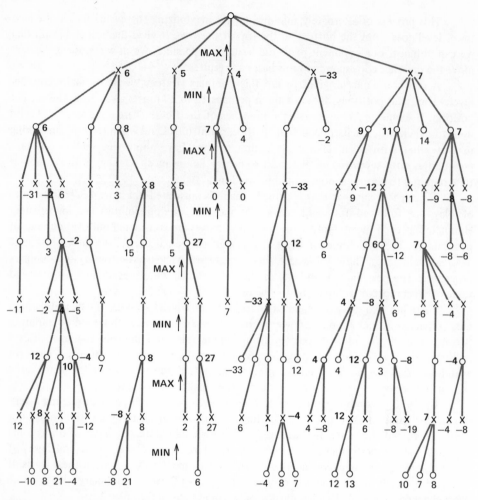

FIGURE 4-3.7 A tree of moves where most branches have been pruned by various kinds of rules. The evaluation at the terminal points is in bold face and the results of the minimax procedure are shown for the intermediate points. Values are not shown if no branching occurs.

more complex than checkers. The number of distinct games is estimated to be about

$$10^{110} = 100,000,000,000,000,000,000,000,000,000,000,000,000,000,$$
$$000,000,000,000,000,000,000,000,000,000,000,000,000,000,$$
$$000,000,000,000,000,000,000,000$$

Earlier we outlined the staggering amount of computations required to examine all the games of checkers. If one needed to examine only one-billionth of one-billionth of one-billionth of one-billionth of the percentage of chess games as needed for checkers and if computers were a thousand times faster in examining chess than checkers, then the amount of work left is still almost beyond comprehension. Suppose there were twenty billion people on the earth with everyone operating such computers, and suppose there

FIGURE 4-3.8 A typical chess situation. There are 64 squares on the board and each player starts with 16 pieces: 8 pawns, 2 castles, 2 knights, 2 bishops, a king, and a queen.

were a billion planets in this galaxy with the same activity, and suppose there were a billion such galaxies engaged in this effort. Suppose further that the effort lasted for 50,000 billion years. Then the calculations would be about 1 percent completed.

The approach described for checkers can be and has been applied to chess. In fact a great deal of effort by many groups in many countries has been spent on this project. A display from a current chess-playing computer program is shown in Figure 4-3.9. The results are much less satisfactory than for checkers, but still there are high hopes that programs will be able to seriously challenge very good (if not the world's best) chess players by 1980. This would be quite a triumph for the person who develops the computer program.

FIGURE 4-3.9 A computer's display of two situations in a chess match. Several times this one has won the Association of Computing Machinery annual chess tournament for computers. The left position is the one where Spassky resigned in his final 1972 game with Fisher. This program predicted that Spassky, not Fisher, would win.

We can foresee that as people try harder and computers become more powerful, people will be able to write programs that play a very good game of chess, eventually better than a person can play. This is not something that chess players need to fear. After all, runners and high-jumpers do not concern themselves about the fact that we can build machines to run the mile in one minute or to jump 80 feet high. The competition that concerns them is between people. Automobile racing is an example of competition involving a combination of man and machine. Perhaps game playing with computers might develop in this spirit.

4-4 NATURAL LANGUAGE TRANSLATION— THE COMPUTER'S FAILURE?

The translation of artificial computer languages is one of the routine steps in computer applications. In the early 1950s the use of computers to translate natural languages (Russian into English, for example) was considered. Some people were very enthusiastic and believed that the language barrier could be removed by computer translations within a few years. Numerous projects were started throughout the world, especially in the United States, England, and Russia. Everyone realized that a large effort was required and thus it was no surprise when the total budgets reached several million dollars per year. This money came primarily from the central governments who realized that successful translations by computers would well be worth a 25 to 50 million dollar investment in research.

The basis for the optimism was the recognition of the tremendous advantage that the computers have over people in learning vocabulary. Vocabulary is by far the most difficult part of learning a foreign language, at least for people. However, one can put a 10,000 or 20,000 word Russian-English dictionary in a computer memory and it has "learned" the vocabulary. The early workers realized that grammar also plays an essential role, but they were confident that they could handle the variations in grammar between two languages.

Before 1960 one could find newspaper accounts saying that "machine translation is no longer a theory but an accomplished fact." These accounts were incorrect and machine translation is still not an accomplished fact today. The quality of computer translations produced after ten years of research and development was much poorer than that of human translations. Furthermore, machine translations were more expensive than human translations. Crude translations do have their uses so this effort was not completely wasted. Nevertheless, the early optimistic predictions failed to materialize.

One difficulty was in the grammar. Vocabulary is easy for computers and hard for people, so perhaps we should not have been surprised that grammar, which is easy for people, turned out to be hard for computers. Looking back, it is easy to say that this should have been foreseen, but it is a well-known fact that hindsight is much clearer than foresight.

Most of us have had long training in grammar patiently studying verbs and nouns and adverbs and direct objects and prepositional phrases and so on. Most of us showed little appreciation for the subject because we did not see how this information was used. After all, we could speak English well enough and thus we were already using the grammar even though we did not know all (or even any) of the rules we used. Nevertheless, grammar is essential to understanding and/or translating a language. Thus a computer must have a complete set of grammatical rules if it is to make a good translation.

What Does a Sentence Mean?

Let us consider a short sentence in English and see how grammar plays a role in determining the meaning.

Time flies like an arrow

This sentence has at least five different interpretations as follows:

1. The common metaphor meaning that time passes quickly.
2. Certain insects (time flies) enjoy an arrow.
3. Use the same method to time the flight of flies that is used to time the flight of an arrow.
4. The magazine (*Time*) flies like an arrow when thrown.
5. Time goes in a straight manner.

Three of these interpretations (1, 4, and 5) correspond to the same grammatical structure:

	Time	flies	like an arrow
grammar	*noun*	*verb*	*qualifying phrase*
1.	clock-time	passes	quickly
4.	magazine	flies	straight and fast
5.	clock-time	goes	in a straight manner

The grammatical structure of the other two interpretations are:

	Time flies	like	an arrow
grammar	*noun*	*verb*	*object*
2.	insects	enjoy	something

	Time	flies	like an arrow
grammar	*verb*	*object*	*qualifying phrase*
3.	measure time	of insect flight	this way

The first of these five possibilities is the most likely and would be accepted if the sentence appeared alone. However, the sentence could be placed in a context where one of the other meanings is appropriate. For example, if students at a football game were throwing paper airplanes and other objects, one of them might well use this sentence if he happened to have brought *Time* magazine to the game with him. Some of the other meanings are less plausible but are grammatically correct and conceivable. It is an interesting exercise to imagine different situations where each of the possible meanings would be appropriate. This sentence is admittedly unusual, but sentences with *more than one possible meaning* occur regularly in any natural language.

With this difficult sentence in mind, let us visualize how a straightforward machine translation might proceed. First, examine all the words in the sentence, find their meaning (or meanings) and possible grammatical uses (verbs, nouns, articles, and so forth). This information is then processed to obtain one or more possible meanings. If only one meaning is found, then the translation is finished. Thus we would not expect a machine translator to have trouble with a sentence like:

The house is red.

We would also expect to have a correct translation of an absolute nonsense sentence like:

Rotating dissatisfactions eat supersonic churches clearly.

Difficulty arises with the following simple sentences:

The school is close.
The school is full of roaches.

The word "school" might refer to an educational institution or to a group of fish. There is no indication of the correct choice in the first sentence, but an educational institution must be meant in the second sentence because a group of fish cannot be made up of roaches, unless, of course, there is a roach fish [which there is—it is a fresh-water fish (replace "roaches" with "suckers" for a salt-water variety)] .

The Central Problem: Ambiguity

A sentence is *ambiguous* when it has more than one possible meaning and by now one sees that a central problem in natural language translations is ambiguity. How does one select the correct meaning of a statement when more than one possibility exists? Nobody knows the answer. But it is recognized that a better understanding of grammar is one of the keys to the solution of this problem.

There are two terms widely used in describing the translation of languages (either natural or artificial). The first of these is *syntax* which refers to the way words are combined to form phrases and sentences. It also includes the rules for punctuation and the rules for forming paragraphs out of sentences. The second term is *semantics* which refers to the meaning of the words and sentences. The final goal of machine translation is, of course, to preserve the semantics.

One can give an oversimplified summary of the early straightforward approaches by stating that investigators felt that the semantics problem would be solved by using a dictionary and the syntax problem by a little bit of ingenuity and simple rules. After years of effort it was realized that there is a large interplay between syntax and semantics and that machine translation efforts did not include an adequate knowledge of syntax (or grammar) to unravel this interplay.

Since language in general and grammar in particular have been studied for many centuries, people interested in machine translation began to investigate the traditional work in grammar. The traditional work resulted in extensive and elaborate grammars for various natural languages. These grammars have proved inadequate in a variety of ways, but a common weakness is that they are based on a human understanding of language. That is to say, the grammars might be useful to a person who already knows about languages, but they do not contain enough information to permit automatic machine translations.

The result of these considerations and the lack of rapid progress in language translation was that research of the grammars of natural languages became very active. This research in the area of *linguistics* has been fruitful and it is fair to say that a much deeper knowledge of grammar has been found. Computer systems for machine translation now contain several thousand different rules to help determine the structure and meaning of sentences. Some people feel that ten times this many rules are really needed. Unfortunately, these advances in research plus several more years of multi-million dollar budgets have not resulted in a very significant improvement in the quality of the translations obtained. In the middle 1960s there was considerable controversy due to this fact. Some people said that machine translation was hopeless and that the government should stop wasting its money. Others still insisted that the answers were just around the corner. The middle ground between these two extremes can be summarized in the following way:

1. A cutback should be made in the support of large projects aimed at producing quality translations in the near future.
2. A greater emphasis should be placed on basic research into the grammar and meaning of natural languages.
3. Studies should be made of the possibilities of combined machine and human translation schemes.

The third point is typical of the conclusions reached in a number of sophisticated computer application areas. One should aim to devise an operation where the strengths of computers and people are mutually complementary. Let the computer do the things it does well and let the human do the things that he does well.

Does one conclude from all of this that the computer has been a failure in natural language translation? In a strict sense, the answer is certainly yes. At this time computer translation programs cannot produce reasonable translations of a general selection of material. The biggest error however, was in the lack of understanding of the nature of the natural language translation problem. Even some of the pessimists of the early 1950s were over-optimistic. It is now realized that the processing of natural languages is one of the most subtle and complex processes known and it was foolhardy to think that one could unravel these processes in a mere ten years.

The project to put a man on the moon was an enormous triumph for science and technology and yet this project was much easier than translating Russian into English by computer. The space program required numerous discoveries and advances in technology, but these were small in comparison with the 250 years of accumulated knowledge and understanding of science that could be applied. On the other hand, the machine translation efforts had to start from scratch and it took several years for anyone to appreciate the enormous difficulty of the problem. It took almost 20 years for everyone to appreciate it. (We believe that the early pessimistic statements were based on anti-machine bias rather than insight into the problem).

Recall from Chapter 3 that we predict that computer programs will be able to make good translations of conversations in two different languages. This situation is easier than the translation of written material because ambiguities can be removed by asking for clarification. Even so, this capability will represent a very large advance over the capabilities of the early 1970s.

Context and Semantics

Although the bulk of the current research and progress is in the syntax (or grammar) of natural languages, the final and most difficult barrier will be in the semantics. Recall the example of "Time flies like an arrow." The main method to remove the ambiguity and to select the correct meaning of this statement is to examine the *context* of the statement. This is a method humans use and one that can be incorporated into a computer program for machine translation. Thus, if the paragraph containing this sentence has the words "fly" and "flies" used as nouns and the word "time" as a verb or the noun "timing," then it is logical to select the third possible meaning of this sentence: the meaning involving the timing of something (probably flight) that flies do. In this case the study of the grammar (syntax) would remove the uncertainty in the meaning (semantics).

The second possibility can be eliminated quickly because the computer's dictionary would not have an entry for insects (or anything else) called "time flies" even though "butterflies," "houseflies," and "horseflies" are real words.

A study of the context might also remove the ambiguity between the three interpretations with the same grammatical structure. If the word "time" is identified as a magazine or even just capitalized, then one expects this sentence to involve the throwing of a magazine rather than the passing of time. If clock-time is selected as the meaning of "Time" (as it would be in the absense of contrary evidence) then the ambiguity in the qualifying phrase "like an arrow" need not be removed in the translation. Instead this phrase is translated directly and the reader of the translation can make his own choice as to the meaning.

The preceding discussion illustrates how a deeper grammatical analysis can be combined with an analysis of the context in order to select the correct meaning. The successful exploitation of this approach can raise the quality of machine translations considerably. There are, nevertheless, two major difficulties left. The first of these is the size of the context. It is a fact that a person can be reading page 287 of a book, come across a phrase the correct meaning of which is determined only by one sentence on page 72 and he can instantly select the correct meaning. It is not known how the human brain accomplishes this. A practical machine translation program cannot use a simple-minded searching method to examine the context. If it did, it would end up analyzing 215 pages of material before it removed the ambiguity. This inefficiency would no doubt raise the cost of translation to a prohibitive level. One of the most important open problems in language, computing, psychology, and information theory, is to discover how the brain accomplishes such a feat. None of the currently proposed theories seems likely to be correct.

The final problem is the most difficult and it leads many people to conclude that high quality rapid machine translations might not be available for a very long time. Some ambiguities in meaning cannot be removed by syntax analysis or by context analysis alone. They can only be removed by applying a level of knowledge and understanding *about everything* comparable to that of a human being. In other words, the intellectual ability of a human being must be incorporated in a program to do machine translation if high quality translation is to be achieved. Consider the following pairs of simple sentences:

> *The school has both boys and girls.*
> *The school has both herring and mackerel.*

> *The pen is filled with black ink.*
> *The pen is filled with black sheep.*

The meanings of these sentences are clear because we know

> boys and girls go to educational institutions
> herring and mackerel are fish (which are never educated)

> ink goes in writing instruments
> sheep go in enclosures

Thus we see that knowledge comparable to the whole human experience is needed in order to select the correct meanings for these sentences.

Finally, we see that the "plausible meaning" analysis described above must be combined with context analysis. Consider the following three pairs of sentences:

> *The honor guard was dressed in elegant uniforms and marched down the wide avenue. It was one of the most impressive rows ever seen in Boston.*

> *When the Harvard and Yale crews met, the outcome was in doubt until the very last moment. It was one of the most impressive rows ever seen in Boston.*

> *Mr. and Mrs. Snozzlepunch were at it again, dishes were breaking and pans were flying out the windows. It was one of the most impressive rows ever seen in Boston.*

The second sentence is identical in each case and the correct meaning of the ambiguous word "rows" is indicated by the first sentence. The three possible meanings are "a number of objects in an orderly sequence," "an instance of rowing boats," and "a noisy quarrel." The third meaning has a different pronounciation, but a machine translation program will not detect that. While the meaning is clear in each case, it cannot be determined by a grammatical or syntactical analysis of the sentences. It can only be determined by knowledge, knowledge which humans possess but which computers, as yet, cannot be given.

4-5 PLAYING THE STOCK MARKET GAME

Our approach to the stock market as a game might offend many of the millions of people who play it. Yet it has all the characteristics of a game, one where the money is real, fortunes can be made or lost, and lives can be ruined. There are many strategies: some very active players buy and sell almost every week, sometimes every day; others buy stocks and put them away for years.

The basic commodity in the stock market is a *share* of a company. The shares are originally sold to raise money for the company which, in turn, spends the money on factories, stores, and wages. This is simply a piece of ownership and these shares are bought and sold in an open auction or exchange. There are hundreds of rules and fine points that govern the auction, but the principle is the basic one of buyers and sellers agreeing on a price through offers of the type: "I offer to sell 800 shares of General Motors for $73 per share," "I offer to buy 200 shares of IBM Corp. for $377 per share." If someone accepts the offer, then a sale takes place—otherwise nothing happens.

The stock market is a huge operation, there are close to 5000 companies whose stock is actively involved (although most of the activity is concentrated in about 800–1000 companies). The number of shares in one of these companies ranges from half a million or so up to 300 million. In order to make this auctioning operate there are two central exchanges, the New York Stock Exchange (NYSE) and the American Stock Exchange (AMEX), and the "over-the-counter market." Each of these organizations serves to bring buyers and sellers—or rather their offers—together in order to make sales.

The objective of playing the stock market game is simple: *to make money by selling stock for more than it cost to buy.* Thus, one's efforts in the game are concentrated on predicting the future behavior of the prices of stocks. Extensive studies have shown that, on the average, everyone can win in the game. If one bought stocks in 1925, 1935, 1945, or 1955 at random (perhaps by throwing darts at the list of stocks) and kept them, then one would have made about 9 percent annual return on the original investments. While 9 percent per year does not make one rich quickly it is a very substantial return. For example, $10,000 invested for 20, 30, 40, or 50 years at 9 percent gives final amounts of $56,000, $133,000, $314,000, or $744,000, respectively.

Some people manage to do much better than 9 percent per year, others manage to do much worse. This variation is one of the fascinations of the game. Figure 4-5.1 shows that prices of different stocks can behave very differently over the same period of time. Companies give the owners of some stocks cash dividends which are sometimes significant amounts, but this source of profit is not considered here because it is a secondary effect for the majority of the players of the stock market.

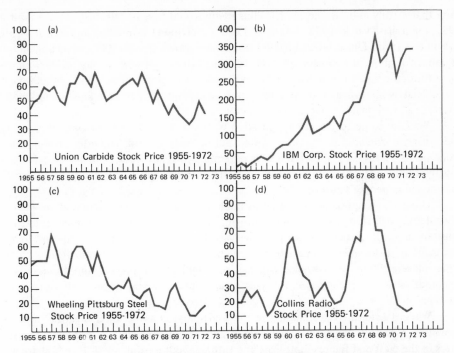

FIGURE 4-5.1   **History of prices of four stocks with four different behaviors. (a) A very stable stock; (b) a steady growth stock; (c) a steadily decaying stock; (d) an erratic stock showing wild oscillation.**

Table 4-5.1 below summarizes the effects of buying each of the four stocks shown in Figure 4-5.1. Two plans of playing, or investing, are considered; first buying $10,000 worth in 1955 and holding for 17 years and second buying $2,000 worth at the start of the year in 1955, 1960, 1965, and 1970.

Table 4-5.1.
Example results of playing the stock market with two different plans and four different stocks for a 17-year period.

		(a)	(b)	(c)	(d)
First plan	Original worth	$10,000	$10,000	$10,000	$10,000
	Final worth	$10,000	$213,000	$3,750	$6,500
	Rate of return	0%	20%	−5-1/2%	−2-1/2%
Second plan	Original worth	$8,000	$8,000	$8,000	$8,000
	Final worth	$6,750	$59,000	$4,700	$3,800
	Rate of return (Approximate)	−1.8%	21-1/2%	−5-1/2%	−6-1/2%

Note that a truly skillful player of Collins Radio would have bought it in 1955, sold it in 1957, repurchased it in 1958, sold it in 1960, repurchased it in 1964, and sold it for the last time in 1967. This original $10,000 would have grown to $570,000 for an annual rate of return of about 40 percent over the 12 years. There is a way to buy and sell among these four stocks so that an original $10,000 investment grows to over $15,000,000 in 17 years. That is an annual rate of return equal to about 59 percent. This is the kind of results that stock market players dream about.

We now come to the crucial question of this game: *what makes some prices go up and others go down?* The answer is simple, but not very helpful. The price of everything, string beans, statues, steel, and stocks is determined by how much people are willing to pay. Nothing, not even money, has an intrinsic value, and values are psychologically determined in people's minds.

One's first impression of the stock market is one of facts and figures about profits, sales, debts, cash flow, markets, and so forth. This is an attempt to determine an intrinsic value for a stock. Experience shows, however, that the essential ability required to win this game is to be able to evaluate the psychological effect of facts and figures on the other players. Thus we visualize a game with millions of players and thousands of commodities where each player is trying to anticipate the actions and behaviors of the other players.

While it is hard to overemphasize the psychological aspect of this game, there are two other aspects that are extremely important. The first of these is *fundamentals* and refers to the facts and figures, both past and future, about a company. Clearly a share of a company that earns $10 per share per year and pays $5 per year in dividends is worth more than $5. Just how much more, though, depends on one's assessment of the future of this company. If its gold mine is to be exhausted in a year or two, then this share is not worth much more than $5 or $10. If its oil field is just opening up with future years profits likely to be higher, then this share is worth $200 or $300. A company which has just discovered a cure for the common cold or a way to make grass stop growing when its 1-1/4 inches high is clearly on the road to riches. This will be recognized by a large number of people and one can expect its stock to zoom in value. Most stock market players believe they are guided by fundamentals and thus a proper evaluation of fundamentals is necessary even for players who rely on another approach to the game.

The *technical* aspect is the other important feature of the stock market and this involves the analysis of the past behavior of stock prices without regard to fundamentals, psychology, or anything else. Thus technicians, or *chartists*, study graphs like Figure 4-5.2 and they derive many other charts from these graphs and other data about the stock market. The essence of their approach is as follows: The fundamental information is already known and incorporated in the prices of the stocks. The psychological evaluations are also already included there. Thus if one can correctly analyze past price behavior, one has all aspects of the stock market included and one can make good predictions about future prices.

The technicians use their charts and graphs to generate "buy signals" and "sell signals" which they then follow. There are dozens of different theories about the technical behavior of the stock market and hundreds of books have been written explaining various ones of them. Some theories generate a buy signal at the same time that others generate a sell signal. Most theories are rather complicated and have slight

```
SII 2S267l8 PD 40 1l2 OXY 19 CU 2S31 1l4 XRX 1087l8 USM 24 1l4
BNY 27 1l4 INF 8 TWA. W 1 97l8 SYO 2S11 1l8 CRE 83l4 INI 303l4 INF 9
```

```
  ▪T         X    LAST    BID    ASK    VOL    TIME
            PB   43 1l2  43 1l2  433l4   206    3 0 0
            PC   435l8   435l8   437l8   529    3 0 ▪
            ND           43 1l4  435l8
```

```
  IBX  +123 1l4    CMF  +310 1l4    MBS  + 27 1l4
  MAI  + 31 1l8    TC   - 15        FAL  -  6 1l4
  GM   + 83 1l2    F    + 67 5l8    C    + 307l8
  FLY  - 35 1l2    BR   + 10 1l2    GE   - 607l8
  FM   + 433l8     FLG  - 29 1l2    DIS  -1067l8
  T    - 43 1l4    UCX  + 273l4     NOC+ - 23 1l4
```

FIGURE 4-5.2 **Example of computer console display of stock market information. The top lines show the New York Stock Exchange "ticker," the next group of numbers give information about the trading on American Telephone and Telegraph (its symbol is T). The bottom group shows the current prices of 18 stocks. One must learn various symbols and codes to use such a system. (Courtesy of Bunker Ramo Corp.)**

variations. The result is that two experts using the same technical theory can disagree on whether one should buy or sell.

One can summarize this brief discussion about price behavior by saying that there is a multitude of approaches and no one has been able to justify any one of them as completely reliable. The stock market players can choose between elaborate or simple-minded strategies, between hot tips or thick reports, between wishful thinking, random impulses, pseudoscience, or systematic confusion. The result is that the millions of players have thousands of different strategies in operation and the game is ever changing and very challenging.

The Application of Computers

We now turn to the question of how to use a computer to help play this game. Even with our rough outline of the stock market, one sees that there is a mass of information and data involved which the players must consider. Even the most basic information about a company fills a couple of pages and includes several tables or graphs. Significant changes in this information occur regularly (every few months) and a large staff or a computer is the only way to keep this information up-to-date and readily available.

Consider for a moment how a stock market player operates. He has accumulated some money and somehow selected the stocks he owns, perhaps only 2 or 3, perhaps 10 or 20. The player must now follow very closely the stocks he owns. A computer display (Figure 4-5.3) may provide him with nearly instantaneous information about the stock market. He will sell his stock in a company if some adverse situation develops or if he feels the stock's price has peaked. This task involves only a small amount of information, but a player who uses a complicated technical approach can easily spend an hour or two each day in updating and studying his charts for only ten stocks.

The player should also follow a much larger group of stocks, namely those that he might buy someday. If something dramatic happens in this group, he might sell one of his mediocre holdings and switch into a more promising stock. This group of stocks should be large and even a full time player of the stock market is hard pressed to keep track of several hundred stocks. The average stock market player does not spend full time on the game and, of course, he does not keep track of many stocks except those he owns. A player must have a considerable investment in order to justify the expense of using a computer, but a part time player can keep up-to-date on several hundred stocks with the aid of a computer. There is a certain problem in getting the data (such as the daily prices of the stocks) into the computer, but most of this can be done automatically if one is willing to pay for it. The cost is about $200 per month.

Once the computer system is provided with current information, then one can obtain programs to create all kinds of graphs, compute all kinds of averages, indices, or other numbers and to search for all kinds of special situations or events. The player can then ask questions like

which stocks rose more than 10 percent this month
which stocks had a 50 percent increase in volume of sales this week
which stocks are 15 percent or more above their 100 day moving average
which stocks reported earnings this month which are 20 percent or more above last
  year's earnings

The response to each of these questions is a list of stocks. The player then decides to examine some of them in more detail and obtains a display such as shown in Figure 4-5.3. Even more detailed information, including brief statements of opinions, could be displayed and the serious player will no doubt refer to a variety of information before he makes a final decision.

The computer system described above is just the first level of computer application to playing the stock market. It organizes and processes the huge masses of data involved and allows a player to selectively and rapidly examine a large number of possibilities. The professional players of the stock market already have such systems and one can expect them to become more sophisticated and much more widespread. However, the bulk of the stock market players are casual players who do not have the interest nor the money to obtain such a system.

The second level of computer application is to go beyond the data-processing approach and actually simulate the behavior of the stock market. In order to do this one has to have a *model* of the market and of all its principal components. Then, of course, one has to know how these components interact. We have wanted to emphasize the

NYSE SYMBOL RCQ. - 74/01/03 - DAILY + VOLUME + TREND LINE

FIGURE *4-5.3* **A display of the recent history of the price behavior of a particular stock. The ends of a bar show the highest and the lowest price of the stock for that particular day.**

complexity of the stock market, yet we have actually given a very simplified description. This means that a good model of the stock market, one able to make reliable predictions about future prices, must be very complicated indeed, more complicated than one would expect from reading this brief section. There is a tremendous reward, both in money and in personal satisfaction, for any one who creates a good model and we can expect a great deal of effort to be expended in experimenting with such models. The various theories of the technicians and chartists are rudimentary attempts to model the stock market and these theories will be expanded, revised, and perhaps perfected some day into a good model. Ironically, the creation of a good model of the game will kill the game, for it will take away the mystery and competition. If everyone knows how the stock market is going to behave, then, of course, the opportunities to get rich quickly will largely disappear and putting money in the stock market will not be much more exciting than putting it in the bank. Since the game is, we believe, primarily psychological in nature, we expect to wait a long time before it is successfully modeled.

4-6 COMPUTERS IN EDUCATION

Before we discuss possible roles of computers in education we should briefly examine the education establishment itself. It is huge and absorbs a significant percentage of society's energy. Some basic data are given in Table 4-6.1.

Table 4-6.1

Some basic data on the size and cost of the education establishment in the United States. The data is for 1970 and includes estimates for all schools; public and private, degree-granting and not, vocational and professional schools.

	Elementary Education Ages 5-13	Secondary Education Ages 14-17	Undergraduate Education Ages 18-21	Post Graduate Education Ages 22-26
1970 Enrollment	37,000,000	14,500,000	7,400,000	1,200,000
Percentage of Age Group	100	92	51	7
Teachers and Staff	1,400,000	1,100,000	750,000	
Cost	$47 billion		$26 billion	
Cost per Student	$915		$3,100	
Students per Teacher	25	20	11-1/2	

Any organization of this size has tremendous inertia and the education establishment is no exception. Education at the elementary and secondary levels is highly regulated by a network of state laws specifying courses to be taken and requirements for teachers. Higher education is regulated primarily by the faculties of the schools involved, and in a university these regulations fill a large book. Postgraduate education is, on the average, the most individualized and unregulated but even here there are numerous requirements (and hurdles) aimed at maintaining "professional standards." The net result is a conservative establishment that can only change slowly. It requires truly dramatic and strong forces to obtain rapid response in all the independent entities that control education.

A serious student of education is simultaneously deluged by facts, theories and ignorance. Each year many volumes of data appear that detail various aspects of education. This data tends to be of the "nuts and bolts" variety—for example, what percentage of the 8th grade students in LaPorte County (Indiana) have parents on welfare, how many hot lunch programs in New Mexico serve over 500 students a day, how many graduates of Los Angles high schools attend a college or university outside California. At times it seems that there are almost as many theories about education as there are people who think about it. Even the number of well-reasoned theories is so large as to require great effort to digest all of them. Education is clearly very complex and many-faceted and we expect many theories. It is, however, discouraging to find two well-reasoned and widely-held theories that are completely contradictory. It is in trying to pick and choose among the theories that one meets ignorance and lack of solid information. One finds that little is known about the quality of education and the effectiveness of the education establishment. Part of the difficulty is that quality and achievement in education are hard to define precisely and even harder to measure. Yet it seems that one must be able to answer such questions as the following (but a poll of education experts produces answers of "yes", "no", "maybe" and "don't know" to *each* of them):

1. Is the phonetic approach to reading using the "Initial Teaching Alphabet" more effective than other methods?
2. Do college freshmen learn more in classes of 30 students than in classes of 300 students?
3. American high school students take 4 or 5 subjects and concentrate on them for a semester or year and then go on to a different set. Europeans take 10 to 15 subjects simultaneously (at least 1 or 2 hours per week on each) for a period of several years. Is the American system more effective?
4. Does one learn more in a student-led exploration of a subject than in a lecture-demonstration presentation of it?

Another part of the difficulty is that some segments of the education establishment are not interested in such questions. Finally, the powers in elementary and secondary education discourage and even prevent attempts to systematically measure the quality of education and achievement in the system. The net result is that there are some very difficult, crucial, and basic questions to be answered before we understand the educational process.

Three Levels of Computer Applications

We discuss three levels of the computer impact on education. One has to be very optimistic to believe that computers (or anything else) are going to rapidly revolutionize the education establishment, but each of these can, in time, have a significant impact and the result will be revolutionary. The pace might be so slow as to be called evolutionary instead. The first level of application is in administration, record keeping, and accounting. The money saving potential exists here just as in other places, but there are more direct educational benefits. The records of students can be more detailed and accessible and this results in better counseling and placement. Student programs can be more varied and school scheduling more flexible if the accounting and records are done by computer. The result should be better education.

The second level of computer application is directly in the teaching/learning process. The first efforts are already underway and involve the automation of some of the more routine functions. This includes "drill sessions" in areas like foreign language vocabulary, arithmetic facts and problems, spelling, and so forth. (See Figure 4-6.1) These functions can be automated and achieve as much, perhaps more, effectiveness as teacher directed drill with workbooks, and so on. A variety of "question and answer" systems (usually called programmed learning) may be used to teach a subject and to evaluate a student's knowledge of it. Some such systems already exist and they are quite effective in certain subject areas. An example of a student console is shown in Figure 4-6.2. The effectiveness depends in large part on the talent and effort of the creator of the system. A tremendous amount of time is required for writing, debugging, testing, and evaluating a segment of such instruction; commonly it is on the order of 100 hours for each hour of instruction.

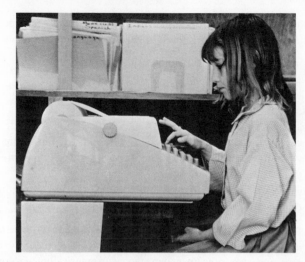

FIGURE 4-6.1 A third grade pupil working on a computer-aided instruction (CAI) system. The teletype console shown is the one described in Appendix 2. (Courtesy of P. Suppes, Stanford University.)

A different application at this level is the use of simulation models as aids to teaching. For example, students in accounting can work on the accounts of realistic simulated corporations. Not only is the experience more realistic, but much the tedium of arithmetic and recording of numbers is removed. Students in civil engineering can design a tall building, then subject it to an 80 mile per hour wind and examine the stresses that result in the frame. An interesting variation of this approach is in "game-playing" simulations of situations of personal interaction. Thus a simulation of a city might include provisions for students to play the roles of mayor, taxpayer, city employee, welfare recipient, and so on. The game is started by presenting several alternatives of

FIGURE 4-6.2 A fairly elaborate education terminal that provides sound and still or motion pictures during the instruction session. (Courtesy of Westinghouse Learning Corp.)

action to each player and then determining the new situation that results from the actions chosen. As the game progresses each player can see the city change and develop as a result of the choices made. This approach has been used in the areas of corporate operations, national defense, international politics, prison administration, and so forth, and some people are very enthusiastic about the new insights they have gained in these games.

The third level of computer application is the development of programs which will teach with a level of flexibility, resourcefulness, and effectiveness comparable to that of a human teacher. Even though some predict this capability to be available in a few years, it seems more likely that we will have to wait until we understand the human learning process better. It seems safe to predict that the methods to be used by a computer in teaching will not be simple imitations of human teachers. This capability might evolve through some breakthrough in understanding but it is more likely to arrive by a steady, evolutionary improvement of the capabilities of the more routine, second level computer programs for teaching.

Three Sources of Anxiety

There is considerable anxiety as well as hope for the application of computers to education. The hopes are based on the suspicion that the current education establishment is neither very effective nor very economical. The optimists feel that the current system is so poor that significant improvements can be made long before the best approaches are perfected or all the difficulties understood. It is noteworthy that this has happened in some areas (though not as broad as education) and one cannot ignore this possibility. If the second or third generation of computerized teaching systems are this effective, then those that will appear by the end of this century will be revolutionary indeed.

There are three sources of anxiety about computers in education. The first of these is the fear that the computerization of education will lead to centralized impersonal regimentation. Even worse is the fear that the centralized control will be captured by undesirables who will impose an anti-social, immoral, or inhuman education on the entire population. We have already noted that computerization does not imply regimentation but it does allow it. We believe that computerization of education has the potential of allowing much greater individuality and freedom, but this will not happen automatically.

The second source of anxiety is that computerized education will be less effective but will be adopted anyway. This is partly based on the belief that the educational establishment is not objective in its evaluation of teaching methods and that it has, from time to time, adopted fads that were later discarded. The "computer in education" fad might sweep the establishment (slowly, of course) and harm the education of a generation of students.

The third anxiety is that even if computerized education works, its adoption will bankrupt the country. Note that the cost per student in elementary schools is still only a few hundred dollars a year and the purchase of one modest console for each four or five students could double this cost. It seems very remote that the taxpayers will authorize a 100 percent increase in taxes for education no matter how much better education becomes.

In this section we have only considered the possible impact of the direct application of computers to the educational process. We have already projected that by the end of this century the entire American population will have rapid (possibly almost instantaneous) access (via computers) to a body of information equivalent to at least a good encyclopedia. If this is the case, then there might be no point in children learning how to spell thousands of words, or learning to add mixed fractions, or memorizing historical dates. Why struggle to learn a foreign language when you can just ask your computer for the answer? The point of these remarks is that the *content* of education may change even more and faster than the *methods* of education.

4-7   THE URBAN CRISES—CAN COMPUTERS HELP?

People are rapidly moving into cities all over the world and the resulting conglomeration of pollution, crime, poor housing, and inadequate transportation is called the urban crisis. One could fill a library with chronicles of this crisis and theories on how to solve it. An oversimplified summary is that the crisis is growing more acute and methods used so far to combat it have had little or no effect. This crisis is not a feature of affluent, industrialized society; it exists in Addis Ababa, Calcutta, and Sao Paulo as well as in New York, Tokyo, and Rome. (See Figures 4-7.1, 4-7.2 and 4-7.3.) The projected growth of the cities will make this crisis *THE* problem of society. In 1900 about 40 percent of the U.S. population lived in urban areas and the same percentage lived on the farms. The U.S. government estimates that 85 percent of the population will be in urban areas in the year 2000 and city dwellers will outnumber farmers by 15 to 1. A projection of the urban regions in the United States is shown in Figure 4-7.4. This projection was made by the U.S. Department of Housing and Urban Development.

It is clear that computers are *not* going to solve all these problems by themselves. It appears though that the situation is similar to that of landing a man on the moon: computers are one of several essential components of a successful program. We can identify three levels of computer applications to this crisis. The first is to improve the effectiveness of the administration of city governments and services. The second level is to model, analyze, and simulate in order to gain a better understanding of how a city "lives." The third level is to help control the city, to serve as the nerves and memory of the city administration.

Three Levels of Computer Applications

The first level of application is well advanced in some cities and started in almost all. This application seems mundane, unexciting (perhaps it is), and unlikely to get at the roots of the crisis. Nevertheless, the improvement of efficiency and effectiveness in city administration is a crucial first step in the resolution of this crisis. Analysts of government have concluded that local governments are, on the average, the most disorganized and uncontrolled administrations in society. It is literally true in most instances that no

FIGURE 4-7.1   An aerial view of Los Angeles showing the expanse of single family homes that makes its population density lower than most large cities. (Courtesy of Gruen Associates.)

FIGURE 4-7.2   An aerial view of Brasilia showing the design of large apartment buildings on spacious grounds and with wide avenues. Brasilia is a new city and follows one coordinated master plan for growth. (Courtesy of Gruen Associates.)

FIGURE 4-7.3 **A crowded street scene in New York City.**

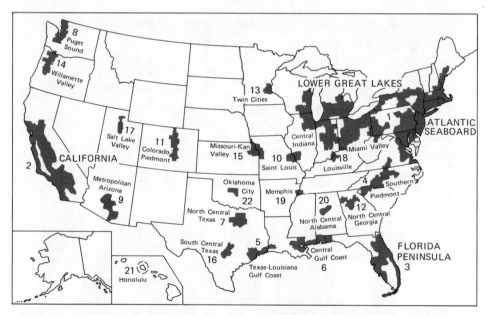

FIGURE 4-7.4 **A projection of the 22 largest U.S. urban regions in the year 2000. An urban region is a continuous region (including adjoining rural areas) where cities and urban places are dominant. There is a high concentration of urban activities and even the bulk of the people in the rural parts of a region work in the cities. Over 75 percent of the population is projected to be in these 22 urban regions, and over 60 percent is projected for the three largest regions.**

one—mayor, city councilman, school board member, or taxpayer—can say what quality of service is provided or at what cost. Note that these organizations can say how much is spent on tires, chalk, typewriters, and tongue depressors and how many people work in the street department or were arrested for running red lights. The amount of money spent here is huge, over $100 billion per year in the United States, and even modest increases in efficiency can provide billions for better services.

One of the great disappointments is that there seems to be no "economy of scale" in urban government. We know that Ford or General Motors can build and sell 2,000,000 cars cheaper than 20 companies can build and sell 100,000 cars each. A supermarket can sell a jar of mustard cheaper than a small market and still make as much profit. A town of 31 people cannot have police protection at a reasonable cost, but a town of 20,000 can. However, once a city becomes large an opposite effect seems to take place. One survey in the United States showed that police protection costs about $5 per person in cities with a population of 100,000 to 300,000 persons, $18 per person in cities with 500,000 to 1,000,000 in population and almost $40 per person in New York City. It is certainly wrong to believe that size is the only factor involved but the relationship is striking. It is hard to believe that the police service rendered in New York City is eight times better than that in Santa Barbara, California or Austin, Texas. This increased cost per person occurs in service after service: trash removal, sewage disposal, highway construction, welfare services, health services, and so forth. (See Figure 4-7.5.)

Can the application of computers improve the administration of cities? There is no reason to believe otherwise. Some cities have already done so and business and industry have adopted computerized administrative procedures precisely because they are cheaper and more reliable. Will this have any real effect on the urban crisis? Isn't this just doing the same old ineffective things with a little more efficiency? This level of computer application is not going to result in any immediate dramatic effects but there are three reasons to pursue this line (in addition to saving some of the taxpayer's money). First, it might slow the deterioration of city life, allowing time to discover some more fundamental lines of action. Second, it will force at least some people in city government to study their operation and to attempt to identify their objectives. This can only be beneficial. The third reason is more subtle and more significant. Many people believe (and have some supporting evidence) that when an organization changes its operational methods—even for doing the same things—then, in the long run, fundamental changes occur in the organization itself.

Serious efforts have already started on the second level of computer application, the modeling and simulation of the city. (See Figure 4-7.6) A model of a city consists of a large set of equations to express the relationships between the various components of city life. A city is tremendously complex and even a simplified model involves several hundred relationships. For example, one recent model identifies 31 distinct effects that draw underemployed people to a city. New York City has about 70 distinct programs to assist landlords (it is one of the few American cities with rent control laws) and any complete analysis of housing in New York must incorporate *all* of these programs.

An example of the complexity of a really detailed simulation is that of the Long Island Railroad. It required 12,000 punched cards of data just to specify the commuter system and its operation. Some of the crucial information was difficult to obtain and no one realized that this information was necessary to understand the railroad's operation.

Rural and small towns 1900	Distance traveled: 50 feet Pounds/person per week: 5 Population/square mile: 5-500 Trash disposal work: .01

Small and medium towns 1930	Distance traveled: 2 miles Pounds/person per week: 10 Population/square miles: 6000 Trash disposal work: 60

Medium city 1960	Distance traveled: 5 miles Pounds/week per person: 20 Population/square mile: 25,000 Trash disposal work: 1250

Large city 1970	Distance traveled: 25 miles Pounds/person per week: 25 Population/square mile: 250,000 Trash disposal work: 80,000

FIGURE 4-7.5 An illustration of the growth in the effort required to dispose of trash. The work of trash disposal is measured in ton-miles of hauling per week per square mile of area. The cost has grown from almost nothing in 1900 to more than $1 per week per person in 1970 (for a large city). These estimates do not include commercial or industrial trash.

The people who made the simulation underestimated the amount of data needed and the difficulty in obtaining it. This is typical and many ambitious projects are delayed, short-circuited, or invalidated by the lack of complete and accurate data. In this case, good data was obtained and the simulation model put on a typical medium sized computer. It took longer to run the railroad by simulation than it took in real life! This was no doubt caused by an inadequate amount of high speed memory, but even the slow speed memory is very fast by human standards. A complete, item by item, simulation of the transportation system in New York City would be many times bigger than this one and it would require a very large amount of computer power.

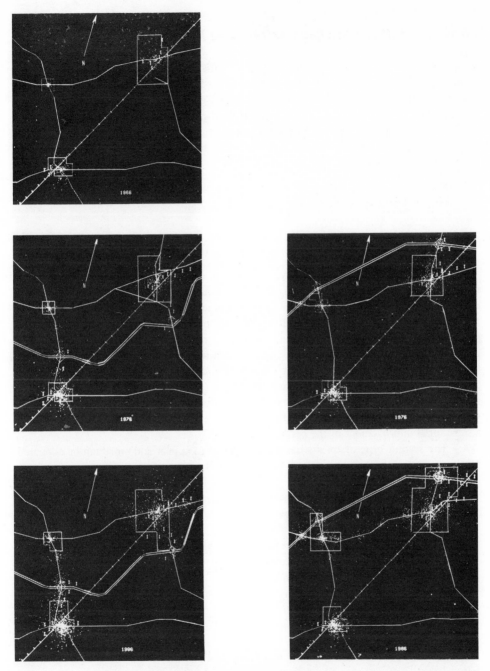

FIGURE 4-7.6   A sample of result of a computer program that simulates the growth of a city. This computer model makes projections about the resulting changes in the city as a result of two different expressway developments. (Courtesy of J. R. Voss, Ohio State Univ.)

Current Results of and Counter-Intuitive Processes

The current first attempts at models of cities have many inadequacies. They are incomplete and oversimplified. They lack realistic data about many aspects of city life. Many relationships and factors used are mere guesses, unsupported by any data, experiments, or detailed study. Such a description could lead one to conclude that these attempts are a waste of time or only serve to pave the way for better results at some later time. However, the results of these efforts could be the single most important step in alleviating the urban crisis for these studies might:

Show that the operation of cities is even worse than suspected and that phenomenal improvements may be possible.

Show that one's naïve intuition is not applicable to many areas of city life and that many proposed "cures" only worsen the situation.

The first of these results may provide the ammunition needed to bring about reorganization of the cities. This reorganization must be both internal and external. For example, there are 251 different local governments in the Chicago metropolitan area and the problems of pollution, transportation, education, slums, and so on in Chicago are not going to be solved until there is a single, unified administration of the city. Each of these 251 governments is a small political empire which has its diehard supporters. Many will fight to the bitter end to defend their freedom and independence from the octopus of big-city government and can you blame them? The effort to unify the cities will involve all the forces of smog, traffic jams, taxpayer revolts, race riots, and garbage strikes and yet success is likely to come only if there is strong evidence that unification can result in a substantial improvement of the common cause.

The second type of results has already begun to appear and more can be expected. These results might be summarized by saying that some urban processes are counter-intuitive. A few examples of this are given in an earlier chapter and a few more are listed below. Note that the statements below are not yet established facts but they are rather only possibilities supported by some evidence:

Traffic: Bigger highway and freeway systems lead to larger traffic jams.
Unemployment: (a) More extensive benefits and retraining programs lead to higher unemployment.
           (b) Providing new jobs yearly for 10 percent of the unemployed aggravates the poverty problem.
Taxes: Reducing the property taxes on buildings leads to more tax income from the tax on buildings.
Housing: (a) Urban renewal and slum clearance leads to the spread of slums, urban decay, and further hardships for the poor.
           (b) Providing low-cost housing each year for 5 percent of the underemployed leads, in 30 years, to a 30 percent drop in the number of skilled workers in the city, to denser slums and fewer jobs for the underemployed.

Once these possibilities are widely appreciated, we can expect government (at all levels) to think, study, analyze, and experiment before instituting great programs. The federal government has, in the past, launched full scale, billion dollar programs whose design was the result of last-minute compromises between several parties, some of whose interests were entirely different from the program's. It is small wonder that some of these programs were ineffective or even counter-productive.

A rosy picture has been painted so far for the application of computer simulations to the urban crisis. This optimism is to be tempered with both patience and skepticism. The two results discussed above are both negative and no matter how valuable it is to know one is doing the wrong things, this is not the same as knowing what the right things are. While bigger freeway systems may lead to monumental traffic jams, so does the lack of a freeway system. Quick and easy positive results from computer simulations and modeling will be rare. The dynamic processes of a city are extremely subtle and deeply involve the emotional and psychological behavior of people. This behavior is exactly the thing that has been most difficult to understand, analyze, or simulate with or without computers. A tremendous effort is required to develop a science of urban dynamics and growth but the rewards for success will repay it many times over. In anticipation of the day when this science arrives, a name has already been invented: *ekistics*—the science of human settlements.

The third level of computer application is in the actual control and operation of the city of the future (Figure 4-7.7). We contemplate an urban region of perhaps 50 or

FIGURE 4-7.7   **A motorcycle policeman on duty to monitor and control traffic. Perhaps a computer controlled surveillance network can do a more effective job and release the policeman for other (and safer) duties. (Courtesy of Los Angeles Police Department.)**

100 million people with a unified government of some sort. The dynamics of urban life are fairly well understood and scientific principles are in practice. The complexities of the control of the city will involve computer power in large quantities. We cannot be very specific about this application because we know very little of its detail. It will, no doubt, involve tremendous files of information on the status of the city, a vast communication network to obtain and provide information, and complex, high speed processors to analyze situations that arise.

What Will It Be Like in 1984?

Many will view such a city with revulsion because individuals will be reduced to mere numbers manipulated by some computer. The dangers inherent in this situation are real, but so are the opportunities. In order to analyze and appreciate the effect on individual freedom, one should compare the current situation with those of 50 and 100 years ago and what is possible 50 years from now in the "computerized" city. The history books say little about the status of the *average man*, but we believe that the current industrialized societies offer an unprecedented level of freedom to the average citizen. His mobility in society has never been greater, but even so we are far removed from Utopia. The average person neither has friends in city hall nor the energy and resources to fight it. He deals with a clerk with no authority and usually little desire to accommodate his special circumstances. He is more likely than not just a nameless (but not yet numbered) object processed by the city machinery. In other words his unprecedented level of individual freedom is not very high, at least for that part of his freedom dependent on city government. The situation is quite different for the *elite*; the professors, the rich, the student leaders, the union organizers, the money-men, the blue-bloods, the theologians, and so forth. The ranks of the elite have grown over the centuries, but their freedom of individual action might have actually declined. It certainly has on a basis relative to the average man. They have always had privileges and friends in city hall or the resources to circumvent its power. Note that the voices one hears are almost exclusively those of the elite and one wants to consider whether the protest raised is against general mistreatment by computer or against equality in treatment by computers.

We do not mean to say that the computerized city is going to be good automatically. George Orwell's "1984" vividly portrays a society completely and inhumanly controlled by "Big Brother." Such a society is very possible and the role of "Big Brother" could be played by a computer system. On the other hand, a computerized city has the potential to be vastly more personalized than the current ones are. It is easier to be inflexible than flexible, impersonal than personal and the people must continually insist that flexibility, personal attention, and equality be incorporated into the computerized city.

SUGGESTED READINGS FOR PART I

The following books are sources of additional reading and information about the impact of computers (and science in general) on society. Most are nontechnical and intended for general audiences. A short comment is given about each book.

Baer, Robert, *The Digital Villain.* Reading, Mass.: Addison-Wesley Publishing Company, Inc., 1972.

> "Notes on the Numerology, Parapsychology, and Metaphysics of the Computer" is the subtitle and indicates that it is a witty book. A wide variety of present and potential impacts are viewed (mostly as bad) and interwoven with some material on programming and computer systems.

Bemer, Robert, *Computers and Crisis.* Association of Computing Machinery, 1971.

> The proceedings of the 1971 national meeting of the Association of Computing Machinery. It is expressly intended for the general public and systematically covers the interface between computer science and society.

Bernstein, Jeremy, *The Analytical Engine: Computers Past, Present, and Future.* New York: Random House, Inc., 1966.

> A general, nontechnical introduction to computing which contains a great deal of historical detail.

Bowen, Howard and Garth Mangum, *Automation and Economic Progress.* Englewood Cliffs, N.J.: Prentice-Hall, Inc., 1966.

> Report of the prestigious National Commission of Technology, Automation, and Economic Progress. Contains several particularly relevant chapters such as:
>
>> Technological Change and Unemployment
>> Applying Technology to Community Needs
>> Computer Aspects of Technological Change

Burdick, Eugene, *The 480.* New York: McGraw-Hill, Inc., 1968.

> A novel which explores recent strategies (many of them computer based) in political campaigns.

Carovillana, Robert and James Skehan, *Science and the Future of Man.* Cambridge, Mass.: M.I.T. Press, 1970.

> While not specifically concerned with computers, this book presents thoughtful contributions and discussions by a distinguished group with various backgrounds and viewpoints.

Communications of the Association for Computing Machinery, Vol. 15, No. 7, July 1972.

> A special, enlarged edition which commemorates the 25th anniversary of the Association. Contributors were invited to give some perspective for the present and

future of computing and they succeeded. While the articles are primarily general in nature, they are too technical for a general audience.

Diebold, John, *Man and the Computer.* New York: Frederick A Praeger, Inc., 1969.

The subtitle "Technology as an Agent of Social Change" indicates the general nature of the book as it is quite wide ranging in its consideration of the impact of science and technology on society.

Ferkiss, Victor, *Technological Man, the Myth and the Reality.* New York: New American Library (Mentor), 1970.

A well-balanced presentation of the strengths and weaknesses of current thoughts about the relationship between technology and society. An extensive bibliography is given.

Greenberger, Martin, *Computers and the World of the Future*, Cambridge, Mass.: M.I.T. Press, 1962.

Partly of historical interest, this book indicates what distinguished leaders in the field were forecasting in the early 1960s. Some of the articles are still very relevant such as:

> What Computers Should Be Doing
> The Computer in the University
> A New Concept in Programming

————, *Computers, Communications, and the Public Interest.* Baltimore, Md.: Johns Hopkins University Press, 1971.

A collection of papers which presents a number of viewpoints on the social implications of computing, especially the computer utility and related ideas.

Hamming, Richard, *Computers and Society.* New York: McGraw-Hill, Inc., 1972.

A book which covers a wide range of interrelationships between society and the computing profession. The author's goal is to exclude any material that will be obsolete or irrelevant in the year 2000.

Information. A Scientific American Book. San Francisco: W. H. Freeman and Company, 1966.

The contents of *Scientific American*, September 1966. Written for a scientific audience, but does not assume an acquaintance with computing.

Martin, James, *Telecommunications and the Computer.* Englewood Cliffs, N.J.: Prentice-Hall, Inc., 1968.

A study of the relationship and role of communications in the computing society. The study is thorough and assumes some familiarity with computers.

Martin, James, and Adrian Norman, *The Computerized Society.* Englewood Cliffs, N.J.: Prentice-Hall, Inc., 1970.

A lengthy analysis of computer applications, many in considerable detail. The later parts of the book discuss some adverse effects of these applications and possible protective measures that might be taken.

Myers, Charles, *The Impact of Computers on Management.* Cambridge, Mass.: M.I.T. Press, 1967.

> Some of the contributions are fairly sophisticated, but several are suitable for general audience, particularly the introductory chapter and
>
> Implications of On Line, Real-Time Systems
> Changes in Management Environment and Their Effect on Values

Oettinger, Anthony G., *Run Computer Run.* Cambridge, Mass.: Harvard University Press, 1969.

> A brief analysis of the difficulties one faces in attempting to introduce computers into the educational process. It is written for a general audience.

Orwell, George, *1984.* New York: Harcourt Brace, Jovanovich, Inc., 1949.

> A classical account of the control of society by a "Big Brother" which is very much like a huge bureaucratic computer.

Pylyshyn, Zenon, *Perspectives on the Computer Revolution.* Englewood Cliffs, N.J.: Prentice-Hall, Inc., 1970.

> A large collection of articles on the development of ideas and applications of computers. The articles are for a general audience and emphasize the interaction between man, machine, and society.

Rothman, Stanley, and Charles Mosman, *Computers and Society.* Chicago: Science Research Associates, Inc., 1972.

> The first part of this book is a text on the technology of computing and the second part uses social science to study the social implications of computing.

Sackman, Harold, and Norman Nie, *The Information Utility and Social Choice.* Montvale, N.J.: AFIPS Press, 1970.

> A series of articles which considers the impact of the computer utility concept. This concept foresees information services (computer based) that are readily available to the general public.

Sanders, Donald, *Computers and Management.* New York: McGraw-Hill, Inc., 1970.

> A review of the impact that computers are having (and will have) on management and business organizations.

Taviss, Irene, *The Computer Impact.* Englewood Cliffs, N.J.: Prentice-Hall, Inc., 1970.

> Twenty-six contributions which explore the impact of computers on society. The articles are divided into four groups—The Computer Potential, The Economy, The Polity, The Culture—and are oriented toward a general audience.

Westin, Alan, *Privacy and Freedom.* New York: Atheneum Publishers, 1967.

> A book which explores the issues of privacy in the context of large data banks of information under computer control.

5 *First Elements of Basic*

5-1 INTRODUCTION

The second part of this book is primarily concerned with "how to solve problems using computers." There is almost as much emphasis on "how to solve problems" as there is on "using computers." By learning both, the student will appreciate and understand that the computer is one of the most versatile and powerful tools available for solving problems and processing information. Furthermore, the student can then better understand the impact of computers: how the use of computers has revolutionized and will further revolutionize many aspects of business, science, and the life of every person.

The use of a computer to solve a problem involves five rather distinct steps and only *one* of these is unique to the computer. Consequently, part of the study we now begin applies to problem solving in general and is useful in many areas.

The first of the five steps is *to formulate the problem carefully and to determine exactly the objective to be reached.* This step seems to be an obvious and easy one (sometimes it is). But, usually it is more subtle and difficult than one might first think. Carelessness in this first step is one of the primary causes of the much publicized "computer goofs." These errors occur because of a lack of careful study and analysis of the problem; some circumstances or situations were not foreseen and provided for. Then, when one of these situations does occur, the result is nonsense. The blame is, of course, placed on the computer rather than where it belongs—on the people who use the computer.

The second step is *to construct a mathematical model for the problem.* This involves identifying important variables and relationships among the variables.

The third step is *to find a method or procedure to solve the problem or to process the information.* These procedures are often called *algorithms*, for example, the sequence of calculations to determine interest paid by a bank (see Section 0.2), or the sequence of steps one uses to put a list of names into alphabetical order. These first three steps must be carried out whether or not a computer is used.

The fourth step, the one peculiar to using a computer, is *to prepare instructions for a computer* to carry out the algorithm. This step is called computer *programming* or computer *coding.* It amounts to *translating* the algorithm into a *language* which the computer can understand. The usual activities of a computer programmer include, not only the programming, but also the considerable amount of work required to find the method and to organize the information. In fact, in many instances, the computer programmer has responsibility for these first four steps as well as the next one.

The final step is *to evaluate the results* of the first four steps by making comparisons and tests. This step is necessary to ascertain that the formulation, the model, the algorithm, and the program are correct. Frequently the first results from the computer are completely unrealistic, showing that something is wrong. Errors can be caused by mistakes in the formulation, in the model, in the algorithm, or in the program. Errors in programs are called "bugs" and the process of removing them is called "debugging." Once gross errors and blunders have been identified and removed, one can hope to have reasonable and useful results. But, even at this point, there are often small imperfections or inaccuracies in the results. It might take a period of months (or even many years) to perfect the analysis of a very complicated problem as well as the methods and programs used to solve it.

In summary, the five steps in problem solving using a computer are:

1. Careful formulation of the problem and determination of the objectives.
2. Construction of the mathematical model.
3. Discovery of a method (algorithm) to solve the problem.
4. Preparation of a computer program.
5. Evaluation of results.

This chapter discusses the fourth of these steps. We describe how to write computer programs in the *Basic programming language*. We discuss relatively few of the Basic instructions in this chapter, but we present enough to enable the student to solve some fairly complicated problems. In Chapter 8 we return to the programming aspect of problem solving and describe additional Basic instructions.

The example problems presented in this chapter are rather simple problems so that the first three steps of problem solving using computers are easily carried out. The student can then concentrate on the fourth step, preparation of a computer program. In Chapter 6 we discuss ideas about algorithms and program construction and in Chapter 7 some of the aspects of the first and second steps of problem solving are presented.

PROBLEMS

5-1.1   Write an algorithm for writing the capital letter A with a piece of chalk on a chalk-board.

5-1.2   Suppose you want to find a discussion of a certain topic in a text book. The index says that it is discussed on page 218 of the book. Write an algorithm to locate that page (the book has 364 pages).

5-1.3   Write an algorithm for unlocking and opening a door. You execute each step of your algorithm. Does it work in all cases? Does it work if the door is already unlocked (have you included appropriate steps to take care of such a situation)? Does it work if the door is already open?

5-1.4   Review Chapter 0, Section 0-2 and write a set of instructions which, when carried out, would determine the best buy for catsup:

Brand A	10½ ounce bottle	@	18¢
Brand B	1¼ pound bottle	@	2 for 67¢
Brand C	500 gram bottle	@	30¢

(There are 16 ounces or 453 grams in a pound.)

5-1.5   When walking up an icy hill, a man walks three paces up and then slips four feet back down the hill. Each of his paces is 3 feet. Write a list of instructions which would determine the number of paces he must take to travel N feet up the incline. Test your algorithm for N = 10 feet, N = 16 feet, N = 6 feet. What do your instructions give for N = 9 feet?

5-1.6   Construct an algorithm for alphabetizing a list of the names of the presidents: Washington, G.; Adams, J.; Jefferson, T.; . . .

5-1.7   Construct an algorithm for finding the number of days between two dates, for example, June 22, 1066 and April 1, 1947. Neglect the changes in the calender made in the middle ages; take into account leap years and that century years are not leap years unless the year is divisible by 400.

5-1.8   Construct an algorithm which would enable you to determine the number of tablespoons of milk in a can which contains a given amount of milk, for example, the can holds one gallon, three quarts, one pint, and three ounces of milk. There are two tablespoons in an ounce, sixteen ounces in a pint, two pints in a quart and four quarts in a gallon.

5-2 A SIMPLE PROBLEM AND BASIC PROGRAM

Let us now consider a very simple problem. Notice the three different Basic programs which solve it.

The problem is: If the hourly rate of pay of a worker is $2.80 and he works eight hours a day and five days a week, what is his daily and weekly pay?

The programs are:

```
10 LET R = 2.80          10 LET R = 2.80            10 LET A = 2.80
20 LET W = R*40          20 PRINT R,R*40,R*8        20 LET A1 = A*40
30 LET D = W/5           30 END                     30 LET A2 = A1/5
40 PRINT R,W,D                                      40 PRINT A,A1,A2
50 END                                              50 END
```

Program 1   Program 2   Program 3

We now use English to describe what these Basic statements mean. The first statement specifies the rate of pay (called R or A) to be 2.80. The programs on the left and right then compute the weekly pay (called W or A1) and daily pay (called D or A2). All three programs then print out the values computed. The middle program did not give a name to the weekly and daily pay, but directly specified the required calculations in the print statement. The final statement in each program indicates that the program is finished and the computations are to stop.

Note that each statement in these programs is numbered. These numbers are also called *labels*. These numbers specify the order in which the statements are to be processed or executed. Thus statement number 10 is processed before number 20. The order in which the statements are punched on cards or typed on a terminal is immaterial, it is the statement numbers that determine the actual order that the statements are executed in the calculation.

A *computer run* or *job* is a program (plus any data, control cards, or other items needed with the program) submitted to a computer. The *output* is the results returned to the programmer. The output of programs in this book are printed on paper, but outputs could be displayed on a TV screen if one has such a terminal.

When one submits the middle program to the computer to be run, then the total program and output appears as follows.

```
10  LET R = 2.80
20  PRINT R,R*40,R*8
30  END


            OUTPUT

2.800000           112      22.400000
```

The computed output is exactly the same for the other two programs, but the program listing is, of course, that of the program actually submitted. The program is printed along with the computed results so one can see and study them together. Let us examine these programs and their operation in more detail. Each line of these programs is a Basic *statement*.

Statement 10 of each program contains the name of a *variable* (R or A) and it is used for the hourly rate of the worker. This statement causes a *word* in *memory* to be reserved for the variable; any use of the name (either R or A) later in the program refers to the current value of the variable. This statement also tells the computer to put (*store*) the value 2.80 in that word in memory; that is, R and A are *assigned* the value of 2.80, and the statement is an *assignment statement*. The *keyword* LET is always used to start an assignment statement.

It is important to note that the symbol R (or A) is associated with a particular memory word (or location) and *not* with a particular value (say 2.80) which may be written there at the moment. In later programs the values written in a word change during program execution and a variable name (say R) refers to the value which happens to be written in this word at this particular moment during the execution.

Programs 1 and 3 are identical except that different names for the variables are used. We discuss only Program 1. Statement 20 of Program 1 is also an assignment statement. The variable (word in memory) W is assigned the value of the product of 40. and the value of R (2.80); the "*" denotes multiplication. Thus, 112.00, which is 40. times 2.80, is stored in W.

Statement 30 of Program 1 assigns 22.40 (112. divided by 5) to D.

Statement 40 of Program 1 tells the computer to print the values contained in the words R, W, and D, so the values 2.80, 22.40, and 112.00 are printed on some output device such as a line printer or a teletype terminal. The resulting output is shown above.

Statement 50 of Program 1 tells the *language translator*, which translates the Basic language program to a machine language program, that the end of the program has been reached and to stop the calculation.

Program 2 is a different program which produces the same results as Program 1. One can see that different sets of instructions can be used to solve the same problem. Program 2 does not assign the values 112.00 and 22.40 to variables but rather has these values computed and printed out in one statement, namely statement 20.

5-3 PREPARATION OF A PROGRAM IN MACHINE-READABLE FORM

After a programmer writes a program (on a sheet of paper), he must prepare it for the computer. That is, he must put the program onto something which the computer is capable of reading. There are many ways to present a program to a computer, but in each of them, the hand-written program is transferred to some physical object or objects such as punched cards, a punched paper tape, or a magnetic tape.

The most common method of presenting a program to a computer is with a deck of punched cards, with each statement of a Basic program punched on one or more different cards. The format of any Basic program, no matter how it is presented to a computer, is the same as the format used on punched cards even, for example, if magnetic tape or a remote computer terminal is used instead of the cards.

A card is shown in Figure 5-3.1. Each card has 80 columns and 12 rows and a small rectangular hole can be punched in any column and any row by a *keypunch machine*. The collection of punches in a single column represents a single character and each of the possible characters like 0, 1, 2, A, B, C, +, =, and so on has a unique representation by holes. (See Figure 0-4.1 for the representations.) Thus, as explained in Chapter 0, information (hand written Basic statements) is encoded onto cards. Note that the keypunch machine prints the characters corresponding to the holes punched in the cards on the top of the card. Thus the programmer reads the printing while the computer reads the combination of holes.

The following rules apply to transferring Basic language statements onto cards:

1. The statement may start at any point (column).
2. A statement number must appear.
3. A *keyword* must follow the statement number. So far we have seen only three keywords: LET, PRINT, and END.
4. Blanks (or spaces) may be inserted anywhere in the statement. This is usually done to make the program more readable, but if an extra blank accidently appears, it does not affect the statement.

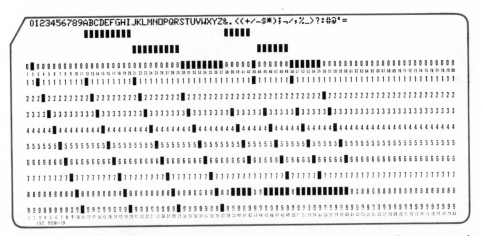

FIGURE 5-3.1 **The standard 80-column punched card showing the holes punched for a statement in Basic.**

5. We emphasize that the Basic statements are processed according to the statement numbers, not according to the position of a statement in the program deck.

A deck of cards with a Basic program punched on them is called a *source deck* and the program contained on them is called the *source program*. (See Figure 5-3.2.)

A number of computer installations have terminals, each of which has direct access to the computer. A typical Teletype terminal is shown in Figure 5-3.3. The programmer types a Basic program on the terminal (instead of preparing punched cards) and then the computer processes the program, executes it, and returns the results directly to the terminal which prints them.

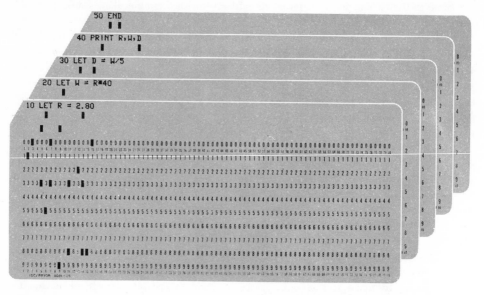

FIGURE 5-3.2 **The punched cards that made up a program deck for a Basic language program.**

FIGURE 5-3.3 **A typical Teletype terminal for direct access to the computer. (Courtesy Teletype Corp.)**

This direct communication between terminal and computer requires a number of commands in addition to those in the Basic language. The exact form of these commands varies from installation to installation, but their effect is the same. The use of a Teletype terminal and a typical set of these commands is discussed in detail in Appendix 2.

5-4 COMPILERS AND TRANSLATORS

Each computer has its own particular machine language. The only programs which a computer can execute without translation are programs written in its machine language. Consequently, for a computer to carry out instructions, one must either write a program in machine language or translate programs written in other languages, like Basic, into machine language. That is, the information and instructions contained in the Basic program must be expressed in the language which the computer "understands" (see Chapter 0).

Writing programs in machine language is a very specialized and tedious task. No English words or mathematical symbols, like +, -, =, are used; only digits are used in these languages. Furthermore, each machine language instruction is very primitive and even a simple calculation requires the use of many digits. Hence machine language programs have many more instructions than Basic programs. In order to write a machine language program, one must know in precise detail how the computer works.

To enable a large number of people to program, programming languages such as Fortran, Algol, Basic, Cobol, PL/I, and over 100 others have been developed. These languages are closer to English and mathematics. Statements written in Basic have much the same appearance as formulas and cryptic English statements.

The Basic language and its first translator were originally developed at Dartmouth College in 1965 under the direction of Professors John G. Kemeny and Thomas E. Kurtz, to provide a good language for teaching computing. This original work was supported by the National Science Foundation as part of its program to improve science education in the United States. The name Basic is an acronym for *B*eginner's *A*ll-Purpose *S*ymbolic *I*nstruction *C*ode.

The original goal of creating a teaching language meant that Basic had to be simple. This simplicity makes Basic unsuitable for many applications and thus a wide variety of "embellishments," "improvements," and other added features have been added at various places. These additions are meant to make Basic suitable for "real" applications and yet retain the simple nature of the language. These attempts have been successful for a variety of situations, and Basic is now widely available for commercial use as well as for teaching computing.

The features that have been added to the original Basic language are not at all standardized and vary widely from place to place. In order to learn which added features (if any) are available at a particular place one must normally obtain a reference manual from the local computing service.

After a Basic program is put into machine-readable form, punched on cards, for example, the cards are placed in a card reader and the information is put into the memory of the computer. A computer program, called a *compiler* or *translator*, examines this information and translates the Basic instructions into equivalent machine language instructions; it also allocates memory locations for all of the variables and numbers used in the program.

Thus, a translator is a computer program whose instructions are to read a source deck and to generate machine language instructions which carry out the Basic instructions. The machine language program which is generated in this process is called the *object program* or the *object code*. Once this machine language program is produced the computer is then told to carry out the instructions of the program, to execute the program. Hence, the computer does exactly what the Basic program instructs it to. Moreover, it does *only* what these instructions tell it to do.

Thus, with the help of a translator, a computer can aid in the task of using a computer to solve problems, notably by using computer time in translating, in order to reduce the total elapsed problem-solving time. Because the programmer can write programs in a language closer to English and mathematics, he can concentrate his efforts on the other parts of problem solving listed in Section 5-1.

But, there are other very important advantages of writing programs in programming languages such as Basic rather than in machine language. Such a program can be modified more easily in the future and it can be read more easily by other programmers. Furthermore, the same source program can be used on several different kinds of computers even though their machine languages are different, because each computer has its own translator which translates source programs into the appropriate machine language programs. The results are great savings in time, effort, and cost, because a program written at one installation with one kind of computer can be used, and perhaps modified, at other installations with different kinds of computers without first having it reprogrammed.

5-5 OPERATING SYSTEMS AND CONTROL STATEMENTS

When a small computer is used to process a Basic language program it often happens that each user is expected to operate the computer directly. In that case, the programmer must place the translator and his program into the computer's memory. The program is then translated and executed.

Larger and more expensive computers are usually run by full-time computer operators. To help reduce computer time for setting things up for the many different jobs to be executed, an *operating system* (or *executive* system, or *monitor* system) is used. Like a compiler, an operating system is a computer program. Among many other functions, the operating system sees that:

1. The required language translators are loaded into the computer's memory as needed.
2. Each user's input and output is properly identified.
3. Records are made of the amount of computer time used by each user and the accounting is done for each user.
4. Users do not make unreasonable demands on the computer time or output. If unreasonable demands are made, the job is terminated so that the computer can go on to the next job.

The operating system must be given instructions and the programmer does this by inserting a few more statements in with his source program and input data. These statements are called *control statements*, or, when punched cards are used, *control cards*. Typically, several of these statements are inserted immediately in front of the source program, another might be used to separate a source program from input data, and another to indicate the end of the input. These statements are in a "Job Control Language," sometimes called JCL. The control statements specify things like:

1. The programmer's name.
2. The account number, or job code, of the user.
3. Limits on the execution time, the amount of printed output, the amount of punched card output, and so forth, to safeguard against waste in case of program errors.
4. Which translator to use.
5. The beginning of a source deck.
6. The beginning of input data.
7. The end of input data.

If such control statements are required, they must be provided with each program submitted to the computer and they must be prepared according to the format specified at the local installation. These control statements are completely independent of the Basic language. Control cards differ from installation to installation and we illustrate in Figure 5-5.1 one set of control cards which might be used to run a source deck with input data. We use a dollar sign ($) to denote a control card.

After a programmer prepares a source deck and inserts the proper control cards, he submits the deck to the computer. The program is compiled and executed. Then the deck and the output are returned to the programmer. The manner and place for doing these things are specified by the installation. The programmer can learn complete details about this at his computing center.

```
$   Name.   John P. Jones
$   Account.  69427
$   Limits.  10 pages, 20 seconds.
$   Language.  Basic.
$   End of control cards
    10 LET   X = 4.13
    20 REMARK   NEXT STATEMENT IN BASIC PROGRAM
    ---
    190 REMARK   NEXT TO LAST STATEMENT
    200 END
    300 DATA  6,12
    399 DATA  15.2, -11.23
$ End of computer job
```

FIGURE 5-5.1 **A Basic program along with a typical set of control cards for a computer run.**

It is common for a number of decks from different programmers to be processed and run all at once (in some sequential order). This mode of operation is called *batch processing*. The time one has to wait for the return of the output is called the *turnaround time*. This turnaround time varies from place to place and, at a single installation, from day to day. In some cases, the turn-around time is as short as a minute or two; anything less than 15 minutes for turnaround time for batch-processed jobs is exceptionally good. The most common turn-around time is from one to three hours and, occasionally, it is as long as twenty-four hours and even longer for programs which use a large amount of computer time.

Although we have used the word "system" in relation to an "operating system," this word is also occasionally used in a much broader sense. It sometimes encompasses the computer, the compilers, and the operating system, all specific to the same computer, perhaps even unique to one installation.

5-6   *PROGRAM DIAGNOSTICS AND DEBUGGING*

All computer languages—machines as well as languages like Basic—have very rigid rules. They are unlike natural languages, such as English, in that statements in natural languages might be ambiguous and statements are often understandable even though they are grammatically incorrect, some of the words are misspelled or omitted, and some of the puncutation is missing or incorrect.

But if there is an error in punctuation or syntax in a Basic statement, the translator will not be able to understand that statement and, hence, it will be unable to complete the translation of the program into machine language. When such an error occurs, the translator will send a message to the programmer that a mistake has been made, what the mistake is (or, more precisely, what the translator's interpretation of the mistake is), and often, in which statement the error occurs.

These messages from the translator to the programmer are called *diagnostics* and they are printed as part of the output. When the programmer receives diagnostics on his printed output, he must locate the errors, correct the program, and submit the corrected source program to the computer.

Errors in a program are frequently called *bugs* and the process of removing them is called *debugging* the program. This process normally consists of submitting a program for translation and execution, receiving diagnostics, locating and correcting the errors, and resubmitting the program. This is repeated as often as necessary to remove all of the bugs. During the process of debugging, it is convenient to have a listing of the program as part of the output to help locate errors.

Unfortunately, the translator can *not* identify every error—only those pertaining to *syntax* or *grammatical structure*—so the debugging process usually does not end when diagnostics do. One can translate each statement into machine language; the *semantics*, or *meaning*, of the program might be something other than originally planned. For example, when punching the deck for Program 1 of Section 5-2, the programmer might accidentally punch R = 2.70, instead of R = 2.80; the translator can not detect such an error because the punched card contains a correct statement in the Basic language.

Thus, a diagnostic-free program might produce "wrong" answers. The answers are wrong in that they are not the desired ones, but the fault is not in the computer nor in the language translator. The fault is with the author of the program who either has a faulty method, has failed to correctly transform the method into a program, or has introduced some other error (like punching 2.70 instead of 2.80). As we have tried to emphasize, the computer will do *exactly what the programmer tells it to do, no more nor less.* We now phrase this as: the computer will do exactly what the programmer *tells* it to do, not necessarily what the programmer *wants* it to do.

The language translator itself can be a great help in learning a computer language. When there is doubt about a statement or combination of statements in a language, a test case can be constructed and run in a program. The resulting diagnostics, if any, or the values computed and printed out can be studied to see if the computer's interpretation is the same as the programmer's. This is a type of *computer experiment.* The programmer makes hypotheses and draws conclusions and then tests these by writing and running a program. The results of the program might refute his hypotheses or, on the other hand, give him experimental evidence (and sometimes even confirmation) that his hypotheses are valid.

In fact, the use of computers as an *experimental tool* is an extremely important aspect of computing. The famous mathematician, John von Neumann expressed this by remarking that a computer can be used as a wind tunnel. A *mathematical model* of a physical phenomenon can be constructed and programmed and various experiments on it can be done by the computer; typically, the cost is much less than if a physical model were built. A larger variety of experiments can be performed with the computer and the computer model can be varied more easily—all of the testing is of the "nondestructive" type. Some simple computer experiments are suggested in Problem 5-6.4 at the end of this section.

PROBLEMS

5-6.1   Find out what operating system control statements are needed, if any, to run Basic programs at your installation.

5-6.2   Prepare Program 2 of Section 5-2 in machine-readable form, add appropriate control statements, and submit the program to your computer. Verify that it does indeed run on your computer and that it prints correct results.

5-6.3   Make up new variable names for Program 2 of Section 5-2 and run the programs. Since the rules for making up names have not yet been discussed, you might be told by your computer (via diagnostics) that you have used illegal Basic statements.

5-6.4   To discover various requirements of your compiler in regard to the form of Basic programs, modify Program 2 of Section 5-2 in the ways listed below; make one run for each of the modifications, make only one such modification in Program 2 in each run. If your installation uses batch processing and has turn-around time longer than a few minutes, you might make several copies of your original deck and then make these changes, one each, in the copies of your deck. Then submit all of the programs at one time. Note that these are examples of computer experiments mentioned above. You should make a guess about what will be the result of the changes *before* you look at the output.

   a.   Omit the statement "10 LET R = 2.80."
   b.   Do not put a statement number on the PRINT statement.
   c.   Delete the comma between the R and W in the PRINT statement.
   d.   Change the number of statement 20 to 200.
   e.   Put blanks between the letters of "PRINT" in statement 40.
   f.   Place the card with statement 40 in the deck upside down.
   g.   Replace the "5" with "0" in statement 30.
   h.   Place the PRINT statement at the beginning of the program.
   i.   Omit the END statement.
   j.   Interchange "R" and "2.80" in the first assignment statement.
   k.   Interchange "R" and "40." in the second assignment statement.
   l.   Put a decimal point after "40."
   m.   Replace "2.80" with "2.70."
   n.   Replace the "R" in the PRINT statement with "P."
   o.   Replace the "T" in the PRINT statement with "D."

5-6.5   In Programs 1, 2, 3 in Section 5-2, only the arithmetic operations of multiplication, "*", and division, "/", were illustrated. The operations of addition and subtraction are indicated by "+" and "−," respectively. Thus, LET A = B + C means: add the numbers in B and C and place the result in A; LET D = E − F means: subtract F from E and place the result in D. Write a program that takes three exam scores of 97., 86., and 57. and computes the average of these scores by giving a weight of 1. to the first two and a weight of 3. to the third. Have the program write out the exam scores and the weighted average. Run the program.

5-6.6   Write and run a program that takes three numbers, A, B, and C, and multiplies A by 3. then adds 2. times B divided by 5. to the result and then subtracts C from the result to obtain a final result. Have the computer write out the values of A, B, C, and the final result. Have the computer do the computations for two sets of values for A, B, and C: 12., 25., 16., and 4., 12., 10. .

5-6.7   Write and run a program which determines the best buy for catsup; use the data in Problem 5-1.4.

5-6.8   Verify that the order of the statements is determined by the statement numbers. Take one of the sample programs and rearrange the cards (or type the statements in with a different order). Then run the program again. Run the program a second time using completely different statement numbers (say 11, 47, 48, 919, and 982) which give the same order to the statements.

5-7   CHARACTERS, NUMBERS, AND NAMES IN BASIC

The characters that are available for writing Basic programs are those that are on the mechanical devices used. These characters may be divided into four groups:

Letters of the alphabet:	A B C ... X Y Z
Digits:	0 1 2 3 4 5 6 7 8 9
Special characters:	= + / , $ and so forth
Blank	

All the common devices have the 26 letters of the alphabet (in capitals only), the 10 digits, and the blank. The set of special characters is more variable; however, the "normal" set for programming in Basic is as follows:

Mathematical:	$+ - * / \uparrow = > <$
Punctuation:	. , ;
Grouping:	( )
Other:	" $

The most common keypunch machine does not have all of these special characters, so that people using this machine must make some substitutions. Typical of these substitutions are:

**	for	$\uparrow$
'	for	"
LT	for	$<$

Some of these are quite satisfactory, other are not. The complete set of special characters on this keypunch (the IBM 026) is

$$+ - * / = . , ( ) ' \$$$

The newer IBM 029 keypunch has all of the normal Basic characters. The common terminal keyboards have a number of additional special characters (# ? : [ ] \ "Bell") which are often used in the commands related to direct access to the computer.

The blank may be used freely at any point within any statement to improve its readability. With only one exception (discussed later) the blank is not significant in a Basic statement. Thus the following three Basic statements are identical in meaning.

```
125 LET A2 = B2 * (X-Y)
125LETA2=B2*(X-Y)
12  5LE  TA 2 = B 2*( X -Y    )
```

The names of variables in a Basic program contain one or two characters. The first character must be a letter of the alphabet and the second character (which is optional) must be a digit. The names are invented by the programmer as he writes and he may choose them any way he pleased within these rules. A name that is "made up" is called a *symbolic name*. Note that Basic contains other names that are an integral part of the language (for example, LET, PRINT, END).

Symbolic
Names

One or two characters; the first one is a letter, the second one (if present) is a digit.

EXAMPLES

A	X	B4	A9
U2	I	G2	Z

A *constant* is any consecutive list or string of digits which may have a decimal point in it. The maximum number of digits allowed depends on the particular computer and language translator being used. A common maximum length is eight and this value is used throughout this book. A plus or minus sign may be placed in front of the constant (for example, +120, −12.02).

Constants may also be written with an integer exponent. This is particularly convenient for very large or very small numbers. Table 5-7.1 below gives some examples of numbers written in three ways: the usual way, the mathematical notation for exponents, and the Basic language notation for exponents. Note that the number of digits of precision might be less (say six) in this notation.

Table 5-7.1
Examples of the integer exponent notations.

Usual Notation	Mathematical Notation	Basic Notation
1000	1×10^3	1E+3 = 1E3
.001	1×10^{-3}	1E−3
1,000,000,000	1×10^9	1E+9
1,250,000	$1.25 \times 10^6 = 125 \times 10^4$	1.25E+6 = 125E+4
.000001234	$.1234 \times 10^{-5} = 1234 \times 10^{-9}$	.1234E−5 = 1234E−9
123.456	$.123456 \times 10^3$	.123456E+3

This notation is not only convenient for very large or small numbers, but also essential. Thus the number one billion requires a string of 10 digits which exceeds the maximum permitted length of 8 digits. Likewise, the fifth number in Table 5-7.1 requires 9 digits and thus can only be written with the exponent notation in a Basic program. The letter E may be read as "times 10 to the power."

Constant

One to 8 digits, with or without sign and with or without a decimal point. May also include the letter E followed by a plus or minus sign and an integer. The maximum size of the integer allowed after the E varies, but it is commonly less than 38.

EXAMPLES

1	-37	12345678	-101202
1.0	-37.37	1234.5678	-1012.02
1.0E + 13	-37.37E37	1234.5678E+9	-101.202E-13

5-8 LET *AND* REMARK *STATEMENTS*

The building block of a Basic language program is a *statement*. The most common statement is the *assignment statement* which causes a variable to be assigned a value. The standard form of this statement is as follows:

(label)   LET   (variable) = (expression)

The *keyword* LET is used to indicate that an assignment is to be made for the value of the variable whose name follows the word LET. The value to be assigned is computed from the expression on the right of the = sign.

LET
or
Assignment
Statement

The keyword LET followed by a variable name, followed by an = sign and ending with an expression.

EXAMPLES

```
10  LET  A = A2 + 4.2
20  LET  B = (X-Y)*(X+Y)
22  LET  Z4 = A-B*(X - 4.1234)
```

Every statement in a Basic program must be numbered or labeled. The label is a number between 1 and some maximum limit. A common maximum limit is 99999 although some systems prohibit labels larger than 9999. Labels are often called *line numbers* or *statement numbers*.

Label

A number which precedes each statement in a Basic program. The label is an integer between 1 and some limit, usually 99999. These labels control the order in which the statements are executed.

EXAMPLES

```
    3     LET    A = 17.3
12345     PRINT     A, A1, A1*A
  987     LET    B = A - A1
 1000     END
```

It is good practice to label the statements in a program in steps of 5 or 10. Then there is room to insert more statements without changing the labels already present. Consider the following simple example.

```
1 LET A = 16.04          10 LET A = 16.04
2 LET B = A*5 - 7.3      20 LET B = A*5 - 7.3
3 PRINT  A*B-D,D+4*A,B   30 PRINT A*B-D,D+4*A,B
4 END                    40 END
```

The programs are identical except for the labels, and both have the same error: D has not been assigned a value. One can fix the program on the right by simply adding the statement

```
25 LET D = A+B/2-4.5
```

Note that this statement can be placed *at the end* of the cards or at the end of the teletyped program. The order of execution is determined by the labels, and the added statement will be executed before the PRINT statement.

This simple correction cannot be made for the program on the left because their is no "room" between statements 2 and 3 to add another statement. Thus a new statement must be added and the labels on the last two statements must be changed.

One may also use the labels in large programs to help organize the program into parts. Consider a program which has several distinct parts: the first digit of the labels can indicate to which part a statement belongs. Thus the labels of the statements in the initial part are less than 100, those in the first computation are between 100 and 199, those in the next computation are between 200 and 299, and so forth.

Computations can be made using the four basic arithmetic operations: + *addition*, *subtraction*, * *multiplication*, and / *division*. The operation of ↑ *exponentiation* is also available and corresponds to the computation of powers or exponentials in mathematics. Thus we have

$$X^3 = X*X*X = X↑3$$

Note that exponentiation allows one to compute various roots of numbers. We have

$$\sqrt{X} = X↑(1/2) = X↑.5$$
$$\sqrt[3]{X} = X↑(1/3) \approx X↑.3333333$$

and so forth.

Expression

An expression is a collection of variables and constants with arithmetic operations indicated. The expression is correct or legal if the result of performing the operations is a single value.

EXAMPLES

```
3*X+B                 4*Y*(8+3*X-Z↑5)           (K2/5 + 6/ J2)/X1
A-B+C/D↑E          (((A)) + ((B) + (C+D)))/E            515.2
```

The rules for forming expressions are the same as those of ordinary mathematics. These rules, which are called *precedence rules*, are summarized as follows:

Operation	Precedence
↑ exponentiation	first
/ division	second
* multiplication	third
− subtraction	fourth
+ addition	last

These rules give the order in which operations are performed. Thus in $3 * X + B$ the multiplication (third precedence) is done before addition (last precedence). A frequently used modification of these rules is discussed at the end of this subsection.

Parentheses are used to further specify the order of performing the computations, and the rule associated with them is as follows: *All operations within a matching pair of left and right parentheses are performed before any operation is performed on the parenthesized quantity.* This results in the evaluation of the innermost subexpression first, then the next innermost and so forth. Thus, in the expression

$$A * (B + (C - D/2))$$

the innermost subexpression $C - D/2$ is evaluated first. Note that the division is done before the subtraction because of the precedence rules. The resulting value is then added to B (as this is the next innermost subexpression), and then this result is multiplied by A.

The precedence rules do not specify what to do when several operations of the same precedence appear together. This does not cause any difficulty with addition, subtraction, or multiplication because the result is the same no matter in what order the operations are peformed (for example, $7 + 8\,63 + 12$ or $7 * 8 * 63 * 12$). This is not so with division or exponentiation. Consider

$$2/4/8 .$$

If the left division is done first, then the result is 1/16. If the right division is done first, then the result is 4. Likewise consider

$$2↑3↑2 .$$

If the left exponentiation is done first, the result is $8↑2 = 64$, while the opposite order gives $2↑9 = 512$. Many computer systems resolve this difficulty by adopting another rule: *All equal precedence operations are done in a left to right order.* This means that

$$2/4/8/3$$

would be interpreted as

$$((2/4)/8)/3 .$$

Note that the use of this rule allows one to say that + and − have the same precedence. Thus $16 + 5 - 3 + 8$ is evaluated correctly either by the rule that − has precedence over + or by the left-to-right rule. The left-to-right rule is frequently used along with modifying the precedence rules to say that + and − have equal precedence and * and / have equal precedence. If the left to right rule (or, perhaps, some similar rule) is not used, then these expressions are illegal and a diagnostic would be issued.

When in doubt about how an expression might be evaluated, parentheses should be inserted to remove that doubt.

It is often convenient and sometimes essential to include a description in a program of what the program does. In theory, of course, one can figure it out by reading the program. In practice, a few hints are very helpful. There is a statement in the Basic language just for this purpose, the *remark statement*.

Remark

A remark statement is indicated by the three letters REM which may then be followed by anything. The statement causes no action by the computer and is only to give information to a reader of the program.

EXAMPLES

```
25   REMARK - THIS IS THE MAIN CALCULATION
66   REM -- A4  IS THE AVERAGE GRADE
12   REM *** PRINT THE  $+/$.*  ANSWERS HERE ***
```

The thoughtful and generous use of remarks in a program can make it very readable. This is particularly important if a program is to be used by various people or over a long period of time.

The following program illustrates some of the features of Basic. It does not perform any particularly meaningful computations.

```
 1 REMARK - THIS PROGRAM ILLUSTRATES A FEW THINGS
 2 REM        ABOUT BASIC DISCUSSED SO FAR.
 3 REM
10 REM     *****   ASSIGNMENT STATEMENTS    *****
12       LET A = 12.345678*4 - .4259E+2
14       LET B1=  A*(2.15/(A+6.1))↑.5
16       LET C3=  A-B1↑2 + 7.2*(A-B1↑(A+.004))
18 PRINT A,B1,C3,A-B1,17.1
20 REM
22       REMARK STATEMENTS MUST HAVE LABELS
24 REM
26 REM    ALL PROGRAMS MUST COME TO AN
30       END


                    OUTPUT

6.792712     2.773896   -7346.167024     4.018815     17.100000
    A            B1           C3             A-B1          17.1
```

PROBLEMS

Some or all of the programs suggested below can be combined into a single program. However it may happen that a particular system will not detect every error in a program that has many different kinds of errors.

5-8.1   Invalid names are usually detected by a language translator. Write a program with several arithmetic statements in it, each using some invalid variable name.

5-8.2   Write and run a Basic program that has some misspellings in the keywords PRINT, LET, REM, and END.

5-8.3   Determine experimentally the length of the largest positive integer by writing a program that involves constants of ever-increasing lengths. What does the language translator do with an integer constant that is too large?

5-8.4   Write and try to run a program that has expressions in which parentheses do not balance.

5-8.5   In a mathematical text, an expression such as $A(B + C)$ has meaning. Write a Basic program with $A2(B + 4)$, $B(4 + B)$, $X(A - B)$ and similar expressions in it. What conclusions do you draw from this experiment?

5-8.6   Insert all of the implied parentheses in the following expressions:

(a)   A*B↑C+D/E

(b)   A−B+C*E*D/F↑G

(c)   X*Y−Z↑A+2*N/K+3.4

(d)   X+Z−K/M+1

5-8.7   Delete all of the redundant or unnecessary parentheses in the following expressions:

(a)   ((X+Y)−Z)*(X/Y)↑Z

(b)   ((A)*(B↑C)↑D)/E

(c)   (X+Z)/(Y−((X+Y) − 2*(Z/K)))

(d)   ((((X+Y)↑(K+1))*H4)*2+3)/(A−4)

5-9   PRINTING AND READING

We have already seen the PRINT statement used in the example programs. These programs only printed numbers (either from variables or expressions), but it is also possible to print messages. One may place messages just as one places expressions in the PRINT statement. Other names in common use for messages are: *strings, character strings, literal strings, Hollerith variables,* and *Hollerith strings.*

Message

A message is a list or string of characters in quote marks. Any Basic characters may be used in the message except quote marks.

EXAMPLES

```
"THE ANSWER IS"              "X1 = "
"NO SOLUTION FOUND"          "A,B,Q,P1 ARE = "
```

PRINT

The word PRINT followed by a *list* of items separated by commas. The items in the list may be variables, numbers, expressions, or messages.

EXAMPLES

```
22  PRINT  X, 17.42,  X + 1.2 * Y, "HELP ME"
33  PRINT  "X2 = ",  X2,  "Y AND Z = ",  Y, Z
44  PRINT  "ANSWER NO.",  K,  "  IS",  A3
```

The items in the PRINT list are printed out in print *zones*. The details of how this is done vary from place to place, but the general idea is as follows. Each line to be printed is divided into a number (usually 5) of zones of fixed length (usually 15 spaces). The first item is printed in the first zone, the second in the second zone, and so on. If there are more items in the list than zones, then a new line is started. A number of examples of PRINT statements and the results are given below.

```
10 PRINT A1,A2,A3,A4,A5,A6,A7,A8

   1             2             3             4             5
   6             7             8
```

```
20 PRINT "X,Y,Z =",X,Y,Z

X,Y,Z =         222          481          -77

30 PRINT "X","Y","Z"
31 PRINT  X,Y,Z

X               Y            Z
 222            481          -77
```

There are still several points to be mentioned about the PRINT statement.

1. If a message is longer than 15 spaces then it uses additional zones until enough spaces are obtained to print the message. There is normally a limit on the length of messages, sometimes it might be only 15 characters.
2. Most systems print numbers and messages *justified to the left* (pushed as far left in the zone as possible). A few may use right justification or centering.
3. The first position of a zone is reserved for the sign if a number is printed. If the number is positive, then this first position is blank.
4. Some systems also have *short zones* available for printing more numbers on a line. There are fewer than 15 spaces in short zones, perhaps 8 or 10. To obtain short zones one replaces the commas by another character, say a semi-colon.
5. Most systems use the exponent form to print very large or very small numbers. Thus the numbers

$$123456780000. \ , \qquad .000001233321$$

would be printed out as

$$1234567E+11 \ , \qquad 1.23332E-6$$

Recall that some Basic systems print fewer digits in the exponent form.
6. The PRINT statement normally causes the printing to start on a new line. In particular the statement

```
20 PRINT
```

simply causes a blank line to appear.
7. The PRINT statement does not start printing on a new line if the statement ends with a comma (or semi-colon for short zones). This is illustrated below

```
10 PRINT "  X-VALUE"           10 PRINT "  X-VALUE",
20 PRINT X                     20 PRINT X

   X-VALUE                        X-VALUE      18.47
18.47
```

The terminal or *dangling comma* does not prevent a new line from starting if there are no more print zones available. If a simple PRINT (as in Item 6) is used after a terminal comma, a blank line does not follow, but rather printing starts on the next line.

There are many situations where one wants to have a program process information that changes from time to time or run to run. A simple example occurs in a company's payroll computation. There, the rate of pay and hours worked would change from employee to employee but the formulas and rules to be used are the same for each one. There are two statements in Basic that allow this to be done, the READ and DATA statements.

There may be many DATA statements in a program and they are used to create a *data stack*. The READ statement described below then reads information from this data stack. This concept is illustrated in Figure 5-9.1.

DATA

The keyword DATA is followed by a list of constants separated by commas. The constants are placed on the bottom of the data stack in the order in which they appear.

EXAMPLES

```
303  DATA  17, 18, 909, -66.1, 123.321
492  DATA  808.305,  1.23E+6,  -999,  1.0004
```

There is no limit on the size of the data stack (except for the size of the computer involved), and the number of items specified in each DATA statement is arbitrary. Note that one *cannot* put expressions in a DATA statement, not even something as simple as 1/2 or 1/3. Thus for 1/3 one would have to use .33333333.

The data stack can be created at any point of the program, and the DATA statements need not be placed together. One must, of course, pay close attention to the sequence of the labels of the DATA statements as this determines the order in which the numbers appear in the data stack. It is common practice (and also good practice) to place the DATA statements at the end of the program just before the END statement.

Once the data stack is created, then the values in it may be assigned to variables by means of a READ statement.

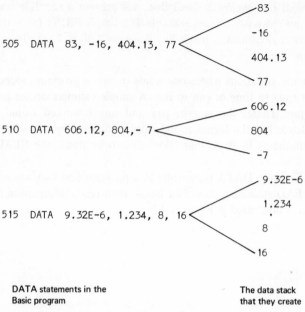

DATA statements in the
Basic program

The data stack
that they create

FIGURE 5-9.1 **The relationship between DATA statements and the data stack.**

READ

The keyword READ is followed by a list of variable names separated by commas. Values are taken off the top of the data stack and assigned (in order) to the variables in the READ list. A number taken off the data stack is not replaced.

EXAMPLES

```
606  READ  A,B,C,X          99  READ  Z9
225  READ  K1,K2,Y,K3       88  READ  N
```

Two typical combinations of READ and DATA statements are shown below.

```
10 READ A,B,C               20 READ X1,X2,A
88 READ K                   60 READ B,Q,A
98 DATA 12,14.1,-6,4        96 DATA 1.6,1.72,44,6.302
                            97 DATA 1.1E+6,49,-99
```

Statement number 98 on the left creates a data stack with four values. The READ statement number 10 uses the top three and makes the following assignments of values: A = 12, B = 14.1 and C = -6. The data stack then contains only one value, 4, and this is assigned to the variable K at statement 88.

The program segment on the right has a data stack with 7 values. The top three are assigned to X1, X2, and A at statement 20. The next three (which are now the top three) are assigned to the variables B, Q, and A at statement 60. Note that A is assigned a value by two different READ statements. Presumably some computation was made between statements 20 and 60 which used the first value before the second one was assigned. There is still one number (-99) in the data stack at the end of this program segment.

A program is stopped if an attempt is made to read from an empty data stack. This convention is reasonable and it is convenient in many situations, since reading an empty data stack almost always indicates a blunder or the end of a number of identical calculations.

An Example Program

Consider the calculations needed to make out the weekly payroll checks of a certain company. The input information is the hourly rate of pay and the number of hours worked. The program is to compute the gross weekly wage as the product of these numbers and then compute the income tax withholding (20 percent), the Social Security Tax (5 percent) and the amount of the paycheck.

```
 1 REMARK   ***    SIMPLIFIED PAYROLL    ***
 2 REM       H = HOURS       R = HOURLY RATE
 3 REM       G = GROSS PAY   I = INCOME TAX
 4 REM       N = NET PAY     S = SOC. SEC. TAX
10 READ H,R
15 LET  G = H*R
20 LET  N = .75*G
25 PRINT " GROSS"," INCOME TAX"," SOC. SEC."," NET"
30 PRINT  G, .2*G, .05*G, N
35 DATA    38, 2.65
40 END


                       OUTPUT

     GROSS           INCOME TAX    SOC. SEC.    NET
     100.7           20.14         5.035        75.525
```

The output gives a complete and readable account of the program and its results. If a similar computation is to be made for another employee, then one need only change the information in the DATA statement. Another feature of Basic is presented in the next section that allows one to obtain these results for a large number of employees with one computer run.

PROBLEMS

5-9.1   Write a program that prints squares or triangles, such as

```
,  ,  ,                    +
,  ,        or       +    +
,  ,  ,            + + + + +
```

5-9.2   Write a program that prints a short table of squares and cubes of integers. The output should appear as follows

NUMBER	SQUARE	CUBE
1	1	1
2	4	8
3	9	27

Compute and print out the table for the integers 1 to 9.

5-9.3   Write a program similar to the example in Section 5-9 with the following changes:

(a)   An employee identification number is read in
(b)   The income tax withholding is 15 percent
(c)   The Social Security Tax is 5.2 percent
(d)   There is a state disability insurance tax of 1 percent
(e)   The output provided is "EMPLOYEE," "GROSS," "TOTAL TAXES," and "NET PAY."

5-9.4   Write a program that computes and prints a short table of numbers as follows. Say the first number is A, then print A, A $*(A + 1)$ and A $* (A + 1)*(A + 2)$ in one row. Then take the value of A for the next row to be the last number of the preceding row. Do this for 5 rows and start with A = 1. The output should appear as follows:

A	A*(A+1)	A*(A+1)*(A+2)
1	2	6
6	42	336

5-9.5   The language translator can detect illegal items in a DATA statement. Run a program with some illegal items in a DATA statement and observe the diagnostics produced. Example illegal items to try are:

$$13/5 \qquad 17.035.1 \qquad 12,405 \qquad \$6.35$$

5-9.6   Write a program that prints the letter X in the middle of the first zone and the word CENTER in the middle of the second zone. The program is then to print the word ZONE centered under the word CENTER.

5-9.7   Write a program that reads five integers. It then writes out the original numbers, the sum of their squares, and the product of their squares with appropriate headings. After writing out the above, the program should read in seven more integers. Again, it computes the sum of the squares and the product of the squares. It then prints these numbers, their sum, and their product with appropriate headings.

5-9.8   Write a program that reads in a number and prints out the following four lines of output:

> THE NUMBER INPUT IS _____
> THE SQUARE OF THIS NUMBER IS _____
> TEN TIMES THIS NUMBER IS _____
> TEN PERCENT OF THIS NUMBER IS _____

Run the program with input of 16, 1.2, and −7.

5-9.9   You have just received a bill from B. I. Cuspid, your dentist, for $12.15. Write a computer program which prepares a check for the bill. Include all the appropriate entries: date, name of dentist, "$12.15," "Twelve and 15/100," and so on, and have these printed at the appropriate places by the printer.

5-10   PROGRAM CONTROL AND DECISIONS

So far it has been possible to create only "straight-line" programs where the statements are executed one after another until the END statement is reached. There are many situations (examples are given below) where one needs to make different computations depending on the circumstances that arise. In order to do this one has to have additional statements. The fundamental statement in Basic for controlling the sequence of computations in a program is the IF-THEN statement. This statement allows one to make *logical decisions* and introduce *branching* into the program. The nature of the statement is illustrated by the following little program which selects the largest of two given numbers.

```
10 READ A,B
20 LET  M = A
30 IF   M>B    THEN 50
40 LET  M = B
50 PRINT " THE MAXIMUM OF" A,B," IS",M
60 DATA  88,67
70 END
                    OUTPUT

THE MAXIMUM OF     88         67 IS        88
```

The value of M is going to be the maximum of the two numbers A and B. We see that the IF-THEN statement allows us to skip over part of the program if A > B and the value of M remains set to that of A.

In order to make decisions or tests one uses *relational expressions* after the IF in the IF-THEN statement. These expressions involve one of the six relational operators or symbols. These operators are defined and illustrated in Table 5-10.1.

Table 5-10.1
The relational operators and some relational expressions

Relational Operator	Name	Relational Expressions Example Use	Meaning of Expression
=	Equal	A = B	A is equal to B
<	Less than	A < B	A is less than B
<=	Less than or equal	A <= B	A is less than or equal to B
>	Greater than	A > B	A is greater than B
>=	Greater than or equal	A >= B	A is greater than or equal to B
<>	Not equal	A <> B	A is not equal to B

Relational Expression

A relational expression is of the form:

(expression) (relational operator) (expression)

The expressions are ordinary arithmetic expressions and the relational operator may be any one of the six listed in Table 5-10.1. Note that a relational expression has a logical value of either *true* or *false*.

EXAMPLES

```
X + 1.2 = Y*Z - 4          (N4 - N/3)/6.1 > = 17.4
N - 3 < K* (K + 1)         (X1 - X2)*A   > 19.2
N  <>  0                        K  < =100
```

IF-THEN

The IF-THEN statement is of the general form

IF (relational expression) THEN (label)

If the relational expression is *true then* a *transfer* is made to the statement whose label is given. That is to say that the normal sequence of execution of the statements is broken and the next statement to be executed is the one whose label is specified.

EXAMPLES

```
IF  K < 0  THEN  999          IF  A <= M+N THEN 408
IF  X-1 > Y*(X+1) THEN 110    IF  J <> K  THEN 500
```

Computing centers that use the older IBM keypunch machines do not have the symbols < and > available. The usual substitutions made for the six relational operations are EQ, LT, LE, GT, GE, and NE, respectively.

The example program given above is special in that we merely wanted to skip over part of the program. A more common situation is where one wants to make one calculation for some cases and another calculation for other cases. In other words, we want to branch the program into two separate parts. In order to achieve this and other kinds of program control the GO TO statement is provided in Basic.

GO TO

This statement uses the keyword GO TO followed by the label of some other statement. When this statement is encountered in execution the next statement executed is that whose label is given.

EXAMPLES

```
GO TO 999                     GO TO 800
GO TO 20                      GO TO 2
```

To illustrate the use of this statement in conjunction with the IF-THEN we consider part of a payroll calculation where we pay time-and-a-half for work over 40 hours per week.

```
 5 REM   R = HOURLY RATE   H = HOURS   P = PAY
10 READ R,H
20 IF H>40 THEN 50
30 LET P = R*H
40 GO TO 60
50 LET P = R*40 +1.5*R*(H-40)
60 PRINT " THE PAY IS", P
70 DATA 2.40, 41.5
80 END
```

We see that the combination of the IF-THEN and the GO TO allows us to compute the pay P from the rate R and hours H in one of two ways and then to come back and print out the result of the computation.

A somewhat longer example program is given below which performs a typical income tax computation. We assume a very simple tax situation here, but it contains some of the elements of a realistic one. The income tax on *taxable income* is computed as follows:

taxable income		tax	of excess over
over	but not over		
$0	$5000	10%	$0
$5000	$10000	$500 plus 18%	$5000
$10000	$20000	$1400 plus 30%	$10000
$20000		$4400 plus 50%	$20000

The taxable income is obtained from the *gross income* by subtracting certain deductions. The rules for this are specified below:

1. *Married*:   deduction of $2,000.
2. *Children*:   deduction of $2,000 for the first,
               deduction of $1,000 for the second,
               no deduction for other children.
3. *Medical bills and gifts*:   deduction of all such expenses which are in excess
               of 6 percent of gross income.

The program is given on the opposite page.

This program starts with a remarks section which defines the variables appearing in the program. The next section (statements 10 to 75) reads the data and computes the total deduction D. This section sets D = 0 first and then adds various amounts to D as they are found to be allowed. This type of program control uses the IF-THEN statement for the branching and decisions. The third part (statements 100 to 140) computes the net income N and the tax T. The program branches into four parts depending on the tax bracket. The GO TO is then used to bring everything back to statement 200 where the results are printed out.

The GO TO is used at statement 210 to transfer back to the beginning of the program and to restart the computations. Note that there are four sets of data so that four separate tax computations are made. The data stack is empty when the READ statement is reached for the fifth time and the program stops at this point. This repetition of the entire program is one of the simplest examples of iteration, a topic which is discussed in detail in the next section.

The program shown has an error in it, the kind that causes "computer goofs." Consider Mr. Jones, who is married and has two children. He was very ill last year and able to work only a few months. As a result, his gross income was only $4256.00 and his medical bills were $3172.43. The above program computes his deductions to be 4000.00 + 3172.43 = $7172.43 and his tax to be minus $291.64. He might hope that the government will pay him this amount, but the tax system does not work that way. The error may be removed by placing a test on the net income N at statement 101.

```
 1 REM *****   INCOME TAX PROGRAM  *****
 2 REM
 3 REM     G = GROSS INCOME
 4 REM     M = 1 IF MARRIED, 0 IF NOT
 5 REM     C = NO. OF CHILDREN
 6 REM     B = BILLS FOR MEDICAL + GIFTS
 7 REM     D = DEDUCTIONS
 8 REM     N = NET INCOME
 9 REM     T = TAX TO BE PAID
10 REM - READ DATA, COMPUTE DEDUCTIONS
20 READ G,M,C,B
30 LET D = 0
40 IF M = 0 THEN 60
50 LET D = D + 2000
60 IF C<1    THEN 70
62 LET D = D + 2000
64 IF C<2    THEN 70
66 LET D = D + 1000
70 IF B< .06*G THEN 100
72 LET D = D + (B-.06*G)
75 REM              HAVE FOUND D
100 LET N = G-D
102 IF  N<5000   THEN 140
104 IF  N<10000 THEN 130
106 IF  N<20000 THEN 120
110 LET T = 4400 + .50*(N-20000)
112 GO TO 200
120 LET T = 1400 + .30*(N-10000)
122 GO TO 200
130 LET T = 500   + .18*(N-5000)
132 GO TO 200
140 LET T = .10*N
200 PRINT " G,D AND T =" G,D,T
210 GO TO 20
300 DATA 6145,0,0,405
310 DATA 14027.50,1,4,  689.50
320 DATA 26587.03,0,2,  1654
330 DATA 9825.13,1,1,  842.67
400 END
```

Before going on let us introduce a simple statement which is occasionally convenient. The STOP statement simply terminates the execution of the program. It is identical to a direct transfer (GO TO) to the END statement. Its use is to make a program more readable by not forcing the reader to ascertain that a GO TO transfers to the END statement.

STOP

The keyword is STOP. It terminates the execution and is equivalent to a GO TO to the END statement.

EXAMPLES

108 STOP   225 STOP

5-11   *ITERATION AND ITERATION LOOPS*

Iteration or the repetitive execution of groups of statements is one of the most important facets of computing. Computers can do thousands of calculations in a split second but this power would not be of great value if one had to write thousands of statements. Thus one wants to obtain a set of instructions that the computer can use over and over again. A great many situations are exactly of this type because they involve the *identical* processing of a large number of similar items. Some typical examples of this are:

> credit card billing
> payroll processing
> bank account statements
> student grade point averages
> warehouse inventory reports
> moon rocket control computations

To illustrate this in a simple situation look at an example program for the payroll computations of an imaginary company. This program prints out an appropriate heading and then processes all of the DATA statements (one per employee). The data includes an employee identification number, his rate of pay, and the number of hours worked. The output produced is gross pay, the tax deductions, the medical insurance deductions, and the net pay. There is an income tax withholding of 12 percent of the first $50.00 and 20 percent of the rest, a state employment insurance tax of 1½ percent, and a Social Security tax of 5.2 percent. The insurance deducted is 6 percent of the gross salary with a maximum of $6.50.

The calculation part of the program is rather short (only about 15 lines), the rest of it is either remarks or data. Note how the 15 statements that do the work can be used over and over again as long as there is data left in the data stack. We have only shown 9 employees for this company but a larger number is more likely, perhaps several thousand for a large company.

```
  1 REM *            PAYROLL
  2 REM * INPUT   I=EMPLOYEE ID, R=PAY RATE, H=HOURS
  3 REM * TAXES   T1=INCOME, T2= UNEMPLOY  T3=SOC SEC
  4 REM *           N=INSURANCE
  5 REM * OUTPUT I,G,TOTAL TAXES,N,NET PAY
 10 PRINT " "," SUPERSOUP CORP PAYROLL"
 12 READ D1,D2,D3
 14 PRINT " DATE ",D1,D2,D3
 15 PRINT
 16 PRINT " EMPLOYEE"," GROSS"," TAX DEDUCT"," INSURANCE"," NET PAY"
 20 REM         READ NEXT DATA SET, COMPUTE GROSS PAY
 21 READ I,R,H
 25 IF H>40 THEN 40
 30 LET G = R*H
 35 GO TO 50
 40 LET G = R*40 + 1.5*R*(H-40)
 49 REM                          COMPUTE DEDUCTIONS
 50 IF G>50 THEN 60
 55 LET T1 = .12*G
 56 GO TO 70
 60 LET T1 = 6.00 + .20*(G-50)
 70 LET T2 = .015*G
 80 LET T3 = .052*G
 85 LET N = .06*G
 90 IF N< 6.50 THEN 100
 95 LET N = 6.50
 99 REM                    HAVE DEDUCTIONS
100 PRINT I,G,T1+T2+T3,N,G-T1-T2-T3-N
110              GO TO 21
199 DATA  8,17,1973
200 DATA 1604, 3.75, 40.0
205 DATA  812, 5.21, 32.0
210 DATA 1122, 2.40, 41.5
215 DATA  971, 2.75, 16.0
220 DATA 1404, 4.05, 40.0
225 DATA   88, 6.25, 40.0
230 DATA 1532, 3.75, 43.0
235 DATA 1269, 4.05, 40.0
240 DATA  943, 3.90, 38.0
900        END
```

Further, note that when next week's payroll is to be done, all one has to do is prepare new data and insert them. Thus even for a small payroll this program would be executed several thousand times in the course of a few years. It is exactly this iteration or repetitive use of the program that makes it so valuable. Once one has specified how the payroll computation is made and expressed this in a program, then one can use it over and over again without arithmetic mistakes, miscopying mistakes, and the other human errors in accounting. The primary source of errors will, in fact, still be the human errors that occur in preparing the data for the program.

The first few lines of the output of this payroll program are shown below. Note the heading that is printed out initially. This is followed by a table of the output generated by the program.

SUPERSOUP CORP PAYROLL				
DATE	8	17	1973	
EMPLOYEE	GROSS	TAX DEDUCT	INSURANCE	NET PAY
1604	150	36.05	6.50	107.45
812	166.72	39.51424	6.50	120.70576
1122	101.40	23.0736	6.084	72.2424

Many large organizations have special forms that are used instead of paper with such a program. These forms are actually blank checks and these are separated after the correct amounts have been filled in by the computer. This eliminates the need to recopy the results computed by the program as well as the mistakes that would be made in that recopying.

The simple iteration example above involves the repetition of the reading of data and processing that information. There is more to iteration than a set of operations to be repeated—there must also be a mechanism for stopping the iteration. We illustrate this stopping mechanism in Figure 5-11.1.

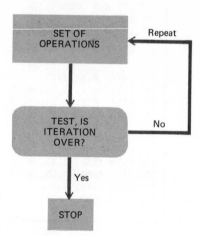

FIGURE 5-11.1 **Flowchart of a simple iteration.**

The type of diagram in Figure 5-11.1 is called a *flowchart* because it indicates the flow of the computations in the program (see Chapter 6 for more discussion). The looping through the set of operations seen in this diagram suggests the common name of *iteration loop*. The test for the termination of the simple iteration example was: "Are there more DATA statements to process?" This test can be rephrased as "Is the data stack empty?."

It is appropriate to ask the question: Why do we bother to introduce the concept of iteration? Certainly for the algorithms considered above, it is not required to clarify or simplify the statement of the methods. In fact, it seems as if we have needlessly complicated very simple and straightforward situations.

There is one obvious reason to justify this approach. It is a fact of life that present computers require rather detailed instructions about what they are to do. Thus, we must break programs down into rather small steps in order for present computers to proceed. If we want something done 7317 times, we must tell the computer to do it each of these 7317 times. The use of iteration loops allows us to do this without actually writing down 7317 instructions for the computer.

This obvious reason obscures the important reason for studying iteration. The concept of iteration is required for clarity of thought in programming. Iteration is a fundamental procedure and we must be able to think in terms of iteration loops in order to be adept at constructing programs. When writing programs that involve some repetitious calculations one must have a clear idea of what is happening (and when) and at times one must stop and lay out the logical relationship in the iteration. Large programs tend to have many iteration loops with various interconnections that can lead to considerable confusion if one does not take care.

A general iteration loop is more complicated than that shown in Figure 5-11.1. Let us now consider a problem and an iterative method to solve it which illustrates all the parts of an iteration loop. Suppose X is an interest rate (say 5 percent so that $X = .05$) and A is the amount of money one would like to have for each dollar invested (say $A = 2$ so that we want to double the money invested). The problem is to find the number I of years that the money must be invested in order to achieve the desired amount A. Thus for $X = .05$ and $A = 2$ we find that $I = 15$ because $(1.05)^{14} = 1.98$ and $(1.05)^{15} = 2.08$.

An equivalent problem is as follows: Suppose X is a population growth rate per year (say 3 percent so that $X = .03$) and A is the factor of increase in population ($A = 2$ corresponds to doubling the population). The problem is to find the number I of years for the population to increase by the factor A. Thus for $X = .03$ and $A = 2$ we find $I = 24$ because $(1.03)^{23} = 1.97$ and $(1.03)^{24} = 2.03$. This problem can be simply rephrased as a mathematical problem

Determine the smallest integer I *so that*

$$(1 + X)^I > A.$$

One way to solve this problem is by an iteration loop. The steps are:

1. Read X and A.
2. Set $I = 1$ and test $1 + X > A$, if so then print I and stop.
3. If not then increase I to 2 and test

   $(1 + X)^2 > A$, if so then print I and stop.

4. If not then increase I to 3 and test

   $(1 + X)^3 > A$, if so then print I and stop.

5. ...

A value of I is eventually found so that $(1 + X)^I > A$, and this value is the smallest such integer and the solution of the problem. The above steps may be written more precisely and briefly.

1. Read X and A.
2. Set $I = 1$.
3. Test $(1 + X)^I > A$; if true then go to step 5.
4. Increase I by 1 and return to step 3.
5. Print the value of I and stop.

This method is incorporated in a Basic program as follows:

```
        10 REM      PROGRAM WITH AN ITERATION LOOP
        20 READ X,A
        30 LET  I=1
      →40 LET T = (1+X)↑I - A
        50 IF T > 0 THEN 80
Loop    60 LET  I=I+1
      └─70   GO TO 40
        80 PRINT " THE SMALLEST INTEGER IS",I ←
        90 DATA .05,2
        99 END


                       OUTPUT
        THE SMALLEST INTEGER IS          15
```

Exit from loop

Note that statements 40 and 50 can be combined into one statement:

```
45 IF    (1+X)↑I > A THEN 80
```

This results in a simpler and more efficient program, but it is not done here so as to illustrate the various parts of 3 general iteration loop. These five parts are listed below along with the corresponding statements in the Basic program.

1. Initialization	LET I = 1
2. Operations to be executed	LET T = (1+X)↑I−A
3. Test (for termination)	IF T > 0 THEN 80
4. Modification (for next repetition)	LET I = I+1
5. Exit	GO TO 40

These parts are illustrated in flowchart form in Figure 5-11.2

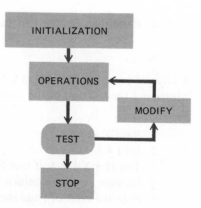

FIGURE 5-11.2 **Flowchart which shows the five parts of a general iteration loop.**

We now consider some variations of the program shown earlier and a difficulty that might arise. If one has X as a negative number (or zero) then the quantities $(1 + X)^I$ do not increase as I increases. In this case the test $(1 + X)^I > A$ would never be true and the iteration would never stop. Such a situation is called an *infinite loop* and it is to be carefully avoided in computing. Of course, a program does not stay in execution forever. There are limits placed on how long each program is allowed to run and the computer system stops any program at this limit.

There are two ways to protect against infinite loops and both of these are frequently used. The first of these is to test all the variables to be sure that an infinite loop cannot occur. The second is to put a fixed limit on the number of iterations in a loop. The previous program is shown below with both of these protection devices used.

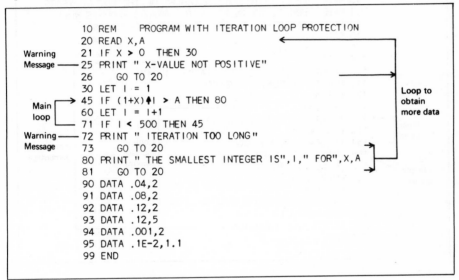

The first protection occurs at statements 21, 25, and 26. If X is not positive the program returns to the READ statement *after* printing a message. It is a very good practice to print messages at the point an error is detected as this greatly aids in program debugging, and so forth. The second protection occurs at statements 71, 72, and 73. If I is greater than 499 the program prints an appropriate message and again returns to the READ statement.

This second type of protection is useful because some errors produce a very large number of iterations. For example, one might want to set $X = .1E-1$ and hit the wrong key to set $X = .1E-9$. This would result in millions of iterations and effectively produce an infinite loop even though it would eventually stop—if one has enough money to pay for the computer time.

Another modification has been made in addition to providing protection against infinite loops. Instead of stopping after one set of values for X and A, the program returns to the READ statement for another set. This simple iteration is continued as long as the data stack is not empty. This creates a situation known as *nested iteration loops*. That is to say that one iteration loop is inside another iteration loop, that is, the set of operations of one loop (called the *outer loop*) contains another loop (called the *inner loop*).

The nesting of iteration loops is very useful in computing and we see it again in a further modification of the above program. This modification is to print out tables of the number of years required for a dollar invested to increase up to $2, $3, $4, and $5 for interest rates of 1 percent, 2 percent, 3 percent, 4 percent, 5 percent, 6 percent, 7 percent, and 8 percent. The first (outer) iteration loop is chosen to vary the interest rate through the 8 desired values. The next loop (which is in the middle) varies the amount of increase through the values 2, 3, 4, and 5. The inner loop then determines the number of years required. Note that this program does not obtain values of X and A from the data stack, but rather they are generated in the iteration loops.

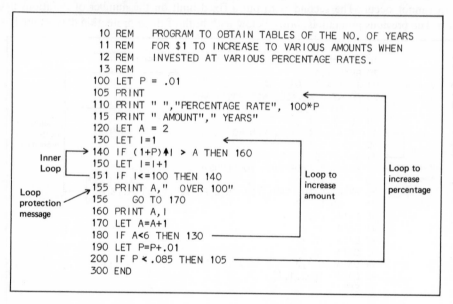

The first part of the output is shown below. One could make the output neater by printing out a heading of the values 2, 3, 4, and 5 for A and then printing the number of years below that. This requires considerably more programming with the features of Basic now available. Features introduced in Chapter 8 allow this to be done easily.

	PERCENTAGE RATE 1
AMOUNT	YEARS
2	70
3	OVER 100
4	OVER 100
5	OVER 100
	PERCENTAGE RATE 2
AMOUNT	YEARS
2	36
3	56
4	71
5	82

This program has iteration loops nested three deep and might possibly take a considerable amount of computer time to run. We know that the operations in the outer loop are executed eight times. Every time the middle loop is used, its operations are executed four times. Thus the total number of values of I to be found is $8 * 4 = 32$. We do not know how many iterations there are in the inner loop. There are no more than 100 so that the test $(1 + P) \uparrow I > A$ is not made more than 3200 times. If the average number is 10 (rather than the limit of 100) then the test is made 320 times.

There are two points worth noting about the amount of work involved here. First, if we wished to have the tables at slightly finer intervals in percentages and amounts then the amount of work increases very much. Thus for interest rates from 1 percent to 10 percent in steps of ½ percent, and amounts from 1.5 to 5 in steps of .5, the number of values of I needed is $19 * 8 = 152$. This is an increase of almost 500 percent. Second, we can cut down on the amount of work very significantly by being a little more clever. As we are increasing the value of I, we can note when we pass $A = 2$ and print this out. Then instead of stopping, we continue increasing I until we pass $A = 3$, and so forth. This reduces the number of iterations in the middle loop to one and cuts the work from 152 to 19 (or by 87 percent) in the case of finer tables.

PROBLEMS

5-11.1   Explain how a Basic program with a $>=$ in an IF-THEN statement can be modified to perform the same, but to use only a $<$ in the IF-THEN statement.

5-11.2   Write a Basic program that reads a DATA statement to obtain an integer value of X that is between 0 and 999,999. The program is to print out the number of digits in X.

5-11.3   Write a Basic program to obtain diagnostics for the following errors:

(a)   An illegal label (-17 LET X = 3, for example).
(b)   A direct transfer (GO TO or IF-THEN) to a nonexistent label.
(c)   A program without an END statement.
(d)   Two statements with the same label.
(e)   An erroneous relational expression (for example => or >>).

5-11.4   Write a program that reads an unspecified number of DATA statements, each with four test grades in it. You are to compute and print with appropriate messages the average grade for each of the four grades in the statement.

5-11.5   Write a program that reads in an integer N from data and computes $N! = N \cdot (N - 1) \cdot (N - 2) \cdots 3 \cdot 2 \cdot 1$. Recall that $0! = 1$ by definition. If N is negative or N! is too large to be represented in your computer, print N and an error message that indicates why N! could not be computed. If N! can be computed, print N and N!. In either case after printing one of these messages, your program should go back and read in a new value for N until the data stack is empty.

5-11.6   Find the sum of all the odd integers from 1 to 1001.

5-11.7 Write a program that reads a value of X with $0 < X < 1$ and then finds the integer I so that $0 < I * X < 30$ and such that $I * X$ is as close to 30 as possible. Put in protection against bad data for X and run your program with several values (both good and bad) for X to show that it works properly.

5-11.8 Find the sum of the first 10 numbers in the sequence $1, 4, 9, 16, 25,...,n^2$.

5-11.9 Assume that you are a clerk in a store and a man hands you a $20 bill to pay for a purchase of X dollars. Determine what bills and coins you give him as change. Print out lines of output as follows:

RECEIVED	$20		COST = $11.47
CHANGE:	0	$10 BILLS,	1 $5 BILLS,
	3	$1 BILLS,	2 QUARTERS
	0	DIMES,	0 NICKELS
	AND 3 PENNIES.		

Check, also, to see if you received enough money.

5-11.10 Modify the program in this section for computing tables of returns on investments at various interest rates so as to compute the entries with the more efficient method discussed in the text.

5-11.11 Write a program that reads in any two dates after the year 0 and computes the exact number of days between the given dates. Write out the dates and the number of days between them before reading in two more dates. Recall that 1900, and so on, are not leap years and ignore the days lost when the present calendar was adopted in the Middle Ages. The program is to read in the dates in the form of year, month, day (for example, 1617 11 28   1945 8 15). The result is to be printed with an appropriate message.

5-11.12 Write a program that reads a **DATA** statement which gives the number of pins a bowler knocked down with each ball he threw during a game. There are 10 frames in a game. If it takes a bowler two balls to knock down 10 pins in a frame (a spare), his score for that frame is 10 plus the number of pins he knocks down on his next ball. If it takes him only one ball to knock down 10 pins a frame (a strike), his score is 10 plus the number of pins he knocks down on his next two balls. If he does not knock down all 10 pins in a frame (a miss), his score is the number of pins he did knock down in that frame. After reading the data, compute the bowler's score. Write out the data input, the computed score, the numbers of the frames in which he made spares, and the number of the frames in which he made strikes. Read new data and repeat until the data stack is empty. Run your program with a number of cases which show that it works properly.

5-11.13 Write a program that reads in a number X with value $0 < X < 1$ and determines how many leading zeros X has. *Hint*: If X has P leading zeros then $10^P * X > 1$ but $10^{P-1} * X$ is not greater than one.

5-11.14 Write a program that reads in a number X with value $1 < X < 10$ and determines the integer part of X (for example, 2.73 has integer part 2, 7.04 has integer part 7). *Hint:* If X has integer part I then $X - I \geq 0$ but $X - I - 1 < 0$.

5-11.15 Write a program to prepare the table indicated in Problem 5-9.4. Print out the first 10 rows of the table and use an iteration loop to do it.

5-11.16 Write a program to compute a table of returns on an investment of $1. The output should have 5 columns with the first column containing the number of years invested (range from 1 to 30 years). The next four columns are to be the value of $1 invested at interest rates of 3 percent, 4 percent, 5 percent and 6 percent. Print out an appropriate heading for the table and for each column of the table.

5-11.17 Suppose that you are just married and want to buy $1200 worth of furniture for your apartment. You do not have $1200, so you decide to use your "Supercharge" credit card to buy the furniture. The "Supercharge" card charges you 1½ percent per month on the amount you owe them.

Write a program that determines how long you have to make payments and how much interest you have to pay for each of the following schemes for repaying this debt:

(a) Suppose you pay $50 per month until the furniture is paid for.
(b) Suppose you pay exactly 10 percent of the balance due each month until the balance is less than $50. At this point you pay the remaining balance.
(c) Suppose you pay $120 per month until the furniture is paid for.

6 Algorithms and Program Construction

5 Algorithms and Program Construction

6-1 ALGORITHMS

As mentioned in Chapter 1, the word "algorithm" is derived from the name of a ninth century Arab mathematician—Al-Khuwarizmi—who devised a number of methods for solving certain problems in arithmetic. The methods were presented as a list of specific instructions, and thus his name has become attached to them.

An algorithm is much like a recipe, a set of instructions, or specifications for a process for doing something. That something is usually solving a problem. There are, however, extra connotations to the word algorithm, which invest it with several properties, as discussed below.

First an algorithm must be unambiguous; since we are operating in a certain framework or context, each instruction in an algorithm must not allow more than one interpretation. The following examples illustrate this point.

AN INSTRUCTION IN A COOKING ALGORITHM

Bad: Put some spice in the batter.
Good: Add 1 teaspoon of ginger to the batter.

AN INSTRUCTION IN A COMPUTING ALGORITHM

Bad: Take two numbers and add them.
Good: Take x add 10 to it, square the result, and call the new result y.

Note how much neater the mathematical expression of this algorithm is:

$$y = (x + 10)^2 .$$

The prime examples of algorithms are properly constructed computer programs and it is because we want to construct such algorithms (or programs) that we are interested in discussing their properties.

It is surprisingly difficult to be unambiguous. Consider the number of times that one receives (or gives) confusing instructions. A program that is correctly translated into machine language is rarely ambiguous because computers only accept simple instructions. (Even so, more often than we like, we find that the computer does something completely unexpected when we thought the instructions were airtight and foolproof. This is the result of programmer errors and not of ambiguous instructions, however.)

In addition to being unambiguous, an algorithm should always come to an eventual end. Furthermore, when it stops, it is somehow supposed to report whether or not it has achieved its objective. It is quite easy to write a set of instructions which does not bring the computer to a normal termination.

Let us now examine some problems and algorithms.

Problem: Is 7319 a prime number?

Algorithm: Divide 7319 by each of the numbers 2,3,4, ..., 7317, 7318. If any division is exact (the remainder is zero), the answer is no; otherwise it is yes.

This is an absolutely unambiguous solution procedure for the problem. There are much more efficient algorithms, but this one does provide the solution to the problem.

Problem.   Make a million dollars.

Procedure.   Take ten million dimes and go to Las Vegas. Play the dime slot machine there until you have either (1) twenty million dimes or (2) no dimes at all.

Note that this procedure is unlikely to solve the problem. In general, we do not require an algorithm to do so, but we are most interested in algorithms which always do solve the problem. This procedure for making a million dollars fails to be an algorithm because it might never terminate; we could play the slot machines forever without either losing or making a million dollars (the slot machine owners in Las Vegas arrange things so that it is unlikely that this procedure fails to terminate).

One of the most satisfactory definitions of the word algorithm is based on the intuitive concept of a machine (or mechanical process). We envision idealized machines that never make a mistake or have a mechanical failure. These machines have a means for receiving instructions, and they react to these instructions in a certain deterministic way. A simple way to visualize how a machine receives instructions is to imagine that it has push-buttons on it. When a button is pushed, the machine responds. This is an oversimplification because we want the machine to be able to react in different ways *according to the state that it is in*. Thus, when you push a car accelerator, the movement (forward, reverse, or none) depends on whether the car is in gear and, if so, in which gear—reverse or forward—whether the motor is on, and so forth. Instructions which depend on the condition or state of the machine are compatible with the idea that the *machine is completely deterministic*. We emphasize that the machine operations involve no random or uncertain processes. Thus, a process with actions dependent on the outcome of flipping coins or on a random number generator does not satisfy this condition.

An algorithm is a list of instructions for such a machine or mechanical process, the execution of which must result in a termination at some point. This description fits many real machines. Two such machines are a desk calculator (the operations involve arithmetic and entering numbers into the machine) and a typewriter (the operations include hitting the keys, setting margins, shifting, and returning the carriage). These real machines are, of course, not infallible as the idealized machines used to define algorithms.

Our interest here is with machines that perform mathematical and logical operations. The foremost example of a real machine to which this description applies is the computer. Indeed, it is not too far wrong to say that computer science is the study of what can be done—and how to do it—with mathematical machines (either real or idealized). However, this view of computer science is perhaps too narrow, for present computers can already perform a variety of "nonmathematical" operations (for example, draw pictures, turn off ovens, open doors, and order spare parts). We have already noted that future computers will be able to perform a very broad range of actions.

6-2 FLOWCHARTS

So far, we have described algorithms in one of two ways. First as a combination of natural English and mathematical notation. There are several drawbacks to this method:

1. The description is usually not concise.
2. The English language is ambiguous.
3. These descriptions do not reveal the basic structure of the algorithms. They are hard to grasp.

The second way is by a computer program. There are also several drawbacks to this method:

1. The description is usually not concise.
2. These descriptions do not reveal the basic structure of the algorithms. They are hard to grasp.
3. Many people do not understand computer programs and it takes considerable study to learn to understand them.

Occasionally a third "language" is used for describing and expressing algorithms: the flowchart. This language does not resemble English, or most artificial language, but it is effective for communication.

Flowchart Language

A flowchart consists of a diagram of lines connecting boxes that contain statements (often abbreviated) in natural language or jargon. The boxes contain groups of steps of · the algorithm, and the lines indicate the relationships between the groups. The statements in the boxes are simply the instructions in the algorithm. They are to be performed in *top-to-bottom* order. The lines have arrows on them which indicate the order in which the instructions in the various boxes are executed. We can follow the lines and see the "flow" of the algorithm, thus the name flowchart.

One feature of a flowchart is that a question may be put into one of the boxes. Frequently, the question is phrased so that only one of two answers is possible: either yes or no. Various lines leaving such a box are labeled (for example by yes or no), and that line corresponds to the answer to the question. We distinguish the boxes where decisions are made by rounding their corners. One says that a *branch* occurs at such a box. The values of variables in an algorithm may change from pass to pass through a box and, as a result, the answer to the question may change. This causes one to take different branches and to follow different paths through the flowchart as the algorithm proceeds.

Consider an algorithm for fixing a flat tire (see Figure 6-2.1). We can read the algorithm quickly and see its general structure. A description of the algorithm in ordinary English is considerably longer, and the relationship of the various parts of the algorithm is not nearly as apparent.

One of the essential distinctions between the flowchart language and natural language occurs at the branches. Natural language (and a programming language like

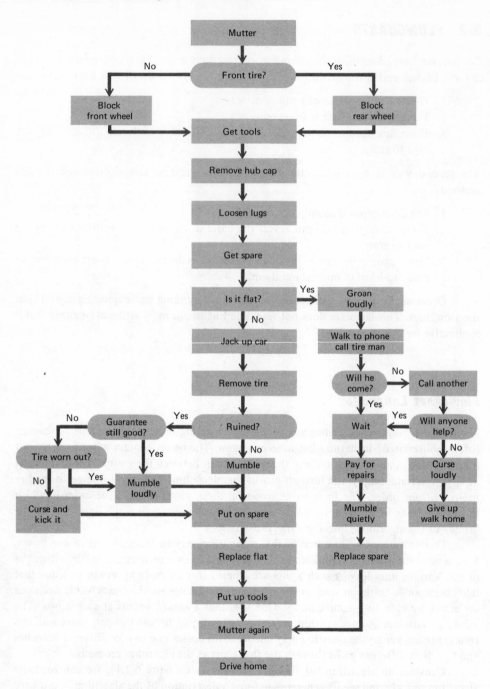

FIGURE 6-2.1 **Flowchart of an algorithm for fixing a flat tire.**

Basic) is sequential in nature. Statements in a natural language must be made one after the other; two or more statements cannot be made simultaneously. Thus when a branch is to be made, only one alternative can be read immediately and all others must be read later. In a flowchart, the branch is represented naturally as a diagram and the two (or more) alternatives are presented simultaneously. (Examples are seen in Figure 6-2.1 at the boxes which contain: "Front tire?," "Is it flat?," "Ruined?.") This fact is often described by saying that flowcharts allow a two-dimensional expression of algorithms, whereas natural language (and most other languages) give a sequential, linear, or one-dimensional expression of the algorithm.

Since branching occurs on the basis of various tests or questions, the location and relationship of the branches indicate the logical structure of the algorithm. The primary use of flowcharts is to express the logical structure in a form that is better understood by people.

The systematic use of flowcharts increased with the beginning of automatic computation in the late 1940s. For a period it was thought that a flowchart should be made for every computer program. Keep in mind that in the late 1940s instructing computers (that is, writing programs) was much more complicated than it is now. There was a much more formal flowchart language than that presented here. It included many shapes of boxes to indicate the various types of elementary steps in the algorithm, and many elaborate flowcharts were made. However, experience soon showed that all the details were not required, and many people wrote computer programs without first making flowcharts. Thus the role of flowcharts in programming computers is smaller than many people anticipated some years ago. Note that flowcharts are routinely applied in a number of areas outside of computing.

The main use of flowcharts in computing now lies in two areas:

1. The communication and analysis of the logical structure of programs by people.
2. The documentation of complicated programs. This latter use is actually a special case of the first.

The first use is particularly important during the construction of programs. At that time programmers often do not know what a program is doing—or should be doing—and it is very useful to draw rough flowcharts to visualize the structure of the program and the flow of the process.

Flowcharts are frequently the easiest way to describe and understand programs, particularly complicated ones.

PROBLEMS

Describe an algorithm and make a flowchart of it for each of the following five problems.

6-2.1   Getting to class.
6-2.2   Adding two five-digit numbers.
6-2.3   Enrolling for classes.
6-2.4   Making coffee.

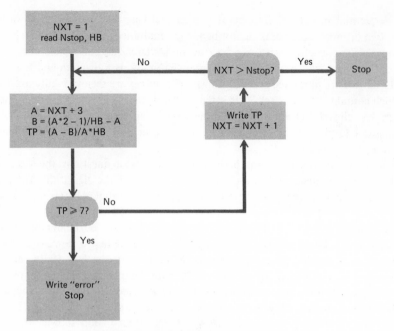

FIGURE *6-2.2* Flowchart for Problem 6-2.6.

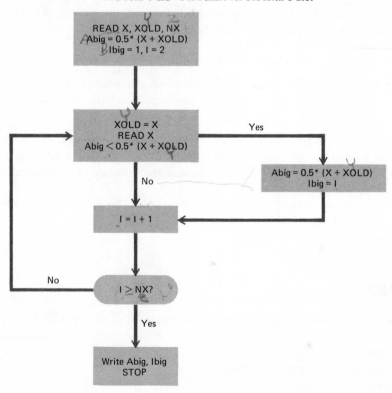

FIGURE *6-2.3* Flowchart for Problem 6-2.7.

6-2.5   Solving a problem in physics, economics, or balancing a checking account.

6-2.6   Translate the flowchart in Figure 6-2.2 into a computer program and run it with some data.

6-2.7   Translate the flowchart in Figure 6-2.3 into a computer program. Run it for NX = 20 and some set of X values. It is to compute the largest value of the average of two successive pairs of X values and print out this value and an indicator of where it occurred.

6-3   COMPONENTS OF PROGRAMS

Two examples are considered in this section and programs are developed to solve the problems in them. Each problem is of some interest in itself and the programs obtained might well be useful. However, the main motivation for considering these examples is that they involve techniques that occur over and over again in programming. They seem always to be modified in some slight detail in each application, but they are among the basic building blocks of programs.

EXAMPLE 6-1

Sums and Averages

The simple situation arises when we have a known number of items and want to find their sum and average. Thus if we have five quantities A1, A2, A3, A4, and A5, we can use

```
100  LET   S  =  A1+A2+A3+A4+A5
105  LET   A  =  S/5
```

to do the calculation.

Frequently this approach is not feasible; either there are so many terms in the sum that it is inconvenient to write them all, or we do not know how many terms there are when the program is written. Thus an instructor might want one program to compute his average grades for each term. His number of students varies and he decides to punch their grades on cards at the end of each term and to have his program compute the average.

In order to do this he must know when his last grade is read, otherwise his program stops when it runs out of data. One can indicate this by putting an impossible value at the end of the deck and then check each value to see if it is this value. Let us assume that he places a grade of -99 as the last card in his deck of grade data. His strategy is shown in the flowchart in Figure 6-3.1.

We see that two crucial variables are introduced—SUM and COUNT. SUM is the total of the grades read in so far and COUNT is the number of grades. Each of the variables is set equal to zero before any grades are read. The algorithm given in this flowchart can be written in Basic; of course Basic variable names have to be used for SUM, COUNT, and GRADE.

```
10  REM         INITIALIZE VARIABLES
20  LET C = 0
30  LET S = 0
40  REM         READ A GRADE
50  READ G
60  REM           TEST FOR THE END
70  IF G = -99 THEN 120
80  LET C = C+1
90  LET S = S+G
100     GO TO 50
110 REM         FIND AVERAGE AND PRINT
120 LET A = S/C
130 PRINT " THERE ARE"; C;" GRADES"
140 PRINT " WITH SUM="; S;" AND AVERAGE"; A
150     GO TO 500
200 DATA 88
250 REM   *** MORE DATA HERE ***
299 DATA -99
500 END

THERE ARE  22  GRADES
WITH SUM =  1642  AND AVERAGE  74.636
```

EXAMPLE 6-2.

Maximum and Location of the Maximum

This example is a slightly more complicated variation of the previous one. Now we want to find the largest number in a list of numbers and where it occurs (that is, is it the first, the second,..., the last?

Let us reconsider the situation in Example 6-1 and assume that the instructor wants not only the average grade, but also the highest grade, and the ID number of the student who made it. The flowchart of Figure 6-3.1 still indicates the general strategy; we need merely to put more in the box where the SUM is computed. Assume that the data contain not only the grade, but also a student ID number as the second item. Now two more variables are introduce, HIGH, the highest grade found so far, and IDHIGH, the ID of the highest grade found so far. The key box in Figure 6-3.1 is then enlarged to be as shown in Figure 6-3.2.

One question still remains; namely, what are the proper initial values for HIGH and IDHIGH? We see that IDHIGH does not have to be initialized at all since

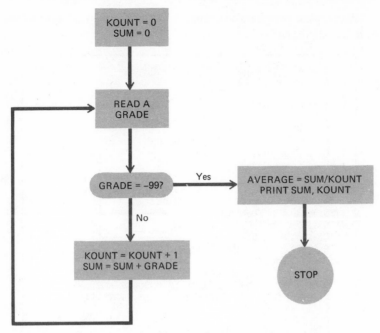

FIGURE 6-3.1   Flow chart of a program to compute the average grade.

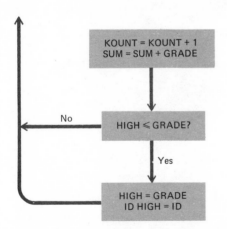

FIGURE 6-3.2 Replacement for the lower box of Figure 6-3.1.

it does not depend on previous ID's. We want HIGH to start out so that GRADE is always the largest of HIGH and the first value of GRADE. This would happen if HIGH starts out as minus infinity, but most computer systems do not have such a number. We can set its initial value to anything that we are certain will be smaller than any possible grade. Let us assume that the lowest possible grade is zero, so an initial value of −1 is small enough for HIGH.

A complete program for Example 6-1 and Example 6-2 is given below, again with Basic variable names:

```
  1 REM        INITIALIZE VARIABLES
 10 LET C = 0
 20 LET S = 0
 30 LET H = -1
 40 REM            READ GRADE, ID NUMBER
 50 READ G, I
 60 REM              TEST FOR THE END
 70 IF G = -99 THEN 160
 80 LET C = C+1
 90 LET S = S+G                            Loop to process
100 DEF FNM(X) = .5*(X+H+ABS(X-H))         grades
110 LET H = FNM(G)
120 IF G < H THEN 50 ─────────────────────>
130 LET I1 = I
140    GO TO 50 ───────────────────────────>
150 REM              FINAL OUTPUT
160 LET A = S/C
170 PRINT "    THERE ARE";C;" GRADES"
180 PRINT "    WITH SUM ";S;" AND AVERAGE"; A
190 PRINT "    HIGHEST GRADE IS";H;" BY";I1
199    GO TO 500
200 DATA 88, 192643
250 REM   *** MORE DATA HERE ***
299 DATA -99, 0
500 END

    THERE ARE  22  GRADES
    WITH SUM =  1642   AND AVERAGE  74.636
    HIGHEST GRADE IS    96   BY    136048
```

Note that if there is a tie for the highest grade, this program prints the last one of those that tied.

PROBLEMS

6-3.1　(Simplified Income Tax)　The tax is based on the adjusted income. The rates are given by the following table:

Tax Rate on Adjusted Income

Adjusted Income		Tax Rate
between	$0 and $2,000	15%
	$2,000 and $5,000	$300 + 20% of excess over $2,000
	$5,000 and $10,000	$900 + 25% of excess over $5,000
	$10,000 and $15,000	$2,150 + 30% of excess over $10,000
	$15,000 and $25,000	$3,650 + 40% of excess over $15,000
	over $25,000	$7,650 + 50% of excess over $25,000

The adjusted income is obtained by subtracting the following deductions from the actual income:

Personal Deductions

Taxpayer	$0
Wife	$5,000
First child	$2,000
Second child	$1,000
Third child	–$2,000 (i.e., add $2,000 to income)
Fourth child	–$2,000 (i.e., add $2,000 to income)
Each additional child	–$1,000 (i.e., add $1,000 to income)

Other deductions to be subtracted from actual income are:

(a)   All gifts to charity.

(b)   All state and local taxes.

(c)   Medical expenses in excess of 5 percent of actual income.

Write a program that reads in the following information:

actual income,

number of personal deductions (the taxpayer counts as 1) and marital status.

amount of gifts to charity, total of all state and local taxes, total medical expenses.

This information should be placed on one card and printed out with appropriate messages as soon as it is read in. The income tax due is to be computed and printed out as follows.

INCOME TAX DUE IS XXXXX.XX DOLLARS

Hint: This program is very similar to the example given in Section 5-11.

6-3.2   You are married and have two children. How much more tax would you have to pay if you have a third child? Use the tax rules of Problem 6-3.1. Estimate your gifts, state and local taxes, medical expenses, and average salary during the next 20 years. Use three different salary estimates: low, medium, high.

6-3.3   (*Table of the Present Value of Money*) A dollar to be received next year is not worth as much as a dollar to be received today. Likewise, a bill of $10 to be paid 5 years from now is less than a bill of $10 to be paid now. One can put a lesser amount in savings and the interest earned can be applied to the bill as well as the original amount. The present value of money to be paid or received in the future depends on two things: the interest rate and the length of time involved. If the interest rate is R% and the number of years is Y, then the present value of X dollars is

$$X/(1. + .01*R)^Y.$$

Write a program that computes and prints out a table of the present value of $1000.00 for four rates of interest, 2 percent, 4 percent, 6 percent, and 8 percent and for periods of 1 to 40 years. The table is to have appropriate headings for each of the five columns required. These are the number of years (on the left) and the present values for each interest rate.

6-3.4 (*Table of the Present Value of Regular Payments*) If one is to receive or make regular monthly (not yearly) payments for a long period of time, then these payments have a present value. This is the sum of the present value of each payment as described in the preceding problem.

Write a program that computes and prints out a table of the present value of $100.00 a month payments for four interest rates, 2 percent, 4 percent, 6 percent, 8 percent and for periods of 1 to 30 years. Even though the payments are made every month, print values only for every year (that is, after 12, 24, 36,... payments). Appropriate headings are required as in Problem 6-3.3.

6-3.5 (*Table of the Future Value of Regular Payments*). If one makes regular payments (say into a savings account) over a long period of time, then the amount at the end is larger due to the interest earned. If the interest rate is R%, then the future value of a payment of X dollars after M months is

$$X * (1. + .01 * R/12.)^M.$$

Write a program that computes and prints out a table of the future value of regular monthly payments of $100.00 for four interest rates, 2 percent, 4 percent, 6 percent, 8 percent and for periods of 1 to 30 years. Even though the payments are every month, print values only for every year (that is, after 12, 24, 36,... payments). Appropriate headings are required as in Problem 6-3.3.

6-3.6 It is a common practice for savings institutions to credit the interest earned only a few times a year even though monthly payments are made. Write a program to recompute the quantities in Problem 6-3.6 for 6 percent interest where the interest is added only once every 3, 6, or 12 months. The formula involved changes to

$$3. * X * (1. + .01 * R/4.)^Q$$

for the 3 month case where Q is the number of quarters (3-month periods) and the formula gives the future value for all three monthly payments made in the quarter. You are to find similar formulas for the 6- and 12-month cases. Put appropriate headings on the printed output.

6-4 THE ORGANIZATION OF COMPONENTS
INTO COMPLETE PROGRAMS

Three general aspects of programming are discussed in this section. First we consider the objectives that one has in writing a program and present situations where each of these objectives is critical. Then we discuss general strategies to meet these objectives. Finally, a few observations are made about common weaknesses in the "style" of programming, particularly those found in beginners' programs.

It might surprise readers at this point to learn that there are objectives in programming besides getting the programs to work. Certainly that is the ultimate objective in beginning programming assignments and one's proficiency is normally judged on whether the program works or not. However, after some experience in programming one sees that there are many programs that work for the same problem and some of these are much better than others.

One might make an analogy (slightly farfetched) with golf, where the objective is to hit the ball into each of the holes on the course with flags sticking out of them. Even a novice golfer can achieve this objective if he is patient and tries long enough. However, there is still a big step between this and being a good golfer who achieves the objective with many fewer strokes. The knowledge and skill required to write programs that work (even bad ones) is much more than required for golf, but, as in golf, meeting this first objective still leaves one with a big step to take.

There are two important general requirements for a good program: efficiency and understandability. It is not so easy to precisely measure either one of these. One commonly measures efficiency by the amount of computer time required to solve the problem. At one time this was a very reasonable measure, but the situation is more complex now primarily because computer systems have become much more complex and simple running time does not accurately reflect the cost of the resources used. However efficiency is measured, it is a primary criterion for judging the value of a program.

The second requirement for a good program, understandability, is not as widely recognized and is much harder to measure. Experience has shown, however, that this can be just as important as efficiency. The ultimate objective is, of course, to have a program that is efficient, which is easy to understand, and which works in a straightforward, natural way. The construction of such programs is an art which must be cultivated by conscious effort and practice. The relationships among these objectives are illustrated in Figure 6-4.1.

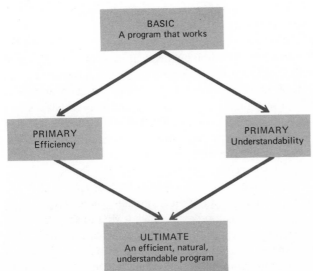

FIGURE 6-4.1 The objectives in the construction of programs.

Let us now consider some common situations and the resulting values of these objectives. One of the most common is the *short, one-shot program*. Such a program is not a big calculation and once the answers are obtained the program is not likely to be run again. This situation includes the typical homework assignments in an computing course, only the fundamental objective of a working program is really of value. There is not much point in spending time and effort on efficiency and clarity in a program that does only a short computation and which is to be run only once. Nevertheless, programmers should adopt the policy of making their programs efficient where this can be done easily and in the same time that it takes to write a sloppy inefficient program. An instructor in a course might well ask for efficiency and clarity in homework assignments; this is to give students practice and to help them develop good programming habits.

There is another quite different situation where efficiency and clarity assume secondary importance. This is for programs that solve an important problem for the first time. This occurs often at the frontiers of knowledge and, naturally, the first and foremost requirement is to be able to obtain the solution somehow. Even here, clarity plays a role because such programs are sometimes rewritten several times and by several people. If one attempt results in an unintelligible program, then this might prevent a necessary improvement from being recognized and made.

Efficiency becomes the most important objective when extensive use is made of a program. Typical examples include programming language translators, payroll and accounting programs, programs that handle requests in an airline reservations system or a stock market price quotation system, programs that perform basic design computations for a company's products, programs that do very long and complicated scientific computations, and programs that control the processes in an oil refinery. In these and similar situations the effort spent in increasing the efficiency of the programs involved is rewarding. In fact in some of these cases, efficiency might be the only difference between a program that "works" and one that does not. Thus an airline reservation system cannot allow 10 or 15 minute delays in responding to requests. Nor is it worthwhile to have a weather prediction program that takes 36 hours of computer time to make a 24 hour forecast. Weather prediction computations are very long and this possibility is not exaggerated (in fact, it has actually happened).

Understandability is very important for a program which has a relatively long life span during which it undergoes gradual modification by different programmers. A typical example is the payroll accounting program for a company. Such a program has an indefinite life span, yet it probably must be changed every time the state or federal government changes the tax laws, every time a new union contract is negotiated, every time a new pension or insurance plan is adopted, and so forth. Often the changes required are quite minor—only a few lines. But it might be very difficult to locate the right lines in a program that is many pages long, without comments or otherwise incomprehensible. Many organizations have had the bitter experience of being forced to completely rewrite a program from scratch because they could not make a required minor change in an old program. In fact, there are many stories about a job security strategy that involves this situation. One somehow gets assigned to write a program which is vital to the company's (or organization's) operation. One then writes it with no comment cards, with all the variables named Q1, Q2, Q3, Q4, and so on, and, at every opportunity, does things in a peculiar way. It also helps to sprinkle in complicated statements that are not used at all.

After the program is working well and everyone realizes that the company cannot live without it, one becomes much too busy to ever write a report about how the program works or how to modify it. This way the programmer becomes an irreplaceable, indispensible key employee (hopefully, also unfirable), the only person who can modify and update this crucial program.

Another situation where clarity is important is in the construction of complicated mathematical models. Imagine, for example, an economist who is constructing a mathematical model for the economic behavior of a small town. His program must, of course, represent all the important economic features of a small town. This economic behavior is quite complex and the economist will probably have to modify his model many times before he is satisfied. It is clearly to his advantage to make his program clear and understandable as he has to read and reread it during the modifications. Most inexperienced programmers fail to do this even though it reduces their work in the long run. Everyone clings to the hope that there is just one more bug in the program before it is finished, and thus it is not worthwhile to put in a comment card explaining what these *ad hoc* three lines of code do.

Even if the economist is able to learn to live with his program, the day will come, he hopes, when he will tell the world about his new and extraordinary model. The world, of course, will want to examine it closely and will rightfully be unimpressed by an unintelligible program.

It is the task of the programmer to judge his particular situation and to place correct emphasis on efficiency and clarity. Experience in programming allows each programmer to develop his own "style." His programs incorporate his favorite little constructions and idiosyncrasies. Hopefully, he develops the ability to write good code unconsciously, just as a good writer writes good prose unconsciously. The development of this ability requires practice (and usually a lot of it), but practice alone is not enough. The programmer must continually examine his programs critically if he is to improve.

It is not possible to give a few paragraphs that say how to write good programs any more than it is possible to say how to write good short stories in a few paragraphs. However, the key requirement is to be able to visualize the *entire* computation in one's mind. It is frequently helpful to make one or two rough flowcharts of the program in order to get a better view of what is to be done. If the programmer does not have a good view of the whole program, then the program will be a set of disconnected pieces that are unlikely to fit together smoothly or efficiently.

The concept of *structured programming* is designed to force a programmer to visualize the entire computation and to organize it in an understandable way. The idea is to determine various levels of detail in the program. On the first or top level one lays out the general tasks to be performed and the details are not present at all. The next example (see Figures 6-4.2, 6-4.3 and 6-4.5) may be used to illustrate this top level. Note that the structure of the computation is already laid out by these flowcharts even though no details are given. Once this top level is determined, then one goes down to the next level and lays out the structure of those computations. The number of levels, of course, depends on the complexity of the program and in very large programs there may well be four, five or more levels of detail before one arrives at actual program statements in a computer language. Note that this approach forces one to think completely through the computation before a single line of computer code is written.

The maximum in efficiency usually requires that the computations and processing be carefully integrated and coordinated with one another. Thus if a quantity is needed both for the fourth and seventh steps of a computation, it should be computed at the fourth step, stored, and saved until the seventh. Furthermore, if most of the ingredients of a part of the computations required in the seventh step are available at the third step, then one should finish that part of the seventh step in the third step and save the results until needed in the seventh step. It is easy to believe that the objective of efficiency works against the objective of clarity and simplicity.

It is interesting that these two objectives can also work together. It frequently occurs that the most efficient code is simple. That is to say, the most efficient code consists of a number of simple statements. However, it might be hard to understand the logical structure of the code and thus hard to see why it produces the correct results.

The maximum in understandability usually requires that the program be modular. That is, the program is broken down into a number of modules (pieces of code) each of which has a readily understandable purpose. This organization is almost essential if the program is to be modified from time to time. While modularity does tend to be slightly inefficient, it is rarely necessary to make great sacrifices in efficiency in order to achieve it. Nevertheless, the desire for modularity often leads to inefficient programs because the programmer chooses a set of modules that are inappropriate for the computation to be made. In other words, if one does not have a good visualization of the computation, one might well break it up into pieces or modules that make maximum efficiency impossible. Modularity is closely related to the structured programming approach mentioned above and one of the important benefits of structured programming is to help identify the natural pieces of a program that should be made into modules.

A frequent fault with beginning programmers is to identify the main steps in the computations with the quantities to be computed. This leads to a program organization as shown in Figure 6-4.2. This type of program organization is often correct, but sometimes it leads to inefficiency. We present two examples where this organization is inefficient.

First, consider an insurance company that has a lot of accident records on punched cards. The company wants a number of statistics about single car accidents. Figure 6-4.3 illustrates a possible organization of a program to obtain four items of information from the company's records. A sample of the cards (3 cards per accident) is shown in Figure 6-4.4. This example shows the poor program organization that is common among inexperienced programmers. The difficulty is that the programmer has failed to realize that the crux in this program is processing the information on the cards. If this is seen as the main feature, then the organization appears as in Figure 6-4.5. A more detailed flowchart would, of course, show that the box "Find what information . . . " breaks up into a number of boxes with decisions. Efficiency is gained at this point by choosing to make the decisions in the right sequence.

Another illustration of the lack of correct organization occurs in sorting a list, say arranging a list of numbers into order (for example, the scores on a test). One approach is to search for the highest score; then when it is found, search for the next highest score, until it is found. One can continue in this way until all the numbers are in order. It is easy to take this idea and make a computer program carry it out. The program is a simple one. Yet this is a very inefficient method and for large lists it can result in using hours of computer time when better methods could do it in minutes, or even seconds.

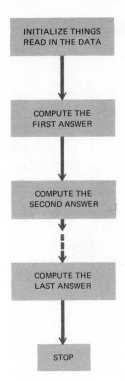

FIGURE 6-4.2   The straightforward, one answer at a time organization of a program

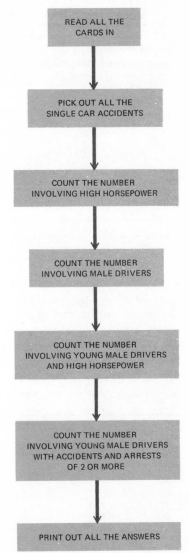

FIGURE 6-4.3   The result of using the "one answer at a time" organization for locating some statistics about single car accidents from an insurance company's records.

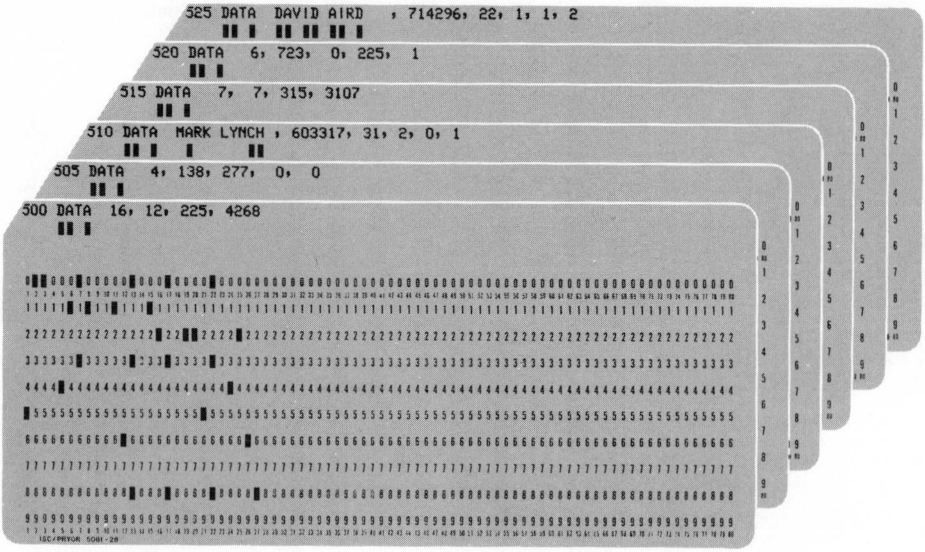

FIGURE 6-4.4 **The card information for two accidents.**

A much better approach involves putting the numbers into groups first. If the test scores range from 0 to 1000, one could go through the tests and put all the 900's together, all the 800's together, and so forth. Then one can go through each of these 10 groups and put all the 90's together, all the 80's together, and so forth. Finally one can make a third pass through the groups (there are now a hundred of them) and put all the 9's together, the 8's together, and so forth. At the end the test scores are in order.

If one had 2000 scores, this second scheme would result in 6000 examinations of test scores. Each score is handled three times. The first scheme would involve about 2,000,000 examinations of test scores.

Another frequent fault in beginners' programs is confusion in the logical statements. A symptom of this is excessive use of IF-THEN's and GO TO's. Excess, of course, is to be judged in view of the task at hand. Note that the nature of Basic is such that one uses GO TO's with considerable frequency. As an example of how bad things can be (and often are), consider a computation where $Z = 4*X + Y$, but Y is to be increased by 1 if X is zero or positive. Two program segments are shown for this; the one on the left is clearly poorly constructed.

```
 10 IF X>0 THEN 70              10 IF X<0 THEN 30
 20 IF X=0 THEN 60              20 LET Y = Y+1
 30 IF X<0 THEN 40              30 LET Z = 4*X+Y
 40 LET Z = 4*X+Y               40 REM   *** PROGRAM CONTINUES ***
 50      GO TO 100
 60 GO TO 70
 70 LET Y = Y+1
 80 LET Z = 4*X+Y
100 REM    *** PROGRAM CONTINUES ***
```

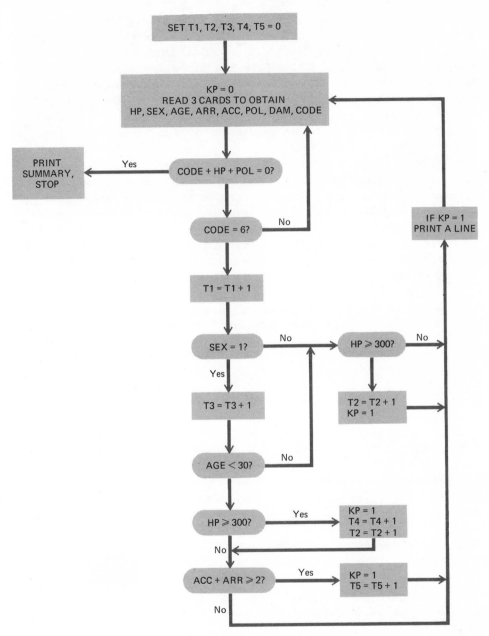

FIGURE 6-4.5 **An alternate organization of the processing the insurance company's accident record file.**

A construction like that on the left above, results in programs that are hard to understand. Any confusion in the logic will, of course, have the same effect. Other direct causes of unintelligibility are: random numbering of statements, no comments, and unnatural names of variables. Last, but not least, of the sources of lack of clarity are programming tricks (intentional or otherwise) that accomplish the desired results in an unnatural or obscure way. Some programmers pride themselves on being able to write programs that do unexpected things, but this can cause real difficulties when these programmers must work with other programmers or when a change in the computer system stops their trick from working.

All of the discussion of this section relates in one way or another to *programming style*. It has been recognized that there are good and bad styles in programming just as there are in writing and speaking. Beginning programmers normally have very poor style (or programming habits) and some people never learn good style. One might believe that style in programming is just a cosmetic or aesthetic factor of little importance. That is not true, good programming style leads to faster and more reliable programming. There is a difference factor of 10 or more among the efficiencies in a typical group of programmers with comparable training and experience. This difference can be attributed partly to style; every person who steadily does programming should continually question and criticize his own style. He should ask himself: Have I made it clear what I am doing? Have I done this neatly and efficiently or have I just thrown some statments together which somehow work? There are many aspects of style beyond those mentioned here and once a basic ability in programming has been achieved, the next step is to acquire good style.

PROBLEMS

6-4.1   Consider a set of punched cards with the following information on each card:

(a)   Five test scores,
(b)   A student ID number.

Write a program which does the following:

(a)   Prints out the information on the cards and the average test score for each card.
(b)   After all cards are read, print out the average for each of the five tests and the average of the students' averages.

Assume that there are N (also read in) cards and supply appropriate headings and messages in the printed output.

6-4.2   A department store keeps its records of sales made in each department on punched cards. Each card contains the following information:

(a)   Department code (3 digits),
(b)   Date (in the form 2,16,72 for February 16, 1972).
(c)   Sales for the date (that is, dollars and cents).

Write a program that processes these cards and produces the following information:

(a)   Total monthly sales for each department,

(b)   Daily total sales for the store. Arrange the cards so that all cards of the same date are together.

(c)   Total monthly sales for the department store.

(d)   Sales tax to be paid to the state (3 percent of sales).

(e)   Sales tax to be paid to the city (½ percent of sales).

Each of these items is to be printed on one line with an appropriate identifying message. For one test run assumes there are only 3 departments (codes 1 to 3) and 20 days of selling. For a second test run assume that there are 31 departments and 2 days of selling. You are to invent appropriate data for the program to process.

6-4.3   Assume that you are the registrar of a small college. For each student enrolled you have a deck of cards of the following types:

Type 1:   ID number
          Class
          Major
          Number of courses, N

Type 2:   (one card for each course, all behind the Type 1 card)
          Department code
          Course number
          Credits hours

The last card is identified by a student number of -1.

You want a program that computes the tuition for each student, the total tuition to be collected, and the number of regular students. The tuition if $60.00 per credit hour up to 11 hours. The tuition for 12 or more hours is $720.00 and a student is called a regular student if he pays this full tuition. Write a program that processes these cards and produces the desired information. Give appropriate headings and messages for the printed output. Make a test run for 10 students who are enrolled in 1 to 5 courses with total credit hours ranging from 3 to 18.

6-4.4   Write a program that processes the same data as in Problem 6-4.3 but which produces a list of the number of students enrolled in the courses in the college. Assume, for a test run, that there are 4 different departments each giving 4 different courses.

6-4.5   The results of a 10-question true-false test have been punched on cards along with each student's ID number. The answers are encoded with 1 for a "true" and zero for a "false." The first card in the deck has the correct answers, the last card has a 2 as the first number. Write a program which reads this deck of cards and produces the following output:

(a)   The number of correct responses for each student (along with his ID number).
(b)   The percentage of correct answers for each question.

The output should have appropriate headings and messages.

6-4.6   Suppose you are going to Las Vegas to gamble. Each day you gamble you expect to lose about 10 percent of the money you have that morning. On your last day you set aside enough money for the fare home and play roulette at high stakes for one hour, then quit. The fare home is $275 and your expenses are about $30 per day.

(a)   You want to determine the amount of money you should take with you for a 10-day visit so that you can expect to have $500 left to play roulette with on the last day.
(b)   Suppose you take your wife or husband with you. Your expenses become $50 per day and the fare home is $500. Each day you let your spouse gamble with half the money you have over $1200. You expect your spouse to lose 25 percent of this money each day. You want to determine the amount of money you should take for the visit of Part A.

In the process of solving this problem you are to write a subprogram which computes a variable R whose value is the amount that remains at the end of the last day if the amount of money you take is T. Write such a subprogram for each case and run it with a main program and show that it works.

6-4.7   (*Random number generation*) Consider the numbers between 1 and 100,000. A number is said to be chosen randomly from this set of numbers if any of the numbers is equally likely to be chosen. A number of important computer applications require choosing many random numbers from a specified set of numbers. Such algorithms are called random number generators. One of the simplest schemes to generate a sequence of random numbers is as follows. Call the random numbers R_i, i = 1,2,... and set

$$R_1 = A$$

$$R_{i+1} = C*R_i \bmod(B) .$$

Recall from algebra that $x \bmod(B)$ is the remainder when x is divided by B. Examples are $431 \bmod(100) = 31$, $2 \bmod(6) = 2$, $7 \bmod(3) = 1$, $19 \bmod(5) = 4$. The algorithm depends on the three constants A, B, and C. The choices

$$A = 61, \quad B = 100,000, \quad C = 91,$$

are suitable to generate a few thousand random numbers between 0 and 100,000.

(a)   The procedure $x \bmod(B)$ is not an elementary Basic operation. Give a method to compute $x \bmod(B)$ in Basic.
(b)   Use the method of part A to construct an algorithm to generate a set of K random numbers.

6-4.8   Suppose you have an algorithm to generate random numbers between 0 and 100,000. Show how it can be modified to generate random numbers between any two values A and B. Give a flowchart for your algorithm. *Hint*: If R is between 0 and 100,000 then R*.1 and R − 50,000 are between 0 and 10,000 and between −50,000 and 50,000, respectively.

6-5   PROGRAM DEBUGGING AND TESTING

This section presents a selection of ideas and techniques that have proved useful in debugging and testing programs. The selection starts with the simpler and more common approaches, but there is little systematic organization in these techniques. They make up a "bag of tools" that a programmer learns how to use as he becomes more proficient. There are two points for the beginner to keep in mind as he faces the seemingly endless frustration of program errors:

1. Experience plays an important role in debugging ability. One sees a problem and reflects on situations where a similar problem has occurred. Professional programmers with 20 years of experience should still be perfecting their ability in this respect.
2. Some bugs are *extremely* difficult to find. There are instances where teams of expert programmers have spent weeks and months to locate a single bug. About 99 percent of the bugs in a beginners program are simple and easy to locate (for a professional). Occasionally, however, you may have a bug which cannot be located by a beginner. The beginner (or the professional, for that matter) should not hesitate to ask for help after he has spent a reasonable effort on locating a bug. Later we discuss how merely asking for help can locate a bug—even when no help is received!

Diagnostics and Consulting Services

A translation program that encounters an error issues diagnostics which indicate what it thought about the error. A mark of a good translator is good diagnostics. Language translators exist which may, at the bottom of the program, state "ERROR IN TRANSLATION." Such a message is no clue at all as to the error in the program. A good diagnostic is something like:

| "UNBALANCED PARENTHESIS" | for example | 6.2/(X+1.5 |
| "ILLEGAL CONSTANT" | for example | X + 17.032.96 |

These immediately tell the programmer what to look for and the errors are quickly removed. A good diagnostic also indicates the statement containing the error.

Unfortunately, there is no hope of having a language translator that always gives the correct diagnostic message. A program may have so many errors that the translator becomes "confused" and issues diagnostics that are wrong or even where no errors exist. A high quality translator is not easily "confused" by a multitude of errors.

Even more unfortunately, there are translator's in common use which give unreliable diagnostics. For example, it might report "ILLEGAL CONSTANT" every time that parentheses are unbalanced. Or it might report "MISSING FVD COMPONENT" (which is meaningless to everyone but the programmer of the translator) whenever an equal sign is left out of an assignment statement.

The net result of this situation is that someone who makes steady use of a computer system must learn how to interpret the language translator diagnostics.

Most computing centers of any size maintain some kind of consulting service, primarily for beginning or casual programmers. One of their strong points is in the explanation of diagnostics. They see them day after day and have learned that "MISSING FVD CONSTANT" means an equal sign is left out and that "ERROR 00078" means that one tried to read a nonexistent card. One can expect consultants to quickly locate the more common kinds of errors, but one can also only expect limited help for more difficult errors. Consultants can rarely spend an hour or two in studying a program in order to understand its overall operation and this is frequently required before difficult bugs are located.

One of the most fruitful strategies for "consulting" is to become a member of an informal group involved in programming. This group might consist of several students on the same floor of an apartment, or a group that gathers around the coffee machine in late afternoon. If this group includes a few people with a genuine interest in programming and even a little bit of knowledge, it can be a very useful education and consulting organization.

Techniques for Locating a Program Bug

The day soon comes (it is usually about the second or third day after all the diagnostics are gone) when one has a bug that one must find himself. We now consider three important techniques for locating a program bug. They are intermediate output, test of simple cases, and hand calculations. The most important of the three is the first.

INTERMEDIATE OUTPUT. A program is normally written to solve a problem and output the answer. If a program is producing incorrect answers, then the error in the method or algorithm must be located. Of course, the current program should be studied to verify that a blunder has not been made. In theory all errors can be located by reading the program, but many errors are very difficult to locate this way.

A much more efficient way is to request intermediate (and temporary) output at several key points in the program. These print statements are removed after the program is debugged. The variables printed should be such that the programmer has some idea of what their value should be. Then he can, hopefully, detect where the incorrect values first occur and narrow the search for the location of the bug or error. If this technique does not succeed at first, he should increase the number of places where variables are written out. This approach is something like the game of 20 questions; the idea is to continually narrow down the location of the error. It is not unheard of in complicated programs to have 10 or 20 pages of intermediate and debugging output when the final program has only a single page of output. Fortunately, most bugs can usually be located with just a little intermediate output.

The usefulness and importance of this technique is illustrated by the fact that many instructors in computing courses refuse to examine a program until the student has inserted a reasonable amount of intermediate output. Furthermore, they often insist that the initial data (if any) read in also be printed out. It is unwise to assume the data punched on cards or typed-in are entered correctly unless this is verified by a print-out.

SIMPLE CASES. The idea behind this technique is to choose special cases with one or more of the following properties:

1. A number of parts of the program are not used.
2. The programmer already knows what all of the intermediate results should be.
3. He knows the answer to the problem from an independent source.

Each of these properties can be an aid in detecting errors in a program. The third property merely allows the programmer to check for the existence of an error somewhere. The other two properties are helpful in isolating the location of the error, particularly if the programmer has some intermediate output.

HAND CALCULATION. Hand calculation means that the programmer goes through the program step by step. At each step he performs the necessary calculations (a slide rule is usually accurate enough) and records the values of all of the pertinent variables. The objective is not to check on the arithmetic of the computer, which is almost infalliable, but to force the programmer to focus his attention on each detail of the program. A secondary objective is to obtain a complete set of intermediate output.

Because this technique is time consuming and tedious, it is often used only as a last resort. Neverthless there are times when it is the proper thing to do. The usual result of such a calculation is that the programmer suddenly recognizes that the program says to do the wrong thing. The error frequently occurs in a statement that has been examined a number of times and verified as correct each time. After a statement has been accepted as correct once or twice, it seems that the mind is unable to examine it critically any longer.

We see that the hand calculation is primarily a psychological technique. The human mind has a great (and extremely useful) facility to see things as they should be rather than as they are. Thus, for example $(X+Y^2)$ and PR1NT are read as $(X+Y)^2$ and PRINT. Two techniques to overcome this psychological difficulty are offered.

READ THE PROGRAM BACKWARDS. The mind manages to correct the errors present because it knows what should appear. When one reads a program backwards, the mind becomes somewhat disoriented and has to examine what is actually printed. Unfortunately, this technique is only beneficial the first time and, if one has read the program many times, the mind can quickly accommodate itself to reading it backwards.

EXPLAIN THE TROUBLE TO SOMEONE ELSE. The scene should go something like this:

> "Hey, Joe, would you look at this cotton-picking program. It always comes up with over 390 days in a year." Joe listens patiently for a few minutes, asks a few unhelpful questions and finally says: "How about this statement, it might be that you didn't get the number of days in February right. Did you add a day for leap years"? You reply "Sure, I did. Look, right up here I check to see if the year is divisible by 4 and then . . . I . . . add. Blast it all, I added a month instead of a day!"

You had probably looked at the calculation of the leap year several times. After all, you expect that to be a little tricky. You now have it in your mind that this is done correctly and your mind ignores what the program actually says. Now, however, you have to *prove* to Joe that you did it right and you have to point out how you did *each step* right. Of course, it is then that you see the step that is not right.

Infinite Loops that Cause No Output

A fairly frequent problem is to have a program returned which ran out of time and which failed to print a single thing. An infinite iteration loop, of course, is the primary cause of programs running out of time and yet many people find it hard to accept this possibility. They say that either they do not have any loops or they are not infinite. Frequently the offending loop can be located by simply stating: "I know there is an infinite loop there somewhere, now let's find it." This positive approach soon leads to the solution of the problem.

The next step is to put an *intermediate output* statement in each loop that simply prints the number of times the iteration is performed.

One very puzzling situation occurs when the very first statement of a program, should write two lines and yet the program has run out of time and written no output. This can occur as follows: The output of the program is placed in a temporary place (called a *buffer*) which holds, say, up to 10 lines of output. Whenever this place is full, the 10 lines are then sent out to the standard output route. A frequent defect in computer operating systems is that they fail to process this output buffer correctly *when* the program stops abnormally. So, in our case, the two lines of output are placed in the buffer, the infinite loop is entered, and the program stops abnormally because it ran out of time. The friendly operating system discards the buffer and the programmer cannot imagine what happened. Note that putting in the intermediate output statements will fill the buffer up and the programmer will obtain some output.

The above situation is something that should never have to be explained to a user of a higher level language. He should not need to know that such a buffer exists (never mind how or why it is used), but, alas, we still have not perfected computer systems completely. So one must be prepared for programs to operate in an unexpected, or even apparently impossible way, especially if we know that there is something wrong with the program.

Hidden Error Sources

One of the features of difficult bugs is that the error is in one place and the trouble appears in a completely different place. Fortunately for beginning programmers, these errors usually arise in long, complex programs using advanced language features. One does not write such programs to begin with, so these bugs are uncommon (but not unheard of) in beginning courses. A simple situation where this can occur involves a program with two parts which we call PART1 and PART2. The "flow" of the computation is as follows:

Read Control Variable Values
Read Data Set #1
Do PART1
Do PART2
Read Data Set #2
Do PART1
Do PART2
Read Data Set #3
. . . .

The program now operates as follows: Data Set #1 is read, processed, and the correct output appears. Data Set #2 is read, the processing stops in the middle of PART1 and the output that does appear is "garbage." So, there must be something wrong in the middle of PART1.

More runs are made, always with the same result. The first data set is correctly processed and the program fails on the second. Furthermore, the place at which it fails changes from run to run, but it always fails.

This error may be located in PART2. Suppose the control variable V is read in at the start and immediately printed back out so we know it is correct. Suppose now in PART2 that one has a variable V1 used in collecting information to be printed in the summary after all the data sets are finished. You want to have

$$V1 = X + Y$$

where X and Y are part of the data set, but, due to a keypunch error you actually have

$$V = X + Y$$

The fact that V1 is incorrect does not show up until the end of the run. But, before that occurs, the value of V is changed and when it is used in PART1 it causes the program to "blow up."

No amount of checking of PART1 will locate this bug because PART1 is perfectly correct. The bug will be located only when one reflects: "PART1 appears to be correct, but it isn't. So, there must be something wrong somewhere else that is affecting PART1. Now what could that be?" Note that the liberal use of intermediate output is a good aid in locating this bug. One might choose to see V itself or something which is simply related to V. Once one realizes that the value of V has been changed, then one merely searches the program to find where the change occurs.

This example is one of the simplest ways in which the error source can be hidden. In a complex program the error can be hidden so well that it takes considerable searching by a crew from Scotland Yard headed by Sherlock Holmes himself in order to unravel the mystery.

Think. What Will This Change Do?

One of the common weaknesses in beginner's debugging is the tendency to change something, almost anything, and submit the program again. Unfortunately, this tendency is encouraged by the fact that it sometimes works. An unrecognized error in a statement is often removed just by rewriting the statement in some slightly different way. The effectiveness of this approach is low and it should be avoided.

It is easy to say that one should think through the effects of a change about to be made. This is asking a lot of a programmer who is unsure of many aspects of programming, computing, and his problem. The beginning programmer is, of course, usually in this situation. Nevertheless, one should specifically and consciously ask oneself what a particular change is going to do. If one is completely unclear, it is time to ask for some help, read the text again, analyze the problem some more, or take some other positive action.

Debugging Versus Testing

So far we have concentrated on one kind of testing—that which is needed to locate errors in a program. The simple programs in a beginning course have a very nice property: *They are either correct or they have bugs in them.* Once all the bugs are removed, we have a correct program. As one becomes involved in more sophisticated computer applications, one sees that this situation disappears. There are two reasons for this:

1. One does not know what the program is supposed to produce and it is not possible to say whether a particular result is correct or not.
2. The program is so long and so complex that one cannot hope to remove all the bugs. One merely hopes to remove all of the "bad" ones and bring the level of performance of the program up to a useful level.

The topic of program testing in general is beyond the scope of this book, but we can illustrate these reasons for an example. Consider two programs:

Program TICTAC: Its objective is to play Tic-Tac-Toe with a person via some kind of interactive system.

Program CHESS: Its objective is to play chess with a person via some kind of interactive system.

The program CHESS clearly should be much more complicated than TICTAC, but even TICTAC requires a reasonable effort. Now we know (see Chapter 4) a strategy to play Tic-Tac-Toe that never loses. Thus we are not satisfied with TICTAC until it is "perfect." If it loses or fails to win when it has a chance, then the program has a bug in it.

No such strategy is known for chess and thus most moves that CHESS makes cannot be judged as correct or incorrect. The effectiveness or quality of the program CHESS is measured by its won-loss record for a large number of games. Imagine now that at one point in the program, one wanted to set X equal to K+1 but, instead, one has X equal to K-1. If this is in a sensitive part of the program, this error might cause CHESS to lose almost all games. This then, is a "bad" bug and must be removed before CHESS is acceptable.

On the other hand, this error might be in part of CHESS that examines special situations, ones that arise in only 2 percent of the chess games played. Now, even if this error causes an immediate loss of the game, it only affects 2 percent of the games. It requires considerable experience with CHESS just to suspect that this bug exists. Suppose that this error merely causes a different choice of move out of five reasonable moves in this special situation. It might now take a careful analysis of thousands of games to detect this error. Indeed, it might well be that this erroneous choice is better than the one the programmer intended!

Complex programs like CHESS can run to 5,000 or 20,000 or even 50,000 statements. There is very little hope to remove *all* the errors in these statements. Such programs are so complex that a bug might lead to erroneous results in only one out of a million times the program is used. This means the program could be used steadily (10 times a day for 20 years) and the chances of this bug *ever* appearing are about one out of fifteen.

Testing, then, is the overall evaluation of a program performance. There are many points in a complex program where equally reasonable choices could be made. Even if the "best" choice is not made, one does not consider this a bug. Testing includes the evaluation of these alternative choices. A program can be well-tested, useful, and productive and still have bugs in it, perhaps dozens of them. Such bugs must be such that either they appear very rarely or their effect is almost always very minor.

The main sources of error in programs are listed below. The list begins with the most frequent and ends with the least frequent.

> Blunders and keypunch errors
> Faulty method
> Faulty use of programming language
> Data incorrect or in the wrong order
> Error in the language translator
> Error in operating system
> Machine error.

Errors in language translators and operating systems are very infrequent in most computing centers, even though programmers have a natural tendency to blame their troubles on the computing center. Before jumping to conclusions, the programmer should pin down the supposed error with a special test program that clearly shows the presence of an error.

Machine errors are extremely rare and can be checked by rerunning the identical program. If an automobile were as reliable as an average computer, car trouble would be so rare that few people would have car trouble at any time in their life. If the failure rate in a computer were one out of a billion operations, then machine errors would occur about *a hundred times a second*. A computer may do only a million instructions a second, but each instruction involves on the order of 100 different operations by the computer. The actual failure rate is something like one out of 50 quadrillion operations. Such reliability is possible only with electronic devices.

7 *Problem Solving and Computers*

7-1 INTRODUCTION

There is a natural tendency, especially for beginners, to become very engrossed in the programming process and to overlook the other aspects of problem solving. The aim of this chapter is to discuss how computers fit into the overall problem-solving process along with the other important parts. These parts are: precise formulation of the problem, construction of a *mathematical model*, construction of an *algorithm* and corresponding program, and *evaluation* of the validity of this model. This chapter concentrates on the formulation, the model, and its evaluation. Each of the steps must be done well or the results will be poor. Furthermore, one cannot compensate for an inadequate mathematical model by doing a superb programming job. Conversely, a superb mathematical model can be made useless if not adequately translated into a program.

Occasionally there are highly publicized examples of horrible "goofs" by computers. In almost all cases, the mistakes are made by people, not by computers. It is, of course, much easier to blame the computer. In many instances the mistakes are not even in the "using the computer" phase of problem solving at all. They occur, rather, in an *incorrect* formulation of the problem or in an *incomplete* mathematical model. The fact that these errors occur usually indicates that there has been *inadequate* testing and evaluation of the resulting programs. It is almost impossible to have complete testing of a large and complex program, but in some instances almost no testing is done. It is similar to building a car from scratch, then driving it around the block in low gear and reporting that it is all checked out and working perfectly.

7-2 PROBLEMS AND MATHEMATICAL MODELS

Most problems go through five main stages. They are:

1. Precise formulation,
2. Construction and analysis of a mathematical model,
3. Development of a method to solve the problem,
4. Computation of a solution,
5. Analysis of results.

A more detailed breakdown is given at the end of Section 7-4. The first stage is often *not* mentioned in the classroom or in textbooks. The development of the mathematical model is a common part of an instructor's lectures. Usually the instructor/lecturer concentrates on the third and fourth points, which make up what we would call "problem solving."

These five stages occur in all problems, from way-out scientific problems to common, everyday problems. In the first stage we recognize that something needs to be done, and we try to define it exactly. Then we consider some cause-and-effect assumptions—"if I do this, then that will happen." These assumptions are the basis for the mathematical model even though they might in fact be very unscientific rules of thumb, or wishful thinking. Nevertheless we begin to mull these things over in our minds and analyze the various possibilities. This analysis can be considered a systematic analysis even though it might actually be illogical and unmathematical. Most people do not want to do any computation so that such calculations are usually reserved for the solution of financial problems.

One of the greatest sources of difficulty is understanding the nature of the problem. Frequently this understanding is the key to solving the problem. One might expect this to be true in some "nonscientific" areas such as personal relationships, juvenile delinquency, and poverty, but, it is also true in the supposedly well-determined, formalized, scientific and engineering areas. It is a common experience of consultants (supposedly hired to help solve problems) to discover that people who bring them a problem actually do not know what the problem is. There is probably no single method for obtaining a precisely formulated problem from a vaguely formulated one, but it is important to be aware of this aspect of problem solving. A person should first try to express in clear terms exactly what must be done. If one experiences difficulty in attacking a problem, it might indicate that the problem is not yet clearly stated.

The development of the mathematical model involves two distinct parts. The first is the identification of the pertinent and important variables in the problem; the second is the identification of relationships between these variables and the solution of the problem. In many business applications, these relationships are the results of tax laws, accounting principles, company operating policies, and so forth. The variables identified here are the basic pieces of data that go into the problem. These might be, for example, rates of pay, interest rates, equipment costs and depreciation rates, inventory levels, and so forth. In most scientific areas the relationships are the various laws of physics, chemistry, and so on. In the "well-understood" areas of science, the identification of these variables and their relationships is standard, and much of the early training of scientists consists in their becoming familiar with standard mathematical models.

Problems tend to be one of two kinds based on whether or not the model is known. In the first kind, the important variables are known and the relationships are clearly specified. That is, the mathematical model is well understood and obtaining the required answers to the problem is what is called for. Typical examples of this kind of problem are:

1   computations for the company's payroll checks,
2   preparation of invoices,
3   calculation of repayment schedules for loans,
4   calculation of tables of freight shipment rates,
5   calculation of the load that a simple bridge of standard design will support.

One could view these problems as completely solved except for organizing and carrying out the actual calculations.

In the other kind of problem, by far the most common one, the important variables and relationships are not yet clearly identified and understood. The work at the frontiers of scientific study is primarily concerned with understanding these relationships. Thus the economist investigates, for example, the relationship between unemployment, interest rates, and inflation. The management scientist investigates, for example, the relationship between advertizing strategy and sales. The agronomist investigates the relationship between various fertilizers and crop yields. The geologist studies the relationship between terrain features and mineral or petroleum deposits. It is easy to visualize these studies at the frontiers, but not so easy to see that many common, ordinary problems are also of this kind. Typical examples are:

1. How does one efficiently organize the data and computations for a company payroll?
2. How does one efficiently keep track of the accounts receivable and prepare the bills to be mailed out.
3. How does a florist decide how much new capital is required for him to open up a branch florist shop?
4. How does one decide whether the extra speed of air freight delivery is worth the extra cost?
5. How does an engineer decide whether to use two large bolts or three smaller bolts at a particular place in a piece of machinery?

Problems such as these are really difficult and similar ones occur over and over again in every kind of activity. It is important to realize that the most difficult part of these problems is the identification of important variables and relationships. Note that most of these problems are not "solved" in the ordinary sense and the successful problem solver is the one who can consistently make good guesses at their solution.

Once the problem is precisely stated and reduced to a set of exact relationships and equations we have a mathematical model for the problem. Then we can do some systematic analysis. That is, we can apply the various procedures and rules of logical reasoning in an effort to bring the problem (as represented by the mathematical model) into a more understandable form. The amount of analysis varies from almost nothing to volumes.

There are two principal goals at this point. The first is to simplify the mathematical model until a form is reached from which the solution may be obtained. The second goal—often more important—is to obtain a simple form of the problem so that the mind can grasp the mechanism by which the variables influence the solution.

Last, but not least, is the calculation of specific answers. Here, numerical, or actual, values (for example, 1.625) of the variables are used, whereas symbolic names (for example, X, Y) might have been used earlier. Computing machines have enormously increased the amount of computation that can reasonably be done making many previously unsolvable problems solvable.

It is important to have a clear picture of the relationship between the real world and the mathematical models of it. This relationship is simply illustrated in the following diagram:

$$\text{Real World} \atop \text{Problem} \quad \xleftrightarrow{\text{Idealizations}} \quad \text{Mathematical} \atop \text{Model}$$

One of the effects of the high computational power of computers now available is that we can (and do) perform computations involving complex mathematical models. This activity is interesting and well defined; that is, we have a self-contained, complete, explicitly stated problem (to find answers from the mathematical model) and we can go to work on it. Sometimes people become so engrossed in this phase of problem solving that they lose sight of the inaccuracy of the mathematical model. Thus, there is a real danger of expending considerable effort on obtaining the solution to the mathematical model to a much greater accuracy than the model represents the real world.

The last two sections of this chapter present mathematical models of fairly complex situations. One purpose of these sections is to show how a computer program is constructed, but they also show many of the difficulties in constructing mathematical models. Indeed, there is a very close relationship between programs and mathematical models. Frequently the computer program is the *only* place where *all* the details are specified about variables, assumptions, and relationships.

EXAMPLE 7-1

A Mathematical Model for Depreciation

A fact that one learns soon in life is that automobiles are worth less as they become older; they *depreciate*. A common rule of thumb for this depreciation is "the value decreases 30 percent a year." If V_0 denotes the original cost of the car, then during the first year its value decreases by $.3V_0$. So, at the end of the year, its value is $V_0 - .3V_0 = .7V_0$. At the end of the second year, its value is $.7 (.7V_0) = (.7)^2 V_0$; at the end of the third year, its value is $.7 (.7^2 V_0) = (.7)^3 V_0$; and so forth. With V_N denoting the value of the car at the end of the N-th year, we have

$$V_N = .7^N V_0.$$

This last equation is a mathematical model of depreciation.

Suppose you buy a car for $3240 and keep it for five years. This mathematical model says that the car's value V_5 is

$$V_5 = (.7)^5 * 3240 = .16807 * 3240 = \$545.$$

Now if you actually try to sell this car, you may find that it is only worth $475 or perhaps $600. In any case, it is not likely to be worth exactly $545 since the value predicted by this mathematical model is only approximate because our model is only an idealization of the actual depreciation of automobiles.

We remark that the model $V_N = .7^N V_0$ can be expressed in slightly different notation, that is, $V(N) = .7^N V(0)$. The use of $V(N)$ for V_N is the Basic language notation for a variable with a subscript (see Chapter 8).

EXAMPLE 7-2

A Mathematical Model for Motion

One of the most famous examples of a mathematical model is Newton's law of motion, which is often expressed as "force is equal to mass times acceleration." The mathematical expression of this law is

$$f = ma.$$

Here f stands for *force*, m for *mass*, and a for *acceleration*.

We now know that this relation is only approximate, for the theory of relativity says that there are other factors that enter into the situation. And who is to say whether there are yet other effects that are not taken into account by the theory of relativity?

Newton's law is introduced in elementary physics courses, and one of the standard problems that students are asked to solve is the "rock-throwing" or "rock-falling" problem. This application involves additional idealization about the real world. Consider the specific problem: A rock is released from a 1000-foot-high tower and the force of gravity makes it fall. How long does it take to fall to the ground? We find from Newton's law and experiment that the force of gravity per unit mass results in an acceleration of 32 feet per second per second. By a little bit of analysis we find that the *distance d* it travels in *time t* with constant *acceleration a* is given by the formula

$$d = \frac{at^2}{2}.$$

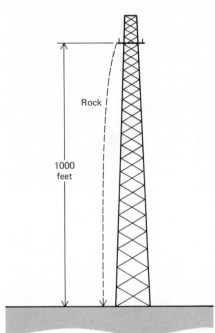

In this example we know that d = 1000 and a = 32. Thus we find that the time of fall t is

$$t = \sqrt{\frac{2000}{32}} = 7.9 \text{ seconds.}$$

Now if we actually drop a rock from a 1000-foot-high tower and measure the time of fall, we find that it is more than 7.9 seconds. Our mathematical model does not include the effects of air resistance. The error is not in Newton's law, but in our neglect of this factor which significantly influences the motion. By neglecting the air resistance we used the wrong force. Thus this idealized mathematical model is too crude to give accurate results of the real world problem of falling objects; if the rock were dropped 1000 feet in a vacuum, then the model would give an accurate result.

7-3 COMPUTERS IN THE PROBLEM-SOLVING PROCESS

It is easy to see how computers are involved in the problem solving process—because they can compute answers. However, there are other ways that computers affect problem solving and these actually have a much greater impact.

First, beyond computing faster and more reliably, the power of the computer allows one to do less systematic mathematical analysis. In the past, much of the effort in the analysis was aimed at obtaining a form of the mathematical model where the calculation of the answers would be simple. Now one need not spend so much effort on analysis which simply reduces the calculations. But, there is another aim of mathematical analysis, to gain insight and understanding, which is not affected by this use of computers.

Much more significant is the fact that one can attack and handle more complicated mathematical models. In the past, one often had to make certain assumptions and idealizations simply to reduce the computational work, to get any answers at all. Now, people can and do attempt to obtain solutions from mathematical models that are very complex. Thus a simple listing of the variables involved, the assumptions made, and the equations, relationships, and tables used, might well make up a report of 50 or more pages.

The idea of a mathematical model is not widespread and it probably is unfamiliar to most readers of this text. Thus this discussion might seem vague and fuzzy. However, the idea of a mathematical model is so important in the study of computing that it should be introduced early and mentioned frequently. As the reader further studies computing, he should keep two questions in mind: What is the mathematical model here? What assumptions have been made? Note that in computing there will always be at least one form of the mathematical model: the computer program. The computer program contains all of the variables, the assumptions, and the relationships of the mathematical model. Programs are not so easy to read and a great deal of the difficulty in computing comes from small assumptions (made while writing the computer program) which are either incorrect or unknown to the users of the program. This is particularly apt to occur if there is not a complete formulation of the mathematical model in a more readable form. Of course, one rarely makes a formal mathematical model for a short program, but many programs (especially the more important ones) are long and complicated and one needs a formal listing of the variables, assumptions, and relationships in order to really understand what is going on.

There is yet another significant result of using computers. Even though we have just stressed the importance of making a mathematical model, it is frequently not done even in important projects. We can view the model as a complete description of what the computer program is to do and thus the absence of a model means that the writer of the computer program will also make part of the model. These parts are usually small, but there have been occasions where important company policy decisions were made by a relatively junior person who happened to be writing the relevant computer programs.

Here are two examples of applications of computers and what effects might result.

EXAMPLE 7-3.

Putting the Company Payroll on the Computer

The calculations for a company payroll are probably the most straightforward and well practiced in the whole company. After all, the payroll department has been issuing the checks every week or month for years. When management is considering using a computer for the payroll, they are concerned with comparing the costs of doing it by hand with the costs of doing it by computer. The analysis of these costs varies from company to company (one might even write a computer program to help in the analysis), but medium and large companies all seem to conclude that it is cheaper to do it on a computer. Once the decision is made, management tells the chief accountant to do it, the chief accountant tells the head payroll clerk to do it, and assigns a programmer to help out. No one expects that company policy decisions need to be made or that explicit requirements for the payroll program need to be considered by management. They simply want the program to do the same thing that is being done by hand and they feel that is all that needs to be said.

They are correct for the 99 percent of the checks that are routine, but the other 1 percent lead to complications. These special cases are usually referred to someone in authority and some action is taken to handle this specific case. This action can vary and involves modifying records, waiving requirements and rules, and so forth. Many of these actions are much more difficult in the computer program. After all, the rules and requirements are incorporated in the program and most programs have no provisions to "suspend" these rules. The result is that the person who writes the program makes critical decisions (often without realizing it) for the 1 percent or so of the cases that require special handling.

It is unlikely that anyone in management would authorize (or even allow) the company to withhold more Social Security taxes in a year than is required by law. Yet this happened to one of the authors of this book in the amount of 4¢. It turned out that this happened to about half of his fellow employees in amounts of 1¢ to 5¢ (the company never took out too little). This never should have occurred but some programmer was careless in writing the part of the program that deducts these taxes. Moreover, a complaint to the payroll department had no effect because they had no provisions in their programs to correct such an error (which, of course, they had never believed would happen). The payroll department's reply to the complaint was that one could get the 4¢ refunded from the government when one filed his income tax return. Most people have enough trouble with this tax return without trying to figure out how to get 4¢ back, so they just forget it. In giant companies with hundreds of thousands of employees, the extra amount taken out might total as much as $20,000. We wonder who gets the $20,000 per year, the company or the government?

EXAMPLE 7-4.

Putting Inventory Control on the Computer

Imagine a company warehouse that stocks several hundred different items. There is someone who is in charge and who, in particular, decides when to order new items when the stocks get low. Now this company has all its records about deliveries to and from the warehouse already in the computer. Thus one can write a program that figures out how much of each item is in the warehouse and that initiates a new purchase order when the stock of certain items gets low. Now consider what the computer programmer will do when he writes this program.

He needs to know at what level to reorder supplies and how long delivery takes. He gets this information from the man in charge of the warehouse and the scene is something like this:

"OK", says the programmer, "when do you reorder size #8 round head bolts?"

The warehouse manager thinks a moment, then replies, "When we have only 15 cases left." (Actually, he reorders whenever that bin looks almost empty.)

"How long does it take you to get the order?"

"Well, we get them in 6 or 7 days. Never more than 10 days. Why don't you put down 10 days to be safe."

So the programmer incorporates in his program:

reorder level of size #8 round head bolts = 15 cases
delivery time = 10 days.

Things go well until the company's main assembly line is shut down for four days because they ran out of #8 round head bolts.

The resulting investigation leads to transfers, demotions, and lots of loud talk, but not to the reason the shutdown occurred. In fact, the bins look empty to the warehouse manager when 18 or 20 cases are left, not 15 as he had guessed. Furthermore, because of August vacations and the Labor Day holiday, it took 13 days to get the new order of bolts. The manager always took this slow period into account in his reordering, but since it was January when he was talking to the programmer, it didn't come to his mind. The whole debacle is, of course, somehow blamed on the computer and the warehouse manager tells his wife, "I knew that #@!?# thing would foul it up sooner or later." It is interesting to note that this debacle will occur only when the time to reorder these bolts falls within a certain three-day period in August. Since these bolts are only ordered about twice a year, the company could have, with a little luck, used this program for 30 or 40 years without any problem. Unfortunately, this company's luck was not so good.

These two examples hopefully show that there is much more to putting things on a computer than just getting the arithmetic done faster. The implications are many and varied and often completely unforeseen.

7-4   THE SOLUTION OF A REAL PROBLEM

Let us now consider a real problem in some detail and follow through its "solution." The problem chosen is a familiar, everyday one that many people attempt to solve. It is important to realize that the textbook problems that one meets early in one's education are *not* typical of real problems. These textbook problems have usually been carefully analyzed and have almost always been simplified, broken into small pieces, and put into a precise form. They are designed to be easy to present in the classroom, rather than to be realistic. The real problem we consider now has no "standard" solution or "standard" technique of analysis.

Original Problem Statement.   How do I minimize my automobile costs?

The problem is normally stated this way, but the form is not yet precise because it has some unstated assumptions. As the problem now stands, the solution is clearly not to own an automobile.

In order to obtain a precise formulation, we explicitly state some assumptions (different people would use different assumptions here). First, we *assume* that we own an automobile at all times. Second, (for simplicity) we *assume* that we buy a new car, keep it until the "proper" time, and then buy another new car. Finally, we *choose* to measure cost by the long-term average annual cost. With these assumptions, we can state the problem in a precise, if more complicated, form.

Precise Problem Statement   How long should I keep a new car before trading it in on another new car so as to minimize my average annual cost?

We have identified the time, or the number or years, to keep the car as the unknown solution to the problem. The next stage is to identify the factors that affect the solution. The principal variable is the average annual cost. The variables that affect this cost are depreciation, operating costs (gas, oil, insurance, taxes, and so forth), and repairs. Each of these costs depends on the age and the mileage of the car. We *assume* that the car is driven 12,000 miles a year. This assumption allows us to relate operating costs and repairs to time.

The values of the variables which affect the annual cost change from year to year and, looking ahead to a computer program for solving the problem, we see that the annual cost can be computed in an iteration loop. In the Y-th iteration the costs for the Y-th year will be determined as well as the average annual cost for the first Y years.

Denote the amount of these costs by D, O, and R, for depreciation, operating expenses, and repair costs, respectively, and denote the total cost during a year by C. The first part of the mathematical model of this situation is

$$C = D + O + R$$

During each iteration, the values of D, O, and R will be determined by an appropriate mathematical model and in each iteration, C will be evaluated.

The average annual cost for the first Y years is the sum of the annual costs divided by Y. Let A denote the average annual cost. Suppose the Y-th iteration is being executed and the annual cost, C, of the Y-th year has been computed. At this point, the value of A would be the average annual cost for the first Y-1 years; it was computed during the previous iteration. To determine the sum of the costs for the first Y-1 years, we multiply A by (Y-1). Then we add the current value of C to the result to get the cost for the first Y years. Finally, we divide the result by Y to obtain the new value of A which is now the average annual cost for the first Y years. Thus, in the Basic language, this part of the mathematical model is

$$LET\ A = (C + (Y-1)*A)/Y$$

Observe that during the first iteration, when Y is equal to 1., the factor (Y-1) is equal to zero and the value of A is set equal to C, the cost for the first year.

The next step is to specify the dependence of the quantities D, O, and R, on time. Those people who have studied this problem know that it is not possible to determine such costs exactly. Thus we must assume some idealized situation in order to develop the mathematical model further. The following assumptions seem reasonable:

Depreciation   We *assume* that the depreciation in the Y-th year is 30 percent of the value of the car at the beginning of the year. We introduce V as the value of the car at the end of the Y-th year and have

$$D = .3 \, V$$

Of course, before we begin the iteration, V must be set equal to the original cost of the car.

Operating Cost   We *assume* that

$$O \; = \; 450 \quad \text{for } Y = 1 \text{ and } 2$$
$$O \; = \; 500 \quad \text{for } Y \geqslant 3$$

Repair Cost   We *assume* that

$$R \; = \; 0 \quad\;\; \text{for } Y = 1 \text{ and } 2$$
$$R \; = \; 100 \quad \text{for } Y = 3$$
$$R \; = \; 200 \quad \text{for } Y = 4 \text{ and } 5$$
$$R \; = \; 300 \quad \text{for } Y \geqslant 6$$

Our mathematical model is now complete and it consists of the equations for C and A and the three sets of assumptions for depreciation, operating cost, and repair cost.

We are interested in determining for what year (what value of Y) the average annual cost is a minimum. We start computing with Y=1 and then successively increase Y (up to some reasonable limit) and for each Y we compute the value of A. We then examine the resulting values of A for the various values of Y and select that value of Y which gives the minimum average annual cost. Thus, we have constructed an algorithm to compute the minimum cost and the best value of Y.

The only unspecified piece of data is the original value. We assume it to be $3000 and one easily obtains the following table of values for the average annual cost:

Y = Year	1	2	3	4	5	6	7	8	9	10	20	100
A = Average Annual Cost	1350	1215	1157	1120	1079	1058	1036	1016	998	982	895	819

We find that the mathematical model leads us to conclude that we should buy a car and keep it forever! This is unreasonable and indicates that some essential ingredient is missing from the mathematical model. (Note that we are analyzing the results of our model—this is the fifth of the steps itemized in Section 7-2.) In particular, now that we think of it, repair costs increase sharply at a certain point because of the unavailability of spare parts and the frequency of major repairs. We take this into account in our mathematical model by modifying out assumption about repair costs as follows: for $Y \geqslant 10$

Modified Repair Cost

$$R = 400 \quad \text{for } 11 \leqslant Y \leqslant 13$$
$$R = 600 \quad \text{for } 14 \leqslant Y \leqslant 19$$
$$R = 750 \quad \text{for } \ Y \geqslant 20.$$

This reexamination leads to the modified table of costs:

Y = Year	10	11	12	13	14	15	20	100
A = Average Annual Cost	982	976	972	967	977	986	1022	1204

Now the mathematical model leads us to conclude that we should keep a car until it is about 13 years old. Since the model is admittedly rough, we should actually conclude that somewhere between 10 and 15 years is the "optimum" time.

Almost everyone wants to minimize his cost, yet few people keep their car this long. The question is then: Is there something still wrong with the model or do people really not care this much about cost? The model described here is reasonably accurate and the reason people do not keep their cars about 13 years is that they consider factors other than money. It seems reasonable that the important missing factor is the intangible value of having a car that is

1. flashy,
2. reliable,
3. clean,
4. worry-free, and so forth

In order to have a more realistic model, we must assign a monetary value to these intangibles. Since different people have different value systems, let us assume we have three types of individuals:

Big Shot

Average Joe

Penny Pincher

We *assume* that these individuals are willing to pay a premium in order to have a newer car. We include this is our model by putting in an intangible cost, T, of owning a car that is in its Y-th year. This cost is the amount we would pay *not* to have a car that is Y years old.

Intangible Cost   We *assume* the following values for the three types of people.

	Big Shot	Average Joe	Penny Pincher
Y = 1	0	0	0
Y = 2	200	0	0
Y = 3	400	100	10
Y = 4	700	100	20
Y = 5	1000	200	30
Y = 6	1500	200	40
Y > 6	1500	200	50

The average annual costs for this new mathematical model are given as follows:

	Year									
	1	*2*	*3*	*4*	*5*	*6*	*7*	*8*	*9*	*10*
Big Shot	1350	1315	1357	1445	1539					
Average Joe	1350	1215	1190	1170	1159	1158	1150	1141		
Penny-Pincher	1350	1215	1160	1127	1091	1075	1058	1041	1025	1012

We would generally conclude from our mathematical model that a Big Shot should not keep a car more than 2 years, the Average Joe can trade his in any time he feels like it after 3 years, and the Penny-Pincher is still going to keep his car for about 12 years.

We now have a mathematical model which gives reasonable results. These results are not necessarily accurate, but this particular problem contains many unpredictable elements and it is not meaningful to talk about accurate results.

There is an interesting view of the process of adding the intangible cost to the model. This is not, of course, an actual expense in the same sense as gasoline. It is however, an indication of how much it costs not to follow the least expensive course of action. Thus we can view this analysis not as a search for the cheapest strategy, but rather as a search for how much more expensive is the strategy already chosen than the least expensive strategy. This kind of analysis can sometimes give worthwhile insight into the consequences of one's decisions.

A Basic program is given below which combines all three of the mathematical models developed for this example. There is a variable, M, which takes on values 1, 2, and 3 and, when this program is run, it selects the results for all three models. For the sake of simplicity only the intangible case of "Average Joe" is included. Note that this model, while certainly not super-simple, is much more compact and less ambiguous than the English description in the text. It is also easy (once one is familiar with the program) to modify the model in various ways.

One can visualize that this program developed in the following manner. First, the original model led to a program without statements 235 through 350 or the loop on the variable M. Then statements 235 through 299 and the loop on M were added to obtain the second model. Finally, statements 300 through 350 were added to obtain the final model (for Average Joe). Other statements were modified to "support" these changes. For example, the variable T was added to C in statement 400.

```
10 REMARK - PROGRAM FOR THE AUTO COST PROBLEM
20 REMARK - M=1 FOR FIRST MATH MODEL
30 REMARK - M=2 FOR ADDED REPAIRS ON OLD CARS
40 REMARK - M=3 FOR INTANGIBLE COST ADDED
50 REMARK - V = VALUE
55 REMARK - D = DEPRECIATION
60 REMARK - Y = YEAR
65 REMARK - O = OPERATING COST
70 REMARK - R = REPAIR COST
75 REMARK - N = INTANGIBLE COST - FOR AVERAGE JOE
80 REMARK - C = COST IN Y-TH YEAR
85 REMARK - A = AVERAGE ANNUAL COST UP TO YEAR Y
99 LET M = 1
```

```
100 PRINT "RESULTS FOR MATH MODEL",M
110 PRINT "YEAR","AVERAGE COST"
120 LET V = 3000
130 LET Y = 1
140 REMARK            COMPUTE D,R AND O COSTS
200 LET D = .3*V
205 LET V = V - D
210 LET O = 450
215 IF Y<= 2 THEN 265
220 LET O = 500
225 IF Y=3 THEN    275
227 IF Y<= 5 THEN 285
230 LET R = 300
235 IF M=1 THEN 300
240 IF Y<= 10 THEN 300
245 IF Y<= 13 THEN 292
250 IF Y<= 19 THEN 295
255 LET R = 750
260 GO TO 300
265 LET R·= 0
270 GO TO 300
275 LET R = 100
280 GO TO 300
285 LET R = 200
290 GO TO 300
292 LET R = 400
294 GO TO 300
295 LET R = 600
299 REMARK            FINISHED D,R AND O COSTS
300 IF M< = 2 THEN 400
304 LET N = 0
305 REMARK            INTANGIBLE COST - AVERAGE JOE
310 IF Y<=2 THEN 400
320 IF Y<=4 THEN 350
330 LET N = 200
340 GO TO 400
350 LET N = 100
400 LET C = D + O + R + N
410 LET A = (C + (Y-1)*A)/Y
420 REMARK        PRINT SELECTED VALUES OF A
430 IF Y=40  THEN 460
440 IF Y=100 THEN 460
450 IF Y>20  THEN 500
460 PRINT Y,A
499 REMARK        TEST FOR END OF LOOPS ON Y AND ON M
500 IF Y > = 100 THEN 600
510 LET Y = Y+1
520 GO TO 200
600 IF M=3    THEN 700
610 LET M = M+1
620 GO TO 100
700 END
```

This example illustrates the important steps in solving a problem from beginning to end. The steps are:

1. Recognize the problem.
2. Identify the important variables and introduce quantitative measures

3. Formulate the problem precisely.
4. Make idealizations and assumptions about the variables and their relationships. (Other variables are often identified here.)
5. Make a mathematical model.
6. Make an analysis of the model.
7. Compute some specific results.
8. Check these results for reasonableness. If they are unreasonable, reexamine steps 2, 3, and 4 (also 6 and 7).
9. Check these results for accuracy by comparing them with observations and measurements from the real world. If the accuracy is inadequate, reexamine steps 2, 3, and 4 (also 6 and 7).
10. Tentatively accept the mathematical model and the results it predicts about the real world.

Once the problem is recognized, we begin to formulate it in precise terms. This means that we identify exactly what must be done and settle on a means of measuring the variables in the problem. From this process we can formulate the problem precisely. Often at this stage some assumptions or idealizations about the real problem are introduced to simplify matters. Once there is a precise problem statement, pertinent variables and relationships among them can be identified. Again, we often introduce assumptions at this point. For example, we might know that two variables are related (car-repair bills depend on the age of the car) but we might not know how they are related; thus we assume a relationship that appears reasonable. From an analysis of the mathematical model we can compute its solution.

It is advisable (in fact, essential) in "vague" or "fuzzy" problems to check the solutions for reasonableness. If they appear reasonable, we may tentatively accept them. If they are unreasonable, then we must reexamine the whole process of problem formulation and solution. Thus it is particularly important to clearly display any assumptions or idealizations made. It is likely that one of the assumptions has led to the unreasonable answer. The process of making mathematical models, checking the results against reality, and refining the model can be never ending.

Consider the example of Newton's laws of motion. For many years many people believed that these laws were exact models for motion in the physical world. Then people began to observe things that did not agree with the model. As more and more such observations were made, people began to look for a new model; Einstein's theory of relativity is one of the results of this research. Another is quantum mechanics. People are still checking these new models for "reasonableness," and it is optimistic to think that either the theory of relativity or quantum mechanics will pass all the tests put to it.

Most mathematical models, even in science, stand on much less firm ground than the theory of relativity. Thus, when difficulties begin to appear in correlating answers with observed results, we should not hesitate to question the validity of the mathematical model involved. In the less-understood areas, such as economics and social phenomena, we should be prepared to reexamine the mathematical model with considerable frequency.

PROBLEMS

7-4.1   Give two examples of special situations that could arise in a company's payroll operation and that might require special action. Discuss the pros and cons of making a payroll program able to handle all types of special situations that might arise.

7-4.2   Suppose that the Social Security taxes are 5.2 percent of all wages up to $9600.00 earned in a single year. The payroll program should thus deduct 5.2 percent of each paycheck up to the time an employee goes over the $9600.00 level. A special calculation must be made for the pay period in which an employee goes over $9600.00 in the current calendar year. Describe a method for computing this tax which deducts exactly the right amount. Write a program that uses your method. Run it to verify that it is correct for employees who earn the following amounts per month: $976.00, $796.00, $808.08, $1247.15, $2666.67.

7-4.3   Consider Example 7-4 of the inventory control being put on the computer. Describe some steps that can be taken to protect the company against a disaster like the one described. Note that it costs money to keep a large inventory. Thus one object of putting the inventory on the computer is to keep as small an inventory as possible without running out of critical supplies.

7-4.4   Reread the discussion in this chapter of the automobile cost problem and locate one or two assumptions in the mathematical model that you find unsatisfactory. Explain why you find the assumptions unsatisfactory and suggest (if you can) better assumptions.

7-4.5   It is stated in the text that it is unreasonable and unimportant to get "accurate" results from an analysis of the automobile cost problem. If you believe this is true then explain why. If you do not believe it is true then also explain why.

The following problems are given in a vaguely defined form. You are to take the incompletely defined problems and introduce various reasonable assumptions, idealizations, and so forth, to obtain precisely defined problems. Once you have a precise statement, you are to identify the important variables and find, or assume, some specific relationships among them that lead to a mathematical model of the problem.

Note that some of the problems are actually immensely complex and you will probably need to make several idealizations in order to keep the size of the problem statement reasonable. You are not required to do any computing. You are, in effect, to do the first five steps of problem solving listed near the end of Section 7-4.

7-4.6   Building costs are quite high, but rent is also very expensive. Construct a mathematical model to help decide which is more economical for you: to build or rent a house.

7-4.7   You are a girl's advisor in a major college. A young lady comes to you for advice about the field in which she should major. Describe the important variables that enter into this decision and make a mathematical model that can be used to analyze the decision problem.

7-4.8   "Beware the Population Explosion!" This is a headline in nearly every publication today. Describe a mathematical model of the situation causing the population explosion. Define some precise indicators of the severity of this so-called explosion, and show how you would evaluate the indicators. Some of the following variables and data might enter your considerations.

		U.S.A.	*Mexico*	*California*
Area, sq. mi.	1950	3,625,000	758,000	156,000
Population	1950	151,000,000	25,700,000	10,500,000
	1960	179,000,000	38,000,000	15,000,000
Annual increase, %		1.4	3.4	3.7
Family size	1950	3.37	5.51	3.85
	1960	3.35	5.40	3.75
Births	1950	4,167,000	1,750,000	328,000
	1960	4,100,000	1,830,000	385,000
Deaths	1950	1,452,000	400,000	141,000
	1960	1,712,000	403,000	147,000
Pop./sq. mi.	1960	50.5	50.4	100.4
Immigration	1950	104,000	52,000	375,000
	1960	265,000	68,000	694,000

7-4.9 An instructor has grades at the end of the semester as given in the table below. He assigned regular homework plus two special, more difficult, problem sets and gave four pop quizzes. The two hour-exams seem quite satisfactory, but the midterm exam had several poorly stated questions on it which misled several students. The final exam was too difficult and all but the very best students made very low grades. Present what you feel to be a reasonable method for grading the students, and apply it to the grades listed below. Do you find that your method results in a good ranking of the students?

	Student 1	*Student 2*	*Student 3*	*Student 4*	*Student 5*	*Student 6*
Regular homework (225 points)	182	212	64	168	71	219
Special homework (50 points)	31	45	28	33	13	49
Pop quizzes (40 points)	28	36	32	29	16	38
First hour-exam (100 points)	68	57	91	62	37	88
Midterm exam (150 points)	112	98	103	91	60	61
Second hour-exam (100 points)	59	55	87	61	32	88
Final Exam (150 points)	16	11	89	19	6	57

7-4.10   You are a sophomore majoring in math. You do not like it and want to change your major to business, with sales option, or engineering. How do you make your choice?

7-4.11   A farmer has 640 acres producing wheat. He has a 10-year-old combine that is still usable for several seasons even though it is rather slow and inefficient. A new machine is quite expensive but will cover his farm in about one half to two thirds the time required for the old one and will give about 5 percent more recovery of grain. What would you advise him to do: use the old one or buy the new one?

7-5   APPLICATION: WHALES VERSUS PLANKTON

In this application we shall study the whole process of developing a mathematical model and then writing, debugging, and testing a complete program. The application appears simple on the surface and the final program obtained is only a page long. Nevertheless, the presentation is quite long because we must consider a number of details about the application. Furthermore, thorough testing of even this short program requires several test cases. This application illustrates a common situation in programming, one in which the programmer becomes involved in an analysis that has nothing to do with computers or programming. The application may be of interest in itself to some readers, but, since it merely serves as an example, it may be skipped without omitting any topics in programming.

We have constructed a computer program to study the biological interaction betweeen whales and plankton. This program is a mathematical model of the environment of whales and plankton. See Figures 7-5.1 and 7-5.2. Our model has two main assumptions:

1. The plankton are born and live to die of old age except for the presence of the whales which eat them.
2. The whales reproduce, live, and die naturally as long as there is enough plankton to feed them all, but some whales starve if the plankton supply is insufficient.

At the end of this section we discuss how this approach may be applied to other situations (for example, coyotes and rabbits, pastureland and sheep) and extended to more complex systems (for example, Whales plankton, and whale fishermen).

To make this study over a long time span, we first consider what happens during a short time interval, PERIOD. If the number of whales and plankton is known at a given time, TIME, the number at the end of the time interval is given by formulas of the model. So, starting at TIME equal to zero, the population of whales and plankton can be determined at the end of successive time intervals, that is at times PERIOD, 2.*PERIOD, 3.*PERIOD. . . . The population behavior predicted by this approach might not agree with reality; it depends on how accurate the mathematical model is. Indeed, changes in the model produce considerably different results and one can attempt to check the models by comparing the results with observed data taken in the past.

FIGURE 7-5.1   A finback whale breaking water. This whale feeds by swimming with its mouth open and using its teeth as a sieve to collect plankton and krill. Its teeth are specially adapted for this purpose. (Courtesy of National Maritime Fisheries Service)

FIGURE 7-5.2   An enlarged view of the plankton that a baleen whale feeds upon. Many of the plants and animals of the whales diet are so small that they cannot be seen by the unaided eye. (Courtesy National Maritime Fisheries Service)

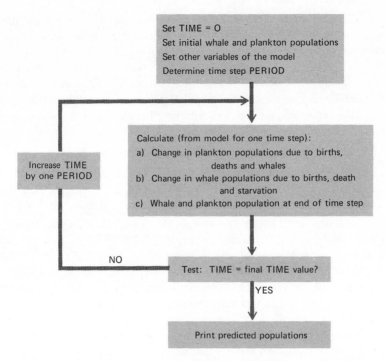

FIGURE 7-5.3 **A flowchart of the general approach to studying the interaction of whales and population. This approach is developed into a mathematical model and, in turn, a computer program makes the calculations.**

The general organization of this study is illustrated in the flowchart of Figure 7-5.3.

We now need a more detailed analysis of the situation in one time period. After taking the two main assumptions, and making them more precise, we put them into mathematical formulas for the model. The model also requires other assumptions to be introduced here.

In biological systems, the number of births and deaths due to old age during a short time interval is proportional to the number of members. If one population is twice the size of a similar one, then the larger one will have twice as many births and twice as many old-age deaths as the smaller one. The number of births and deaths is also proportional to the time interval—twice as long implies twice as many. If the net rate of population increase ([birth–deaths] per unit time) is denoted by RATE, then the net increase during a time interval PERIOD is RATE*PERIOD*population. If RATE is positive, then there are more births than old-age deaths and the population grows; but if RATE is negative, then deaths exceed births and the population decreases. We *assume* the RATE does not vary with time in our study. In fact, RATE can change with time for a population. For example, the RATE for human population increases when a cure for cancer is introduced and it decreases when new birth control methods are widely used.

We use RATEP and RATEW to denote these rates for the plankton and the whales, respectively. We use PLANKT and WHALES to denote the population of plankton and whales; they are measured in tons per cubic mile of ocean and number per cubic mile, respectively. As the first part of the model, we have the increase during PERIOD due to births less old-age deaths as RATEP*PLANKT*PERIOD for the plankton and RATEW* WHALES*PERIOD for the whales. The population at the end of PERIOD is equal to the population at the beginning plus the change during PERIOD. Thus the equations that give the relation between the populations at the start and end of the time step are

$$\text{WHALES} = \text{WHALES} + \text{RATEW*WHALES*PERIOD}$$
$$\text{PLANKT} = \text{PLANKT} + \text{RATEP*PLANKT*PERIOD}$$

These equations are *only* for natural birth and death effects and now we must include other terms that model the interaction between the two populations.

During the interval PERIOD, the whales eat some of the plankton. We assume that each whale would like to eat a certain amount, DINNER*PERIOD, of plankton during PERIOD; so, if there is a plentiful supply of plankton, the amount eaten by all of the whales is DINNER*WHALES*PERIOD. The average large whale eats 300 tons of plankton a year and we set DINNER = 300 in the computer program. However, the amount of plankton which can be eaten depends also on the amount of plankton. If the amount of plankton available is small, a whale has a harder time finding his dinner and so eats less. The amount which can be eaten also depends on the number of whales and the length of the time interval. We *assume* the amount of plankton which can be eaten is EAT*PLANKT*WHALES*PERIOD. The variable EAT measures what fraction or percentage of the plankton is found and eaten by a whale when there is a shortage of plankton. Thus, the amount of plankton which is eaten is either DINNER*WHALES* PERIOD or EAT*PLANKT*WHALES*PERIOD, whichever is smaller. Plenty of plankton implies that the whales eat their fill, so the first value is the amount eaten; but a scarcity of plankton implies that some of the whales go hungry and the second value is the amount eaten. Noting that WHALES*PERIOD is a factor in both of these expressions, we see that the term to be added to the model for the plankton population is

WHALES*PERIOD*(minimum of DINNER and EAT*PLANKT)

This term is illustrated in Figure 7-5.4.

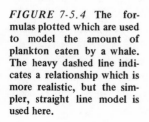
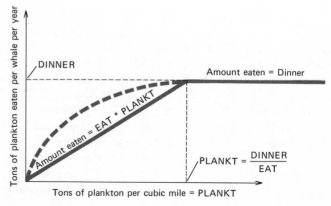

FIGURE 7-5.4 **The formulas plotted which are used to model the amount of plankton eaten by a whale. The heavy dashed line indicates a relationship which is more realistic, but the simpler, straight line model is used here.**

As long as DINNER is smaller than EAT*PLANKT none of the whales die of starvation. But if this is not the case, then some of the whales cannot find enough to eat and eventually starve. The number which starve depends on the deficiency of the food supply, that is it depends on the value of (DINNER – EAT*PLANKT)*WHALES* PERIOD. This is the amount of extra plankton needed to fill the whales. When this is a small value, the whales are only a little hungry and it takes a long time for them to starve, but if this is a large value, then they hardly have anything to eat and they starve quickly. The food deficit in percentage terms is

$$\left(1 - \frac{EAT*PLANKT}{DINNER} \right)$$

when this number is positive. We *assume* that the fraction of whales which die during PERIOD is proportional to this food deficit percentage and we use STARVE for the proportionality factor. Thus the term to be added to the model for the whale population is

$$0 \qquad\qquad \text{if DINNER} \leqslant \text{EAT*PLANKT*}$$

$$STARVE*\left(1 - \frac{EAT*PLANKT}{DINNER} \right)*WHALES*PERIOD \qquad \text{Otherwise}$$

This term is illustrated in Figure 7-5.5.

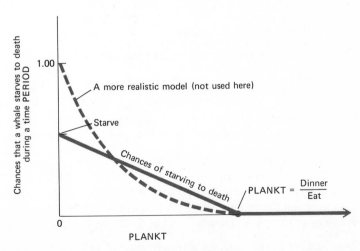

FIGURE 7-5.5 The formulas plotted which are used to model the proportion of whales that die of starvation. The heavy dashed line indicates a relationship which is more realistic, but the simpler, straight line model is used here.

By combining the relationships listed above, we obtain a simplified model of the change of plankton and whales during the time interval. We have:

At the beginning of a time interval PERIOD the plankton and whale populations are PLANKT and WHALES. At the end of the interval, the populations are:

Plankton:

PLANKT + RATEP*PLANKT*PERIOD – DINNER*WHALES*PERIOD

if DINNER ⩽ EAT*PLANKT

PLANKT + RATEP*PLANKT*PERIOD – EAT*PLANKT*WHALES*PERIOD

if DINNER > EAT*PLANKT

Whales:

WHALES + RATEW*WHALES*PERIOD   if DINNER ⩽ EAT*PLANKT

WHALES + RATEW*WHALES*PERIOD

$$- STARVE*\left(1 - \frac{EAT*PLANKT}{DINNER}\right)*WHALES*PERIOD$$

if DINNER > EAT*PLANKT

The relationships in this model can be expressed in Basic almost directly. The variable names in Basic are the first letters of the variables used above except that RATEP and RATEW are R1 and R2 and PERIOD is I (for Interval) in the Basic program.

```
205 REM          PLANKTON POPULATION CHANGE
210 IF D<= E*P THEN 240
220 LET P = P + (R1*P - E*P*W)*I
230       GOTO 260
240 LET P = P + (R1*P - D*W)*I
250 REM           WHALES POPULATION CHANGE
260 LET W = W + R2*W*I
270 IF D<= E*P THEN 290
280 LET W = W - S*(1. - E*P/D)*W*I
290 LET T = T + I
```

To study this interaction is the heart of a program. There are still a number of things to do to complete the construction of this program:

1. Write the initialization part (set initial values).
2. Control the steps in time and termination of the iteration loop.
3. Put in PRINT statements at the appropriate places.
4. Put in intermediate output PRINT statements to aid the debugging.
5. Find some test examples (simple ones) to check out the program.

The initialization of the program is simply a list of assignment statements for all the variables involved. Alternatively we could read these values in as data if we wish. The size of the steps in time is determined by PERIOD (denoted by I); we also must place a limit on the time span of the study, say TMAX.

There are four types of output from this program.

1. Information about the particular model used, that is, the values of the variables at the start and the values of the various proportionality factors.
2. Information about the final situation (at time TMAX).
3. Information about what happens during the time span of this study.
4. Information to debug the program.

The first two sets of information are obtained by putting print statements at the beginning and end of the program. The best way to assess what happens during the study is to have a graph or plot of the whale and plankton populations. Some such plots are given later, see Figure 7-5.6. Unfortunately, we do not have a "PLOT" statement in our programming language, so we must settle for printing out a table of values which can be used for a plot. This table lists TIME and the values of WHALES and PLANKT, all at appropriate times.

Let us pause for a moment and consider the choice of value for PERIOD (because this affects the table we are about the print out). If PERIOD is too large, say 100 years, then the results of our model are useless because the actual changes within a PERIOD are much more complicated than our model. If PERIOD is too small, say one day, the results may be much more accurate, but the amount of computer time required for the study is very large. Thus we must choose an appropriate value for PERIOD, neither too large nor too small. Since we do not yet know what this appropriate value is, we must arrange the printing of the table independently of the number of time steps.

We introduce yet another variable TPRINT which is the length of the time steps we want in the table of values. Now the variable TIME is increasing by PERIOD in each loop of the iteration, so we must find a way to know when time has increased by TPRINT since the last printout. We do this by introducing a variable TLAST and then test to see if TIME–LAST is greater than or equal to TPRINT.

An important point to note here is that the "auxiliary" requirements of the computer program (such as printing, logical control, and so forth) usually require that we introduce a number of variables in the program that have little to do with the problem itself. The printing is accomplished by the following piece of program. Again we must introduce Basic language variable names for TPRINT, TLAST and TMAX (We use T1, T2 and T9).

```
300 REM          TABLE PRINTING CONTROL
310 IF T-T2 < T1 THEN 340
320 LET T2 = T
330 PRINT T,W,P
340 REM    *** PROGRAM CONTINUES ***
```

Note that we must set TLAST equal to TIME as well as print the table values out.

Finally let us consider output for debugging the program. In general, debugging requires two kinds of output, first the values of variables at the start (especially all values read in) and various items scattered throughout the computation. This particular program already provides a considerable amount of output, but there are two more useful points for intermediate output. These are:

1. Initial values of all "auxiliary" variables. These are variables which do not interest us *after* the program is debugged. However, they should be checked *during* debugging.
2. Values of some of the terms that appear in the statements in the heart of the program.

These statements are included and noted in the program given below.

We have covered all the points for writing the program. One must now collect these components and put them together. The resulting program is on the opposite page.

The program is written and entered into the computer; now we need to debug it. The first step, of course, is to remove any language errors. The program above has no such errors, but it is unusual to start with such a program. There normally are some wrong parentheses, misspelled words, or something of this sort. The language translator detects these errors and issues diagnostics which, hopefully, pinpoint the errors it has found.

Once these errors are removed, we must check for mistakes in logic, copying down equations, and so forth. We list a set of test cases which are so simple that we know the answer to the population interaction.

Case 1:

Nothing happens at all.

Set   PERIOD = 1.   TPRINT = 4.   TMAX = 60.
        RATEP = RATEW = EAT = DINNER = STARVE = 0.

Then WHALES and PLANKT stay fixed. This case serves to test:

1. Reading of the data,
2. The construction of the interation loop; that is, does it start and stop at the right time?
3. The print statements.

Case 2:

No interaction between the whales and plankton.

Set PERIOD   = 2.5   TPRINT   = 5.   TMAX = 100.
      RATEP   = .03   RATEW   = -.02
      EAT = DINNER   = STARVE   = 0.

Since there is no interaction, the plankton population should grow by 3 percent a year and the whale population decrease by 2 percent a year. This case serves to test:

1. The print statements (again),
2. Parts of the logic and equations in the model.

```
  1 REM                WHALES AND PLANKTON POPULATION STUDY
  2 REM                 MODEL VARIABLES (PARAMETERS)
  3 REM  P  = PLANKT       W  = WHALES
  4 REM  R1 = RATEP        R2 = RATEW
  5 REM  E  = EAT          D  = DINNER
  6 REM                    S  = STARVE
  7 REM                 PROGRAM VARIABLES
  8 REM  T  = TIME          I = PERIOD (TIME INTERVAL)
  9 REM  T1 = TPRINT ( INTERVAL FOR PRINTING TABLE )
 10 REM  T2 = TLAST ( LAST TIME A TABLE VALUE WAS PRINTED )
 11 REM  T9 = TMAX ( TIME TO TERMINATE THE STUDY )
 20 REM         READ MODEL AND PROGRAM VARIABLES
 30 READ P,W,R1,R2,D,E,S
 40 READ I,T1,T9
 50 PRINT ≠     P≠,≠     W≠,≠     R1≠,≠     R2≠
 60 PRINT P,W,R1,R2
 70 PRINT ≠     U≠,≠   E≠,≠   S≠
 80 PRINT D,E,S
 90 REM  *** DEBUG *** CHECK DATA READ IN
 92 PRINT ≠ I - T1 - T9 =≠,I,T1,T9
100 REM         INITIALIZE TIME
110 LET T = 0
120 LET T2 = 0
200 REM         EQUATIONS FOR TIME PERIOD
205 REM         PLANKTON POPULATION CHANGE
206 REM  *** DEBUG *** EQUATION TERMS
207 PRINT D*W,E*P*W,R1*P,R2*W,S*(1.-E*P/D)*W
210 IF D<= E*P THEN 240
220 LET P = P + (R1*P - E*P*W)*I
230      GOTO 260
240 LET P = P + (R1*P - D*W)*I
250 REM         WHALES POPULATION CHANGE
260 LET W = W + R2*W*I
270 IF D<= E*P THEN 290
280 LET W = W - S*(1. - E*P/D)*W*I
290 LET T = T + I
300 REM        TABLE PRINTING CONTROL
305 REM  *** DEBUG *** PRINT CONTROL
306 PRINT ≠T , T-T2=≠, T,T-T2
310 IF T-T2 < T1 THEN 340
320 LET T2 = T
330 PRINT T,W,P
340 IF T< T9 THEN 210
400 REM             FINAL PRINTOUT
410 PRINT
420 PRINT
430 PRINT ≠AT TIME≠,T,≠ A CUBIC MILE CONTAINS ≠
440 PRINT ≠ ≠,P,≠ TONS OF PLANKTON≠
450 PRINT ≠ ≠,W,≠ WHALES≠
500 REM         MAKE ANOTHER RUN WITH MORE DATA
510      GO TO 30
600 DATA 600,.4,.10,.08,300,125,.30
610 DATA 1., 2., 100
800 END
```

Case 3:

Extreme interaction between the whales and the plankton. We take two subcases; the first is where the whales eat all the plankton immediately and starve quickly. Both the whale and the plankton populations should decrease quickly. For this subcase we set

WHALES	= 1.	PLANKT	= 100.			
PERIOD	= 1.	TPRINT	= 2.	TMAX	=	50.
RATEP	= .03	RATEW	= -.02			
DINNER	= 300.	EAT	= .75	STARVE	=	.8

The second subcase is where there is initially very little plankton, but their rate of increase is much faster than the rate at which the whales eat them.

WHALES	= 1.	PLANKT	= 10.			
PERIOD	= 1.	TPRINT	= 1.	TMAX	=	50.
RATEP	= .3	RATEW	= -.02			
DINNER	= 300.	EAT	= .25	STARVE	=	.6

The whale population should decrease rapidly. Then after there are very few whales left, the plankton population should explode. Once the plankton population has reached a large size, the whale population should decrease slowly at the -2 percent rate due to the natural excess of deaths over births.

These two subcases test the logic of the heart of the model. Specifically:

1. At the start DINNER is larger than EAT*PLANKT so the maximum eating term is included for the plankton model and the starvation term is included for the whales model.
2. At the end of the second subcase, we have DINNER smaller than EAT* PLANKT so the other branches are taken in the IF statements.

Once these three cases are run satisfactorily, we can begin to have some confidence that the program is correct. An important point to note is that *we have tested every statement in the program.* Moreover, we have partially tested the mathematical model. We know what would happen in these extreme cases and, by the output, we can verify that the program produces reasonable results for these cases. We can start to make some experiments about the possible kinds of interaction between the whale and plankton populations.

Before examining the results of this study, we point out that the results are purely hypothetical and have no relationship with the actual situation of whales and plankton in the ocean. The reason is that the model for the study does not include many important factors. In particular, whale fishing in the last 300 years has dramatically affected the whale population and now the food supply for whales is not a factor. The surival of the whales depends on some method to reduce and control the number being caught by fishermen.

Nevertheless, the program allows us to make an interesting "what if" study, namely what if the whale and plankton populations were primarily influenced by their interaction. Large scale, serious computer studies of this nature are also "what if" studies and they can never include *all* the factors and influences of a complex, real world situation. They can, however, give one much insight and information about how the real world operates—or might operate.

The results of four computer runs with the program are plotted in Figure 7-5.6. The population characteristics or parameters are listed below (DINNER is 300 in all cases).

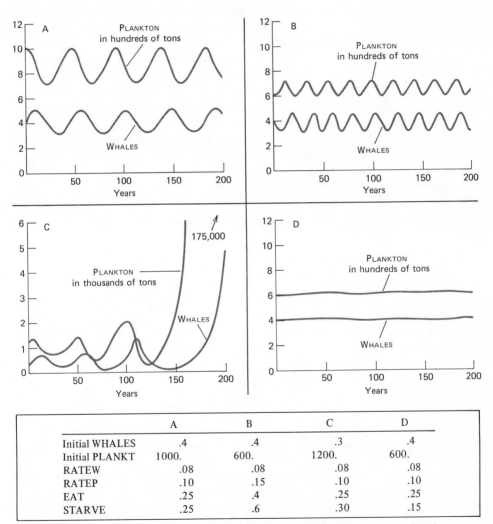

	A	B	C	D
Initial WHALES	.4	.4	.3	.4
Initial PLANKT	1000.	600.	1200.	600.
RATEW	.08	.08	.08	.08
RATEP	.10	.15	.10	.10
EAT	.25	.4	.25	.25
STARVE	.25	.6	.30	.15

FIGURE 7-5.6. Plots of the whale and plankton population behavior as predicted by the computer study of this section. Plot C shows an unstable population interaction that eventually "explodes." The other three show possible stable population behaviors.

The first two cases illustrate the "balance of nature" in that the interaction keeps both populations within a narrow range. The interaction in Plot B is somewhat stronger (EAT and STARVE are both larger) and the oscillations are somewhat more rapid. In both cases the populations vary by about 25 percent, the first over a period of about 30 years and the second over a period of about 12 years. Smaller values of RATEW and RATEP (which would be more realistic) make the period of the oscillation longer.

Plot C illustrates an unstable population interaction, one that is clearly unrealistic. This, of course, means that the values of the parameters are unrealistic. An important point to note is that the parameters of this case are not very much different from the case of Plot A. Thus, we might conclude from this, that an "outside" small disturbance in the populations could change a stable situation into an unstable one, with disasterous results.

The last plot shows a case where the populations are in almost perfect balance and, as time progresses, the two populations remain almost constant.

It is worth noting that the values of the parameters in these four examples are very similar. The population behaviors are, however, dramatically different. The values of EAT and STARVE are only crude estimates of the "correct" values and, of course, they in turn are used in a crude model of the population interaction. It is clear, for example, that other factors would become significant in the case of Plot C long before the two populations "exploded." It would, however, require a much deeper study in order to identify the exact nature of these factors. In the meantime, this study does suggest that the "balance of nature" is sensitive to "outside" changes and that a small change could have disasterous effects in the long run.

The technique used in this study can be modified to study the interaction between many other populations. Examples where one has an almost identical analysis include:

> coyotes and rabbits,
> birds and insects,
> lions and zebras.

As with whales and plankton, these populations have many interactions and influences that are not included in this study.

A slightly different kind of interaction occurs between hunters and game, but the resulting mathematical model is the same. Consider, for example, deer hunters and deer. We list the variables in the whales and plankton study and show the corresponding variables in a study of hunters and deer.

Whales and Plankton		*Hunters and Deer*
WHALES	HUNTERS	
PLANKT	DEER	
RATEW	RATEH =	Normal rate at which young people take up hunting and older people quit.
RATEP	RATED =	Rate of increase of deer population due to natural births and deaths.
DINNER	LIMIT =	Season limit on deer per hunter imposed either by law or by choice of hunters.
STARVE	QUIT =	Rate at which people give up hunting when they do not get the limit.
EAT	KILL =	The fraction or percentage of the deer that are killed when there are too few for all hunters.

The mathematical equations for the interaction between hunters and deer are the same as between whales and plankton except that the names are changed according to the above table.

We finally consider the interaction between pasture and sheep. The difference between this and the previous study is that when sheep eat grass, they kill only a certain percentage of it. If we let DIE be this fraction (DIE = .5 if half the grass dies after a sheep eats on it) then this variable is introduced into one of the interaction terms. The resulting equations for the amount of pasture and sheep at the end of a time interval are

Pasture:

$$\text{PASTURE} + (\text{RATEP*PASTURE} - \text{DIE*DINNER*SHEEP})\text{*PERIOD}$$
$$\text{if DINNER} \leqslant \text{EAT*PASTURE}$$

$$\text{PASTURE} + (\text{RATEP*PASTURE} - \text{DIE*EAT*PASTURE*SHEEP})\text{*PERIOD}$$
$$\text{if DINNER} > \text{EAT*PASTURE}$$

Sheep:

$$\text{SHEEP} + \text{RATES*SHEEP*PERIOD} \qquad \text{if DINNER} \leqslant \text{EAT*PASTURE}$$

$$\text{SHEEP} + \left(\text{RATES} - \text{STARVE*}\left(1 - \frac{\text{EAT*PASTURE}}{\text{DINNER}}\right)\right)\text{*SHEEP*PERIOD}$$
$$\text{if DINNER} > \text{EAT*PASTURE}$$

The variable names PASTURE, SHEEP, and RATES have replaced PLANKT, WHALES, and RATEW of the earlier study.

PROBLEMS

7-5.1 Study the population behavior of whales and plankton with each of the following modifications in the model

(a) If WHALES < .05 then RATEW is halved.

(b) Introduce a variable named LIMIT and set RATEP = 0 if PLANKT > LIMIT. Values of LIMIT of interest range from 600 to 2000.

(c) Introduce a variable named AMOUNT and double RATEW if PLANKT/ WHALES > AMOUNT. Values of AMOUNT of interest range from 500 to 1000.

(d) Introduce combinations of the above modifications.

7-5.2 Make a series of computer experiments to convince yourself that the model for whales and plankton always gives an oscillating behavior of the populations except in two special situations:

(a) Both populations are exactly constant.

(b) One or both populations go to zero or to infinity as time increases.

7-5.3   Consider the interaction of coyotes and rabbits and obtain rough estimates of the values of the parameters (RATEP, EAT, and so forth) that give stable populations of reasonable size.

7-5.4   Enlarge the study of whales and plankton to include whale fishermen. Introduce the variables:

(a)   RATEF = the net rate that men take up whaling = number entering as youths less the number retiring.

(b)   HAUL = the number of WHALES a fisherman hopes to obtain each year.

(c)   CATCH = percentage of whales caught when there are too few whales for all the fishermen. This corresponds to EAT for the plankton.

(d)   BROKE = fraction of fishermen that give up whaling when CATCH* WHALES is less than HAUL.

Introduce these variables into the equations for whales and add the following expression for the change in fishermen per time interval PERIOD:

$$\text{FISHERS} + \text{RATEF*FISHERS*PERIOD} \qquad \text{if HAUL} \leqslant \text{CATCH*WHALES}$$

$$\text{FISHERS} + \left(\text{RATEF} - \text{BROKE*}\left(1 - \frac{\text{CATCH*WHALES}}{\text{HAUL}}\right)\right)*\text{FISHERS*PERIOD}.$$

$$\text{if HAUL} > \text{CATCH*WHALES}$$

7-5.5   Describe a set of test cases that you would use to initially test the computer program that one would write for Problem 7-5.4.

7-5.6   (*Job and workers*)   A simple study of the labor force, unemployment and jobs may be made with the following variables:

LABOR   = Total labor force.

WORKERS = Number of people at work.

JOBS   = Total number of jobs available.

UNEMP   = Job imbalance (unemployed if JOBS < LABOR, excess jobs otherwise).

RATEL   = Net rate of increase in the labor force from youths entering less retirements.

INFLUX   = Net rate at which people join (or leave) the labor force from the "outside."

EXTERN   = Number of jobs available due to "outside" factors which are unaffected by the local situation.

FW   = Factor that specifies how many jobs one worker generates when he spends his income.

FU   = Factor that specifies how many jobs one unemployed person generates when he spends his income.

These variables correspond to an "island" economy where there are certain local job producing activities and some external ones (from items exported less those from items imported). We *assume* that people migrate to this island when there are many job opportunities and that they move away when there is high unemployment. We express this assumption by the formula

$$INFLUX = .01* \left(.03 - \frac{UNEMP}{LABOR} \right) *LABOR$$

This assumption says: "There is an influx of 1 percent of the labor force for each 1 percent that the unemployment rate falls below 3 percent." A negative value for INFLUX means that people are leaving the island.

We now present one possible set of mathematical formulas that describe the labor situation on this island:

JOBS   = FW*WORKERS + FU*maximum of (0,UNEMP) + EXTERN
WORKERS   = minimum of (LABOR, JOBS)
UNEMP   = LABOR – JOBS

The change in the labor force for one time period is

RATEL*LABOR + INFLUX

Study these formulas and present an explanation of what assumptions and situation they describe. Create an imaginary island and specify a set of values for all the variables that is reasonable and consistent.

7-5.7   Consider the situation in Problem 7-5.6 and obtain the equations that one would use to make a computer study of the labor force on this island as time varies. Incorporate these equations in a computer program to carry out this study.

7-5.8   Consider the situation in Problem 7-5.6 and describe a set of test cases that you would use to initially test the computer program that one would write for Problem 7-5.7.

7-5.9   Take a set of variable values that lead to a reasonable, stable situation in Problem 7-5.6 and then introduce an abrupt, sizable change in the value of EXTERN. Consider both an increase and a decrease and investigate the effect this has on the labor force.

Intermediate Elements of Basic

The features of Basic presented in this chapter complete the standard Basic language. They are adequate for a wide variety of applications. The extra features provided in some systems are extremely useful from time to time, even sometimes essential, although one might program for a long time without using some or any of them. The frequency of use of these additional features depends on the area of application and type of programs with which one is involved.

8-1 ARRAYS

One of the most important and useful features of Basic is the ability to handle arrays. The most common arrays are one-dimensional, such as the sequence

$$A(1), A(2), A(3), \ldots, A(17), \ldots, A(40).$$

which is the Basic representation of

$$A_1, A_2, A_3, \ldots A_{17}, \ldots, A_{40}.$$

A *one-dimensional array* is also called a *list* (and it also corresponds to a *vector* or *sequence* in mathematical terminology). An array has a name (the one above is called A) and the elements in the array are indexed by a counter.

A one-dimensional array is ordered from beginning to end and the position of a particular element is indicated by its index. Thus $A(1)$ is the first element, $A(10)$ is the tenth, and so forth. The usual mathematical notation for arrays places the index as a subscript, that is, $A(1) \sim A_1$, $A(10) \sim A_{10}$, $A(i) \sim A_i$.

An array element is often referred to as a *subscripted variable*. The subscript correponds to the index and the name comes from mathematics terminology.

Two-dimensional arrays (often called *tables* or *matrices*) are also important and are allowed in Basic. These variables have two indices, for example:

A(1,1)	A(1,2)	. . .	A(1,17)	. . .	A(1,40)
A(2,1)	A(2,2)	. . .	A(2,17)	. . .	A(2,40)
. . .	. . .	. . .	. . .	. . .	. . .
A(7,1)	A(7,2)	. . .	A(7,17)	. . .	A(7,40)
. . .	. . .	. . .	. . .	. . .	. . .
A(20,1)	A(20,2)	. . .	A(20,17)	. . .	A(20,40)

This is a two-dimensional array with 20 rows and 40 columns. Typical examples of one-dimensional arrays are:

1. A list of the amount of rainfall for each day in the year,
2. A list of the grades on the final exam in a course,
3. A list of the job vacancies in the state highway department,
4. A list of the district warehouses of a company,

5. A list of dates of the season's horse races.

0401, 0402, 0403, 0407, 0408, 0409, 0410, 0412, 0414, 0415, 0416, . . . , 0923, 0924, 0925, 0929, 0930, 1001, 1002, 1004, 1006, 1007.

The first two digits are the month and the second two the day, so the season starts on April 1 and ends on October 7.

Typical examples of two-dimensional arrays are:

1. A list of the amount of rainfall for each day in the year, at each weather station in a state,
2. A list of the elevation above sea level at 1-mile intervals in a 100-square-mile region,
3. The multiplication table for the numbers less than 10.

1	2	3	4	5	6	7	8	9
2	4	6	8	10	12	14	16	18
3	6	9	12	15	18	21	24	27
4	8	12	16	20	24	28	32	36
5	10	15	20	25	30	35	40	45
6	12	18	24	30	36	42	48	54
7	14	21	28	35	42	49	56	63
8	16	24	32	40	48	56	64	72
9	18	27	36	45	54	63	72	81

Call this array MTABLE and we see that MTABLE(J,K) is simply J times K.

The advantages of indexed arrays include:

1. the ability to systematically process the array or list in iteration loops (one uses the index as the counter in the iteration),
2. the ability to make statements about members of the list which are valid even if the list is changed in length or content. Thus the statement

```
100   LET P(I) = H(I)*R(I) - D(I)
```

gives the pay P(I) of the I-th employee in terms of the hours H(I), rate R(I), and deductions D(I). This holds no matter how many items there are in the list.
3. The ability to add items to the list by changing the variable that indicates the list's length and by placing the new items on the end. In general, items can be changed or shuffled without changing the statements that manipulate the list.
4. The ability to refer to the entire list by name.

The name of an array in Basic must be a single letter, and the fact that A(7) is an array element is known because the single letter A is followed by a pair of parentheses containing the array index (7 in this case). If the array is small (the index is *always* 10 or less), then one can use the array without further programming. A simple program which uses two arrays is given below.

```
                    A(1) TO A(N)   IF
10 READ D(1),D(2),D(3)
20 PRINT " DISNEYLAND CROWDS FOR WEEK OF"
30 PRINT " ",D(1),D(2),D(3)
40 LET I=1
50 READ A(I)          ←┐ Loop to read
60 LET I=I+1           ┘ 7 elements of A
70 IF I<8 THEN 50 ─────┘
75 PRINT
80 LET I=1
90 PRINT A(I),A(I+1) ←┐ Loop to print elements
100 LET I=I+2          ┘ of A two at a time
110 IF I<8 THEN 90 ────┘
200 DATA 12 , 6,  1974
210 DATA 16000,14000,13500,15200
220 DATA 18400,24300,21800
300 END
```

The first array D used is for the date and contains three elements (month, day, and year). The use of an array for the date does not gain any particular advantage in this program. The second array A is for the 7 crowd attendance values during the week. These values are read from the data stack by an iteration loop at statements 40 through 70. The values are then printed out by another iteration loop at statements 80 through 110. The printing gives two values per line as follows:

A(1)	A(2)	16000	14000
A(3)	A(4)	13500	15200
A(5)	A(6)	18400	24300
A(7)	A(8)	21800	0

The value of A(8) is zero because no value was read for it. The first iteration loop could be replaced by

```
44 READ A(1),A(2),A(3),A(4),A(5),A(6),A(7)
```

The amount of typing is about the same either way. However, in the next section we see another kind of Basic statement which makes processing arrays shorter and simpler. Furthermore, the iteration loop can be used for 70 elements in the array just as well as 7, while to type 70 elements individually in READ statements would be a painful chore.

Here are precise definitions for the general use of arrays.

Index

The *index* of an array is a variable which indicates which element of the array is to be used. The index can be any legal expression and it is rounded to the nearest integer if it is not an integer. A one-dimensional array has one index and a two-dimensional array has two indices. An index may be zero, but not negative.

EXAMPLES

```
A(14)         A(K+4)         B(K*X-X↑(J*P-88))
A(K)          B(K*4-3)       B(17.32178)
```

Array

An *array* is a variable with one or two indices; its name is a single letter. It can be used anywhere an ordinary variable can be used. If an array is to be used with an index larger than 10 then a DIM statement must be used also.

EXAMPLES

```
LET  A(7) = A(6) + A(4-J)
LET  Q3 = Q(3)↑3 - 8.1 * X↑A(7)
PRINT  A(12), B(K,18-K+J)
LET  P = B(J+1,A(J-7)) - A(17.3↑K3/(J+22.2))
```

It is important to note that there is no relationship between an ordinary variable A and an array A(K). Nor is there any relationship between Q3 and Q(3). Note also that the index of an array can involve another (or even the same) array as A(1+B(K)) and A(A(1)+A(4)).

DIM

A *DIM* statement consists of the keyword DIM followed by an array with constant indices. The constants determine the allowable range for the indices of the array. The DIM statement need not be used for arrays with dimension 10 or less as all arrays are automatically allowed up to 11 elements (that is, index range of 0,1,2, ... ,10). This is a declaration statement.

EXAMPLES

```
DIM  A(20)            DIM X(5,20),A(20)
DIM  B(400)           DIM Y(200,12),B(400)
```

If an index is used which lies outside the range specified then a diagnostic is issued and the program stops. Some examples of illegal indices are listed below:

DIM Statement	Illegal Indices
none	A(−3), A(12), B(1,11), B(20,2)
DIM A(30)	A(31), A(−7)
DIM B(12,20)	B(15,15), B(30,30), B(−1,10), B(10,30)

The function of the declaration statement DIM is to set aside space in the computer memory to write down the values of the elements in the array. Since the memory space is limited, there must also be a limit on the size of the arrays. The exact limit can be determined only with reference to a specific installation. A computer has a memory or storage capacity of MEM words; each variable in a program is associated with one of these words. In many situations the number MEM words given a user is only a small fraction of the total computer memory. If an array has N elements or items, then it is associated with N consecutive words. Of the MEM words available in the computer memory, perhaps one-tenth are set aside for the computer system. The translated program itself will need some part of the remaining .9*MEM words. What remains can be used for variables and arrays.

Since the number of words needed for the machine language program generated by the translator cannot easily be predicted in advance, more than one attempt at translation may be necessary before the maximum number of words available for variables and arrays can be determined. See the diagram in Figure 8-1.1.

The range of allowed array sizes varies from as little as 1000 elements to over 20,000 with 3000–5000 as a typical size that can be used without problems.

The following program illustrates the use of arrays in the computation and printing of a table of returns on a dollar invested for various periods of time at various interest rates. After this table is printed a second table is computed and printed which shows the

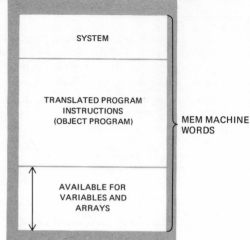

COMPUTER MEMORY ALLOCATED TO THE USER

SYSTEM

TRANSLATED PROGRAM
INSTRUCTIONS
(OBJECT PROGRAM)

MEM MACHINE
WORDS

AVAILABLE FOR
VARIABLES AND
ARRAYS

FIGURE 8-1.1 **Rough illustration of the use of the words in a computer's memory.**

effect of an increase of 1 percent in the interest for an investment of \$24000. The first column of output is the number of years and the next three columns are the effects of increasing the interest from 3 percent to 4 percent, 4 percent to 5 percent and 5 percent to 6 percent. Let A(Y,P) be the amount that \$1 is worth after Y years at P percent interest. Then the formula for this second table is

$$24000*(A(Y,P+1) - A(Y,P)).$$

```
  1 REM    INVESTMENT RETURN TABLES
  4 REM    R,S,T = TEMPORARY VARIABLES
  2 REM    Y= YEARS
  3 REM    A= AMOUNT A DOLLAR GROWS TO
 10 DIM A(20,4)                              ──── Declare the size of A-array
 20 PRINT " "," ","        PERCENT"
 30 PRINT " YEARS", 3,4,5,6
 40 LET Y=1
 50 LET A(Y,1) = (1.03)↑Y        ←
 51 LET A(Y,2) = (1.04)↑Y
 52 LET A(Y,3) = (1.05)↑Y                    Loop to fill up A-array
 53 LET A(Y,4) = (1.06)↑Y                    for 20 years and percents
 55 PRINT Y,A(Y,1),A(Y,2),A(Y,3),A(Y,4)      of 3, 4, 5 and 6
 60 LET Y=Y+1
 70 IF Y<21 THEN 50  ───────────
 80 PRINT
 90 PRINT
100 PRINT " EFFECT OF 1 PERCENT INCREASE FOR $24000"
110 PRINT " YEARS"," 3 TO 4"," 4 TO 5"," 5 TO 6"
120 LET Y= 1
130 LET R=  24000*(A(Y,2)-A(Y,1)) ←
140 LET S=  24000*(A(Y,3)-A(Y,2))
150 LET T=  24000*(A(Y,4)-A(Y,3))           Loop to compute differences
160 PRINT Y,R,S,T                           in A-array times 24000
170 LET Y = Y+1                             for all 20 years
180 IF Y<21 THEN 130 ────────
200 END
```

PROBLEMS

8-1.1 Write a program that sets the I-th element in a list L of length 20 equal to I + 1 and the I-th element of a list R equal to 1 − I. Then print out a table with three columns, the first is L(I), the second is R(21 − I) and the third is the product of the first two.

8-1.2 Write a program that reads in an array A of 31 numbers and then prints out the following 16 numbers.

$$(A(1)+A(31))/2, (A(2)+A(30))/2, \ldots, (A(16)+A(16))/2.$$

8-1.3 Read a 10-element list and compute the average of the elements of the list. Write out the list in reverse order followed by the average with an appropriate message.

8-1.4 Read a set of 16 numbers, then print them in order from the smallest to the largest. If you need help in finding the smallest, see Section 3 of Chapter 6.

8-1.5 What diagnostics does your Basic translator issue when it processes statements like?

    (a)   LET K = A(X,−X)
    (b)   DIM A(K)
    (c)   LET A(1) = A(2) = A(3) = 10
    (d)   PRINT A(1), A(2
    (e)   DIM A(10), A(20), A(15)

Note that c is legal in some Basic language translators.

8-1.6 Consider the following printed output:

17.3	1	7.301
18.8	2	7.321

Indicate which of the following Basic segments might have produced this output:

    (a)   PRINT X,I,B
           PRINT Y,J
           PRINT Z
    (b)   PRINT X,I,Y
           PRINT Z,K,W
    (c)   PRINT X,I(1),Y(4)
           PRINT X(1), "2", X(2)
    (d)   PRINT A2, 1, A(2)
           PRINT X4, K, X(4)

8-1.7 You have three DATA statements which contain values for the variables N, M, D, G4, K(I) for I = 1 to 8 and A(I) for I = 6 to 16. The values are in the order listed here. Give a segment of a Basic program that correctly reads this data and assigns the values.

8-1.8 Consider the following Basic program

```
  1 DIM A(50),B(50),X(50),Y(50)
 10 READ A(1),B(1)
 20 LET K=1
 30 READ X(K),Y(K)
 40 LET K=K+1
 50 IF K<26 THEN 30
100 LET T=1
110 LET D = ((X(T)-A(T))↑2+(Y(T)-B(T))↑2)↑.5
120 LET A(T+1) = A(T)+2*(X(T)-A(T))/D
130 LET B(T+1) = B(T)+2*(Y(T)-B(T))/D
140 LET T=T+1
150 IF D>1 THEN 110
200 LET U=1
210 PRINT U,A(U),B(U)
220 LET U=U+1
230 IF U<T THEN 210
300 DATA 16.3,92.1
350 REM   *** MORE DATA HERE ***
900 END
```

(a) How many values are read in?

(b) How many (in terms of the value of T) numbers are printed out?

(c) How many (in terms of the value of T) lines of printed output are there?

(d) Identify the iteration loops in the program and give the names of their parts and the corresponding Basic statements.

8-1.9 For each of the segments of Basic programs given below give

(a) the number of values read in,

(b) the number of values printed out,

(c) the number of lines printed.

```
 10 DIM X(50),Y(50)
 20 LET J = 1
 30 PRINT X(J),J,X(J+1)+1
 50 LET K = 11
 40 PRINT   A
 60 PRINT Y(K)-A
 70 LET K=K+1
 80 IF K<31 THEN 60
 90 LET J=J+1
100 IF J<9 THEN 30
200 END
```

```
 10 DIM T(100),B(100)
 20 READ N4,N(1),N(2)
 30 LET J=N4
 40 PRINT T(J),B(J)+N(1)
 50 LET J=J+1
 60 IF J< N(2)+1 THEN 40
100 DATA 3,1.62E+3,20,14,8.624
200 END
```

8-1.10 Show how to write out the diagonal elements of a square array or table with a Basic program that uses one PRINT statement. An element is on the diagonal if it is in the same row as column, that is, if its two indices are equal.

8-1.11 An array in which most of the elements are zero is said to be *sparse*. Write a program in which you define a 5 x 5 array, set its elements equal to zero, and then read in the values, along with the subscripts, that constitute the nonzero elements of the array. Write out the data and resulting array. For example, you might set $A(2,3) = 5$, $A(4,1) = -2$ and $A(5,2) = 70$.

8-1.12 For some program that you have already written, determine exactly how many machine words are available for use as arrays. Try rerunning the program with an array that is somewhat too large.

8-1.13 Write a program that reads in a one-dimensional array of up to 100 elements. First, write out the array, then write out the greatest and least elements along with their positions in the array as described below.

If, for example, $A(31)$ was the largest, and $A(62)$ was the least, your output should contain these lines.

$$\text{ARRAY } 31 = 62047 \text{ IS LARGEST}$$
$$\text{ARRAY } 62 = -493 \text{ IS SMALLEST}$$

If you need help in finding the largest and smallest elements then see Section 6-3.

8-1.14 Explain why it is not possible to turn an array, or list around in itself. That is, you are given $L(K)$, $K = 1$ to 10 and you want to get the values of $L(10)$, $L(9), \ldots, L(1)$ in the list instead of $L(1), L(2), \ldots, L(10)$ without using any locations other than those assigned to the array L. Explain how this can be done using just *one* extra variable (word), called T.

8-1.15 Consider Problem 6-4.1 (Student Grading) and show how arrays can be used to make this program simpler, easier to extend to other situations, and more understandable. Write a program to accomplish the same task except that there are eight test scores for each student rather than four.

8-1.16 Consider Problem 6-4.2 (Department Store Sales Records), and introduce an array for the five numbers required as input and the five numbers of output. Show how this simplifies the program and rewrite the program using these arrays.

8-1.17 Consider Problem 6-4.4 (College Registrar Records) and use arrays for the information involved. Show that this shortens the program very much and makes it as easy to handle a college with 20 departments (each with 20 courses) as to handle a college with only 4 departments and 16 courses. Rewrite the program using arrays and make the test runs indicated.

8-1.18 Consider Problem 6-4.5 (True-False Quiz Grading). Introduce an array for the number of people who answer each question correctly and show how this simplifies the program. Furthermore, show how the number of questions can be changed from time to time with a simple change in the program. Rewrite the program for grading a quiz with 25 questions and run a test case as indicated.

8-2 FOR — LOOPS

The control statement FOR allows us to set up a simple iteration loop more conveniently. This can materially shorten a program that handles loops using IF-THEN statements. For instance, three of the four statements used to set an array A to zero on the left below can be replaced by a single FOR statement and associated NEXT statement, as shown on the right.

```
1 LET  J=1                          10 FOR  J=1 TO N ◄──┐
2 LET  A( J) = 0 ◄──┐               20 LET  A( J) = 0    │ Loop
3 LET  J=J+1        │ Loop          30 NEXT  J  ─────────┘
4 IF  J<N THEN 2 ───┘

   Iteration built                     Equivalent iteration
   from IF—THEN                        using FOR and NEXT
```

Not only is the program on the right one statement shorter, it is also easier to read and the total typing is somewhat reduced.

FOR

The general form of the FOR statements is

FOR (variable) = (expression) TO (expression) STEP (expression)

The variable in the FOR statement is initialized with the first expression and proceeds until it reaches or passes the second expression. The steps in the variable are specified by the third expression following the keyword STEP. The word STEP and associated expressions may be omitted if the step is to be 1. The variable in the FOR statement is called the *control variable* or *counter*.

EXAMPLES

```
FOR  J = 1  TO  18
FOR  J = 5  TO  18  STEP 2
FOR  K = X - 3  TO  X*Y+1  STEP  X↑2 -4* J*X
FOR  J =     0  TO      .05  STEP  .001
FOR X4 =    10  TO       1 STEP  -1
```

In the first example J takes on the 18 values 1,2, ... 18. In the second example J takes on the values 5,7,9, . . . ,15,17. It does not take on the value 19 (or 18). The final three examples illustrate that the control variable can decrease as well as increase and that the steps need not be integers.

The FOR statement initiates the iteration loop and specifies the values of the control variable. The range or set of actions in the iteration must also be specified. In Basic, this is done by placing the keyword NEXT to mark the end of the range of the iteration.

NEXT

The keyword NEXT is followed by the control variable of an associated FOR statement. The pair of FOR and NEXT statements specify the *range* of the FOR-loop. The FOR is at the start, the NEXT at the end.

EXAMPLES

```
FOR  J = 1 TO 8          FOR  K = -5 TO 17 STEP 3
     ...                      ...
NEXT J                   NEXT K
```

In the execution of a FOR-loop, all the statements in the range of the FOR are executed in sequence, with the counter or control variable assuming a new value on each pass through these statements. The FOR-loop is terminated when the control variable reaches or passes the terminal value. Then the statement following the NEXT statement is executed. Consider the following statements; they set the array B equal to the array A and also find the sum of the elements of A:

```
 80 LET S=0
 85 FOR J = 1 TO N
 90 LET B(J) = A(J)
 95 LET S = S +A(J) ──────── Accumulate the values of
100 NEXT J                   A(J) with the variable S
105 PRINT " THE SUM IS", S
```

The range of this FOR-loop includes the statements B(J) = A(J) and the one following it. Only after these two statements have been executed N times is the PRINT executed.

The exact action of the FOR statement is shown in the flowchart of Figure 8-2.1.

It is possible to transfer control to any executable statement with an IF or GO TO statement. However, we should not transfer control to a statement within the range of a FOR-loop from outside the range and expect it to work. The only way to enter a FOR-loop is at the FOR statement. This is reasonable since the FOR-loop is only set up by the FOR statement and an entry into the range of the FOR statement results in unpredictable results since the value of the control variable is not determined.

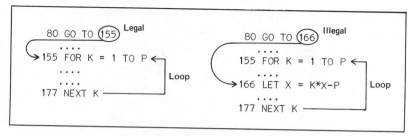

One may leave a FOR-loop at any point by using a GO TO or an IF-THEN statement. When this occurs the control variable retains its current value. If one leaves a FOR-loop by a natural termination, then the control variable keeps the last value it had before the termination test was true. This might not be the terminal value if the step does not make the control variable exactly equal to the terminal value.

Several FOR-loops may be contained within one another, provided that their ranges are properly nested; that is, the range of the "shortest" FOR is fully contained within the range of the next "shortest" FOR, and so on. This is illustrated below.

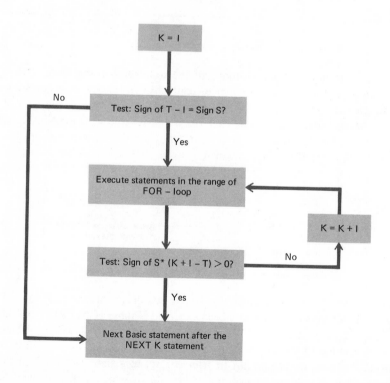

FIGURE 8-2.1   **The operation of the FOR statement FOR K = I TO T STEP S.**

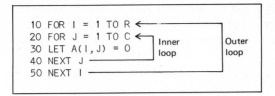

```
10 FOR I = 1 TO R ←
20 FOR J = 1 TO C ←    Inner      Outer
30 LET A(I,J) = 0      loop       loop
40 NEXT J
50 NEXT I
```

The control variable I for the outermost FOR is set; then the innermost FOR is execu'
When it is done, or "satisfied," I is incremented and the process repeats, until fina'
have set A(1,1), . . . ,A(R,C) equal to zero.

The following sample program illustrates the use of the FOR s'
particularly in connection with arrays. The problem considered is the follow'
saves $100 a month (or $1200 a year) and invests it at various interest rat'
much money will one have as the years go by? The mathematical mod(
program assumes that one invests $1200 on the first day of each year ...u that the
interest is credited on the same day for the previous amount. The interest rates chosen are
4 percent (for putting the money in the bank), 8 percent (perhaps for mortgages or
corporate bonds), 12 percent (perhaps for successful real estate or stock market trading)
and 16 percent (for good luck in stock market speculation).

```
 1 REM    RETURN ON $100/MO. INVESTMENTS
 2 REM    P = ARRAY OF INTEREST
 3 REM    S = ARRAY OF SUMS ACCUMULATED SO FAR
 4 REM         FOR EACH OF THE 4 VALUES OF P
10 PRINT " ","RETURN ON $100/MO. INVESTMENTS"
20 PRINT "YEARS","AT PERCENT RATES OF"
30 PRINT " ", 4, 8,12,16
40 READ P(1),P(2),P(3),P(4)
50 FOR K=1 TO 4         ⌐ Initialize S(K) values
60 LET S(K) = 1200        at $1200
70 NEXT K
80 REM           MAIN LOOP STARTS
100 FOR Y = 1 TO 25    ←
110 FOR K = 1 TO 4
120 LET S(K) = S(K)*(1.+P(K))   Compute and add
130 NEXT K                      interest earned
140 PRINT Y,S(1),S(2),S(3),S(4)        Loop on Y
150 FOR K = 1 TO 4     ⌐ Add $100/month
160 LET S(K) = S(K) + 1200  for 12 months
170 NEXT K             ⌐ into S(K)
180 NEXT Y
200 DATA .04,.08,.12,.16
300 END
```

The program is initialized in statements 10 through 70 where the P values are read in and
the sums are set to 1200 for the first year. The main loop starts at statement 100 where
the years Y range from 1 to 25. Statements 110—130 add the interest earned onto the
four sums. Statements 150—170 add on the $1200 after the accumulated sums are
printed out at statement 140.

Note that it is easier to read the values for the P array than it is to set them with four LET statements. A slight modification of the strategy used above results in a somewhat shorter program (though it is not faster to compute). Statements 50—180 may be replaced by

```
 50 FOR K=1 TO 4      ┐ Initialize S(K)
 60 LET S(K) = 0      │ values at $0
 70 NEXT K            ┘
100 FOR Y = 1 TO 25                          ←─┐
110 FOR K = 1 TO 4
120 LET S(K) = (S(K)+1200)*(1+P(K))    Loop on Y
140 PRINT Y,S(1),S(2),S(3),S(4)
150 NEXT Y                                   ──┘
```

Furthermore, one may delete lines 50—70 in most systems because *most Basic language systems initialize all variables to zero.* If this is the case, then this slight modification shortens the original program from 16 executable statements to 10 executable statements. Even though this second program is not executed any faster, it saves time for both the user and the language translater. Such savings in effort are often possible if one puts a little thought into improving the organization of a computation, of a program.

PROBLEMS

8-2.1   A program involving FOR-loops can sometimes be made to execute much more rapidly if there are computations within a FOR-loop that can be done outside it. Discuss how much faster the following statements might run if such changes are made.

```
100 FOR J = 1 TO N
110 FOR K = 2 TO J+3
120 LET B(K) = B(K)+K*(J↑2-A(J))/(16.3+A(J))
130 LET X(J,K) = B(K)*(Y+Z-17.63/(Y-Z)) +A(J)/A(J)*(J-6)
140 NEXT K
150 NEXT J
```

8-2.2   Write a program that reads a set of integer scores all lying in the range from 0 to 100, and have it calculate the frequencies for each score from 0 to 100.

8-2.3   Convert the following FOR-loop into an equivalent set of Basic statements that do *not* include a FOR statement:

```
100 FOR K = 7 TO L4 STEP J-6+X
110 LET A(K) = A(K)/(K+1) - A(K-6)
120 NEXT K
```

8-2.4 Write a program that reads in three integers M, N, and L. Then read in an M x N matrix called A and an N x L matrix called B. Print out the original matrices and the matrix product A*B. The matrix product has the I,Kth element defined by

$$\sum_{J=1}^{N} A(I,J)*B(J,K)$$

and it is an M x L matrix. Create some data for this program and run it to show that it is correct.

8-2.5 A man wishes to retire in 10 years and deposits $25,000.00 at 4½ percent interest compounded quarterly. He then adds $100 at the end of each year for years 1 through 9. At retirement, he finds inflation has deflated the buying power of his money until the purchasing power is no more than his original deposit. What was the average annual percentage of inflation?

Hint: If the rate of inflation is X percent, then at the end of each year his investment loses X percent. Introduce X into your program and adjust the value by trial and error until the final sum is $25,000. Note that the interest earned is added on every 3 months while the inflation and additional savings are included only once a year.

8-2.6 Write a program that converts a number of hours into weeks, days, and hours. Have the output in the form

3092 HOURS IS 18 WEEKS

2 DAYS

20 HOURS

8-2.7 Write a program that reads a date given as 6,5,70 or 12,25,75 and prints out lines like

06 05 70	IS	JUNE 5 1970
12 25 75	IS	DECEMBER 25 1975.

8-2.8 Suppose one has a $26,400 mortgage balance and is paying interest at 7.2 percent per year (or .6 percent per month). The monthly payments are $196.00 per month. Write a program that prints out a table of the interest paid each year and the balance remaining at the end of each year up to the time the mortgage is paid. Also print out the total number of months left to pay on the mortgage.

Note that the part of each payment not needed for the month's interest cost is subtracted from the balance due and the .6 percent rate is applied to the remaining balance. The last payment will be less than $196.00, print out the amount of this payment.

8-2.9 Modify the program of Problem 8-2.8 so as to generate a table of the number of months one has to pay $196.00 in order to pay the mortgage of $26,400. The table is to be for interest rates of 6 percent, 6.6 percent, 7.2 percent, 7.8 percent and 8.4 percent.

8-2.10 Write a program that reads a set of DATA statements with four numbers each. The program is to compute the maximum of the four numbers and print it out with an appropriate message. Further, the program is to find the maximum of all the numbers read from all the DATA statements and print it out in the form:

LARGEST OF ALL IS XXXXXX.XXX.

The program is to recognize four zeros as the last data set and is to terminate without trying to read from an empty data stack.

8-2.11 Write a program to compute Pascal's triangle of binomial coefficients. The first part appears as

```
                1
              1   1
            1   2   1
          1   3   3   1
        1   4   6   4   1
```

and later rows are generated by noting that each element is the sum of the two elements just above it (except for the two 1's on the ends). Give the printed output in the form

N = 0	1
N = 1	1 1
N = 2	1 2 1
N = 3	1 3 3 1

If there are too many numbers for one line, start a second line with indention. Print the first 20 rows of the array.

8-2.12 Write a program that reads in a list of numbers between 0 and 100 and finds the median of the list. The median is the number that is in the middle of the list after it is sorted and arranged from smallest to largest. If the list has an even number of elements then there might not be a middle element (for example, 6,27,42,60,81,88). In this case use the average of the two elements (42 and 60 in the example) next to the middle point of the list. Write the program so that the list may have at most 50 elements. Write out the list and the median and average of the list.

8-2.13 A flowchart is given for adding two integers of arbitrary length. The digits of the first number are in the array T (for top) and those of the second number are in the array B (for bottom). There are K digits in each array and T(K), B(K) are on the left and T(1), B(1) are on the right. The digits of the sum of these two numbers are in the array A (for answer). Write a program based on this flowchart that adds integers of length up to 100.

8-2.14 The Personnel File Problem: *The little black book*

Consider a list of people along with information about their ability, likes, dislikes, experience, and other personal qualities. Assume that from time to time you have to choose a person from this list for a particular task, assignment, and so forth.

(a) Each choice requires a varying combination of the personal qualities in the list. Devise a measure of goodness of choice for a particular assignment. *Hint:* Rank the personal qualities of each person on some scale (say 1 to 5 or 1 to 10) and then specify a set of weights that describes what each assignment requires.

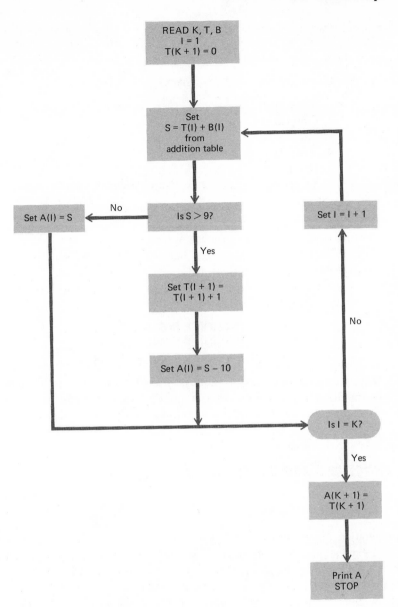

FIGURE 8-2.2 Flowchart for Problem 8-2.13.

(b) *Specific case.* You have a little black book that contains the names, addresses, and telephone numbers of your friends. For each one, you have the following information:

Characteristics	*Likes*
1. Appearance	1. Classical music
2. Compatibility	2. Dancing
3. Conversational	3. Movies—T.V.
4. Financial	4. Parties
5. Moral	5. Sports
6. Scholastic	6. World Affairs

You need dates for (A) the football homecoming game and dance, (B) the Phlat Phrat Braul, (C) a relaxing evening. Whom do you call first (or say yes to first) from your little black book?

Make up a little black book for 12 people and specify a set of weights for each of these dates. Write a program which processes this information and selects the best candidate from your black book. The output should be of the form

> THE CHOICE FOR DATE 1 IS _____
> THE CHOICE FOR DATE 2 IS _____
> THE CHOICE FOR DATE 3 IS _____

8-2.15   Write a program to subtract one integer from another where each number has up to 100 digits. If the result is negative, print a message to this effect.

8-2.16   Write a program to do integer multiplication with up to 15 digits in each factor.

8-3 FUNCTIONS AND SUBPROGRAMS

8-3.1 Built-in Functions

The computational power in Basic so far has been limited to four arithmetic operations +, −, *, / and exponentiation (or powers) ↑. The usefulness of Basic is much enhanced by a number of other computational tools, the *built-in* functions. This set of functions varies from system to system; the set described here includes the more useful ones. The set of built-in functions is naturally divided into two groups, the arithmetic functions and the *mathematical functions* (or *routines* as they are often called).

A simple example of a useful function is the *absolute value*. One can obtain the absolute value as follows.

```
 80  IF X<0 THEN 95
 85  LET X1 = X
 90     GO TO 100
 95  LET X1 = -X
100  REM    *** PROGRAM CONTINUES ***
```

The result of these four statements is that X1 is the absolute value of X. The absolute value function replaces these four statements with one statement as follows.

```
80 LET X1 = ABS(X)
```

Function, Built-in

A built-in function has a name with three letters followed by an *argument* enclosed in parentheses. The argument may be any legal expression and a function can be used in an expression in the same manner as an ordinary variable.

EXAMPLES

```
PRINT  ABS(X+Y),     ABS(1 - X * 4)
LET    K = ABS(T) * 5.2/ABS(T * 7 - 4)
LET    T = ABS(1 + 17.5 * ABS(X - 7.3 * Y))
```

There are six arithmetic (or nonmathematical) built-in functions which are listed in Table 8-3.1.

TABLE 8-3.1
Some of the built-in functions in Basic.

Ordinary Name	Definition	Basic Name
Absolute Value	The magnitude of the argument	ABS
Integer part	The largest integer not greater than the argument	INT
Sign	The sign (+1, 0, or –1) of the argument	SGN
Random Number	A random number lying between 0 and 1	RND
Clock*	The current time of day in the 24 hour/day system	CLK
Time elapsed*	The number of seconds that the program has been in execution	TIM

*This function is not available in some systems.

The following examples illustrate these functions.

ABS(7.3)	= 7.3		ABS(−7.3)	= 7.3
INT(7.3)	= 7		INT(−7.3)	= −8
INT(.73)	= 0		INT(−.73)	= −1
SGN(7.3)	= 1		SGN(−7.3)	= −1
ABS(X)	= X*SGN(X)		SGN(0)	= 0

$$\text{fractional part of A} = \begin{cases} A - INT(A) & \text{if } A > 0 \\ INT(A) - A + 1 & \text{if } A < 0 \\ ABS(A) - INT(ABS(A)) & \text{for all } A \end{cases}$$

The three functions RND, CLK, and TIM do not depend on their arguments, but arguments are needed to conform to the rules of the Basic language. In some systems the argument of RND does play a limited role for the random number generator RND; it allows one to obtain different random numbers on different runs of a program.

The integer part function can be used to determine if a number, N, is a factor of another number, X. One forms the expression

$$X - INT(X/N)*N$$

which is zero if X/N is an integer and not zero otherwise. One could then use this idea to test whether X is a prime number (that is, check all the possible factors between 2 and the square root of X).

In addition to the above built-in functions there are seven common mathematical functions in Basic as given in Table 8-3.2.

TABLE 8.3.2 **Some built-in mathematical functions in Basic.**

Ordinary Name	Definition	Basic Name
Sine, sin(x)	The sine of the angle given in radians, not degrees	SIN
Cosine, cos(x)	The cosine of the angle given in radians, not degrees	COS
Tangent, tan(x)	The tangent of the angle given in radians, not degrees	TAN
Arc tangent, $\tan^{-1}(x)$	The angle (in radians) whose tangent is that of the argument	ATN
Exponential function, e^x	The number e = 2.71828 . . . raised to the power of the argument	EXP
Logarithm, ln(x)	The natural logarithm of the argument, $e^{\ln(x)} = x$	LOG
Square root, $\sqrt{x}$	The square root of the argument	SQR

Some examples of the use of these functions are given below.

```
10 LET Z = SIN(X+1)*COS(X-1)
20 PRINT  SQR(X-1/X), LOG(ABS(3.2*Y))
30 FOR J = 1 TO EXP(K/J) STEP LOG(K+1)
40 LET A = 4.4*SIN(X)↑(SQR(X-1)*2)
```

8-3.2 *User Defined Functions*

Most Basic systems allow additional function definitions in a program. For example, if one were to use the fractional part frequently, one can define

100 DEF FNP(X) = ABS(X) – INT(ABS(X))

and then use the function FNP just as though it were a built-in function. The exact rules governing the definition of functions are given below.

DEF

> The keyword DEF is followed by the function name (three letters starting with FN) and argument with its definition given on the right of an equal sign. The definition must be a single expression in Basic and may use any Basic function, even other ones defined by a DEF statement.

EXAMPLES

```
DEF  FNA(X)  =  X + ABS(X – 3) * SQR(X)
DEF  FNB(X)  =  COS(X+A) * COS(X-A) * .5
DEF  FNR(X)  =  FNA(X) * FNB(X) – X*Y+W
```

The argument of the function being defined is a *dummy argument* (or *placeholder*) and it does not matter what variable name is used. Thus the following statements define exactly the same function.

```
10 DEF FNA(X) = X↑1.5/(X+1)        10 DEF FNA(B) = B↑1.5/(B+1)
```

Note that when the function FNA(X) (or FNA(B)) is used as in FNA(6.3), the value calculated is

$$6.3\uparrow1.5/(6.3+1)$$

which does not depend on whether the function is defined as FNA(X), FNA(B), FNA(K7), and so forth. The expression defining the function may contain the dummy argument and any other variables in the program. The variables (not dummy argument) that appear in the expression must be assigned values before the function is used. The arguments are assigned values when the function is used and the values are simply substituted into the expression in place of arguments.

The usefulness of defining a function comes into play only if it is used at several different points in the program. If it is used only once (or even twice if it is short), it is simpler to put the required expression where it is used rather than define a function.

8-3.3 Subprograms

If a function can be described with a single statement, then it can be defined with a DEF statement. If several statements are required, then it must be defined as a subprogram.

Consider the following example of a subprogram that computes the average of a set of 100 numbers contained in a specified array A.

```
200 LET S = 0 ──────────── Initialize sum to zero
210 FOR K = 1 TO 100
220 LET S = S + A(K)────── Accummulate total
230 NEXT K
240 LET S = S/K ────────── Calculate average
250 RETURN
```

This subprogram appears just as another part of a Basic program except for the RETURN statement. It is used in another part of the whole program as follows.

```
80 REM    HAVE GOT THE ARRAY A READY
90 GOSUB 200
100 PRINT "AVERAGE OF A-ARRAY IS",S
```

When the GOSUB statement at 90 is executed, the control of the program is transferred to statement 200 just as a GO TO statement would do. However, when the next RETURN statement is met (as at statement 250), the control of the program is returned to the next statement following the GOSUB. Thus the program jumps to the little subprogram, computes the average S of the array A and then returns.

GOSUB

The keyword GOSUB is followed by a label. Program control is directly transferred to the specified label, but whenever a RETURN is met the control is transferred back to the statement immediately following the GOSUB.

EXAMPLES

```
        400 GOSUB 250              600 GOSUB 900
```

RETURN

The keyword RETURN signals the end of a subprogram and transfers control back to the point just after the jump (with a GOSUB statement) to the subprogram.

EXAMPLES

```
        400 GOSUB 250            600 GOSUB 900
        ---                      ---
        250 LET K = 2            900 FOR J = 5 TO 86
        ---                      ---
        288 RETURN               972 RETURN
```

Subprograms provide a great deal of power and flexibility in computing. It allows one to construct a program in pieces or as modules. These pieces are presumably well-defined subcalculations and one writes and debugs the program for these parts and then makes them into subprograms. These subprograms are then usable at various places and one need not worry about them while finishing the other parts of the program. Of course, there is the possibility (which occurs all too often) that a subprogram has an error in it which just has not been found yet.

As an example of the use of a subprogram, consider someone whose program keeps taking the square root of negative numbers. This clutters up the output, so it is decided to "replace" the built-in function SQR by a subprogram. This subprogram checks the argument and sets the value of a variable T equal to special value depending on the sign of the argument. The value of this "test" variable is 1, 2, or 3 according to whether the variable X is negative, zero, or positive. The original program had one line in it

```
208 LET Y = SQR(X)
```

which caused the trouble. That line is now replaced by

```
208 GOSUB 600
```

The corresponding subprogram is

```
                    600 REM    SQUARE ROOT WITH TEST VALUE T
                    605 LET T = 3
                    610 IF X > 0 THEN 640 ─┐ Check sign of X
                    615 IF X =0 THEN 635 ─┘
   Negative X ───── 620 LET T = 1
                    625 LET X = -X
                    630 GO TO 640
       Zero X ───── 635 LET T = 2
   Positive X ───── 640 LET Y = SQR(X)
                    645 RETURN
```

This modification protects ones output from being cluttered with little messages about taking the square root of negative numbers and yet it also allows one to find out what is happening by checking the value of T. The next section has an example which makes use of this feature in a realistic situation.

There are two further points about subprograms. First, the functions or subprograms must not be "circular" in their organization. Thus if the definition of FNB involves FNA, one cannot also have FNB in the definition of FNA. Likewise, one cannot have a subprogram that transfers back into another subprogram containing it (except by a RETURN). One subprogram may use another if a circular loop is not defined. Some legal constructions are given below followed by similar, but illegal ones.

```
                    20 DEF FNA(T) = T*ABS(T-7.3)
                    30 DEF FNB(T) = FNA(T)/(T+6.4)
                    40 REM    *** PROGRAM CONTINUES ***
                   120 GOSUB (300)
                  →130 REM    *** PROGRAM CONTINUES ***   ─┐ Go into first
                   (300) LET K = 2  ←                       │ subprogram
   Return to       310 REM    *** PROGRAM CONTINUES ***
   main            315↓LET L = K-4/X
   program         317 GOSUB (400)
                  →319↓LET P = A(L)                        ─┐ Go into second
                   318│REM    *** PROGRAM CONTINUES ***      │ subprogram
                   340▼RETURN
   Return to       (400)│FOR J = 1 TO K  ←
   first           410│REM    *** PROGRAM CONTINUES ***
   subprogram      416▼RETURN
```

Legal Use of Def and GOSUB

```
        20 DEF FNA(T) = T*ABS(T-7.3)
        30 DEF FNB(T) = FNA(T)/(T+6.4)
        40 REM   *** PROGRAM CONTINUES ***
       120 GOSUB 300
       130 REM    *** PROGRAM CONTINUES ***       Go into first
       300 LET K = 2                              subprogram
       310 REM    *** PROGRAM CONTINUES ***
       315 LET L = K-4/X
       317 GOSUB 400
       318 REM    *** PROGRAM CONTINUES ***       Go into second
       319 IF A(L) > 100 THEN 410                 subprogram
  Illegal
  jump back   340 RETURN
  into first  400 FOR J = 1 TO K
  subprogram  410 REM    *** PROGRAM CONTINUES ***
              416 GO TO 319
```

Illegal Use of DEF and GOSUB

The execution of a subprogram *must* be terminated with a RETURN, but it can have more than one RETURN statement if it branches into several parts. For example, a RETURN could be placed in the special "square root with test" subprogram between statements 635 and 640.

Variables that are used in a subprogram are the same as variables elsewhere in the program. Thus the variable X in a subprogram is the same as X elsewhere. This is not the case for dummy arguments of DEF statements where the name used does not play a role.

8-3.4 Application: Processing Data from Remote Monitoring of Bulk Material Supplies

Consider a company that dispenses a bulk material (flour, wheat, sand, iron ore) from containers as shown in Figure 8-3.1.

Under one leg of the container is a pressure-sensitive scale that can be read by remote recording equipment. The company has hundreds of these containers and has decided to replace visual daily inspection by remote sensing and data processing. One key factor is the depth of the material remaining and we consider processing the data to obtain this information. Assume the scale measures weight W in 100 pound units. We must find relationships to relate this to the desired information, depth or D. Such relationships are

$$\text{volume (in cubic feet)} = 50 * \text{triangle area}$$
$$= 50. * D*D/2$$
$$W = .046 * \text{Volume}/4$$

where .046 is the weight (in hundreds of pounds) of one cubic foot of the material. We divide by 4 because the container has four legs. We can combine these equations to obtain

$$D = \frac{\sqrt{W*4}}{\sqrt{25. * .046}} = \sqrt{W * 1.865}.$$

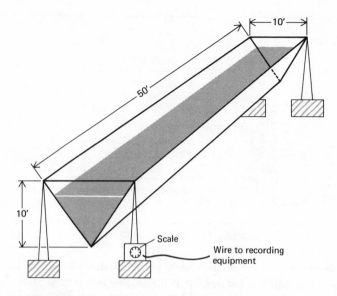

FIGURE 8-3.1   The container, dispenser of bulk material.

The original idea was to have the recording equipment obtain data every day which were then processed to give a computer output listing of the depth in each of the containers. The average depth is also needed to gauge the average level of bulk material in the company. Certain difficulties arose when these listings were first used. First, many containers are out of use at any given moment due to repairs, changes in production, and so forth. These were included in the averages and gave a misleading indication of the supply status in the company. Second, some weights turned out to be negative. This resulted in two things: one was that nasty messages appeared in the middle of the listings which were hard to explain to management. After all, whoever heard of negative weights? The other was that the averages were even more misleading. An investigation showed that these negative weights were caused by a variety of malfunctions in the recording equipment and the scales. Since these malfunctions are expected to be present for a number of months, the program that processes the data is required to check for and eliminate such readings.

The program finally developed is given below. It has the readings in the array R(K) (with up to 800 containers allowed). The function for square roots discussed earlier is used to take the square roots and to avoid the illegal square roots of negative numbers. The result of this subprogram is checked to see if R(K) is valid and, if not, this value is ignored and an appropriate error message printed. The original data W is replaced by the desired information D in the array R(I) and the results are listed with a summary heading.

```
   1 REM    N= NUMBER OF CONTAINERS
   2 REM    R= WEIGHTS READ, LATER
   3 REM       REPLACED BY DEPTHS
   4 REM    G= NUMBER OF GOOD MEASUREMENTS
   5 REM    A= AVERAGE DEPTH
  10 DIM R(800)
  15 READ N
  20 FOR K = 1 TO N ─┐
  25 READ R(K)        ├ Loop to read the array of weights
  30 NEXT K         ─┘
  35 LET G = 0
  40 LET A = 0
 100 FOR K = 1 TO N                              ─┐
 105 LET X = R(K)                                 │
 110 GOSUB 600              ─┐ Go to subprogram   │
 115 IF T=3 THEN 150         ├ then test for type │
 120 IF T=2 THEN 135        ─┘ of situation       │
 125 PRINT "BAD CASE",K                           │
 130       GO TO 160                              │ Loop to process the
 135 PRINT "MISSING CASE",K                       │ weights read
 140       GO TO 160                              │
 145 REM         GOOD VALUES HERE                 │
 150 LET G = G+1                                  │
 155 LET A = A+R(K)                               │
 160 REM     REPLACE VALUES IN R(K) ARRAY         │
 165 LET R(K) = Y*1.865                          ─┘
 170 NEXT K
 200 REM            HAVE PROCESSED ALL DATA
 205 LET A = A/G
 210 PRINT
 211 PRINT
 215 PRINT G," CASES ARE GOOD, AVERAGE =",A
 220 PRINT " DEPTHS MEASURED ARE"
 225 FOR K = 1 TO N STEP 2
 230 PRINT K;R(K),K+1;R(K+1)
 235 NEXT K
 250 STOP
 600 REM    SQUARE ROOT WITH TEST VALUE T ─┐
 605 LET T = 3                             │
 610 IF X > 0 THEN 640                     │
 615 IF X =0 THEN 635                       │
 620 LET T = 1                             │
 625 LET X = -X                             ├ Subprogram
 630 GO TO 640                             │
 635 LET T = 2                             │
 640 LET Y = SQR(X)                        │
 645 RETURN                               ─┘
 800 DATA 25
 810 DATA 10.2,88.1,409.2,16.2,0.0,12.3,0.0,80.6,-42.3
 850 REM    *** MORE DATA HERE ***
 880 DATA 15.6,0.0,58.3,64.9,72.0,-12.0,46.9,10.8,0.0
 890 DATA 45.4,86.1,-142.23,153.6,43.0,68.4,29,7,0.0,-12.0
 999 END
```

The fact that we want the entire list of the array D separate from the list of bad or missing items of data leads to reading in all of the data first, then processing them. It is possible to read and process the data simultaneously and still obtain these two lists separately. However, this approach would require a slightly more complicated (and considerably less natural) program than the one presented here.

PROBLEMS

8-3.1   Give the Basic expressions for the following expressions given in ordinary mathematical notation

(a) $X^{3/2} \sqrt{X^2+Y^2}$

(b) $\sin(a+90)$

(c) $\sin(b-45) \cos(b+45)$

(d) $2 \log(X+1)$

(e) $e\sqrt{X+2} \cos(3x+1)$

(f) $x \log_{10}(x^2-a^2)$

8-3.2   Given the ordinary mathematical notation for the following Basic expressions.

(a)   X*(Y+1)↑(SQRT(X↑2+Y↑2))
(b)   EXP(R*COS(2*R-1))
(c)   (LOG((X+1)/(X-1)))*(1+EXP(X↑2-1)/ABS(X-2))
(d)   4.12*LOG(X*SQR(X↑(5./3.)+1))
(e)   SIN(A+90)↑2+COS(B+90)↑2-2*COS(A+B)

8-3.3   Write a Basic program that uses the quadratic formula

$$X = \frac{-B \pm \sqrt{B^2 - 4AC}}{2A}$$

as a function FNX with an argument S as the sign to be used for the square root. The program should read in values for A, B, and C and print out the roots of the quadratic polynomial Ax^2+Bx+C by this formula. What do you do when the square root is taken of a negative number?

8-3.4   Write a program which processes the 2-dimensional array T with C columns and R rows. This subprogram rearranges the rows so that the specified column D is in descending order. Thus if T is the array

6.2	3.4	25.1	-7.2
14.8	-4.1	16.7	18.2
.7	33.3	1.2	-1.8

then the subprogram with D = 2, R = 3, C = 4 results in T becoming

.7	33.3	1.2	-1.8
6.2	3.4	25.1	-7.2
14.8	-4.1	16.7	18.2

Write a subprogram that generates several arrays with different values for C and R. Print out the arrays and use your subprogram for sorting columns to sort these arrays on two different columns. Print the arrays after each sorting. Suggested values for C, R, and D are:

$$C = 4, \quad R = 3, \quad D = 2 \text{ and } 4$$
$$C = 5, \quad R = 2, \quad D = 1 \text{ and } 4$$
$$C = 3, \quad R = 5, \quad D = 1 \text{ and } 2$$

8-3.5   In recording experimental data, it often happens that the recorded information is to be transformed prior to being used in standard formulas. Suppose five kinds of data are measured. Assign to each a one-digit code. The transformations to be applied are:

> type 1, square root; type 2, add $\pi/2$; type 3, log; type 4, take reciprocal; type 5, cube root.

Write a program that reads the data and data types and then applies the appropriate transformation. Create a typical set of data to test your program and run it to show that it is correct.

8-3.6   Write a program which evaluates the following four numbers and prints them out in increasing order.

$$A = \ln \left(\frac{1}{\sqrt[3]{.00000000584}} \right)$$

$$B = \sqrt[7]{24{,}502}$$

$$C = 6 \cos(251.33) - .43 \sin(2{,}260.3757)$$

$$D = \frac{479{,}058}{76{,}041} + \frac{211}{36{,}911}$$

The output should be in the following form (assuming that $B < D < A < C$ which is not actually the case)

$$B = \text{XXXX.XXXX}$$
$$D = \text{XXXX.XXXX}$$
$$A = \text{XXXX.XXXX}$$
$$C = \text{XXXX.XXXX}$$

8-3.7   Write a program that uses the functions SIN and COS to compute $\sin^2 x + \cos^2 x$ for $x = 0$ to 20 in increments of 0.1. By a well-known trigonometric identity $\sin^2 x + \cos^2 x = 1$ for all x. In order to examine the accuracy of the built-in functions, compute the percentage error for each computation $c = \sin^2 x + \cos^2 x$ using the formula

$$\text{p.e.} = 100 \times |1 - c|.$$

Your output should be in the following form:

X	SIN(X)↑2+COS(X)↑2	PERCENTAGE ERROR
0.00	1.0000000	0.0000000
0.10	1.0000000	0.0000000
and so on		

8-3.8   Write a program that uses the Monte Carlo technique described below to approximate $\pi = 3.1415926$. Consider the unit square $((0,0), (0,1), (1,0), (1,1))$ in the plane and a circle of radius 1 with its center at $(0,0)$. If we randomly generate points in the unit square and count the number that lie within the quarter circle, we get an approximation of the area of the quarter circle from the ratio

$$r = \frac{\text{Number of points within quarter circle}}{\text{Number of points generated in square}}.$$

According to Monte Carlo theory $r \approx {}^{\pi}4$ or the area of the quarter circle. Therefore to get an approximation of π, we use a random number generator to generate 1000 points that lie within the unit square. As we generate the points, we count the number that lie within the quarter circle and form an approximation of π with the formula

$$\pi \approx \left(\frac{\text{Number of points inside the quarter circle}}{1000}\right) * 4$$

Write out 10 approximations of π (using 10 different sets of random numbers) and their average. What happens if 10,000 or 20,000 points are used instead of 1000?

8-3.9   (*Shuffling Cards*)   The random number generator can be used to "shuffle" a deck of cards inside the computer. First, assign numbers to the cards:

$1,2,3,\ldots,12,13$	are the Ace, 2,3, ... ,Queen, King of Spades,
$14,15,16,\ldots,25,26$	are the Ace, 2,3, ... ,Queen, King of Hearts,
$27,28,29,\ldots,38,39$	are the Ace, 2,3, ... ,Queen, King of Diamonds,
$40,41,42,\ldots,51,52$	are the Ace, 2,3, ... ,Queen, King of Clubs.

Use two arrays of size 52. The array A is the "shuffled deck", that is A(1) is the number of the top card after shuffling, and so forth. The array B keeps track of which cards have been put into the shuffled deck. The shuffling goes as follows:

(a)   Set B(J) = 0 for J = 1 to 52 and set K = 0.
(b)   Pick a random number between 1 and 52, say R.
(c)   If B(R) = 0 go to Step (d), otherwise go to step (e).
(d)   Set B(R) = 1, A(K) = R and K = K+1. If K = 52 stop. This adds a card to the shuffled deck. Go to Step (b).
(e)   If R < 52 set R = R+1 otherwise set R = 1. Go to Step (c).

Write a program that implements this method of shuffling cards and which prints out the shuffled deck.

8-3.10 (*Showdown Poker*) Use the program of Problem 8-3.9 as a subprogram to play showdown poker (5 card stud) for $10 a game. The top cards of the shuffled deck are dealt alternately to each of two players until each has 5 cards. Then the highest hand wins the game. The hands are compared as follows (from highest to lowest).

(a) Straight flush: five cards in sequence in the same suit.
(b) Four of a kind: four cards of the same number.
(c) Full house: a pair plus three of a kind.
(d) Flush: all cards in the same suit.
(e) Straight: five cards in sequence.
(f) Three of a kind: three cards of the same number.
(g) Two pairs
(h) One pair
(i) High card

If there are two hands at the same level, then the one involving the highest cards wins. Thus

> 4 Aces beats 4 Kings which beats 4 Queens, and so forth,
> A straight 6,7,8,9,10 of spades beats a straight, 3,4,5,6,7 of Clubs,
> Two pairs—Kings and fives, beats two pairs—Kings and fours,
> Two pairs—Kings and fives, beats two pairs—Queens and eights.

If there is a tie on the same level, then the cards which tie are discarded and the remaining cards are compared to determine the winner. Thus

> King, King, 9,4,3 beats King, King, 7,8,6
> Ace, Queen, 10,9,3 beats Ace, Queen, 10,7,4

If there are two flushes, then the highest card wins.

Your program should have the following parts: a subprogram to shuffle the cards, a subprogram to evaluate a hand and determine which of the 9 levels it belongs to, a subprogram to compare two hands on the same level to find the best (there are 9 of these subprograms), and an overall control program to keep track of the winnings and the status of the game.

The output should be of the form:

PLAYER 1	PLAYER 2
17	8
27	6
42	50
19	26
29	31

PLAYER 1 WINS WITH
THREE OF A KIND
OVER
HIGH CARD OF 13

8-3.11 Translate the following flowchart into a computer program and run it for several values of data; for example

$$
\begin{array}{cccc}
.78, & 3, & 12.1, & 1 \\
16.1, & 2, & 3.7, & 1 \\
14.2, & 2, & 1.32, & 3
\end{array}
$$

This program is to "solve" right triangles. The parts read in are two of the three quantities: one side (ID = 1), the hypotenuse (ID = 2), one angle (ID = 3, value in radians). The output of the program is all three of these values (Aside, HY, and A).

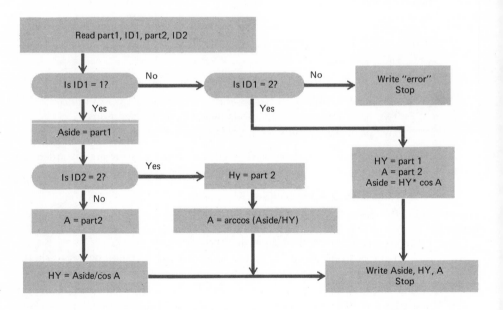

8-4 INTERACTIVE INPUT

The Basic language, frequently available as an on-line interactive system, has a provision to take advantage of this direct access to a computer. The new statement allows a Basic program to behave in an *interactive* way. We see below a Basic program that can react in a way that resembles and is frequently referred to as conversation. The "conversation" might go as follows:

Computer:	"I am the prime number tester"
	"What number would you like tested"
User:	"1081"
Computer:	"Oops, sorry, 1081 has a factor of 23"

The new statement in Basic that allows this is the INPUT statement.

INPUT

The keyword INPUT followed by a list of variables separated by commas. The INPUT acts just like a READ except that the values are typed by the user after the INPUT statement is reached.

EXAMPLES

```
INPUT  X,X1          INPUT  N,B
INPUT  A,B,C,K       INPUT  A(1),A(2)
```

The user has direct access to the computer (usually at a remote terminal) and when the INPUT statement is met the execution of the program is stopped. Then the user must type in values to be read as data by the INPUT statement.

The following example tests whether a number is prime.

```
  5 PRINT
 10 PRINT " I AM THE PRIME NUMBER TESTER"
 20 PRINT " WHAT NUMBER WOULD YOU LIKE TESTED"
 30 INPUT N
 40 DEF FNX(K) = ABS(K) - INT(ABS(K))
 50 LET S = SQR(N)
 60 LET F = 2
 70 IF  FNX(N/F)=0 THEN 130
 80 FOR F=3 TO S STEP 2
 90 IF FNX(N/F)=0 THEN 130
100 NEXT F
110 PRINT "CONGRATULATIONS";N;" IS PRIME"
120      GO TO 5
130 PRINT "OOPS, SORRY, ";N;" HAS A FACTOR ";F
140      GO TO 5
150 END
```

As another example of man-machine interaction, consider a program that matches coins with the user. It does not cheat.

```
 10  PRINT      .
 20  PRINT "I WILL MATCH SILVER DOLLARS WITH YOU"
 30  PRINT "1 IS FOR HEADS, 2 IS FOR TAILS"
 40  LET W=0
100  IF RND(0) >.5 THEN 130
110  LET C = 1
120          GO TO 140
130  LET C = 2
140  PRINT "I HAVE FLIPPED, WHAT DO YOU CALL IT"
150  INPUT U
200  IF C = U THEN 240
205  PRINT " YOU LOSE"
210  LET W = W+1
215  IF C=1 THEN 230
220  PRINT " I HAVE TAILS"
225          GO TO 300
230  PRINT " I HAVE HEADS"
235          GO TO 300
240  PRINT " YOU WIN"
245  LET W=W-1
250  IF C=1 THEN 230
260          GO TO 220
300  PRINT "WANT TO TRY AGAIN - TYPE 1 FOR YES"
310  INPUT A
320  IF A=1 THEN 100
400  IF W<0 THEN 430
410  PRINT " I WON";W;" DOLLARS"
420  STOP
430  PRINT " I LOST"; -W;" DOLLARS"
500  END
```

We can modify the program to cheat just a little bit (say 1 percent of the time) by adding the following statements

```
155  IF RND(0)<.99 THEN 200
160  LET C = 1-U
```

If the computer is a little greedier, the number .99 in statement 155 can be changed to .9 and then it cheats 10 percent of the time.

The possibilities for interesting interaction are great. The main limitation is the amount of effort and ingenuity that one puts into writing the programs. Some possibilities are indicated by the problems.

PROBLEMS

8-4.1 Modify the coin matching program to play the following game. The computer picks a number between 1 and 10 and the person guesses at it. If he guesses right, the person wins $10, otherwise he loses $1.

Play the game long enough to verify that it is unfair to the computer.

The game can be made fair by changing the $10 payoff to $9 or by having the computer "cheat" one out of eleven times. Modify your program this second way to make the game fair.

8-4.2   Write a program that plays the ancient game of paper, scissors, and stones. There are two players and the rules are as follows: Each player picks one of the three items. "Paper" wins over "stone" (because paper can cover stones), "stone" wins over "scissors" (because stones can break scissors) and "scissors" wins over "paper" (because scissors can cut paper). Make the program produce a number of messages and keep track of the amount it wins or loses (as one of the two players) at $1 per game.

8-4.3   Write a program that asks for two dates in the format of month, day, and year (for example, 11,26,1941) and which computes the number of days between the two dates. Recall that 1900 is not a leap year, but that 2000 is. The dates can be in either order and run your program with a number of cases to verify that it works.

8-4.4   Write a program that asks two questions:

How much would you like to borrow?
How much would you like to pay per month?

and then returns with the statement

You will have to pay for XXX months.

Assume that you charge interest at 1 percent per month on the balance. Be prepared for people who want to borrow $10,000 and pay it back at $8.50 per month.

8-4.5   Write a program that tests a person on his facts of multiplication for numbers between 1 and 15. The computer should generate two random numbers between 1 and 15 (say 7 and 12) and then ask:

How much is 7 times 12?

The person types in his answer and the computer checks it. If it is correct the response is "Right" and if it is incorrect the response is "Sorry, but the answer is 84."

Have the program keep score and assign a percentage grade when the person indicates that he wants to stop.

8-4.6   Modify Problem 8-4.5 so that the computer first asks what range of numbers is to be used (for example, 1 to 8, 1 to 10, 1 to 12, or 1 to 15).

8-4.7   Modify Problem 8-4.6 so that the computer asks which kind of arithmetic facts are to be tested: addition, subtraction, multiplication, or division. Be sure to make all of the division problems come out even. That is 64/8 is acceptable but 64/9 is not acceptable as a question.

8-4.8   Modify the 5-card stud poker program (Problem 8-3.10) in two ways. The output should be in the form SPADES 8, CLUBS 11 rather than simply the numbers 8 and 50. Then make the game interactive with betting after each time both players are dealt a card. This means that you must devise a fixed betting strategy for the computer program. A simple strategy to use would be the following:

(a) If you are at a higher level than the opponent bet $1.

(b) If there are 2 or more ways you can reach a higher level then bet $1.

(c) If the opponent bets and you are at a lower level, quit.

(d) If the opponent bets and you are at the same level, but lower, call the bet.

Even with this simple strategy, the program is quite complicated. You can experiment with different strategies to improve the ability of the program.

If several people write poker-playing programs, then it is possible to organize a poker tournament to determine which is best.

8-5   MULTIPLE BRANCHING

Until now we have discussed only the IF-THEN statement for branching. This statement allows a 2-way branch—one either goes to the specified label or to the next statement. There are many instances which require 3-way, 4-way, 10-way, 12-way, and so forth, branches. Examples of some situations which lead to multiple branching are listed below.

4-way branch

Movement:	North, East, South, and West
Seasons:	Summer, Winter, Fall, and Spring
Classes:	Freshmen, Sophomores, Juniors, and Seniors

6-way branch

Helicopter flight: up, down, forward, backward, left, and right

10-way branch

Digital sorting: 1,2,3, . . . ,9,0

12-way branch

Months of the year: January through December

26-way branch

Alphabetizing: A,B,C, . . . ,X,Y,Z

The first step in a Basic program that does multiple branching is to obtain a variable or expression whose value is the branch one wishes to choose. Let us assume that the variable is N. The branches are also numbered and if N = 1 we want to choose the first branch, if N = 2 the second, and so forth. One can "build" multiple branches from 2-way branches as illustrated in Figure 8-5.1.

4-way branch

6-way branch

FIGURE 8-5.1   **A 4-way and 6-way branch built from 2-way branches.**

If one uses K 2-way branches, then one can have at most a (K+1)-way branch. There are different ways to build a multiple branch, some of which are much more efficient than others.

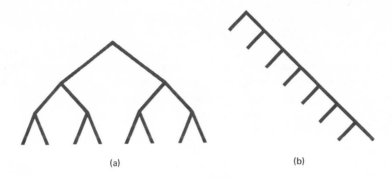

(a)   (b)

FIGURE 8-5.2 Two ways to build an 8-way branch from seven 2-way branches.

Note in Figure 8-5.2 that the branch construction (A) requires one to pass through only three 2-way branches to reach any destination. Branch construction (B) requires one to pass through all seven 2-way branches in order to take one of the branches. It clearly requires more testing and branching on the average than does construction (A).

Each branch point in the above figures corresponds to an IF-THEN statement in a Basic program. Thus a 4-way branch to statements 210, 220, 230, and 240 as indicated by the variable N may be made as follows.

```
199 REM            A 4-WAY BRANCH
200 IF N<3 THEN 203
201 IF N=3 THEN 230
202      GO TO 240
203 IF N=2 THEN 220
210 REM   *** PROGRAM CONTINUES ***
```

Many Basic language systems have a special statement to facilitate multiple branching. The 4-way branch given above can be achieved with one statement.

```
200 ON N GO TO 210,220,230,240
```

This statement type is usually called a *computed GO TO.*

ON-GO TO

The general form of the computed GO TO is

ON (expression) GO TO (list of labels)

The expression is evaluated and its integer part taken. Suppose this is K, then a direct transfer is made to the K-th label in the list following the GO TO. If the value of K is less than 1 or greater than the number of labels an illegal condition exists and the program stops.

EXAMPLES

```
ON  N  GO TO  10,20,50
ON  N+J-3  GO TO  300,606,212,414,606,606
```

As an example of this statement's use, recall that in the program for processing information about bulk-material containers one had to make a 3-way branch based on the situations present (good, bad, or inactive). Statements 115 and 120 in the program can be replaced by

```
115 ON T GO TO 125,135,150
```

In Problems 8-3.9 and 8-4.8 the cards in a deck are coded numerically from 1 to 52. The suit code for a card N is given by the expression

$$S = 1 + INT((N-1)/13)$$

and the position in the suit is given by

$$P = N - 13*(S-1).$$

The computed GO TO can be used to write out (in ordinary English) the description of card N.

```
300 REM           N IS THE CARD NUMBER
305 LET S = 1 + INT((N-1)/13) ─────── Find the suit
310 LET P = N - 13*(S-1) ──────────── Find the number (1 → 13)
315 IF P<11 THEN 340 ──────────────── Check for face card
320 LET F = P-10
325 ON F GO TO 330,332,334
330 PRINT "JACK",
331       GO TO 345
332 PRINT "QUEEN",
333       GO TO 345
334 PRINT "KING",
335       GO TO 345
340 PRINT P,
345 ON S GO TO 350,352,354,356
350 PRINT " OF SPADES"
351       GO TO 360
352 PRINT " OF HEARTS"
353       GO TO 360
354 PRINT " OF DIAMONDS"
355       GO TO 360
356 PRINT " OF CLUBS"
360 REM    *** PROGRAM CONTINUES ***
```

8-6 APPLICATIONS: TABLE LOOKUP AND FILE PROCESSING

8-6.1 Table Lookup

Frequently information is given in the form of tables. In Chapter 7 we saw several small tables associated with the automobile cost problem. There are a variety of ways to use a table and we discuss a few of them here. Table 8-6.1 is a table of life expectancy versus age.

Table 8-6.1
Life expectancy table (U.S. white males) giving expected number of years remaining.

Age	40	45	50	55	60	65	70	75	80	85
Life Expectancy	31.6	27.2	23.0	19.3	15.8	12.8	10.2	7.9	5.8	4.2

Consider a computation in an insurance company where it is necessary to estimate the life expectancy for retired employees.

Given a person's age, call it A, the simplest thing to do is to find the closest age entry in the table and then use the corresponding life-expectancy estimate. There is no single Basic statement for the multiple of 5 closest to a given value of A (which is what we need). There are however, ways to obtain this in Basic—for instance the built-in function INT, as shown below.

```
100 LET A1 = 5*INT((A+2.5)/5)
```

This sets A1 to be the nearest entry in the table to A.

The natural way to find the match of A1 with a table entry is to start at 40 and check each entry until a match is made. The resulting code in Basic appears as follows:

```
100 IF A1 = 40 THEN 140  ⎫
105 IF A1 = 45 THEN 145  ⎪
110 IF A1 = 50 THEN 150  ⎪
115 IF A1 = 55 THEN 155  ⎪
120 IF A1 = 60 THEN 160  ⎬ 9 IF statements
125 IF A1 = 65 THEN 165  ⎪
130 IF A1 = 70 THEN 170  ⎪
135 IF A1 = 75 THEN 175  ⎪
137 IF A1 = 80 THEN 180  ⎭
138            GO TO 185
140 LET E = 31.6
141      GO TO 200
145 LET E = 27.2
146      GO TO 200
165 REM    *** PROGRAM CONTINUES ***
166 REM        STATEMENTS 150 TO 180 SET
167 REM          E FOR    50 TO  80
185 LET E = 4.2
200 REM    *** PROGRAM CONTINUES ***
```

One can make serious complaints about this method. First, it takes a lot of programming. The same checking could be done with many fewer statements (1 will do it instead of 9).

```
          10-way branch
100 ON A1/5-7 GO TO 140,145,150,155,160,165,170,175,180,185
140 LET E = 31.6
141    GO TO 200
145 LET E = 27.2
146    GO TO 200
164 REM    *** PROGRAM CONTINUES ***
166 REM        STATEMENTS 150 TO 180 SET E FOR 50 TO 80
185 LET E = 4.2
200 REM    *** PROGRAM CONTINUES ***
```

This is a situation which shows how useful the computed GO TO can be for multiple branching.

The table look-up can be accomplished even faster if we put the life expectancy values in an array, say T. The program segment might then appear as

```
10 FOR J = 1 TO 10
15 READ T(J)
20 NEXT J
21 LET E = T(INT((A+2.5)/5))
25 REM   *** PROGRAM CONTINUES ***
400 DATA 31.6,27.2,23.0,19.3,15.8,12.8,10.2,7.9,5.8,4.2
```

Correct value for E picked out of T-array with one statement

This approach is much more efficient both in programming effort and in computing time.

Table 8-6.1 is rather coarse and for example, a big change takes place between ages 57 years 5 months and 57 years 7 months. The life expectancy changes from 19.3 years to 15.8 years which is clearly an excessive change for a two month age difference. One way to avoid this sudden, discontinuous change is to use a linear interpolation. To do this one must find the table entries just above and just below the age at hand, then take a weighted average of the table values with the weights chosen to emphasize the closest entry. Let A0 and A2 be the table entries just above and below A. They may be calculated by

```
10 LET A0 = 5*(INT(A/5))
20 LET A2 = A0 + 5
```

Suppose that a table look-up is made to locate the corresponding life expectancy values E0 and E2. The weighted average then is

```
10 LET E = E0*(A2-A)/(A2-A0) + E2*(A-A0)/(A2-A0)
```

which can be expressed more simply (recall that A2-A0 is always 5) by

```
10 LET E = .2*(E0*(A2-A) + E2*(A-A0))
```

The use of this *linear interpolation* causes the variation of table values to correspond nicely to that of the ages.

The table of life expectancy is such that very efficient table look-up is possible with the use of arrays. Some tables are not so systematic and thus actual searching is still required.

In this same company there is a retirement bonus paid which depends on the base salary. The amounts are given in Table 8-6.2.

Table 8-6.2.
Table of retirement bonus for various base salaries (figured as average of last 5 years of annual salary).

Base Salary	0	3000	4000	5000	6500	8000	10000	14000	20000
Retirement Bonus	750	1000	1200	1350	1500	1750	2000	2400	3000

Thus an employee who retires with a base salary of $9627 receives a bonus of $1750.

In order to find the correct entry in this table, one must find the base salary entry which is just below the employee's base salary. You could string nine IF-THEN statements together as we did at first, but this still is a poor way to search this table. Instead, introduce two arrays, one is B of the base salary entries and the other is R of the retirement bonus. A program segment is given below which reads in these entries, an employee's base salary B1, and then locates the retirement bonus to be paid.

```
10 FOR J = 1 TO 9
15 READ B(J),R(J)
20 NEXT J
30 READ B1
40 FOR J = 1 TO 8
50 IF B1 < B(J+1) THEN 80
60 NEXT J
70 LET J = 9
80 PRINT "  BONUS IS",R(J)
```

This program probably does much more computation than is required. For a particular company, it might be that most retired employees have a base salary equal to 8,000 or 10,000. For these people we have to always go through the first five IF's and often the sixth one. This means that most of the time one makes 4 or 5 unnecessary tests. One can greatly increase the average efficiency by simply reordering the table and the corresponding program (one really does not reorder the table but just visualizes it as reordered). The new table is shown in Table 8-6.3 and the corresponding program below. Note that the program does not actually use a rearranged table.

```
30 READ B1
35 IF B1 > = 8000 THEN 55
40 FOR J = 5 TO 1 STEP -1
45 IF B1 > B(J) THEN 80
50 NEXT J
55 FOR J = 6 TO 8
60 IF B1 < B(J+1) THEN 80
65 NEXT J
70 LET J = 9
80 PRINT " BONUS IS",R(J)
```

Table 8-6.3
The retirement bonus table rearranged.

Base Salary	8000	10000	14000	20000	0	3000	4000	5000	6500
Retirement Bonus	1750	2000	2400	3000	750	1000	1200	1350	1500

This table look-up scheme requires a little more programming, but it finds the most frequent cases first and thus is more efficient on the average. A little study shows that we did more than just reorder the table. We split it into two parts with the first IF statement (the 8000 and less part and, the over 8000 part) and then did a systematic search in each of the parts. Furthermore, we searched from high to low in one of the parts because we thought this would be more efficient for that part of the table.

The net result of this scheme is more than just reordering and doing a usual table look-up. Note, for instance, that some cases (base salary = 14000 and 20000) go through nine IF's in the first scheme, but none of them go through more than six IF's in the second one. Furthermore, the most common cases go through only two or three IF's in the second case whereas they go through six or seven in the first approach.

The idea used in the second scheme can be extended to what is called a *binary search*. The word binary refers to breaking the search into two parts. The efficiency of the binary search approach is illustrated in Figure 8-6.1 where a table look-up of life expectancy for ages 30 to 100 is illustrated. Note that even with this larger table, no case ever goes through more than four IF statements. The first scheme proposed would require some cases to go through fourteen IF statements in this situation.

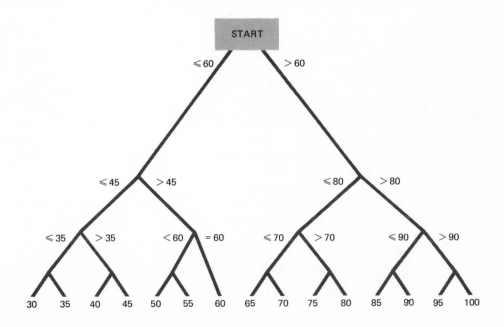

FIGURE 8-6.1   **Search of table of 15 entries using a binary search strategy.**

One of the main points of this example is that there are several ways to do table look-up and some are much more efficient than others. Most important, however, is the idea that one should think about the frequency of use of the various entries and proceed accordingly. Thus in Chapter 7 there is a small table of repair costs versus years for 1 to 100 years. In that problem each entry is to be used once. The last 80 entries are the same and thus we can do the table look-up with one IF-THEN test for 80 percent of the cases if we first test whether the year is larger than 20. The simple linear search (from high to low) is not quite the most efficient scheme for the remaining 20 percent of the cases, but it is nearly so. The conclusion is that even though a binary search is usually much more efficient than a linear one, one must verify that for each table look-up problem in order to be sure.

8-6.2 Information Retrieval from a Card File

Consider an insurance company that wishes to study the occurrences of single car accidents and, in particular, to study their relationship to horsepower and to characteristics of male drivers. This company has a file of thousands of cards where it keeps its accident records. There are three cards for each accident and they contain the following information as indicated:

Card 1: Manufacturer code, Model code, Horsepower. Weight
Card 2: Accident type code, Damage-Car 1, Damage-Car 2, Other Damage, Persons Injured
Card 3: Driver's Name, Policy number, Age, Sex, Arrests, Accidents

The cards for two accidents are shown in Figure 8-6.2

On the basis of the loosely stated requirements and knowledge of the information available, a programmer is instructed to extract relevant information which is of interest to management. The programmer decides that the following information is needed:

1. The total number of single car accidents,
2. The number involving high horsepower cars,
3. The number involving male drivers,
4. The number involving male drivers under 30 and high horsepower,
5. The number involving male drivers under 30 with a total of traffic arrests and accidents of 2 or more.

In addition, for each accident in groups 2, 4, and 5 a line is to be printed as follows

Horsepower, Damage, Sex, Age, Record

(where "record" is the number of traffic arrests and accidents).

In order to process the cards, we must know the following code numbers:

Single car accident: code = 6
Male driver: sex = 1

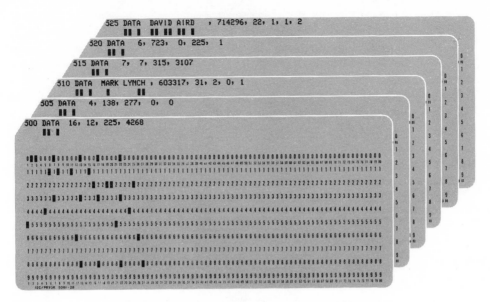

FIGURE 8-6.2 **The card information for two accidents.**

The basic strategy of the program is to read three cards (extracting the proper information) then check to see which, if any, group the accident falls into. If it is an accident of one of these groups, the appropriate totals are increased and, in groups 2, 4, and 5, a line is printed out. The variables

T1, T2, T3, T4, T5

are introduced as the totals for groups 1 to 5. At the end of the card file their totals are printed out as a summary. The end of the card file is signaled by three blank cards. Thus accident type, horsepower, and policy number are all zero, and the program goes into the final summary in this case. Note that it is not safe to check on just one of these numbers as such files often have incomplete information which is just left blank.

The algorithm is given in some detail in the flowchart of Figure 8-6.3. The variables appearing there are, in addition to T1, . . . ,T5,

H	=	horsepower
S	=	driver's sex
A	=	driver's age
A1	=	number of traffic arrests in records
A2	=	number of traffic accidents in records
D	=	damage to car 1
C	=	code for accident type
K	=	switch set = 1 when a line is to be printed.

A program to carry out this study is also given.

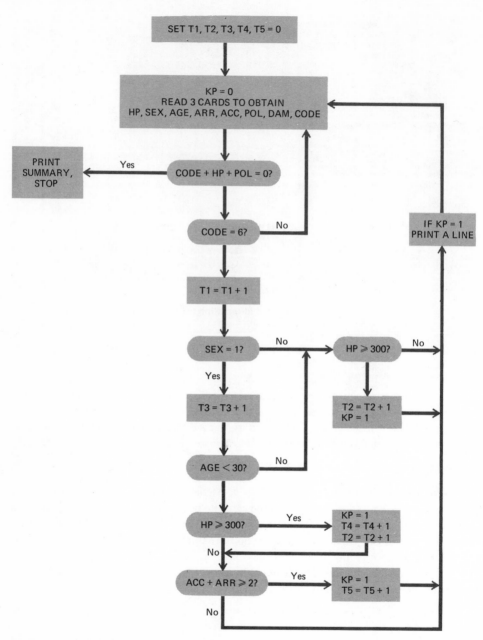

FIGURE 8-6.3   Flowchart of processing the insurance company files to extract information on single car accidents

```
 10 REM                INITIALIZE COUNTERS
 20 LET T1 =0
 30 LET T2 =0
 40 LET T3 =0
 50 LET T4 =0
 60 LET T5 =0
 70 REM                PRINT HEADING
 90 PRINT " HP"," DAMAGE"," SEX"," AGE"," RECORD"
 80 PRINT " "," SINGLE CAR CASES"
100 LET K = 0
111 REM   J1, J2, ETC ARE JUNK VARIABLES NOT USED
110 READ J1,J2,H,J3,C,D,J4,J5,J6,J7,J8,A,S,A1,A2
120 REM                TEST FOR END OF CARD FILE
125 IF H+C+J8 = 0 THEN 400
130 IF C <> 6 THEN 100
200 REM                HAVE A SINGLE CAR ACCIDENT
205 LET T1 = T1+1
210 REM                CHECK SEX
212 IF S = 2 THEN 252
216 LET T3 = T3+1
220 REM                CHECK AGE
225 IF A > = 30 THEN 252
230 REM                HAVE MALE UNDER 30
232 IF H < 300 THEN 240
234 LET T4 = T4+1
235 LET T2 = T2+1
236 LET K = 1
240 IF A1+A2 < 2 THEN 260
242 LET T5 = T5+1
244 LET K = 1
246      GO TO 260
250 REM                CHECK H FOR FEMALES, OLDER MALES
252 IF H < 300 THEN 100
254 LET T2 = T2 +1
256 LET K = 1
260 IF K = 0   THEN 100
300 REM                PRINT A LINE FOR GROUPS 2,4,5
305 PRINT   H,D,S,A,A1+A2
310      GO TO 100
399 REM                FILE IS FINISHED
400 PRINT
405 PRINT " "," SUMMARY FOR SINGLE CAR ACCIDENTS"
410 PRINT
415 PRINT T1;" SINGLE CAR ACCIDENTS"
420 PRINT T2;" HIGH HORSEPOWER CASES"
425 PRINT T3;" MALE DRIVER CASES"
430 PRINT T4;" YOUNG MALE DRIVERS WITH HIGH HORSEPOWER"
435 PRINT T5;" YOUNG MALE DRIVERS WITH RECORD OF 2 OR MORE"
500 DATA  16,  12, 225, 4268
550 REM   *** MORE DATA HERE ***
999 END
```

SINGLE CAR CASES

HP	DAMAGE	SEX	AGE	RECORD
300	1804	1	18	2
301	602	1	29	2
330	1607	1	24	4
400	704	2	19	1

(Continued on next page)

```
                SUMMARY FOR SINGLE CAR ACCIDENTS


        407   SINGLE CAR ACCIDENTS
        267   HIGH HORSEPOWER CASES
        326   MALE DRIVER CASES
        173   YOUNG MALE DRIVERS WITH HIGH HORSEPOWER
        142   YOUNG MALE DRIVERS WITH RECORD OF 2 OR MORE
```

There are two interesting points in the flowchart and program. First we have set up and used a switch (the variable K) to control the printing of the single output line. One might be tempted to print this line at each point where K is set to 1, but that would present two drawbacks. It would require three **PRINT** statements rather than one and there would be two identical lines of output if the accident involved a male driver under age 30 with both a high horsepower car and a record of 2 or more arrests and accidents.

Next, note that all three data cards for an accident are read in the program with one **READ** statement and the items to be ignored on the cards are given to "junk" variables, J1,J2, ...

8-7 GENERAL PROBLEMS

8-7.1   Write one Basic program with each of the following errors in it:

(a)   Undefined label
(b)   One missing quote mark in a PRINT statement
(c)   Variable name with 2 letters
(d)   REMARK misspelled as DIMARK
(e)   Bad arithmetic as in $1.3 + 2*(X-3$
(f)   No END statement
(g)   An illegal character (punch a 7 and a 9 in the same column or something similar)
(h)   Two equal signs in one statement
(i)   PRINT misspelled as PRINR.

If the translator does not detect all of these errors, can you rewrite the program so that it does. Why would the translator fail to find all errors like these?

8-7.2   The following Basic programs have errors in them. Locate each error and write a new program which corrects the errors. The new statements can be anything reasonably close to the given statement. They must, of course, be correct Basic statements. Do not try to understand what the whole program does. Note that no credit is given for such drastic modifications as replacing the whole program by a single STOP statement.

```
  1 REM  THIS PROGRAM HAS ABOUT 10 ERRORS IN IT
 10 DIM A(5),B(20,20),X3(12)
 20 DEF FNX(K) = (A(1)+A(2)*J/(A(3)*ABS(A(4))))/(J↑3+3)
 30 LET K = 0
 40 READ A(4),T,N,X3
 50 LET 1.6 = A(1)
 60 FOR L = 1 TO N-1
 70 LET R = A(L)/*(B(L,L)/7.3) + T*R
 80 PRINT T,R,A(L)/R
 90 NEXT L
100 LET T = B(T,T)
110 IF T < 8 THEN 80
120 LET K = 1
130 FOR A = 1 TO N
140 LET B(A,K) = K/A*T+N-FNX(A/K)
150 IF K > N  THEN 190
160 LET K = K+1
170    GO TO 130
180 NEXT A
200 PRINT  B(N,FNX(N)) IS,B(N,N)
220 IF X3(K) = 0 THEN 40
230 END
250 DATA 1,2,3,6,8,12
260 DATA -1.2,.8.8
```

```
100 REMURK  THIS PROGRAM HAS ABOUT 8 ERRORS IN IT
 10 DIM B(20),X(20),A(12)
 20 LET A(1) = 1
 30 FOR K = 2 TO 12
 40 LET A(K) = A(K-1)- 2*A(K-2)
 50 FOR K = 1 TO 25
 60 LET B(K) = 2*K-3
 70 LET X(K) = B(K)/(3*K+K*(B(K)-12))
 80 NEXT K
 90 REAB R
100 REM       START LOOPS
110 IF  R = 0 THEN STOP
120 FOR K = 0 TO 1 STEP R
130 LET T = A(1) + 16.3/(R*R-1)*B(20)
140 FOR L = 1 TO 10
150 LET X(L) = A(L)*T*+ B(20-L)/T + X(K+1)
160 LET T = X(L)/T*16.3
170 NEXT L
180 PRINT X,T," ARE OK";" R ="; R
190 NEXT K
200 PRINT B,A,D;" FINAL", T↑X(1)/2
210 STOP
220       GO TO 90
230 DATA .1,.2,1/4,.3,1/3
240 DATA -.1,-.2,-1/4,-.3,-1/3
300 END
```

```
 1 REMARK THIS PROGRAM HAS ABOUT 7 ERRORS IN IT
 5 FOR K = 1 TO 40
10 LET A(K) = K-1
15 NEXT K
20 READ X1,X2,T
25 PRINT DATA IS,X1,X2,T
30 DEF FNA(Y) =(X1↑2-X2↑2)/(Y↑2+1)
40    GOSUB 200
50 LET T1 = T+(3/(A(1)+A(2)**3)-K4
60 ON K4 GO TO 60,70,80,80,90
70 LET A(T1+10) = A(T1+10) - 2*FNA(T1)
71 LET X1 = X1-1
72    GO TO 80
80 LET A(1) = A(40)    + FNA(X1+T1)
81 LET A(2) = A(39)-1 + FNA(X2-T1)
82 LET X2 = X2+1
83 PRINT A(1),A(2),X2
84    GO TO 20
90 FINAL OUTPUT
91 PRINT  A,X1,X2,T1
92    GOTO 400
200 LET K4 = A(2)
210 IF K4 > A(K4) THEN 400
220 FOR K4 = 1 TO 100
225 LET K4 = A(K4)+ K4- T
230 IF  K4 > A(2) THEN 50
240 NEXT K4
250 LET K4 = 5
260 RETURN
300 DATA 1,1,4,2,0,4,3,5,-2
400 STOP
```

8-7.3   Which of the following statements about Basic are correct?

(a)   A separate READ statement for each DATA statement is required.

(b)   A STOP statement is required in each program.

(c)   An END statement is required in each program.

(d)   All arrays must have a DIM statement in each program where they are used.

(e)   One must have one's own code for computing the maximum value of K numbers when K is read in from data statements.

(f)   At least one RETURN statement is required in each subprogram.

(g)   Different counters (control variables) are required for each FOR-loop in a nested set of FOR-loops.

(i)   The control variable of a FOR-loop cannot start at a positive number and go down to zero.

(j)   One cannot have a RETURN statement in the middle of a FOR-loop.

(k)   One cannot use an array variable (for example, A(3)) as the control variable of a FOR-loop.

8-7.4   Write a subprogram to compute the number S from the formula

$$S^2 = \frac{1}{n} \sum_{i=1}^{n} (x_i - \bar{x})^2,$$

where x is an array with n elements $x_1, \ldots, x_n$ and $\bar{x}$ is the average value of the x_i's. The number S is called the *standard deviation*. Use the subprogram in a program along with some data which shows that the program is correct.

8-7.5   You have several lists of positive numbers on DATA statements separated by a DATA statement with -1 in it. The situation is illustrated below.

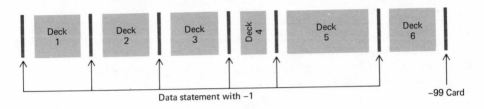

Data statement with -1 -99 Card

The last DATA statement in the program has the number -99. Assume there are no more than 100 numbers in any one list.

Write a subprogram that computes the average and standard deviation of the numbers as in Problem 8-7.4. Use this subprogram in a program to process these data and to print for each list output in the form

LIST 3 CONTAINS 74 NUMBERS WITH
AVERAGE xxxx.xxxx AND S.D. xxxx.xxxx

8-7.6   Write a subprogram that extracts the middle digit from a 3-digit number. The output should be of the form

MIDDLE DIGIT OF 841 IS 4

Hint: Use the INT function in conjunction with appropriate multiplications and divisions by 10.

8-7.7   Write a subprogram that finds the sum of the digits of any integer between 0 and 9999. The output should be of the form

SUM OF DIGITS OF 4129 IS 16

8-7.8   Consider a data set similar to that of Problem 8-7.5 with each number in the list between 0 and 999. Write a subprogram that makes a digit frequency count for each list and prints output of the form

LIST 3 CONTAINS 74 NUMBERS WITH

17 ONES	24 SIXES
23 TWOS	19 SEVENS
28 THREES	17 EIGHTS
16 FOURS	16 NINES
21 FIVES	12 ZEROES

8-7.9 Consider the following statement which generates a new value for R from an old one.

$$LET\ R = 77.*R - 100*INT(.77*R)$$

Set up an iteration loop to compute 500 successive values of R - 50 starting with R = 41. Count the number of times that these values are positive, zero, and negative and print out the counts in the following form

NEGATIVE VALUES FOUND XXX TIMES
ZERO VALUE FOUND XXX TIMES
POSITIVE VALUES FOUND XXX TIMES.

8-7.10 Write a program that prints a neat table with appropriate heading of all the prime numbers less than 500. At the end the number of prime numbers found should be printed out with a message.

8-7.11 Roofing tiles cost $0.20 each and an additional $15.00 per 100 square feet for installation. One tile covers an area of 1 square foot. Sheet copper roofing costs $0.20 per pound and 1 pound covers 1 square foot with installation costing $20.00 per 100 pounds. The life expectancy of tile is 20 years whereas the copper should last 30 years. Insurance on the copper roof costs $30.00 more per year per 1000 square feet than on the tile roof. Which is the more economical over a period of 120 years?

8-7.12 The most common conditional transfers are on a true or false basis and hence they result in 2-way branches. However, general n-way branches are useful in many situations.

(a) Show how any n-way branch can be constructed from a set of 2-way branches.

(b) Give an example where a 10-way branch is natural to use.

(c) Show how a 10-way branch can be constructed from nine 2-way branches so that any path through the branch process actually hits at most four 2-way branches.

(d) What is the largest value of n for an n-way branch that can be constructed from 2-way branches so that at most four 2-way branches are hit on any path through the branch process?

8-7.13 Write a program that reads in three numbers which are supposed to be the lengths of the sides of a triangle. The program is to print out these numbers along with a message indicating the type of triangle formed. One of the following four messages is to appear

ACUTE TRIANGLE
RIGHT TRIANGLE
OBTUSE TRIANGLE
LINES DO NOT FORM A TRIANGLE

Hint: One can test for the cases as follows. Let A, B, C be the lengths and let P be the maximum of A, B, and C. With Q and R denoting the other two lengths one has the following tests

$$P \geqslant Q + R \qquad \text{no triangle formed}$$
$$P^2 > Q^2 + R^2 \qquad \text{obtuse triangle formed}$$
$$P^2 = Q^2 + R^2 \qquad \text{right triangle formed}$$
$$P^2 < Q^2 + R^2 \qquad \text{acute triangle formed}$$

Your program should work for $A = 3.0$, $B = 4.0$, $C = 5.0$, but it might give the wrong answer for $A = 3.002$, $B = 4.006002$, $C = 5.006002$. Explain why. It might also give the wrong answer for $A = .9$, $B = 1.2$ and $C = 1.5$.

8-7.14 We define a magic square as an $n \times n$ square array or matrix where each of the integers $1,2,3,\ldots,n^2$ appears exactly once and all column sums, row sums, and diagonal sums are equal. We give the following algorithm for constructing an $n \times n$ magic square for any odd n.

    I.   Write down the digits in consecutive order, beginning with 1 in the middle of the top row.

    II. Move up one square and to the right one square to place the next integer ($k+1$), unless one of the four special cases below occurs:

(a)   If a move takes you above the top row in the jth column, move to the bottom of the jth column and place the integer there.

(b)   If a move takes you outside to the right of the square in the jth row, place the integer in the jth row at the extreme left.

(c)   If a move takes you to a square that is already filled, place $k+1$ immediately below k.

(d)   If you move out of the square at the upper right-hand corner (off of the diagonal), place $k+1$ immediately below k.

8	1	6
3	5	7
4	9	2

17	24	1	8	15
23	5	7	14	16
4	6	13	20	22
10	12	19	21	3
11	18	25	2	9

Write a program that creates magic squares for $n = 1,3,5,7,\ldots,21$. For each n write out the $n \times n$ magic square, the n column sums, the n row sums, and both diagonal sums.

8-7.15 Radix sorting is the most common method of sorting punched cards. The problem here is to order a list of decimal numbers simulating the method used on a sorting machine. Since the numbers are decimal, we need 10 pockets into which to place numbers. These pockets are labled $0,1,2,\ldots,9$. The algorithm proceeds as follows.

(a)   Examine the rightmost digit of each list element and place it in the pocket corresponding to the digit.

(b)   After (a) has been carried out for all elements of the list, create a new list by placing the contents of the 0's pocket at the top, the contents of the 1's pocket next, $\ldots$, the contents of the 9's pocket last.

(c) Repeat steps (a) and (b) for the digit immediately to the left of the digit just examined.

(d) Keep repeating (c) until all the digits of the largest element have been examined. The last list formed should be sorted.

Example

Original List 171, 805, 624, 562, 476, 409, 624, 437, 248, 003, 669, 552, 437, 743, 797, 020, 109, 217, 317, 816.

After pass 1

Pocket	0	1	2	3	4	5	6	7	8	9
	020	171	562	003	624	805	476	437	248	409
			552	743	624		816	437		669
								797		109
								217		
								317		

List after pass 1 020, 171, 562, 552, 003, 743, 624, 624, 805, 476, 816, 437, 437, 797, 217, 317, 248, 409, 669, 109.

After pass 2

Pocket	0	1	2	3	4	5	6	7	8	9
	003	816	020	437	743	552	562	171		797
	805	217	624	437	248		669	476		
	409	317	624							
	109									

List after pass 2 003, 805, 409, 109, 816, 217, 317, 020, 624, 624, 437, 437, 743, 248, 552, 562, 669, 171, 476, 797.

After pass 3

Pocket	0	1	2	3	4	5	6	7	8	9
	003	109	217	317	409	552	624	743	805	
	020	171	248		437	562	624	797	816	
					437		669			
					476					

Sorted List 003, 020, 109, 171, 217, 248, 317, 409, 437, 437, 476, 552, 562, 624, 624, 669, 743, 797, 805, 816

Write a program that accepts as input an unordered list of positive integers and sorts them using the above algorithm. To demonstrate that the above algorithm was used, pattern your output after the example given above showing the contents of the pockets. List the contents of the pocket after each pass.

8-7.16 An automobile speedometer is connected to one of the tires of a car and transforms the number of revolutions per second of the tire to a speed in miles per hour. But, the size of the tire changes from time to time, it gets smaller as the tread wears down, it gets larger when it is hot, its size depends on the amount of air in the tire, and so forth. Consequently, even if the speedometer accurately measures the number of revolutions per second, its reading might be different from the speed that the car is traveling. Turnpikes and some of the interstate highways have mileposts along the roadway. If a driver keeps the car travelling at a fixed speedometer reading and if a passenger times the intervals between mileposts, then one can determine the actual speed of the car. Write a program which prints the seconds between mile posts for a car travelling at speeds of 10, 20, 30, 40, 50, 60, 70, and 80 miles an hour. The distance, d, is related to the velocity, v, and the time t, according to $d = v*t$. You will want the time in seconds and the velocity in miles per hour, so you will have to multiply the velocity in mile per hour by the appropriate factor to change it to miles per second.

The diameter of a tire is about 29 inches for a full-sized station wagon and about 25 inches for a small compact car. The circumference is equal to diameter times π. Write a computer program which determines the number of revolutions each tire makes when the car goes one mile (there are 5280 feet in a mile). The program should also determine the number of revolutions per second and per minute of each of the two tires when the car is going 30, 50, 70, 90 miles per hour.

Suppose that the diameter of the tire is −10 percent, −5 percent, −1 percent, 1 percent, 5 percent, 10 percent different from the diameter assumed in the speedometer calibration. Your program should determine the actual speed when the speedometer reads 50, 60, 70, 80, and 90 miles per hour.

8-7.17 A chain letter works like this: A friend gives you a list of 12 names and addresses; the friend's name and address is the last on the list. You mail $5.00 to the name and address at the top of the list. You remove the name and address from the top of the list and add your name and address at the bottom. You make 12 copies of the new list and give the list to each of 12 friends. The process outlined above is repeated by each of them. The process repeats, once each day. How many days does it take before you begin receiving five dollar bills in the mail (assume one day mail delivery). Use the computer to determine how much money you would receive and how many different people are involved. When you get the results, give an explanation to justify the fact that it is a federal offense to participate in a chain letter.

8-7.18 A planet is at the perihelion of its orbit when it is closest to the sun; it is at the aphelion when it is farthest from the sun. Here is some information about planets:

Planet	Perihelion (Miles)	Aphelion (Miles)	Duration of year (Earth-days)
1 Mercury	29,000,000	43,000,000	88
2 Venus	67,000,000	68,000,000	225
3 Earth	91,000,000	95,000,000	365
4 Mars	128,000,000	155,000,000	687
5 Jupiter	460,000,000	510,000,000	4,333
6 Saturn	840,000,000	940,000,000	10,759
7 Uranus	1,700,000,000	1,870,000,000	30,685
8 Neptune	2,780,000,000	2,810,000,000	60,188
9 Pluto	2,770,000,000	4,600,000,000	90,700

Read these values into the computer and determine the average distance of each planet from the sun. Determine the approximate distance travelled by each planet during one of its years by computing the length of the circumference of a circle with radius equal to its average distance from the sun (circumference = 2*radius*3.1415926). Determine the average speed of each planet in miles per Earth year, miles per Earth day, miles per Earth hour, miles per Earth minute, and miles per Earth second. How many Earth years would it take to travel a distance equal to each of the nine average radii at a speed equal to the average speed of the earth.

8-7.19   Often one would like to describe some of the features about a set of numbers in terms of a few quantities. The data might be test scores, or bushels per acre of corn from various fields, or the number of words in each sentence in a number of different essays, and so forth. For a given set of numbers, $x_1, x_2, \ldots, x_n$, the *mean* of the set, $\bar{x}$, is the average of the numbers:

$$\bar{x} = (x_1 + x_2 + \ldots + x_n)/n$$

The *mode* is that value which occurs most frequently. The *median* is the value for which there are just as many values below it as above it. The *standard deviation*, s, is defined by

$$s^2 = ([x_1 - \bar{x}]^2 + [x_2 - \bar{x}]^2 + \ldots + [x_n - \bar{x}]^2)/n$$

Write a program which reads in values x_j until a certain value is read, say −99999. The mean, mode, median, and standard deviation should be computed and printed together with the data and value n. Note that

$$[x_j - \bar{x}]^2 = x_j^2 - 2x_j \bar{x} + \bar{x}^2,$$

so that

$$s^2 = (x_1^2 + x_2^2 + \ldots + x_n^2)/n - 2\bar{x}(x_1 + x_2 + \ldots + x_n)/n + \bar{x}^2$$
$$= (x_1^2 + x_2^2 + \ldots + x_n^2)/n - 2\bar{x}^2 + \bar{x}^2$$
$$= (x_1^2 + x_2^2 + \ldots + x_n^2)/n - \bar{x}^2$$

that is, s^2 is the difference between the mean of the squares of the data and the square of the mean.

8-7.20 Write some programs which generate material to help a person learn simple facts about arithmetic. For example, one program could generate output which appears as:

WHAT ARE THE FOLLOWING SUMS	THE SUM IS
1.　　　6 + 7 =	1.　　= 13
2.　　　10 + 0 =	2.　　= 10

and so on.

When using this material, the person covers the right side of the output, figures out the sum, and then immediately checks his result. This is a very effective way of learning for some people. Use the random number generator to pick a pair of integers between 0 and 10 to use to make up each problem, determine the sum, and print a line of output. Then repeat. Do the same thing for subtraction, multiplication, and division. For the division, eliminate problems which do not have an integer solution (like 1/3). You might want to pick more integers than just those between 0 and 10. Do the same thing for the square root of a number; here, pick an integer between 0 and 25, compute its square, and ask for the square root of the square. A more elaborate and helpful program can be written which (1) randomly picks the operation to be tested: addition, subtraction, multiplication, division, finding square roots, (2) randomly picks the numbers involved in the computation, (3) randomly picks the sign of the numbers involved. For example, the output might be of the form:

WHAT ARE THE VALUES OF THE FOLLOWING	THE VALUE IS
1.　　　13*12　　　=	1.　　= 156
2.　　　(-3) - (-4)　=	2.　　=　1
3.　　　-(-6)*2　　=	3.　　= 12

and so on.

To help a person gain facility in rapid mental computation, output of the following forms could be generated:

```
            34
           +21
           ___
  1.                              1.  =  55


            17
           +77
           ___
  2.                              2.  =  94
```

and so on.

or

$$
\begin{array}{r}
334 \\
-133 \\
\hline
\end{array}
$$

1.   1. = 201

$$
\begin{array}{r}
196 \\
-234 \\
\hline
\end{array}
$$

2.   2. = -38

and so on.

9 Computer Languages and Systems

9-1 THE SIMPLE COMPUTERS

9-1.1 Problem: How to Exploit Speed

The fundamental feature of computers is that they can execute certain simple operations extremely fast. In order to understand computer systems one must appreciate just how fast "extremely fast" is. An average computer can add 1 million numbers in 1 second and really fast computers can do 10 or 100 times better than this. In addition, computers can do other things (for example, multiplications, numerical comparisons, branching, and testing) at comparable speeds. Thus one realizes that rather complicated programs can be executed in a few thousands of a second.

R. W. Hamming has taken another viewpoint in order to emphasize the speed of computers. He compares the speed of various operations performed by older, pre-computer methods with those by modern technology. We can estimate the improvement in various areas of modern technology. We see from Table 9-1.1 that the increase in two areas, explosive power and computational speed, is startling. These two technological changes are of such magnitude that they are reshaping our society. If transportation speed in the last 100 years had increased as much as computational speed, then we could travel from Los Angeles to Paris in 1/500 second. Or we could travel from the earth to the moon in 1/10 second or to the sun in 6½ minutes. This is faster than the speed of light.

Great changes in magnitude often do more than just increase size, speed, and so forth. They can, and do, change the basic nature of a situation. For example, a gift of 10¢ would have no effect whatsoever on one's basic financial situation. A gift of a thousand times as much, $100, is nice, but it is unlikely to change one's financial situation. A gift of a thousand times this amount, $100,000, certainly improves one's financial position, but it does not relieve one entirely of financial worries. The entire sum can easily be spent on a new car, a new wardrobe, a new home, and a nice long vacation. Then one is back worrying about money again. A gift of a thousand times more than this, $100,000,000, however would change the basic nature of one's financial situation. It is no longer possible to spend all this money on personal expenses. The cost of a suit of clothes, or a meal, or even a house would become insignificant.

The change in magnitude in computation speed (and explosive power), greater than that of the preceding example, has already altered our view and expectations of how we can use this speed. Many believe that we have only begun to exploit the change in the basic nature of computation.

The goal of the operation of a computer system is to effectively and efficiently harness computational speed. Computational speed by itself is of little value. For instance, an instantaneous desk calculator or adding machine is not much more valuable than an ordinary one since most of the time is spent in punching the buttons, recording the answers, and figuring out what to do next.

To benefit from extremely fast computing speeds, the computing machine (or arithmetic unit) must be able to very rapidly find the numbers it uses and very rapidly record the answers it finds. The operation cannot wait for someone to manually enter

TABLE 9-1.1
COMPARISON OF TECHNOLOGICAL INCREASES

Area	Ancient Times	1870	1950	1970	Factor of Increase in: 2000 Years	100 Years	20 Years
Transportation	40 mi/day	200 mi/day	6,000 mi/day	35,000 mi/day	900	175	6
Work to make a book	10 man-years	10 man-hours	1 man-hour	½ man-hour	175,000	20	2
Life expectancy (U.S.)	22 years	45 years	66 years	67 years	3.05	1.48	1.07
Massive building	Great Wall of China	Suez Canal	Fort Peck Dam	Aswan Dam	Nil	Nil	Nil
Average formal education (U.S.)	None	1 year	10 years	12 years	–	12	1.2
Explosive power	½ lb. of TNT	½ ton of TNT	1,000,000 tons of TNT	100,000,000 tons of TNT	$2 * 10^{11}$	$1 * 10^8$	100
Energy per person*	½ unit	1.6 units	10 units	15 units	20	9	1.5
Computation speed**	.005	.005	40	10,000,000	$2 * 10^9$	$2 * 10^9$	250,000

* The unit for energy is a 1-horsepower motor working 8 hours a day.
**The unit is multiplications per second of two 8-digit numbers.

these numbers or write them down. Instructions must be in a form that the machine can interpret very rapidly. If it must wait for someone to push buttons, the advantage of the great computing speed is lost. The first series of computers—the "simple computers"—were designed, built, and used with these facts in mind.

9-1.2 The Simple Computers

Three principal features of a computer—a central processor, a memory, and a machine language—were the results of the first attempts to exploit the computers' speed. The *central processor* is primarily the "fast calculator" part of the computer. The *memory* is a place where the computer can read and write numbers or instructions. It corresponds to the sheets of paper used by people at a desk calculator, and is the input-output device for the central processor. The *machine language* is the language in which the instructions are presented to the computer. Thus instead of pushing a button to initiate a multiplication, we write the instruction "multiply." Instead of manually entering a number from a sheet of paper on a keyboard, we write "take the number written at such and such a place in memory and put it in the arithmetic unit." Since the computer must be able to respond to instructions in machine language, it has another part, the *control unit*. Its function is to interpret the instructions, execute them, and generally control the whole process. This unit is normally part of the central processor, but it makes the operation of the simple computers easier to visualize if we think of it as distinct.

One of the most widely used early computers, the IBM 650, is shown in Figure 1-3.2. The organization of its components is shown in schematic form in Figure 9-1.1 The basic steps in computing the solution of a problem on this type of computer are:

1. Prepare the instructions.
2. Put the instructions and data into memory.
3. Push the START button.
4. Compute the solution.
5. Get the results out of memory.

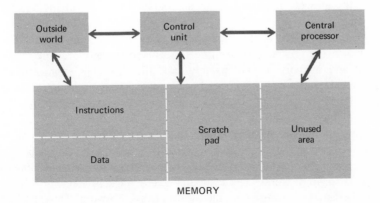

FIGURE *9-1.1* **The organization of a simple computer for the solution of a typical problem.**

FIGURE 9-1.2 The IBM 026 printing card punch is the most common keypunch machine. (Courtesy of IBM Corp.)

In the case of the IBM 650, the instructions and data are written on paper and punched into cards on a keypunch machine (see Figure 9-1.2). These cards are brought to the card reader (the piece of equipment on the right in Figure 1-3.2) and placed in the hopper (at the left end). This machine then reads in the cards placed in the hopper. Once all the cards are in, the computer is started at the location of the first instruction. This is done by using the console. The operator then waits until the computer stops—he can tell this by watching the lights on the console. When the computation is finished, the results are punched into cards by the computer. The hopper in the center of the card reader and punch contains blank cards, and the cards appear in the recess at the right end after they are punched (see Figure 1-3.2).

The instructions must be complete for this process to work. In other words, the control unit reads them one at a time, causes the central processor to execute them, and stops when the answers are found. Thus a program has to be in the language of this particular computer.

Recall that the goal of this organization is to eliminate the human element from the execution of the program. The central processor operates extremely fast, and if the control unit and memory are comparably fast, then the whole program is executed extremely fast. In other words the speed of the calculating machine (central processor) has been exploited.

It is worthwhile to discuss what we mean by "fast" for a memory. There are two distinct points in using a memory where time is involved. The first is in finding the number to retrieve, and the second is in actually retrieving it. One may visualize the memory as a long list where the words are stored. For a typical simple computer the list contains 1000 to 4000 words. The computer keeps track of items in this list by their location in the list. This location is called the *address* of a word. Thus the 1687th word on the list has the address 1687. (Most memories actually start counting at zero instead of one which makes the 1687th word have address 1686.)

Some memories are built so that no searching is required in finding the 1687th word (in memory). Visualize it as a switch that we set to the desired address. When the control unit wants the 1687th word, it is switched to location 1687 on the list and retrieves it. Such memories are commonly made from networks of magnetic cores (see Figure 0-5.4), but advances in technology might replace this construction with another. This fast-access memory is the *main memory*. A memory that requires no searching time is called a *random-access memory*. This terminology apparently comes from the fact that words can be retrieved from memory in any desired (for example, random) sequence at the same speed.

The most common memory without random access is magnetic tape. The words are stored sequentially from the beginning to the end of the tape. Whenever a particular word is desired, the magnetic tape is wound or rewound until that word comes to the reading head. These tapes are usually quite long, and it may take two or three minutes to go from one end of a tape to the other. The searching time is so long that magnetic tapes are not used for the main memory of computers. They are, however, commonly used in other roles.

Another example of a memory that requires searching is the drum memory. Words are stored as magnetized spots on a revolving drum. The main memory for the IBM 650 is a drum that contains 2000 words. There might be 20 bands around the drum, each of which contains 100 words, and there is a reading head for each band (see Figure 9-1.3). When the control unit wants the 1341st word, it asks for the 13th reading head to read it. However, this magnetic reader can read only the word directly next to it. If the 41st word of the band is not there, the reading head must wait for it to come around. Even though the drum may be rotating at 10,000 revolutions per minute, this waiting time can substantially slow down the overall speed of the computer.

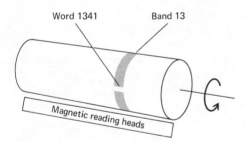

Word 1341   Band 13

Magnetic reading heads

FIGURE 9-1.3 **Schematic drawing of a drum memory.**

Another memory that requires searching is the magnetic disk. Any memory that requires the movement of a physical object is going to be slow compared to the electronic speeds possible in central processors.

The internal operation and the control unit of a simple computer can be visualized in terms of the "little moron" shown in Figure 9-1.4. The little moron inside the computer can read simple instructions written on slips of paper. These slips are kept in storage slots that correspond to the main memory. Both instructions and data are written on these slips. The moron is told to start at some particular address (storage slot), and he reads the slips in the slots one at a time. He goes through the slots in order unless he is told to do otherwise.

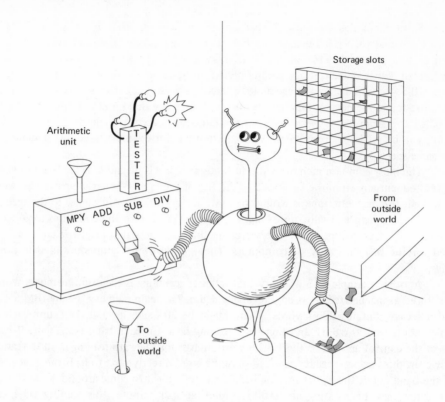

FIGURE 9-1.4 **Schematic illustration of the role of the control unit in a simple computer. The moron follows instructions in the Moron machine language.**

Whenever the moron takes a slip out of a slot, he leaves a copy of the slip in the slot. Whenever he puts a slip into a slot, he throws away the slip already in the slot.

The moron does not know what numbers are, but he can put slips (with numbers on them) into the arithmetic unit (central processor) as instructed. This unit then writes the result on a new slip which the moron can, if so instructed, place in a storage slot. The moron can also look at, and respond to, the lights on the "tester" portion of the arithmetic unit. This is how he can tell if a number is positive, zero, or negative even though he cannot read numbers directly.

The instructions that the moron can understand form the machine language for this simple computer. The actions and instructions for a simple calculation are given in the next example.

EXAMPLE 9-1

The Computation of 2*A+3*B By the Moron

The initial contents of the storage slots (pertinent to this computation) are given below.

Address	Machine Language	Meaning and Remarks
330	056000761	Put the number A into the arithmetic unit.
331	104000765	Multiply by 2.
332	020000763	Store the result.
333	056000762	Put the number B into the arithmetic unit.
334	104000766	Multiply by 3.
335	231000763	Add contents of TEMP = 2*A
336	020000764	Store the result
. . .	. . .	
761	000012006	The number A
762	000201021	The number B
763	000000000	Temporary storage
764	000000000	Final result
765	000000002	The number 2
766	000000003	The number 3

The moron is told to start reading the instructions at address 330. He reads them and executes them, and when he reaches 336, the final result is placed at address 764. The contents of two of the storage slots have changed by the end of the computation as follows:

763	000024012	Contains 2 * A
764	000627075	Contains 2 * A + 3 * B

Note that machine language instructions (and the corresponding assembly language instructions) consist of two parts. The first part indicates what operation is to be performed (for example, 0560 means put a number into the arithmetic unit) and the second part indicates on what the operation is to be performed (for example the contents of address 00761 for the first instruction).

Example 9-1 illustrates only part of what the moron needs to be able to do. A description of a very simple machine language that allows the computer to carry out arithmetic calculations follows.

9-1.3 A Simple Machine Language for the Moron

There are three kinds of instructions in this language; namely, arithmetic, testing and control, and manipulation. For clarity and ease of reading we use an alphanumeric language form rather than the numerical form of actual machine language (as seen in the preceding example). With one exception, the instructions consist of an operation and an address; STOP has no address, only an operation. The thirteen Moron language instructions are as follows.

Instruction	Meaning
ADD, X	Add the contents of address X to that of the arithmetic unit.
SUB, X	Subtract the contents of address X from that of the arithmetic unit.
MPY, X	Multiply the contents of address X by that of the arithmetic unit.
DIV, X	Divide the contents of the arithmetic unit by that of address X.
TRA, X	Read the next instruction from address X.
TZE, X	If the content of the arithmetic unit is zero, then read the next instruction from address X; otherwise, continue to the next instruction.
TPL, X	If the content of the arithmetic unit is positive, then read the next instruction from address X; otherwise continue to the next instruction.
TMI, X	If the content of the arithmetic unit is negative (minus), then read the next instruction from address X; otherwise continue to the next instruction.
STP	Stop.
SRI, X	Start reading instructions at address X.
CLA, X	Place the contents of address X into the arithmetic unit.
STO, X	Store the contents of the arithmetic unit into address X.
OUT, X	Put the contents of address X into the output device.

A program for the Moron, written on slips of paper (or punched into cards), is given to the moron along with a location (slot number) to place them:

$$\text{location address, (instruction, operation address)}$$

$$
\begin{array}{ccccc}
12 & , & (& \text{CLA}, & 106 &) \\
12 & , & (& \text{MPY}, & 707 &) \\
12 & , & (& \text{STO}, & 106 &) \\
\end{array}
$$

The moron goes through the locations in order unless instructed to do otherwise by a transfer instruction. Thus if the moron gets to location 12, it will place the contents of location 106 into the arithmetic unit. It then multiplies that number by the contents of location 707 and, at the instruction in 14, places the resulting number back into location 106.

Data is given to the moron in the form

$$
\begin{array}{cc}
\text{location address,} & \text{number} \\
106, & 12 \\
707, & 6 \\
\end{array}
$$

Thus these data along with the above three instructions would result in the placement of 6*12 = 72 in location 106.

An entire algorithm (program) for the computation of 2*A + 3*B is shown below for A = 12,006 and B = 201,021:

```
330,(CLA,761)          337,(OUT,764)
331,(MPY,765)          338,(STP)
332,(STO,763)          761,000012006
333,(CLA,762)          762,000201021
334,(MPY,766)          765,000000002
335,(ADD,763)          766,000000003
336,(STO,764)          SRI,330
```

It is interesting to compare these instructions with those required in Basic given below.

```
10 READ A,B
20 PRINT   2*A+3*B
30 DATA 12006,201021
40 END
```

Thus for this short computation the moron's machine language requires about three or four times as many statements as Basic. However, the ratio is higher for more complicated computations. There are usually five to ten times as many machine language instructions as there are Basic instructions for a computation.

9-1.4   The Weaknesses of the Simple Computers

Until the late 1950s, the simple computers, the kind just discussed, were the only ones available. Such computers are still manufactured and are quite effective for a large number of applications, but in the late 1950s it became clear that they could not effectively exploit central-processing speed because it takes too long to:

1. prepare the instructions (that is, to correctly write the program in machine language),
2. put the instructions and data into memory,
3. push the start button, and
4. get the results out of memory.

Thus, each step in the solution of a problem was much too long compared to the time the computer took to actually solve the problem. Two changes in the use and organization of computers appeared almost simultaneously in order to alleviate these difficulties. One change was the introduction of higher-level languages, the purpose of which was to substantially increase the efficiency in preparing the instructions for the computer. The other change was the introduction of operating systems, input-output buffering, and batch processing (discussed in Section 9-3). The aim here was to substantially increase the efficiency of input-output and of pushing the start button.

It is noteworthy that these two changes are not really changes in the physical hardware of the computers, but in the manner in which the hardware is used. The IBM 650 has been used both as a simple computer and as part of a system including higher level languages. This does not mean that the hardware did not change, for there were continual increases in the size, speed, efficiency, and versatility of the computers. Nevertheless the new hardware was based on the same concept as that used in building the simple computers. At this point the *computer system* emerged consisting of a physical computing machine and auxiliary devices along with a large number of programs for using them. This collection of programs is called the *software* of the computer system. Originally, the systems part was almost nonexistent. Now the system is recognized as being as important as the physical devices for computing. Certainly the effort put into developing the systems software for a new computer is as large as the effort put into developing its hardware.

PROBLEMS

Make up slips of paper (programs) to get the moron in the simple computer to solve Problems 9-1.1 to 9-1.9. The slips are to be prepared for the moron, in the Moron machine language. Remember: The moron does not do anything without explicit written instructions.

9-1.1   Take the numbers 1382, 7, and 1403 and compute

$$X = 1382+7*1403.$$

9-1.2   Find which of the numbers in slots 92, 63, 112, and 981 is the largest.

9-1.3   Find the largest of the numbers 112, 63, 92, and 981.

9-1.4   Find the sum of the numbers in slots 1, 2, 3, 4, 7, and 9.

9-1.5   Compute the number

$$(17 - 81/403)*6.$$

9-1.6   Find the middle number (median) of the numbers in slots 7, 4, 6, 9, 11.

9-1.7   Find the average of 7, 4, 6, 9, and 11.

9-1.8   Take the number 13,971 and find the power of 10 by which it must be divided in order to get the result between 1 and 10. That is compute P so that

$$1 \leqslant \frac{13,971}{10^P} < 10$$

9-1.9   Discover whether or not

$$\frac{1}{2} + \frac{1}{3} + \frac{1}{5} = \frac{2}{15} + \frac{4}{5}$$

9-1.10   For the above problems you wrote several kinds of instructions, and some were used more often than others. How many different kinds of instructions are needed for Problems 9-1.1, 9-1.2, 9-1.6, and 9-1.9?

9-2 HIGHER LEVEL LANGUAGES

9-2.1 The Hierarchy of Languages

Remember that natural languages are often cumbersome (too long), ambiguous, and do not reveal the structure of algorithms and are therefore unsuited for use in computer programming. Also, we do not know how to construct translators to translate English to machine language. It seems to be extremely difficult to construct a machine to recognize and respond to a natural language like English. (See Section 4-4.)

We do not study languages in any detail here, but rather, in an intuitive way, consider the following levels of language:

1. natural language and jargon,
2. flowchart language,
3. natural programming languages,
4. algorithmic programming languages,
5. machine and assembly languages.

The basic difference between these languages is the power or level of the elementary instructions allowed and the flexibility of the construction of statements. At the top (natural language) we can literally say anything and the construction of statements (sentences) is very free and allows great complexity. At the bottom (machine language) the instructions are extremely limited in power and the statements are short, cryptic and in a very restricted form.

NATURAL LANGUAGE AND JARGON: This is our ordinary language with the four drawbacks listed above. Recall that jargon means the technical language of a science, profession, or special group. The jargon we have used is that of mathematics. It includes not only special words (and special technical meanings for ordinary words) but also special symbols (for example, $+$, $>$, and so on) that are an essential part of the language.

We should not underestimate the ambiguity problem in the natural spoken languages. Recall the following sentence discussed in Chapter 4.

EXAMPLE 9-2

Time Flies Like an Arrow

This statement has, at least, the following interpretations:

1. The common metaphor meaning that time is passing quickly.
2. Certain insects (time flies) desire an arrow.
3. Use the same mechanism to time the flight of flies that was used to time the flight of arrows.
4. The magazine (Time) flies like an arrow when thrown.
5. Time goes in a straight manner.

This sentence, standing alone, is ambiguous.

Even though natural language is inherently ambiguous, it can and has been used for unambiguous communication between people. A sentence such as the preceding one assumes one particular meaning from the context in which it is used. It is easy to note that the mechanism which resolves ambiguity is that of *"meaning in context."* It is very difficult to understand how this mechanism works, which leads to great difficulty in mechanical language translation (for example, English to Russian).

FLOWCHART LANGUAGE: The primary use of flowchart language is to show the logical structure of an algorithm in a form easily recognized by a person. Thus, this language is very appropriate for "thinking" about programs and for communicating with other people. However, it is not so appropriate for machine communication as the machines are not able to "see" the structure of a program from a flowchart. There is some evidence and belief that this is the most "natural" language for programs and algorithms.

NATURAL PROGRAMMING LANGUAGES: We are just now beginning to see the emergence of natural programming languages. They are all oriented to computer usage, and thus the term programming. They are also called problem-oriented languages. Their aim is to use familiar words and phrases from natural language (or jargon) to express programs. To accomplish this, the meaning of the words and phrases are restricted, more stringent rules are placed on the formation of statements, and a much smaller vocabulary is used.

More powerful and versatile instructions are allowed with problem-oriented than with algorithmic languages.

There is, as yet, no widely established example of such a language. Typical statements allowed by such languages are as follows:

1. Set A = solution of $X*X - 3.2 = X\uparrow1.06$.
2. Set P = the payments for a loan of \$3,125.00, 34 months, 12 percent interest.
3. Set A = weight of components 3, 5, 8.

Such languages are not likely to allow many alternatives for making the same statement. The objectives in a natural programming language are:

1. To be unambiguous (this is essential),
2. To be reasonably concise,
3. To use familiar terminology with the familiar meaning.
4. To eliminate unnecessary, artificial, or redundant statements and instructions,
5. To include instructions more powerful than those of current languages.

It is primarily objectives 2, 4, and 5 that distinguish these languages from the next lower level, the algorithmic languages. As more and more languages are developed, the dividing line between these two levels will be more difficult to identify.

ALGORITHMIC PROGRAMMING LANGUAGES: In a certain sense, this class of languages is defined by the example of Fortran (discussed briefly in Section 9-3). Basic is a typical member of this class. An examination of this language shows that it is essentially restricted to arithmetic and use of a few elementary mathematical functions (trigonometric, logarithmic, exponentials). Furthermore, the requirements on the structure of statements are very restrictive, and a considerable amount of artificial and unnecessary punctuation is required. Finally, the execution of programs in Fortran (and in Basic) requires detailed instructions to the computer about certain aspects of the problem, about the data entering the problem, and about the relationships between various parts of the program.

In theory there is no problem in the mathematical-scientific area that can be solved on a computer using a natural programming language that cannot be solved using Basic. The real motivation for developing the natural programming languages is to significantly reduce the human effort in obtaining the solutions. This is achieved by reducing the time and difficulty of instructing and learning how to instruct the computer.

MACHINE AND ASSEMBLY LANGUAGES: The elementary instructions that a computer can perform are very limited. They simply do not recognize statements such as

$$Z = X + Y, \qquad Z = \frac{3X}{7}, \qquad Z = \frac{(3X+Y)}{4}.$$

Before a computer can carry out such operations, they must be broken into smaller steps which involve not only the details of arithmetic but also the internal manipulation of the numbers involved. Thus the third of the statements might take eight to ten separate machine operations. The words in the language recognized by the machine consist of groups of digits, as shown in Part A for Figure 9-2.1. This is a typical machine language. Closely associated with machine languages are the assembly languages which contain statements as shown in Part B of Figure 9-2.1.

Computer instructions in machine language and assembly language are almost in one-to-one correspondence, but assembly language is much easier to read and write. The Moron language discussed earlier belongs to this level of languages.

It is hard to appreciate the difficulties in the use of machine languages without actually using one. There are a fairly large number of instructions, but each has a very limited scope. Thus programs in machine language are much longer, perhaps five to ten times longer, than programs in Basic that do the same thing. For example, it takes 14 instructions in the Moron language to compute $X = 2*A + 3*B$. Furthermore, the user cannot refer to A, B, and X, but must know their addresses. This means that the user must set up his own list of variables and corresponding addresses in the computer memory.

In a nutshell, the user has to know just how the machine shuffles individual words or even parts of words. Every time a word or number is manipulated, detailed instructions must be given for each small step in the manipulation.

Machine languages and assembly languages have several disadvantages. First, it takes a long time just to write a program in these languages. Second, it takes much longer to get the bugs out of the algorithm—there are so many statements, each of which must be exactly right, that errors are almost inevitable and difficult to locate. Third, one cannot understand what a program does (in any general sense) by reading it in machine language which further contributes to difficulty in debugging programs. Fourth, a really complex program might be so long in machine language that it would be almost impossible for one person to absorb and appreciate it all. Finally, it requires considerable study to learn how to use machine language.

Part A

Address	Contents	Address	Contents
04371	410000004373	04424	007400400000
04372	002000004560	04425	100001004430
04373	053500102161	04426	004602000323
04374	050000001424	04427	000000002214
04375	040000002222	04430	060100002266
04376	060100001424	04431	007400400000
04377	050000001001	04432	100001004435
04400	030200000000	04433	004602000324
04401	060100002266	04434	000000002215
04402	050000000000	04435	060100002267
04403	030200001000	04436	050000002236
04404	013100000000	04437	056000002267
04405	026000002266	04440	076300000000
04406	040200002221	04441	013100000000
04407	010000004411	04442	026000002266
04410	012000004413	04443	040200002221
04411	050000002222	04444	010000004450
04412	060100100000	04445	412000004450

Part B

	TNZ	202A	206A	LAC	KNTRT,1
201A	TRA	254A	2316J	CLA	**
202A	LAC	1,1	207A	STO	ROOTS-1,1
	CLA	KNTRT		CLA	ITER2
	ADD	C.3	208A	STO	ORDER-1,1
	STO	KNTRT	209A	STZ	IORD-1,1
203A	CLA	B		CLA	NF
2304J	FSB	**		ADD	C.18
	STO	N.		STO	NF
2306J	CLA	**	210A	NULL	
	FSB	A	211A	TSX	**,4
	XCA			TXI	*+3,,1
	FMP	N.		PZE	211,,LK.DR
	SUB	C.2		PZE	XP
	TZE	*+2		STO	N.
	TPL	206A	212A	TSX	**,4
204A	CLA	C.3		TXI	*+3,,1
205A	STO	INTRT-1,1		PZE	212,,LK.DR

FIGURE 9-2.1 **A sample of machine language (a) and corresponding assembly language (b).**

Another disadvantage of a different type is the fact that machine language is machine dependent. Every time a different computer is used, a different machine language (and therefore a different program) is required. The history of computing shows that computers are changed frequently, and thus the effort required to keep up with the machine languages is very significant.

It is very important to note that one cannot just decide to define a new and better language and then go ahead and use it. Machine language has one property that makes it essential; it is the only language that the machine understands. Thus the introduction of a new programming language requires that it can be translated into the appropriate machine language. Furthermore, it must be possible to do this translation automatically from some specific set of rules. That is, there must be a program (in machine language) to translate the new programming language into machine language. If this translation has to be done by people, then there is little gain in using a higher level language.

The secret of success, then, is to arrange to have the computer do the language translation. This means that a program for the translation has to be written in machine language. With this program the machine can take a program in a higher level language, translate it into its own language, then read and execute the program.

We can now see where the catch lies with natural programming languages. As the language gets more sophisticated, includes a larger vocabulary, and becomes less rigidly structured, the difficulty of translation into machine language increases rapidly. However, since the value of human effort is increasing and the cost of computing is decreasing, it is reasonable to expect that many users of computers in the late 1970s will use natural programming languages designed for the specific problem area at hand. Just as machine and assembly languages are presently used primarily by programming professionals, we can expect in time that algorithmic languages will be used almost exclusively by professionals in programming and algorithm construction.

9-3 *HIGHER LEVEL LANGUAGES — COBOL, FORTRAN, PL/I, AND SNOBOL*

This section presents a very brief discussion of four important higher level languages. The objective is to give the reader an idea of the nature and use of these languages. A thorough description or a real understanding is, of course, not possible in the few paragraphs devoted to each of these languages.

9-3.1 *Cobol*

Cobol—"common business oriented language"—was developed starting in 1959 by the U. S. Government and several computer manufacturers. The objective was to develop a language particularly adapted to business data processing. A set of specifications was issued in 1961 which contained its basic elements and upon which later versions were based.

Cobol is quite different from Basic (which is most closely related to Fortran discussed next) both in appearance and structure. Business data processing typically requires very little arithmetic and a large amount of moving data round and of reading and writing files of information. Furthermore, an attempt was made to have Cobol self-documenting. The hope was that almost anyone, even a nonprogrammer supervisor or manager, could read a Cobol program and follow the data processing. Even though Cobol is more readable than most languages, this ideal of self-documentation was not realized.

Cobol statements are called sentences and many of them do appear as ordinary English sentences. The names of variables can be quite long (up to 30 characters), and in many situations one can add "noise" words which make the sentences closer to English.

Data processing requires extensive input/output and thus Cobol has a very extensive set of input/output instructions and features. These features add to the complexity of the language and contrast sharply with Basic where the aim is to keep the input/output as simple as possible. Even though the appearances are quite different, Cobol does have statements corresponding to the LET, GO TO, IF-THEN, READ, PRINT, and so forth, of Basic. The variables in Cobol can be either numerical or alphanumeric (the messages that appear in Basic PRINT statements are alphanumeric) and various statements are needed to declare the type of variables, either numerical or alphanumeric. A number of Cobol statements are shown in Figure 9-3.1 and an almost complete program is shown in Figure 9-3.2.

```
1. ADD TOTAL_PRICE TO BILL_SO_FAR GIVING AMOUNT_DUE

2. MULTIPLY WEEKS_PAY BY TAXRATE GIVING TAX_DEDUCT

3. MOVE AMOUNT_DUE TO ACCOUNTS_RECEIVABLE

4. IF WEEKS_SALES IS GREATER THAN QUOTA GOTO OVER_QUOTA

5. PART_NAME, PICTURE IS XXXXXXXX

6. DISPLAY "ORDER ENTERED FOR", PART_NAME, " ON " , DATE
```

FIGURE 9-3.1 **Some example Cobol statements.**

The first two statements in Figure 9-3.1 are simple arithmetic assignment statements. The third one simply moves a variable from one information file to another. The fourth statement is the IF-THEN and the GO TO OVER-QUOTA is the usual GO TO except that labels in Cobol are names and not necessarily numbers. The fifth statement declares that PART-NAME is a variable with 8 alphanumeric characters (AXLEROD1 or BOLT-5.5). The final statement prints a line on the standard output unit (usually a printer).

```
PROCEDURE DIVISION
GETTING_STARTED.  OPEN INPUT SALES_FILE, OUTPUT SUMMARY_REPORT.
    READ SALES FILE RECORD.  MOVE ZERO TO TOTAL_ALL_SALESMEN.
NEXT_SALESMAN.  MOVE SALESMAN IN SALES_ITEM TO MAN_NUMBER. MOVE
    AMOUNT TO SALESMAN_AMOUNT.
FILE_PROCESSING.  READ SALES_FILE RECORD: AT END GO TO FINISH.
    IF SALESMAN NOT EQUAL TO MAN_NUMBER GO TO SALESMAN_TOTAL.
    ADD AMOUNT TO SALESMAN_AMOUNT.  GO TO FILE_PROCESSING.
SALESMAN_TOTAL.  MOVE SPACES TO SUMREP.  MOVE MAN_NUMBER TO
    SALESMAN IN SUMREP. MOVE SALES AMOUNT TO AMOUNT IN SUMREP.
    ADD SALES_AMOUNT TO TOTAL_ALL_SALESMEN. WRITE SUMREP.
    GO TO NEXT_SALESMAN.
FINISH. MOVE SPACES TO SUMREP. MOVE 'EVERYBODY' TO SALESMAN IN SUMREP.
    MOVE TOTAL_ALL_SALESMEN TO AMOUNT IN SUMREP. WRITE SUMREP.
    CLOSE SALES_FILE, SUMMARY_REPORT. STOP RUN.
```

FIGURE 9-3.2 **A sample Cobol program which reads the file names SALES FILE and writes the file SUMMARY REPORT. Each record (item) in SALES FILE consists of a salesman's name and a sales amount. Each record (item) of SUMMARY REPORT consists of a salesman's name and his total sales. The last record in SUMMARY REPORT has the total sales for all salesmen.**

9-3.2 *Fortran*

Fortran is the oldest of the higher level languages and it has evolved considerably since its introduction in 1956. In 1970 it still was the most widely used programming language in the world.

The name Fortran is derived from "formula translator" and suggests its orientation toward scientific and numerical applications. It was developed at a time when scientific computing was dominant. Even so, Fortran has been used with considerable success in all the major areas of computing, including business data processing, language translators, systems programming and totally non-numerical applications.

Most programs in Basic can be quickly translated into Fortran on a statement by statement basis. The Basic statements LET, IF-THEN, GO TO, FOR, PRINT, READ, and so forth, have direct counterparts in Fortran. Fortran has much more versatile facilities for printing and reading than Basic, but it also requires detailed specifications to accompany every PRINT and READ statement. Fortran has a number of important facilities for the efficient construction and use of subprograms. The IF-THEN statement in Fortran is more flexible than it is in Basic even though it still falls somewhat short of ideal. Thus one can say, "If X equal 1 then set j equal to 4y+3" as one Fortran statement.

Fortran, as well as most other higher level languages, has a number of different kinds of variables, including four different kinds of numbers (decimal, integer, double precisions, and complex). This adds both versatility and complexity to the language and means that there are many declaration statements present and various rules concerning the interrelations of these variables. Basic has only one kind of number (decimal) and the only declaration in Basic is the DIM statement to declare the size of arrays. A number of example Fortran statements are shown in Figure 9-3.3 and a short, complete program is shown in Figure 9-3.4

```
1.    RESULT = DATA1*2.7-6.4/(COST-XQ43Z*4.076)

2.    GOTO 107

3.    INTEGER X,X1,Y,YY,YXYZ

4.    PRINT 18,RESULT,X,A(14),COST

18 FORMAT(3X,2F10.2,E14.6/2X,4HCOST,F12.5)

5.    IF(K.EQ.0) CALL SUBPRG(TO,PRINT,ANSWER)
```

FIGURE *9-3.3* **Five example Fortran statements.**

The first three statements in Figure 9-3.3 are the assignment, GO TO, and integer declaration statements, respectively. Note that variable names can consist of more than two characters, but the limit is normally six. The fourth statement prints out four numbers, and the details of the way the printing is to be done are encoded in the associated FORMAT statement. The final statement is the IF-THEN, although the word THEN is not used. This statement reads as "If K equals 0 then execute the subprogram SUBPRG and three arguments TO, PRINT, and ANSWER."

```
         INTEGER TOP(1001),BOT(1000),ANS(1001),SUM
    1 READ(5,2)K,(TOP(I),I = 1,K),(BOT(I),I = 1,K)
    2 FORMAT(I5/(60I1))
         TOP(K+1) = 0
         DO 10 I = 1,K
         SUM = TOP(I)+BOT(I)
         IF(SUM.LE.9) GO TO 10
         TOP(I+1) = TOP(I+1)+1
         SUM=SUM - 10
   10 ANS(I) = SUM
         ANS(K+1) = TOP(K+1)
  C       SWITCH ANS(I) END FOR END INTO TOP(I)
         K1 = K+1
         DO 15 I = 1,K1
         II = K1 - I+1
   15 TOP(I) = ANS(II)
         WRITE(6,20)(TOP(I),I = 1,K1)
   20 FORMAT(1H1,10X10HTHE SUM IS/(2X100I1))
         GO TO 1
         END
```

FIGURE 9-3.4   **A Fortran program that reads in two numbers of K (up to 1000) digits and prints out their sum.**

9-3.3   PL/I

The initial development of PL/I started in late 1963 in a committee of IBM users and representatives. The language definition went through many versions and a fairly firm definition appeared in 1966. It is sometimes called "programming language one," but it was not intended that PL/I be an acronym for anything.

The objectives in the development of PL/I were broad and varied. PL/I was intended to be suitable for use by a great variety of users and to be better adapted to the hardware and computer system concepts that appeared in the 1960s. It is specifically designed to be suitable as a replacement for Cobol in business data processing, a replacement for Fortran in scientific computing, and as a partial replacement for machine language and assembly language in systems programming.

The attempt to cover such a range of applications has resulted in a large and complicated language. The problems with obtaining compact and efficient language translators are still not completely resolved. The language is of such complexity that it is not reasonable for a novice in computing to attempt to learn the full language and only professionals in computer science are likely to make use of the full range of facilities offered in PL/I. This situation was realized early and the designers expected that various subsets of PL/I would be selected for various application areas. Thus one subset would be learned and used by people in business data processing, another subset similar to Fortran would be used in scientific applications, and an elementary subset would be learned by students in introductory courses. It was hoped by the originators of PL/I that this new language would eventually replace a large number of languages, including such major languages as Algol, Cobol, Fortran, and Jovial.

The final fate of PL/I is not yet determined, but it has already had a major impact on computing and it is certain to assume a position as one of the most important programming languages.

The facilities in PL/I include all the features mentioned or implied in the previous sections on Cobol and Fortran and there are many additional features. The statements in Basic all have direct counterparts in PL/I and a Basic program is easily translated into PL/I but many programs in PL/I are almost impossible to express in Basic. Sample PL/I statements are shown in Figure 9-3.5.

```
1.  BEST_EST = .5*(OLD_EST + (DATANEW + DATA 445)/2);

2.  PUT LIST ' MY ANSWER = ', 17.2* GUESS1 + FUDGE_FACTOR;

3.  GO TO CASE4;

4.  DECLARE X FLOAT(8), BB FIXED(6,2),DATE PICTURE AAAXXX99;

5.  IF K > 100 THEN GO TO ENDPROGRAM;ELSE K = K+2; GO TO B;

6.  DO CONTROL = 1 TO 50, 60 TO 100 BY 10;
```

FIGURE 9-3.5 Six examples of PL/I statements.

The first statement in Figure 9-3.5 is an assignment statement, the second prints a message and a calculated value, and the third is the usual GO TO. The fourth statement declares that X is a decimal (floating) number with 8 significant digits, BB is of fixed size of six digits, two following the decimal point (for example, dollars and cents) and the appearance of DATE is given by the PICTURE. DATE could be JAN 5,73 or JUN 17,88. The fifth statement is the simple IF-THEN-ELSE and the last statement corresponds to the FOR statement in Basic. The control variable CONTROL goes from 1 to 50 in steps of 1 and then from 60 to 100 in steps of 10. A complete PL/1 program is shown in Figure 9-3.6.

```
MIN_FLOAT: PROCEDURE OPTIONS (MAIN);
    DECLARE (X,SLOPE) FLOAT (10);
        SLOPE: PROCEDURE (X);
                SLOPE = EXP(X + SIN(X))*(1. + COS(X))
                        + 2.*X/(1. + X**2);
                RETURN (SLOPE);
        END SLOPE;
    X = 6.; STEP = 1.;
/* MAIN LOOP STARTS HERE */
    LOOP: DO K = 1 TO 999 WHILE SLOPE - = 0. & STEP > .000001;
            IF SLOPE(X) < O THEN X1 = X - STEP;
                        ELSE X1 = X + STEP;
            IF SLOPE(X)*SLOPE(X1) < 0. THEN STEP = STEP/2.;
            X = X1
        END LOOP;
    PUT SKIP EDIT (' FOUND LOW POINT ' , X)
                (A(17), E(17,10));
END MIN_FINDER;
```

FIGURE 9-3.6 A sample PL/I program to find the lowest point on a curve whose slope is given by the formula in the procedure SLOPE.

9-3.4 *Snobol*

The work on Snobol started in 1962 at the Bell Telephone Laboratories and is based on an older language, Comit. The language has gone through several versions and extensions, the most recent of which is called Snobol 4.

The appearance and format of Snobol is not like other programming languages and its objectives are quite different from Basic, Cobol, Fortran, or PL/I. The aim of Snobol is to provide effective means to process messages, character strings and patterns. Its predecessor, Comit, had no arithmetic capability, it could not even add one plus one. While Snobol 4 does have reasonable arithmetic capabilities, it is not really suited for applications appropriate for Basic. Although the appearance of Snobol 4 is foreign at first, it is a rather natural language for its application area and a useful subset of it can be learned easily. The language does have some subtle and sophisticated features which a novice programmer would find difficult.

Snobol is not nearly as widely used as Fortran, Cobol, PL/I, or Basic, but it is available at a significant number of computing centers and on the majority of the larger computers. Its area of application is perhaps best defined by some sample problems which are easily programmed in Snobol 4.

1. Count the number of times that the letter H is followed by the letter groups EI, AU, or OU in a particular chapter of a book.
2. Count the number of verses in the Bible that contain both the words **PROPHET** and **JERUSALEM**.
3. Count the average number of prepositions per sentence that occur in *War and Peace*.
4. Read information of the type

   07128 JOHN PAUL JONES, AGE 63, JUNE 14, 1972, 497, X

   and print it out in the format

   JONES, J.P., 1972-14-JUNE, No. = 07128,63 = AGE, X***497.
5. Make a grammatical analysis of statements in a programming language in preparation for language translation.

Some sample Snobol statements are given in Figure 9-3.7.

```
DIGIT = '0123456789'

BASIC = INPUT

BASIC ANY(DIGIT) . LABEL LEN(3) . KEYWORD REM . REST

EXECUTE = 'LET' | 'GOT' | 'FOR'

TEST KEYWORD EXECUTE = KEYWORD 'EXECUTABLE' : F(TEST2) S(ANALYSIS)
```

FIGURE 9-3.7 **Five types of statements in Snobol 4.**

Statement 1 in Figure 9-3.7 assigns to the variable DIGIT the character string 0123456789. The second statement is the standard READ statement and BASIC takes on the value of the next record (normally a card) at the input unit. The third statement has four parts as follows:

BASIC	— character string to be examined (assumed to be a statement in the Basic language).
ANY(DIGIT) . LABEL	— "Any digits are assigned to LABEL" (The period is an assignment operator.)
LEN(3) . KEYWORD	— Next 3 characters assigned to KEYWORD.
REM . REST	— Remainder of BASIC assigned to REST.

The effect of this statement for two cases is shown below:

BASIC is:	725 FOR J=1 TO K	4999 LET X1 =Y2
LABEL is assigned:	725	4999
KEYWORD is assigned:	FOR	LET
REST is assigned:	J=1 TO K	X1=X2

The fourth statement defines a pattern (of the simplest type), EXECUTE, which is a 3-letter group of LET or of GOT or of FOR. The final statement is labeled TEST, the character string KEYWORD is tested for the occurrence of the pattern EXECUTE. If this test fails, then a transfer is made to the statement labeled TEST2. This is the meaning of the F(TEST2) after the colon. If the test succeeds, then KEYWORD is replaced by the string KEYWORD followed by the string "EXECUTABLE" and a transfer is made to the statement labeled ANALYSIS. The test succeeds for both the sample values of BASIC given above and the resulting values of KEYWORD are FOREXECUTABLE or LETEXECUTABLE.

Snobol has not been explained enough here for the reader to follow the program in Figure 9-3.8. It shows the distinctive appearance of Snobol 4 and its foreign appearance

```
        LETTERS = 'ABCDEFGHIJKLMNOPQRSTUVWXYZ'

        ONE     = LEN(1) . CHAR

        ONECHAR = NOTANY(LETTERS) . TEMP   ONE NULL . TEMP

READ    OUTPUT  = INPUT                        : F(COUNT)

        DATA    = DATA OUTPUT                   : (READ)

COUNT   DATA ONECHAR =                          : F(TABULATE)

        $CHAR   = IDENT(TEMP) $CHAR + 1         : (COUNT)

TABULATE   OUTPUT =

TABLETTERS   LETTERS ONE =                      : F(END)

        OUTPUT = '    ' $CHAR ' ' CHAR : (TABLETTERS)

END
```

FIGURE 9-3.8 A sample Snobol 4 program to read some data (text), count the number of times each letter appears, and to print the data with a frequency table for the letters.

for those used to Basic, Fortran, or PL/1. This particular program is a little subtle, but the task it accomplishes (in 11 statements) would require much longer programs in the more common arithmetic oriented languages. The first three statements initialize the program and the next four read the text data, print it back out, and count the number of occurrences of each letter. The eighth statement merely prints a blank line and the next two statements print the frequency table. A sample of output from this program is shown below.

ABOUT A HUNDRED BILLION HUMAN BEINGS HAVE WALKED THE PLANET EARTH SINCE THE DAWN OF TIME AND THIRTY GHOSTS STAND BEHIND EVERY HUMAN NOW ALIVE.

    12 A
     4 B
    and so on

9-4 COMPUTER SYSTEMS

The introduction of higher level languages really requires that a "system" be introduced for operating the computer. Such a system is a computer program which handles the manipulation of source programs, language translators, input-output and so on. Since the system is itself a program, it must be written and this process is included in "systems programming" by "systems programmers." However, systems programming would be required even if there were no higher level languages. The fact is that by 1960 computers had become so fast that the analogy with the "instantaneous" desk calculator became valid again. Recall that we started by saying that an instantaneous desk calculator would not be too valuable because most of the time is spent in entering numbers into the keyboard and copying down the results. By the late 1950s a similar situation had been reached with computers except that then most of the time was spent in reading in the program and getting the output. Many problems were solved in less time than it took to read in a few cards of the program and twenty problems might be solved in the time it took a programmer to turn the computer over to the next user.

This does not mean that all problems were solved so quickly, but a large number of real and interesting problems could be solved in a few seconds. For these problems it took much more time to read in the program, push the start button, and write out the answers than it took to compute the solution. Just as before, a means of handling the input and output at electronic speeds is required to effectively exploit the computational speed available.

9-4.1 Systems Programming—The Operating System

The words *systems programming* refer to all of the programs and algorithms required to make the computing system work. This includes the algorithms for language translation, the algorithms for scheduling work on the computer, the programs to "push the start button," the programs to get the programs in and the answers out, and the many other chores that need to be done. The organization of the computer system is more complicated than that required for the simple computers discussed earlier. A sample organization is illustrated by the schematic of Figure 9-4.1.

A general view of such a computer system is shown in Figure 9-4.2. (See also Figure 0-2.3 and Figure 1-3.4.)

OPERATING SYSTEM: The programs that oversee the whole operation make up the monitor system, operating system, or executive system. This system has several functions, which include:

1. Coordination of different memory devices,
2. Supply of auxiliary programs (for example, compilers, subroutines),
3. Control of the input-output devices,
4. Change of representations of information (number formats, and so forth) for input-output,
5. Allocation of charges for computer usage,
6. Scheduling and execution of the programs,
7. Communication with the computer operator,
8. Overall control of the computer system.

We see that the operating system uses part of the main memory even while a typical program is being executed. However, an operating system is often a very large program that would more than fill the normal main memory by itself. The computer system requires an auxiliary memory to keep most of the operating system's subprograms. They are brought into the main memory by the system when they are needed.

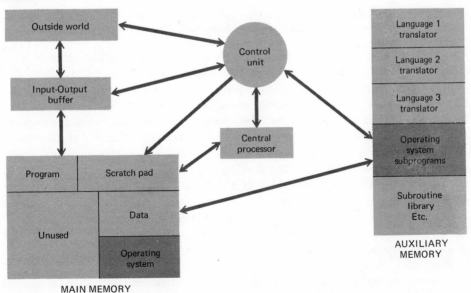

FIGURE 9-4.1 The organization of a typical computer system under the control of an operating system.

FIGURE 9-4.2 A general view of Control Data 6600 computer system. It was the most powerful computer in the world when it was introduced. (Courtesy of Control Data Corp.)

The *main memory* of a computer system of this type typically varies between 10,000 and 65,000 words. The most common size is 32,000 words. At first glance this seems like ample space, but recall that programs in a rudimentary language like machine language require a very large number of statements. Furthermore, many problems manipulate a large number of variables, both from data and from intermediate calculations. Thus problems that require most of the main memory are not at all rare.

The typical range of size for language translators is from 12,000 to 50,000 words, and operating systems run from 25,000 to 100,000 words. This means that the 32,000 word memory which originally looked large is actually fairly small. Thus an *auxiliary memory* is required. There are two differences between the main memory and the auxiliary memory. One is speed—it takes much longer to retrieve something from the auxiliary memory. The other is that the control unit usually cannot directly manipulate words and instructions in auxiliary memory. They must be brought into the main memory first.

We might ask why there are two different kinds of memory since all of the space is required. Why not use a larger main memory? The answer is that fast memory is one of the most expensive parts of a computer. The contents of the auxiliary memory are, presumably, less frequently used, and thus the slower speed or access time for them does not reduce the efficiency by too much. Furthermore, many of the things stored there are large blocks (programs, for example) which are bought into the main memory as a whole. This transfer can be accomplished efficiently because searching is required only for the beginning of the block. Once the first word is located, then all the others are right in line to be retrieved without additional searching. This is particularly easy to visualize in the case of magnetic tapes. Typical examples of such blocks are interpreters, compilers, subroutine libraries, and other pieces of the operating system.

The four principal types of auxiliary memory are magnetic tapes, magnetic disks, magnetic drums, and slow core memories. A group of magnetic-tape units is shown in Figure 9-4.3. There are two reels, and the tape passes over the read-write head as it is spooled from one reel to another. A small magnetic disk pack unit is shown in Figure 9-4.4. There are read-write heads on arms for each disk. Some disk memories are much larger than the one shown in Figure 9-4.4. A schematic diagram of a drum is shown in Figure 9-1.3. A slow core memory is similar to the main memory except it is less expensive, and the time required to retrieve a word is somewhat longer. A slow core memory is usually random access just as is the main memory.

The *subroutine library* contains the standard procedures (for example square root subroutines) of various languages. When we write COS(x) in Basic, a program must be provided by something from someplace to compute COS(x). Note that COS(x) is not found from a trigonometry table, but it is computed by an algorithm. It is the combination of the operating system and the compiler which recognizes that this

FIGURE 9-4.3 **A set of magnetic tape units. They function both as part of the auxiliary and as part of the input-output buffer. (Courtesy of IBM Corp.)**

FIGURE 9-4.4 **A small disk pack unit. These disks are easily exchanged so that this unit may function as part of the input-output buffer as well as part of the auxiliary memory.**

algorithm is needed, locates where it is stored, and brings it to the program when it is needed. The subroutine library might be quite limited or it may contain 100 to 200 subprograms of various sizes. It depends on the particular computer system and the local installation. This library might contain many subprograms that are not built-in procedures in any language. They are useful general-purpose programs placed there for everyone's use and they are already in machine language, ready to use.

The operating system controls the input-output devices attached to the main computer. This control is required because the system is the only thing that "knows" what is going on inside the computer. Thus it knows when more data or more programs should be read in and when some answers should be sent out. There is another facet of input-output that the operating system handles: it changes the representation of various kinds of information needed during input-output. Numbers inside the computer are normally in a form such as

$$100101110001101101101011100$$

Depending on the particular situation, this number could represent 129.6378 or 397,163 or K2. Furthermore, the number 129.6378 might also be written as $.1296378*10^3$. The computer receives various kinds of input, and their representation must be changed to a representation suitable for the computer. This process is more complicated than it appears at first glance, and the algorithms that accomplish it require several thousand statements in machine language.

Since the operating system oversees the computer operation, it knows how long a particular problem runs on the computer. Thus it normally keeps tracks of the charges for computer usage. This part of the system is usually called the *accounting routine*.

Even though the operating system has overall control of the computer system, it sometimes needs to receive instructions from the operator. Similarly, when something goes wrong, the operating system reports this to the operator. One should keep in mind the fact that the operating system does not really "act" in an independent sense. It is simply a large and complex algorithm for the control of a computer system. The effectiveness of this algorithm depends essentially on the people who constructed it. It is certainly no more resourceful than the people who created the system. In fact, it is probably several orders of magnitude less resourceful than these people. It makes up for this lack of resourcefulness by being very fast and able to examine exhaustively a very large number of possibilities in a simpleminded way.

It is noteworthy that the operating system is designed to provide services for the computer user. Its job is to do much of the routine record keeping, button pushing, and program manipulation. The role of the operating system is shown in Figure 9-4.5, where it is visualized as an "executive" in charge of the computer. There are some computing

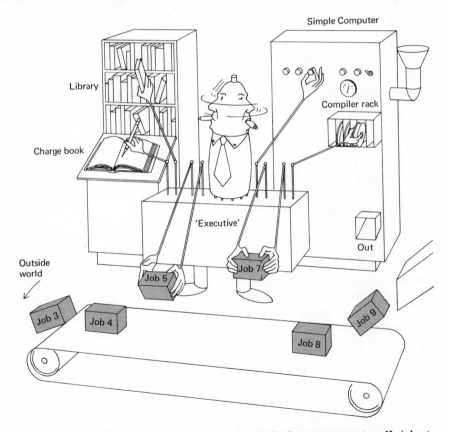

FIGURE 9-4.5 Schematic illustration of the "executive" of a computer system. He is kept busy running and coordinating the various components of the computer system.

centers where a larger computer is controlled by a second smaller computer. In this situation the "executive" is primarily the smaller computer and the larger computer is able to spend more time on the "production" of results.

9-4.2 Batch Processing Operation

The input buffer, basically a system that collects programs to be run on the computer, saves the programs (in various ways) until it has a "batch" ready. This batch is in a form that can be rapidly transmitted to the computer. Once the batch is ready, it is fed into the computer and each program in the batch is run. When the batch is finished, there should be another batch collected, ready to be processed.

The jobs to be run in a particular batch are processed sequentially. They may be visualized as in the following schematic diagram.

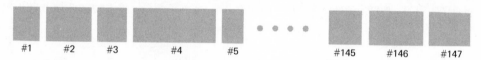

Each of these boxes represents a program to be executed by the computer. In addition to the programs to be executed, there are normally instructions for the operating system. For example, the system is usually told in what language a program is written. Presumably it could read the first part of the program and discover the language itself, but this does not seem to be very efficient.

The information given to the system includes, for example:

1. The user's name,
2. The charge account for the job,
3. Nonstandard input devices used,
4. Type of output and limits on the amount of each,
5. Limit on the execution time,
6. Language of the program,
7. Nonstandard output devices used.

The system accepts this information and uses it in executing and monitoring the job.

It is instructive to see what a typical system does for a program that is written in a higher level language, often referred to as the source program or source deck. The system receives something like this:

```
$           Name John J. Doe
$           Charge to Account 70-4962
$           Output Limits: 30 pages, 100 cards
$           Time Limit: 20 seconds
$           Language = Babel
            Statement 1 in Babel
            Statement 2 in Babel

            . . .
```

	Statement Last in Babel
$	Data for this job follows
*	Data 1
*	Data 2
*	. . .
*	Data Last

The statements marked by a $ are instructions to the operating system. The statements which are unmarked form a program in the Babel language. The statements marked by an * are data to be used by this program for this particular execution.

As soon as the system sees that a Babel program is coming, it brings the Babel translator into the main memory. The translator then begins to read the Babel statements and translates them into machine language. During this translation, much information is collected including:

1. The equivalent algorithm in machine language (the *object program* or object deck, the original Babel language program is the *source program*),
2. The size of the program and its various parts,
3. The names and locations of the variables,
4. Diagnostics: questionable or unintelligible statements in the Babel program,
5. A list of the subprograms needed.

Recall that the translator might have more instructions than can fit into the main memory. So this translation process might become very complicated as various parts of the Babel program, the machine-language program, and the translator are shuffled back and forth between the main memory and the auxiliary memory.

Once the translation is finished, the Babel program (perhaps along with some additional information) is put into the auxiliary memory or is sent to an output device. The machine-language program (object program) is brought into the main memory along with the required subprograms from the subroutine library. Then the system has this program executed by the computer. During the execution the program should call for the waiting data. These data might be in an input device, in the auxiliary memory, or already in main memory. When the execution stops, the system sends out any additional output required and readies itself for the next job.

INPUT-OUTPUT BUFFER. The problem of getting information into and out of a computer without slowing down the whole process is a difficult one. The reason is that programs are originally expressed on some physical forms. The manipulation of these physical objects cannot be done at speeds comparable to the computing speed available. The input-output buffer is a smaller (presumably cheaper) device that performs this physical manipulation for the computer and then presents the problems to the computer at its normal operating speed. In other words the input-output buffer can communicate with both the outside world and the computer and be efficient in both directions.

Although we speak of the input-output buffer as one part of the computer system, it usually consists of a number of different physical devices. A fairly elaborate input-output buffer for a computer system is illustrated in Figure 9-4.6. From this diagram it is easy to see that the input-output facilities for a large computer can be bigger

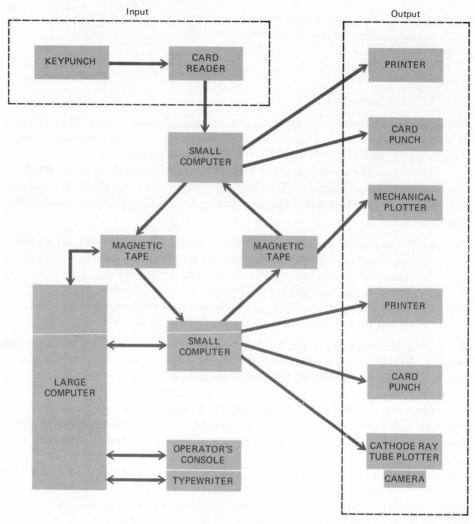

FIGURE 9-4.6 Diagram of an elaborate input-output buffer for a computer system. There are a number of possible alternate ways to organize the input-output buffer.

than the computer itself. Note that the input-output buffer for the IBM 650 consists of a single piece of equipment, a card reader and punch. A number of the pieces seen in Figure 9-4.2 are parts of the input-output buffer.

Some of the components of the input buffer are shown in Figure 9-1.3 (keypunch machine), Figure 9-4.4 (disk pack unit), Figure 9-4.7 (card reader and punch), and Figure 9-4.10 (magnetic tape unit). Other card readers and punches are shown in Figures 9-1.1 and 9-4.2, and rows of magnetic tapes are shown in Figures 9-4.2 and 9-4.3. Note that magnetic tapes and disk packs can be (and are) used either as input-output devices or as auxiliary memory devices.

The four main output devices are printers (see Figure 9-4.8), card punches (see Figure 9-4.7), plotters (see Figure 9-4.9), and scopes (see Figure 9-5.2). Either a small computer or a magnetic tape serves as an intermediary between the large computer and

FIGURE 9-4.7 A card reader and card punch. The cards are read from the stack at the right and punched from the stack at the left. This unit is controlled by a computer. (Courtesy of IBM Corp.)

FIGURE 9-4.8 High speed printers such as this can print from 1000 to 1200 lines per minute. (Courtesy of IBM Corp.)

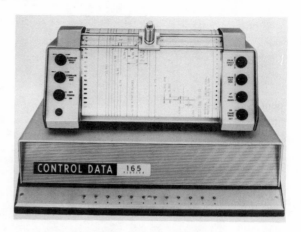

FIGURE 9-4.9 Front view of a small mechanical plotter. The drawing is done with ink and each letter and line is individually drawn. (Courtesy of Control Data Corp.)

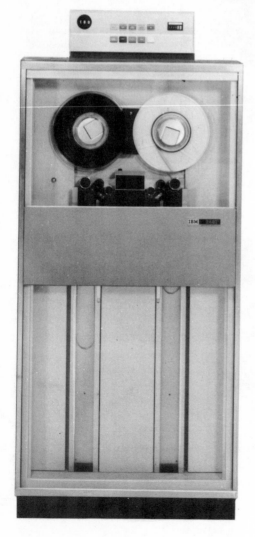

FIGURE 9-4.10 Front view of a magnetic tape unit showing the reading head in between two reels. The tape can move in both directions but can be read only while moving forward. (Courtesy IBM Corp.)

these four devices. When one of these devices is driven by a magnetic tape, there must be some type of computer to read the tape and control the device. In some cases this computer is an integral part of the output device and is a special purpose computer (that is, the only thing it does is to read tapes and control the device). A small general purpose computer is usually used to control printers and card punches. A small computer might operate fast enough to control simultaneously several of these devices. In fact this computer might also be used in the input buffer between card readers and magnetic tapes at the same time it is in the output buffer.

Two typical operator's consoles are shown in Figures 9-4.11 and 9-4.12. The one in Figure 9-4.11 appears similar to that of the simple computer in Figure 9-1.1. The typewriter is the main communication device. This computer might also be directly connected to magnetic tapes, magnetic disks, printers, and card readers and punches. The console in Figure 9-4.12 is a separate unit, but its functions are basically the same. In the background are a set of magnetic tapes, a mechanical plotter, and other components of the computer system.

In order to see why there are so many devices between the computer and the user, consider Table 9-4.1. This table contains the range of transmission rates for various devices. The words in the computer system are usually all the same size and consist of 32

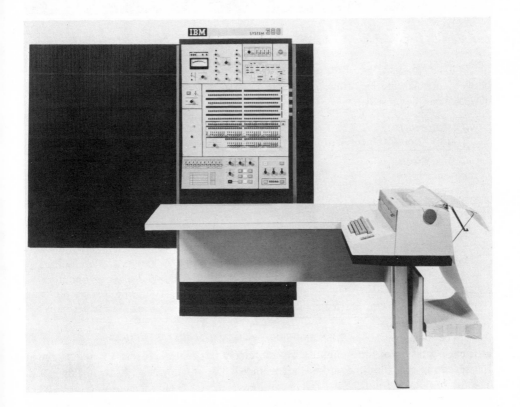

FIGURE 9-4.11 The operator's console and typewriter for a medium size computer. Most of the communication is via the typewriter. (Courtesy of IBM Corp.)

FIGURE 9-4.12   General view of a Honeywell 2000 computer system. (Courtesy of Honeywell Corp.)

to 60 binary digits (9 to 18 decimal digits) depending on the computer. The difference between manual and electronic devices is so large that several "layers" of intermediate devices might be present.

TABLE 9-4.1
Transmission Rates for Various Devices

Coding sheets	10-15 words/minute
Keypunch	5-30 words/minute
Keyboard terminal	20−400 words/minute
Card punch	500−3000 words/minute
Card reader	800−10,000 words/minute
Printer	1,000−25,000 words/minute
Magnetic tape	200,000−1,000,000 words/minute
Magnetic disk	800,000−1,500,000 words/minute
Computer	1,000,000−30,000,000 words/minute
Mechanical plotter	5 minutes per plot
Cathode-ray-tube plotter/camera	5 seconds per plot

The organization of the computer system described in this section results in efficient operation of the computer. The extremely fast central processor is able to run at full speed most of the time without being impeded by the slowness of the outside world. The use of language translators and operating systems introduces a large amount of work for the computer which is only indirectly related to the computation of the solution of a problem. Some of this extra work is simply "overhead" required by a more complex system. Other parts of it (such as translating) contribute to the efficient use of the computer. Thus, even though there is a considerable reduction in the amount of time spent in computing the solution, the total problem-solving process is much more efficient because this computer organization successfully exploits the speed of the central processor.

In spite of the efficiency of this organization, there are still two difficulties present:

1. It takes too long to write programs in these higher level languages.
2. It takes too long in terms of calendar time to solve the problems.

Thus we have increased the efficiency of the computer organization by an order of magnitude, and we still have the original difficulties, namely, input-output and preparation of instructions.

The batch-processing operation of a computer brings into focus an important feature of a computer operation: the *turnaround time*. Recall that this is the time that elapses between the time a job is put into the input buffer and the time it is returned to the user in the output buffer. The turnaround time can vary from ten minutes to several days. It depends on a great variety of factors, but there is one that is crucial. It is the ratio of computing capacity to work load. If this ratio is much bigger than one (that is, if there is considerable excess-capacity), then very short turnaround times are possible. If the ratio is very close to one (that is, if the computer system is saturated), then very short turnaround times are not possible. In this case the computer is running 24 hours a day, and those jobs run in the middle of the night are almost certain to have been submitted during the day.

To appreciate the importance of calendar time in problem solving, consider two people with a problem and an algorithm. The first algorithm is short, but it takes eight runs on the computer to get the program debugged and the problem solved. The second algorithm is longer and it takes 35 runs on the computer to get the program debugged and the problem solved. The 35 runs for the second program includes 8 modifications of the algorithm itself.

A computing center with a rather efficient batch-processing system which is operating close to, but not at, full capacity, might take about 4 days to get the first problem solved. It may take about one minute of computer time for these eight runs. This much computer time may cost from $4 to $10. In many real situations, the user is willing to pay twice or even ten times this amount if he could get the solution in four hours rather than in four days. It might be that a project is completely stopped, waiting for the solution of this problem.

It might take as little as three or four weeks to get the second problem solved. The total amount of computer time may be about 30 or 40 minutes and cost $100 to $300. Again the user may be willing to pay much more if the elapsed time can be substantially reduced. Certainly if eight modifications in the algorithm are required, it is unreasonable to expect to solve the problem in a few hours. But it is not unreasonable to expect to solve the problem in a few days.

The problem is: How do you organize the computer system in order to accomplish this? The next section presents some approaches currently under development to solve this particular problem, and more generally, to better exploit the computation speed of computers.

9-5 *NATURAL PROGRAMMING LANGUAGES AND ELABORATE SYSTEMS*

One of the most obvious facts about algorithmic programming languages is that it is easy to make mistakes in writing programs; that is, mistakes in addition to the ones made because of insufficient analysis or a lack of understanding. These additional mistakes lead directly to an increase in the number of runs through a computer required to solve a problem. It seems reasonable to use programming languages which are as natural as possible.

In a nutshell, the objective is to make the computer understand people's language rather than making people understand the computer's language—or even some compromise such as an algorithmic programming language. Do not expect the use of these languages to remove all of the difficulties in programming. Even experienced people tend to overlook small (and sometimes large) points in writing programs. This means that several debugging runs can be expected even if the computer does exactly what the programmer has in mind. Furthermore, it takes considerable practice to learn how to "think" in the algorithmic terms required for solving problems with computers.

There is, of course, a price to be paid for the use of natural or nearly natural language. It takes the computer much more effort to translate the program into machine language. From one viewpoint, we might say that the decision on the use of these languages should be based on the efficiency of the translation. In other words, can a computer or a person do it more efficiently? However, it is very difficult to find a measure of efficiency here which is reliable and objective and considers all important factors. It is clear that the cost of computing is going down and the cost of human effort is going up. Thus good efficiency requires that we shift more and more of the work from people onto the computer.

The use of natural, flexible, and easy-to-learn programming languages certainly eases the communication difficulties. Such languages are very desirable with batch processing. However, although the batch-processing operation of a computer system is very efficient from the computer's viewpoint, it might not be so convenient for some users. Thus another organization of the computer system appeared in the middle 1960s.

The principal objective of this organization is to make the input-output system convenient for the user as well as the computer. The input-output buffer is changed so that the user has *direct access* to the computer. Recall that most users do not generate enough work to use a computer's facilities efficiently. Thus many users are given simultaneous direct access to the computer. The computer is fast enough to work on many problems in a few seconds, and each user gets immediate (it seems) service on his problem.

This mode of operation is called the *conversational, direct-access,* or *interactive* mode. The number of users that a particular computer can service depends on its size and speed and the average amount of work requested per user. Smaller and slower computers can efficiently service users whose computation load is not sufficient to justify a large computer. In fact direct-access operation may also be used with only one user connected to a small computer.

Even when many users are directly connected to a single computer, there are two distinct methods of internal operation possible. The first, and simplest, is a modified form of 'batch processing. The only difference is in the input-output buffer. A typical organization of the computer is given in Figure 9-5.1.

A simplified description of this type of operation is as follows: The computer is doing batch processing as before. A user is putting in a problem at a console. This problem is being gathered up by the direct-access input-output buffer. When the problem is complete it will be put next in line for batch processing. When the current problem is finished, the computer takes the console user's problem and solves it. The results are returned to the input-output buffer which, in turn, returns them to the console.

One of the keys to the success of this kind of operation is the adequate design of consoles. They range from teletype units (somewhat less versatile than a typewriter), to very elaborate (and expensive) affairs with display (TV) screens, light pens (which communicate with the computer via the TV screens), versatile keyboards, and other devices. Three typical examples are shown in Figure 9-5.2.

The second, and more complicated, method of internal computer operation is a *time-sharing* mode. This mode of operation is motivated by the following possibility. Suppose there are a hundred users at remote consoles and one of them starts a problem that takes five minutes of machine time to finish. Or suppose again that one of the batch-processing jobs takes this long to run. Then most of the hundred users are spending much of this five minutes waiting. Furthermore, the waiting users might have generated enough work that it will take the computer another five minutes to get caught up and back to providing immediate service. Thus, for a period of ten minutes or so, the users are getting very little done.

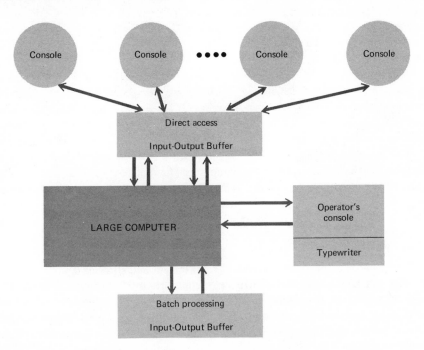

FIGURE 9-5.1 Schematic diagram of the input-output system for a computer with both batch processing and direct access operation.

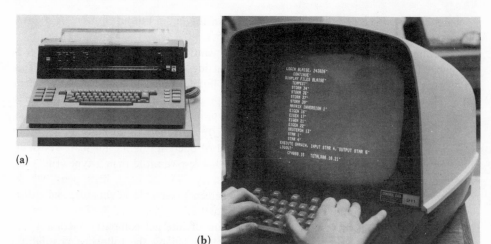

FIGURE 9-5.2   **Three consoles for direct access. (A) A simple typewriter design; (b) a keyboard and display scope; (c) an elaborate console. (Courtesy of IBM and Control Data Corp.)**

It is a trait of human nature to dislike sitting idle and waiting for ten minutes. Since the purpose of the whole operation is convenient and efficient input-output *for the user*, this situation cannot be allowed to occur often. The solution offered by time sharing is to stop the five-minute problem after it has run for a very short time and give some computing service to the other users. Then, a little later, the five-minute problem is run for another short time. These short periods of time are called *time slices* and may be as short as 0.05 seconds. This cycle is repeated until the five-minute problem is finally completed, and it may actually take ten minutes to an hour to finish the problem. If it is a problem from the batch-processing mode, the time lag is not particularly significant. If it is a problem from a console, then one user must wait much longer in order to allow a hundred others to obtain good service.

The time-sharing mode of operation requires a completely different internal organization of the computer system as well as changes in the physical devices. A possible arrangement is illustrated in Figure 9-5.3. The organization illustrated is complicated, and yet many essential details have been left out for the sake of simplicity. One of the important points to be made here is that the computer organization is extremely complex for this mode of operation.

In order to help appreciate this organization of the computer, we briefly summarize the function of the main components illustrated in Figure 9-5.3.

DIRECT-ACCESS INPUT-OUTPUT BUFFER. The function of this unit is essentially the same as that for the previous mode of operation. Each console has an area assigned in

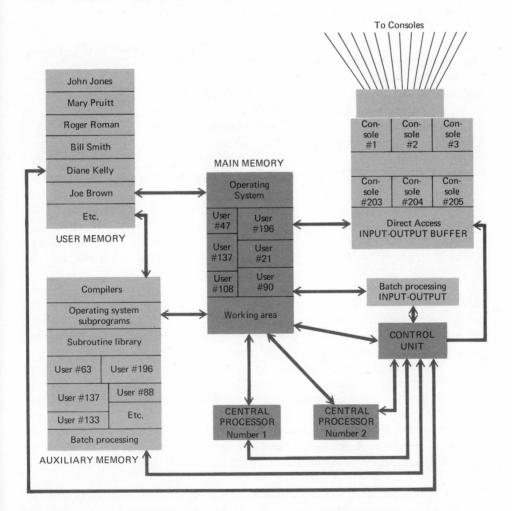

FIGURE 9-5.3 **A possible organization of a time shared, complex computer system.**

the buffer (at least during operation) and information is received and temporarily held there until some processing is required. This device is, in effect, a special purpose computer, and it may do some of the very simple processing itself. When one or more statements are collected and the user wants some computing done, this device sends the statements to the main computer. It then receives the results back from the main computer, puts them in a form suitable for the console, and transmits them to the console.

BATCH-PROCESSING INPUT-OUTPUT.   This part of the system operates as before and brings the problems to the computer which are submitted for batch processing. Even with 200 consoles, there are times when the main computer would be idle. The jobs submitted for batch processing are run during these idle times and provide a "background" computation load. This load ensures that the computer is being used at all times as well as providing service for those users who want to run a job by batch processing.

MAIN MEMORY.   This is the main working area of the total memory. The operating system occupies part of it, and the remainder is divided among several users. The users are allocated only as much space as they require so as to use this premium memory efficiently. All jobs in the main memory are being executed more or less simultaneously; that is, the system is providing each job with small "slices" of time for computation on a rotating basis. With more than one central processor (two are shown in Figure 9-5.3) there is actual simultaneous execution of instructions.

AUXILIARY MEMORY.   This memory has all of its previous functions plus that of the storing the problems that have been partially executed. Since the computer is parceling out its time among all the users, it can interrupt a computation in the middle and put it (and all the intermediate results) into the auxiliary memory. It then brings in another problem and works on it for a few moments. Further, only so much of one program is allowed in the main memory at one time, so that larger programs are divided into two parts, one in the main memory and one in the auxiliary memory.

USER'S MEMORY.   In addition to the other two types of memory it is important to have a place where users can save programs for long periods of time (days or even months). This facility is needed, for example, when a user enters a 150-statement program through a console keyboard and has to leave before he finishes running it. Rather than re-entering the program the next day, he can have it saved for him in the users' memory. There is room in this memory for a number of programs for each user, and thus it is very large. A computing center that has a large enough computing load to justify 200 consoles might well need several thousand individual libraries of user programs, which means that this memory must be able to store millions of words. This is an order of magnitude larger than the auxiliary memory, which, in turn, is an order of magnitude larger than the main memory.

CONTROL UNIT AND CENTRAL PROCESSORS.   The functions of these units are unchanged. The control unit receives instructions from the operating system about the programs and sees that appropriate action is taken. The central processors do the arithmetic, the comparisons, and so forth. They still play the role of the high-speed arithmetic unit originally considered. All of the other parts of the system are to enable us to exploit this tremendous speed.

The time-sharing computer system is so complicated that it is difficult to visualize all that might happen to a particular job as it is processed. It is shuffled many times back and forth between the various devices. During these shufflings it is in various stages of translation into machine language and then execution. The normal amount or slice of time allowed a problem when it is in the main memory is 5 to 50 hundreths of a second, so that a job that takes only a second may be transferred many times. A major design problem with this organization is to minimize the "overhead" created by all of this shuffling and manipulation.

There is a new and interesting problem presented by this organization, that of *memory protection*. This problem is, essentially, how to keep the program of one user from "wiping out" the program of another. In the batch-processing mode, the only thing a bad program can affect is itself and the operating system. Since no one else cares if a user ruins his own program and since copies of the operating system are available, little damage can be done. In a time-sharing operation, one user can ruin another's program unless steps are taken to prevent it. The solution is clear: do not allow any operation of a particular user to write anything outside his assigned area. The job of checking all the writing could conceivably be given to the operating system, but this solution turns out to be very inefficient for most computers. To do the checking efficiently requires changes in electronic devices of the computer.

9-6   CONCLUSION

After reading this chapter one should feel a certain frustration because of the gaps in one's understanding of what "really goes on" in computing systems. This chapter, though long, only skims the surface of the concepts presented, they are much more complex than pictured here. One can easily take several courses in this area and still be left frustrated. In fact, the present complex systems are not yet completely understood by anyone and even more complex systems will be introduced in the future. One of the goals of these systems is to allow the average person to use it without learning about its complexities, but this is very difficult and occasionally one will encounter a completely mysterious situation.

Understanding the impact of computers is much the same. The reader may have achieved some skill in computer programming and studied a number of computer applications. Yet the interactions between computer programming and problem solving or between computer applications and society have not been explored deeply. It is a very long step from a short programming homework assignment to writing a complex, real-world program for keeping a bank's records or for solving a scientist's problem. It is very difficult to analyze and understand the impact of a new computer application that involves other technologies, people's personal behavior, and changing the established pattern of things. Hopefully, the reader is now aware of some of the possibilities and will be able to use his own experience to deepen his understanding of the interaction between computers, problems, people and society.

Keypunch Operation

The keypunch machine allows one to prepare a program on punched cards as shown in Figure A–1. The program is printed at the top of the card to be read by the programmer and is punched in the card (as holes) to be read by a card reader and eventually a computer.

FIGURE A–1.   A typical punched card for a Basic program.

The Basic statements start in column 1, and a card contains one and only one statement. Occasionally, a statement might be too long to fit on one card and then one breaks it into two statements. A few systems might have some special means to punch a long statement on several cards.

FIGURE A–2.   An IBM 026 keypunch machine.

The most common machine used in preparing punched cards is the IBM 026 keypunch shown in Figure A–2. It has a keyboard similar to that of a typewriter and operates much in the same way except for additional mechanisms to control the movement of the cards. A newer model, the IBM 029, shown in Figure A–3, has a keyboard with more characters and a slightly different design.

The normal procedure for punching cards is as follows (see Figure A–4):

1. Load cards in the card hopper on the right.
2. Turn on power (there is a short delay while the machine warms up) and turn the three toggle switches (function control switches) on the top of the keyboard to the off position.
3. Push the FEED key to place a card in the right-hand position.
4. Push the REG key to align (or register) the card with the punches.
5. Type the statement that is to appear on the card. There is a small pointer in the window which indicates in which column one is about to punch a character. Note that the upper case "shift" key is the NUM key.
6. When the statement is finished, punch the REL (release) key. This moves the card to the middle position.
7. One continues in this way until all the cards are punched. In order to get the last cards out of the machine one must push the REL and REG keys twice.

One may *duplicate* a card by placing it in the middle position, a blank card in the right position, and then punching the DUP (duplicate) key as many times as there are characters to be duplicated. A card may be inserted directly in the middle position and is prepared for duplication by punching the REG key.

FIGURE A–3. An IBM 029 keypunch machine.

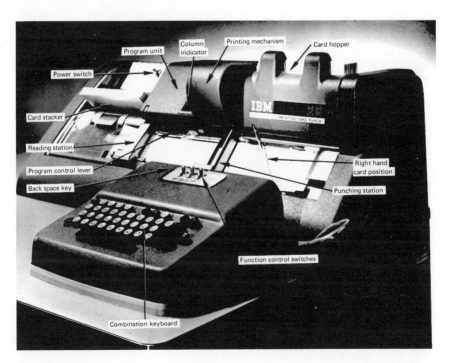

FIGURE A–4. Closeup of the IBM 026 with important components indicated.

One should check the duplicate card, as a misalignment in the original card leads to errors. The IBM 029 is often difficult to align correctly with cards directly inserted in the middle position, and correct alignment may be obtained by inserting the original card directly in the right position and then pushing the following sequence of keys: REG—REL—REG.

It is very common to make mistakes in keypunching and there is a facility to aid in correcting cards. One places the card with the keypunch error in the middle position and a blank card on the right. Push the REG key, then the DUP key until the position of the error is reached. Then type the correct character and finish the card with the DUP key. This works only when one has to replace some bad characters by exactly the same number of correct characters. On most keypunch machines one can also insert or delete characters even though the machines are not designed to allow this. To insert a character, one duplicates up to the insertion point, then presses tightly against the top right of the card in the middle position while typing the character (or characters) to be inserted. The card in the middle *must not move*. The remainder of the card is then duplicated. One deletes characters in a similar way except the card in on the right is held and the space bar is pressed. Recall that in Basic programs one can safely replace unwanted characters by blanks in almost all circumstances.

Other useful features of the keypunch include a *backspace* button (also try this button when the keypunch seems to be locked up) and an automatic feed switch to feed in a new card whenever the REL key is pushed or when a card is completely full. There is a facility to "program" the keypunch which is useful if hundreds of identically laid out cards are to be punched. It is not so useful for Basic cards and the "program" feature should be disengaged by pushing the program control lever down on the left.

Teletype Operation

The teletype machine is the most common device for preparing and running programs with *direct access* to a computer. The Model 33 Teletype is shown in Figure A–5, and it consists of a keyboard similar to a typewriter and a large roll of paper to type on.

FIGURE A–5. *The Model 33 Teletype machine.*

The Basic statements are typed starting on the left, and a line contains one and only one statement. Occasionally a statement might be too long to fit on one line and then one breaks it into two statements. A few systems might have some special means to type a long statement on several lines.

The normal procedure for running a program is as follows:

1. Turn the teletype on with the control on the lower right front of the machine.
2. Make connection with the computer system. This might be automatic or it might be necessary to dial the computer for a telephone connection. The procedures for this step vary from place to place and *specific instructions must be obtained locally.*
3. Make connection with the Basic system. This step involves information (for example, name, account number, type of job, language desired) to be provided to the time-sharing operating system. These procedures also vary and specific instructions must be obtained locally.
4. Create, retrieve, run, save, destroy, modify, or edit Basic programs. This again involves the time-sharing operating system which varies from place to place. However, there are a number of facilities that must be provided by all systems and these are discussed in some detail below.
5. Disconnect the teletype from the computer system and turn the power off.

There are special keys that play a role in the creation of a program. The more important are:

RETURN   This terminates a line in the same way as a *carriage return* on a typewriter. The computer system saves, but does not examine, a line until the RETURN is pushed.

CTRL   This key is usually pushed along with a second key for some type of control action. Such actions might be to gain the computer's attention, to interrupt the execution of a program, or to delete a partially typed line.

LINE RUBOUT   A system will have a means to discard a line any time before the RETURN is pushed.

CHARACTER ERASING   Some key (perhaps ← or #) is assigned the meaning "erase the previously typed character." Thus GOSTB ←← UB is sent to the computer as GOSUB and GOT25 ←← O255 is sent as GOTO255.

The basic facilities needed to operate in a time-sharing system may be divided into groups:

> Program creation and execution
> Program modification and editing
> Program library operation

Program creation and execution involves two commands, usually NEW and RUN. The command NEW signals that a new program is to be created and the system usually responds with a request for its name. After that point the Basic program is typed line by line. The command RUN (perhaps followed by a name in some systems) puts the Basic program into execution and the output is printed on the teletype.

Programs almost never run correctly the first time and the command EDIT is usually used to connect to the editing subsystem. This subsystem provides, as a minimum, facilities to

> delete lines of the program
> insert new lines
> replace existing lines
> list all or part of the program.

The exact commands used vary from place to place and some edit systems provide other convenient facilities.

The program library is needed because otherwise the only record of a program is the teletype listing. Without a library one would have to retype a program every time it is used. The basic facilities provided by a library subsystem include commands to

> save a program in the library
> retrieve a program from the library
> print the contents of the library
> rename a program
> delete a program

Again the exact commands vary from place to place. Note that each user has his own individual library. A large number of users of a system can lead to a very big set of libraries and result in severe limitations on the number or size of programs that one can save in his library. Some programs have a long-term value even though they are not used regularly and many systems allow one to have programs saved on magnetic tape or punched cards. Likewise, these systems should allow one to place programs into one's library from punched cards or magnetic tape.

Most systems provide other things, some of a miscellaneous nature such as

> status of the program in execution
> time of the day
> the user's name, number, and related information
> explanation of how to use the time-sharing system
> catalog of programs in the "public" library
> transmission of messages between the users and
>   the computer operators.

Console A device which gives a person (either the operator or a user) direct access to a computer.

Core storage Memory made out of magnetic cores.

CPU Central Processing Unit; the same as Central Processor.

Cycle time A basic unit of time for computer operations; most instructions require more than one cycle for execution.

Data base A collection of information, usually large and of a general nature, for an applications area.

Data cell An auxiliary memory device characterized by a very large capacity and relatively slow access time.

Data set A device that converts the signals of a business machine into signals that are suitable for transmission over communication lines.

Decision table A format used to describe and display the logic of a decision-making process in a tabular form of organization.

Declaration statement A part of a computer program that defines the nature of other elements of the program or reserves parts of the hardware for special use.

Default option An assumption made by a system or language translator when no specific choice is given by the user or his program.

Delimiter A symbol or word that indicates a breakpoint or termination point in the grammatical structure of a language.

Diagnostic routine A routine designed to locate a malfunction, either in other routines or in the computer itself.

Display A device, usually a TV screen, that shows either messages or graphical output from a computer.

Down time The time during which a computer is malfunctioning or not operating correctly due to mechanical or electronic failure as opposed to available, idle, or stand-by time during which the computer is functional.

Dump A copy of all or a large part of a computer's memory.

Duplex channel A communications channel that allows simultaneous transmission in both directions.

EBCDIC Extended Binary Coded Decimal Interchange Code, an 8-bit code that provides for 256 different characters.

Echo check The checking of information transmission by the immediate return of information received.

EDP Electronic data processing.

Electrostatic printer An electromechanical device that electrostatically charges specially coated paper, which is then dusted with ink particles to bring out the character impressions.

Eleven punch A punch in the second row of an IBM card.

Emulation A process where one computer is set up to behave exactly like a second kind of computer. Programs written for the second computer can then be run on the first.

END-OF-FILE mark A special symbol placed at the end of files of information.

EOF End-Of-File mark.

Error correction A system that detects and inherently provides correction for errors caused by transmission equipment or facilities.

Facsimile Transmission of pictures, maps, diagrams, and so on, by communications channels. The image is scanned at the transmitter, reconstructed at the receiving station, and duplicated on some form of paper.

Fetch To obtain data or an instruction from a computer's memory.

Field A specified area of a record used for a particular category of data.

File A collection of information that is organized for some purpose.

File management The development and use of specific rules, procedures, and methods for creating the file, updating it, and retrieving information from it.

Fixed point calculation   Calculation assuming a fixed or constant location of decimal or binary points in a number.

Flag   A character that signals the occurrence of some condition, such as the end of a file.

Flip-flop   A circuit or device containing active elements, capable of assuming either one of two stable states at a given time.

Floating point calculation   Calculation in which the computer automatically handles the positioning of the decimal point in arithmetic operations.

Graphics   Facilities to provide computer output in the form of displays, drawings, and pictures.

Hard copy   A recording of computer output in a permanent, human-readable form.

Hardware   The mechanical, magnetic, electrical, and electronic devices or components of a computer.

Head   A device that reads, writes, or erases information on a storage device.

Header   The first part of a message containing all the necessary information for directing the message to its destination(s).

Heuristic program   An algorithm that makes decisions on the basis of intuitively plausible, but not guaranteed, criteria which are designed to evaluate the progress made toward the successful completion of a task.

Hexadecimal   A number system with base or radix of 16. The digits are 0, 1, 2, 3, 4, 5, 6, 7, 8, 9, A, B, C, D, E, F .

Index register   A temporary storage device, usually in the control unit, which is used primarily for modification of the direct address portion of an instruction. Index registers are also used for counting and looping.

Indirect addressing   Instructions that contain the address of a memory location which, in turn, contains the address of an item to be processed by the instruction.

Information retrieval   The process of recovering specific information from stored data.

Integrated circuits   A manufacturing process where electronic circuits are produced as a whole rather than assembled from individual components; for example, wires, resistors, transistors, and so on.

Interface   A common boundary between two or more items of equipment.

Interpreter   (1) A program that translates and executes each *source language* expression before translating and executing the next one. (2) A device that prints on a punched card the data already punched in the card.

Interrupt   To stop a process in such a way that it can be resumed.

I/O   Input-Output.

Keyboard entry   A device used to record data on some storage medium by depressing keys on a keyboard.

Keywords   (1) The most informative words in a title or document. (2) Words in a programming language statement which indicate the type of the statement.

Line printer   An electromechanical device that consecutively prints an entire line of output at one time.

Linkage   The codes and statements that connect two independent programs or subprograms.

Load   To fill the internal storage of a computer with data or programs from auxiliary or external storage.

LSI   Large scale integration of electronic circuits.

Macro   An instruction in a source language that is equivalent to a specified set of statements either in the same source language or in an object language.

Main memory   The primary storage device directly under central processor control.

Map   A table that gives the association between program elements and words in memory.

MICR   Magnetic Ink Character Recognition.

Microfilm   Photographic film with extremely reduced images; may be used for computer output or for large capacity auxiliary memory.

Microprogramming   A facility to modify the basic machine instructions for a computer.

Microsecond   One millionth of a second.

MIS Management Information Systems.

Mnemonic A word or name which is easy to remember and identify.

Multiplexor A device that simultaneously transmits and receives from several other devices.

Multiprocessing The simultaneous or interleaved execution of two or more programs by a computer system utilizing two or more central processing units.

Multiprogramming The execution of two or more programs simultaneously by one central processing unit, through the overlapping or interleaving of their execution.

Nanosecond One billionth of a second.

Noise Loosely, any disturbance tending to interfere with the normal operation of a device or system, including those attributable to equipment components, manual interference, or natural disturbance.

Nondestructive read A read process that does not erase the data in the source.

Normalize To adjust the representation of a quantity so that the representation lies in a prescribed range.

Object language The language used to express the results of a language translation process.

OCR Optical Character Recognition.

Octal A number system with base or radix of 8.

Off-line processing Operations performed by auxiliary equipment on data prior to their entry into the central processing unit of the computer. Human intervention is usually required between data entry and ultimate processing. Compare with ON-LINE PROCESSING.

On-line processing The processing of data under the complete and absolute control of the central processor, eliminating the need for human intervention.

Open subprogram A subprogram that is to be relocated and inserted into a routine at each point it is used. Compare with CLOSED SUBPROGRAM.

Overflow The generation of a quantity beyond the capacity of a counter or register.

Overlay The technique of repeatedly using the same blocks of internal storage during different stages of a problem. When one program segment is no longer needed in storage, another program segment can replace all or part of it.

Parallel processing The simultaneous execution of two or more sequences of instructions by a computer having multiple arithmetic or logic units.

Peripheral equipment The auxiliary machines not under the direct control of the central computer, such as tape reader, card reader, or typewriter.

Postmortem dump A dump used for debugging purposes that is performed at the end of a machine run.

Problem-oriented language A programming language designed for the convenient expression of a given class of problems.

Procedure-oriented language A programming language designed for the convenient expression of procedures used in the solution of a wide class of problems.

Random access Pertaining to a memory device where the time for access to information is independent of location of the information or status of the device.

Record A collection of related items of data, treated as a unit. Contrast with FILE.

Recursion A set of operations or program statements where one of the operations or statements is specified in terms of the entire set.

Redundant information A message expressed in such a way that the essence of the information occurs in several ways.

Register A special computer unit whose purpose is to receive, hold, and transmit a specified amount of data as directed. See specific types of registers.

Relocate In programming, to move a routine from one portion of storage to another and to adjust the necessary address references so that the routine, in its new location, can be executed.

Report generation A technique for producing complete machine reports from information which describes the input file and the format and content of the output report.

Reproducer A device that will duplicate in a card all or part of the data contained in another card.

Response time The time interval between the initiation of a request of the information system and receipt of an answer.

RPG Report Program Generator language for business reports.

Scratch pad A small, exceptionally fast memory used by a central processor for holding temporary or intermediate results.

Semiconductor An electronic device that behaves like a vacuum tube but is much smaller, much cheaper, faster reacting, and consumes much less power.

Shift To move the admissible marks in a word one or more places to the left or right. In the case of a number, this is equivalent to multiplying or dividing by a power of the radix.

Simulate To represent the functioning of one system by another, for example, to represent one computer by another, to represent a physical system by the execution of a computer program, to represent a biological system by a mathematical model.

Software The programming systems, libraries, and other programming and nonhardware operating aids in a computer system.

Solid state The electronic components that convey or control electrons within solid materials; for example, transistors, germanium diodes, and magnetic cores. Thus, vacuum and gas tubes are not included.

Source language The language that is input to a language translation process.

Special character In a character set, a character that is neither a numeral, a letter, nor a blank; for example, virgule, asterisk, dollar sign, equals sign, comma, period.

Storage allocation The assignment of programs and blocks of data to specific blocks in a computer memory.

Supervisor The part of the operating system that has internal control over all subsystems of the computer system.

Syntax The vocabulary and grammatical rules required for the correct combination and formation of a computer language.

Tape drive A device that moves tape past a read/write head.

Target language Object language.

Teleprocessing A form of information handling in which a data processing system utilizes communication facilities.

TELPAK A service offered by common communication carriers for the leasing of broadband channels between two or more points.

Terminal An input-output device designed to receive or send source data, as part of a data transmission system.

Tracing A program debugging technique that involves printing out the value of a specified variable every time the value changes.

Track The portion of a moving magnetic storage medium, such as a drum, tape, or disk, that is accessible to a given read/write head position.

Transfer rate The speed at which data can be transmitted through a given type of channel.

Truth table A table that describes a logic function by listing all possible combinations of input values and indicating for each such combination the true output values.

Twelve punch A punch in the top row of an IBM card.

Utility programs A set of programs that provides the very basic facilities of a computer system; for example, copying one tape onto another, copying information from memory onto punched cards.

Variable word length The number of characters used for an item of data is exactly equal to its length, whether short or long. Marks are used to indicate the end of a data item.

Word An arbitrary number of binary digits or bytes handled as a unit by the computer for the purposes of operation, transmission, and storage.

Working storage Memory locations used for intermediate results for a computation.

Index

SUMMARY OF BASIC RULES

Statement Format

Every statement has three parts: a statement label, a keyword and the remainder. The labels are integers (usually less than 99999) which indicate the order in which the statements are processed. Blanks are ignored except in messages but they should be used to improve readability.

Remark

Only the three letters REM of the keyword are required.

Constants

Up to 8 digits are allowed in the usual or exponent notation:

Usual notation:	1000	0.001	123.456	
Exponent notation:	1E+3	1E−3	123456E−3	.123456E+3

Names

One or two characters, the first a letter and the second a digit. Array names are limited to a single letter.

Array

A collection of variables with one or two subscripts (indexes). If the subscript range may be larger than 10, then the maximum range must be declared using a DIM statement, for example, DIM A(30), R(5, 22).

Input and Output

The keyword PRINT may be followed by a list of variables, constants, expressions, or messages separated hy commas. Each item is printed in a zone of width 15 with 5 zones to a line. Short zones are obtained by using a semicolon (or similar character) instead of a comma to separate the items. If the list ends with a comma (or semicolon), the next print continues on the same line.

The keyword READ causes values to be taken from the DATA stack and assigned to variables listed after the READ. The assignment is made in order. The DATA statements create the DATA stack and numbers are added to the top on the stack in the order that they appear in the DATA statements.

Arithmetic Operators

+ (addition)   − (substraction)   * (multiplication)   / (division)   ↑ (exponentiation). Some systems use ** in place of ↑.

Relational Operators

Operator	Simplest Example	Meaning	Alternative Notation
=	A = B	A is equal to B	EQ
<	A < B	A is less than B	GT
<=	A <= B	A is less than or equal to B	GE
>	A > B	A is greater than B	LT
>=	A >= B	A is greater than or equal to B	LE
<>	A <> B	A is not equal to B	NE